MASTERING HOUSEHOLD ELECTRICAL WIRING

BY JAMES L. KITTLE

TAB BOOKS Inc.
BLUE RIDGE SUMMIT, PA. 17214

FIRST EDITION

FIRST PRINTING

Copyright © 1983 by TAB BOOKS Inc.

Printed in the United States of America

Library of Congress Cataloging in Publication Data

Kittle, James L., 1913-
Mastering household electrical wiring.

Includes index.
1. Electric wiring, Interior. I. Title.
TK3285.K57   1983   621.319′24   83-4897
ISBN 0-8306-0587-8
ISBN 0-8306-1587-3 (pbk.)

Contents

Preface

BOOKS ON HOW TO DO YOUR OWN WIRING are many and varied. The predominant fault with some of these how-to books is that they are written by excellent writers who know how to write, but their information is second hand.

Some books are a compilation of many experts' combined efforts all in one big book of do-it-yourself projects. Very few of these authors, writers, or researchers have crawled around in hot (or cold) attics or dug their way under houses without basements, all the while watching for snakes and other crawly things. How many have been an apprentice for six long, hard months doing all the hard, dirty jobs no one else wanted. Try drilling through a 6-inch concrete wall using a ¾-inch star drill and a three-pound sledge. Or have you threaded 2-inch rigid conduit by hand?

I have done every procedure, every method, used every material, devised better, easier ways of doing things, suffered smashed fingers, and banged my head. Construction work is hard, cold, hot, wet, and dangerous. Electrical installation is a science, an art that is very technical and exact. Wires must be connected correctly, labeled properly, and carefully tested before use. This book is designed to help you achieve those goals.

To Marian

Acknowledgments

TO MENTION EVERY PERSON WHO HAS, IN SOME way, made this book a reality is impossible. The two owners of the electrical contracting company, whose names I have forgotten, were the best teachers a young apprentice could ever have. They instilled in me a concern for good workmanship that has ever since been my goal.

The construction foremen for whom I worked in other trades helped me. Electrical inspectors H.A. (Lucky) Swager, director of building & zoning, Zion, Illinois; A.C. Holliday, electrical inspector, Troy, Michigan; and especially Mark N. Shapiro who collaborated with me on the technical aspects and interpretations of the National Electrical Code. Mr. Shapiro is Treasurer of the Reciprocal Electrical Council of the Greater Detroit Area. Two of his functions are the formulation of certain amendments to the National Electrical Code and the reciprocal licensing of electricians so that they may work in any member city. Mr. Shapiro is chief electrical inspector for the city of Madison Heights, Michigan and in addition is the code instructor at the Michigan Electrical Inspectors' School.

The following companies have provided illustrations and text for this book. Their cooperation and courtesy are greatly appreciated:

Arrow Hart Division of the Crouse-Hinds Company, Hartford, Connecticut.

Benfield International Corporation, Jack Benfield, inventor and copyright holder, Ft. Lauderdale, Florida.

Commonwealth Edison, Chicago, Illinois.

Bussman Division, McGraw-Edison Company, St. Louis, Missouri.

General Electric Company, Plainville, Connecticut.

Hawaii Electric Light Company, Inc., Hilo, Hawaii.

Honeywell Inc., Minnetonka, Minnesota.

Intermatic Inc., Spring Grove, Illinois.

Leviton Manufacturing Company, Inc., Little Neck, New York.

National Fire Protection Association, Inc., Quincy, Massachusetts.

Detroit Edison Company, Detroit, Michigan.

RACO INC., South Bend, Indiana, A Hubbell Subsidiary.

GTE Sylvania Inc., Danvers, Massachusetts.

City of Troy, Troy, Michigan, Jay N. Winslow,

electrical inspector supervisor.

Wiremold Company, West Hartford, Connecticut.

City of Zion, Zion, Illinois, H.A. Swager, director of building and zoning.

I would also like to thank: my sons Rex (who gave excellent advice on my drawings), Steve (who advised me on the operation of my camera), and Blake (who took many of the photographs). Joanna Rademacher of the Warren Public Library directed me to research material and helped me select books about writing for publication. The friendship and help of TAB BOOKS Inc. staff, especially Raymond A. Collins, Elizabeth J. Akers, Kim Tabor, and all of the editorial department, in completing and submitting my manuscript is greatly appreciated. Clara, who checked all of my drawings for accuracy, was a great help.

Last but most important, I acknowledge the loving help of my late wife, Marian, who proofread my typed manuscript as long as she was able and her love, which kept me going.

Introduction

THE USE OF ELECTRICITY IN OUR HOMES, FAC-tories, and places of business is so much taken for granted that we forget that without it everyday living and working as we know it would not exist. Electricity in the home *is* a necessity.

Anyone who is handy with tools and used to following directions can do residential wiring correctly and safely by following this book and the rules of the latest edition of the *Electrical Code for One- and Two-Family Dwellings*, published by the National Fire Protection Association, Quincy, Massachusetts. Your house wiring can be remodeled, added to, and modernized. This book will guide you. In addition this book will *save you money*. You will save because you will eliminate labor costs by substituting your labor and because you will buy all materials at *your* cost with no contractor's mark-up added on.

Methods and materials described here have been found to be practical from many years' experience in the fields of electrical contracting and related building trades.

You will be guided through your present house wiring. Each item and device will be described and its purpose explained. Many points and procedures will be emphasized and clarified so that you will be on notice that: "This is the only way to do this procedure; do not attempt to do it any other way." This is not to scare you off. This is to ensure that you understand and follow the procedure. The purpose of this book is to train you so that the wiring that you have done will be approved by the local inspector. The inspector's word is law and your work might not be approved on first inspection.

The inspector is first interested in safety and second the inspector is required by law to be satisfied that the work conforms to the requirements of the National Electrical Code. This book and the inspector's excellent *free* advice will allow you to save money and learn a skill, which will always prove useful. Use common sense, be careful, watch what you are doing, and you will do fine. Do it and save money!

The first thing to do is to carry a notebook and a good flashlight and make a thorough inspection of the wiring in your home. You should at least go through this book and make yourself familiar with the various chapters. You could even take it with you on your inspection. Note everything that does not look right or seems worn, broken, or damaged.

Many houses have wiring done by persons who are not careful or just do not work neatly or accurately. In other words, the work looks sloppy. This could mean standard procedures were not followed and perhaps some wires were improperly connected.

Most local governing bodies will issue a permit for you to do your own wiring. You will be asked to fill out and sign what is called a Homeowner's Permit to do electrical wiring. By signing the permit, you state that you will do *all* the work yourself and not contract the work out to others. Your family members may help, but you are still responsible for the work. Upon completion of the work, the inspector—after inspecting for violations—will either approve or disapprove. The inspector will explain to you what things have to be corrected and how to correct them. Most inspectors are very happy to help you. For your own safety they *want* you to apply for the permit so that they can help you to do the job correctly.

CAUTION: Do not do any electrical wiring without first obtaining the necessary permit. Then call for the inspector to make an inspection of the completed installation. Another reason to have the work inspected is for insurance purposes. Any fire will be inspected by insurance adjusters. If it is suspected that there was no permit *and* no inspection, the insurance company *may* not pay your claim. The fire might have been some distance from any suspicious wiring.

These fire insurance adjusters are very knowledgeable on standard construction methods and they can spot code violations readily. *Be advised of these facts and act accordingly! Be safe!* Do a good job, check your work, be careful, and save money. Happy Wiring!

NOTE: In the United States and Canada, single-phase, 60 cycle ac power-line house voltages vary from one area to another. Voltages might even be varied during different times of the year. Generally, there are only two voltages available for standard residential use: 120 volts and 240 volts. In some areas of the United States, 208 volts ac is available. Do not confuse 208 volts with 240 volts.

From time to time, you will come across references to house voltage listed as 110 volts, 115 volts, 120 volts, 220 volts, 230 volts, or 240 volts. Any appliance rated at 110, 115, or 120 volts is a 120-volt appliance. Any appliance rated at 220 volts, 230 volts, or 240 volts is a 240-volt appliance.

Chapter 1
Inspecting
Your Home

I T IS LIKELY THAT YOUR HOUSE WAS WIRED BY a licensed electrical contractor. Generally they do good work. Still it is wise to check everything. Previous owners might have made improper changes or additions. When checking your wiring, take with you a small notebook to record defects and list the items to be changed. Also list any additions or special improvements you would like to make.

Throughout this book for convenience I refer to nonmetallic cable as "Romex®" to armored cable as "BX" and to flexible conduit (having no wires inside) as "Greenfield."

THE NATIONAL ELECTRICAL CODE

All wiring in the United States should be installed in accordance with the National Electrical Code. The code is, in most cases, made a part of city ordinances by adoption and is incorporated into and made a part of the municipal building code. Other governing entities such as townships and counties, and even states, incorporate the code into their laws and ordinances.

While the code itself is not law, the above entities do incorporate it into their laws and regulations. Each such entity also adds to the code their special additions. These additions also have the effect of law and can be enforced. The code requires only minimum conditions in the wiring methods. The authors of the code are interested in safeguarding people and property from hazards arising from the use of electricity. Sizing and layout of the system are left to the contractor.

The code has been in existence for 80 years. It is updated and added to every three years as required by new technology.

THE METER AND POWER SUPPLY

Start at the meter whether inside or outside of the building. Note the wires coming from the utility pole (service drop). Check their condition. On old homes, the connection to the building wall might be porcelain insulators. Modern practice employs a service bolt and a tension sleeve to hold the three-wire service drop. This connection must be securely fastened to the building framing because of the heavy strain when wires are ice covered.

The wires coming down to the meter or into the house can be either in conduit or cable (service-entrance cable). If your house is quite old, there might be only *two* wires coming from the pole. Consider increasing the electrical ampacity to 60 A as your first project. See that the conduit or cable is fastened securely to the wall. If the meter is inside, which is likely if there are only two wires, you will want to move it outside when you increase the ampacity. Figure 1-1 shows meters on a condominium. Where conduit or cable goes through the house wall, it must be made watertight. Water can travel through an opening and seep into electrical panels. Caulk this area securely.

ALUMINUM WIRING AND ITS HAZARDS

Some years ago, aluminum wire was used in inter-

Fig. 1-1. A meter cluster for a four-unit condominium. The meters on the right are for the water heater. Meters on the left are for power. The top left meter is for the outside lighting.

Fig. 1-2. Two sizes of service-entrance cable. This cable has the neutral insulated because the main breaker is outside under the small covers under each meter. This is a code restriction.

ior wiring in houses. This caused some fires and destroyed many electrical devices such as switches and receptacles. This damage was caused by the nature of aluminum, which tends to flow and deform under pressure and heat. This problem was compounded by electrolysis between the aluminum wire and steel terminal screws on the devices.

Many houses were rewired with copper wire and new devices and related parts were used. There are devices on the market marked "CO/ALR" that have *brass* screws. These devices used with aluminum wire or copper-clad aluminum wire do not cause problems. Figure 1-2 shows types of aluminum entrance cable used presently.

I do not recommend the use of aluminum or copper-clad aluminum wire for 15 A and 20 A branch circuits. It is brittle and does not work well. Aluminum wire is used with good results for the service drop and the entrance cable to feed the distribution panel and entrance panel inside.

THE SERVICE-ENTRANCE PANEL

You will find the service-entrance panel either in the basement or utility room and sometimes in the kitchen. (In my parents' home, it is in an upstairs bedroom.) Note the condition of the panel and also the type. There might be just a main disconnect (switch), or it might be combined with the fuse/circuit breaker panel. The front might be hinged or attached with four or more screws. Turn off the main disconnect or trip the main circuit breaker. The panel might consist of one or more pull-out fuse blocks. One will be marked *Main*. Pull this one out. Touch only the handle. Now, carefully remove the

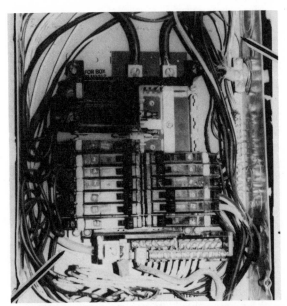

Fig. 1-3. Circuit breaker panel with cover removed. The main breaker is outside (Fig. 1-1). The right arrow is pointing to the equipment grounding bar. The wire is from the meter box outside. The left arrow is pointing to the neutral wire (also from the meter outside). This connects to the neutral bar where all the white wires from the various circuits connect to form the neutral system of the house.

front of the panel. See Fig. 1-3, which shows the wiring found in the circuit box. At the top you will see the feed from the meter. *These wires will still be live.* Be *careful.* As the service supplies 230 volts, there will be *three* wires, black, red, and *bare.* If conduit supplies the service, the wires might be black, red and *white.* The white wire might actually be black with white tape or paint near the end. This is the neutral wire. Figure 1-4 illustrates a circuit breaker panel.

Take a screwdriver with a ⅜-inch wide blade and a good plastic handle (no metal in handle) and tighten all screws having a wire connected to them. Some might need almost a complete turn to make them tight.

Always follow the safety rule of using only one hand when working around and near live (hot, and they are hot) wires. Put your other hand in your pocket, literally, because unintentionally you might reach for metal or some other object and receive a shock or worse. It is also a good idea to stand on a

piece of dry wood when working near live wires. The screws on the three feed wires at the top of the panel will be *hot* so be doubly cautious if you tighten them. The neutral (white or bare) wire might extend down to the bottom or side before being connected. Figure 1-4 shows a panel with type "S" fuses (time delay).

OUTDOOR LIGHTING

In the interest of security and to provide yard lights for convenience after dark, you might want to install outdoor lighting. Perhaps you have lights at the front and rear doors and the garage. If you want, this lighting can be increased to provide lighting around the perimeter of the house and garage.

To control such lighting, either a time switch or a photocell can be installed. For decorative

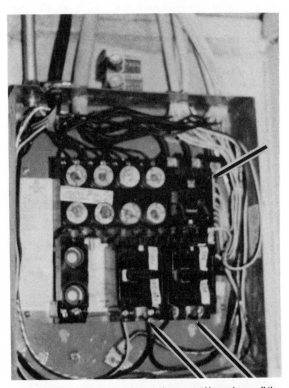

Fig. 1-4. The right arrow points to the neutral bar where all the white wires from the circuits are connected. The bottom, left arrow points to the pull-out fuse block for the air conditioning system. The bottom, right arrow points to the pull-out fuse block for the electric range. The pull-out directly above the range pull-out is for the main fuses for the house.

3

lighting during holidays, a number of outlets can be installed and they can also be controlled the same way.

CHECKING THE BASEMENT

The basement and attic are the easiest places to check because the wiring is exposed and problems can be seen and noted. The distribution panel will have many Romex cables leaving the top and sides. These will be either white, gray, or black. This is the sheath color; it is not the individual color of the wires. Each cable feeds a lighting or power circuit. Inspect and tighten all cable clamps holding the Romex or BX (metal-sheathed cable) to boxes or the panel. Tighten both the cable-clamp screws and the *locknuts* inside the cabinet or box. Some panels are located outdoors and have just the main disconnect breaker there. In some areas, even the distribution panel is outdoors. See that wiring on the basement ceiling is run neatly and is supported and anchored properly every 4½ feet.

Now turn on the main breaker or replace the fuse block. Leave the cover off for now or replace it if there are small children around. Trip one breaker off or remove one fuse. Now go through the house and look for lights that don't work. A fine device for testing outlets is a bulb socket with prongs on the end to plug into an outlet, like a plug on a lamp cord. This device is available at hardware stores.

When you find the *dead* (no voltage) circuit at an outlet, remove the plate and the top and bottom screws holding the outlet in place. Check for current again. *Be safe.* See if the screws holding the wires are tight; if not, tighten them. Also determine if the wire is aluminum. This is important. It is easy to check inside the breaker panel for aluminum wire. If any wire *is* aluminum, examine the outlet itself. If it is marked "CU/AL," the aluminum wire to it won't be acceptable. If it says nothing, then there will be problems. Aluminum wire is white in color or it might have a copper coating on it (copper clad). This is somewhat better, but avoid aluminum wiring entirely if possible. Look at the end of the wire. Copper-clad wire is like plating and the wire end should show white.

CHECKING THE ATTIC

An attic inspection should be much simpler than a basement inspection because, perhaps, only the original wiring is there. Any attic junction boxes or in the basement must have covers on them. There also must be *no* wire connections made that are not made inside junction boxes. This is mandatory. Every wiring connection must be made inside a junction box or other enclosure, such as a switch or outlet box. All Romex within 6 feet of the entrance to the attic skuttle hole must be protected either through bored holes in joists and covered with flooring or protected with running strips along each side of the cable. Use 1-inch-by-2-inch wood strips.

If you can see the ceiling outlet boxes for the downstairs ceiling fixtures, determine if they are solidly supported. Heavy ceiling fixtures over 10 pounds must be supported from the center bottom of the junction box. Do not support them from a strap screwed to the small box ears.

GROUNDING

The main service entrance panel *must* have a ground wire leading to a cold-water pipe. The pipe must be in the ground for at least 10 feet to be considered a sufficient ground. The ground wire must be attached to the water pipe on the *street* side of the water meter. A pipe that is part of and connected to a municipal water supply is an excellent ground. If the grounding wire cannot be connected on the street side of the meter, then a bonding jumper must be installed to maintain a ground in the event the meter is removed from the premises. See Fig. 1-5 for the correct method. One house that I purchased had no grounding wire at all. Another had the ground clamp left very loose. Modern wiring using Romex or BX with a ground as part of the cable assures safety to persons and also helps prevent electrical fires.

DETERMINING THE CAPACITY OF THE SYSTEM

Modern dwellings using many appliances require much more capacity than was required even 10 years ago. A minimum capacity of 100 amps is now

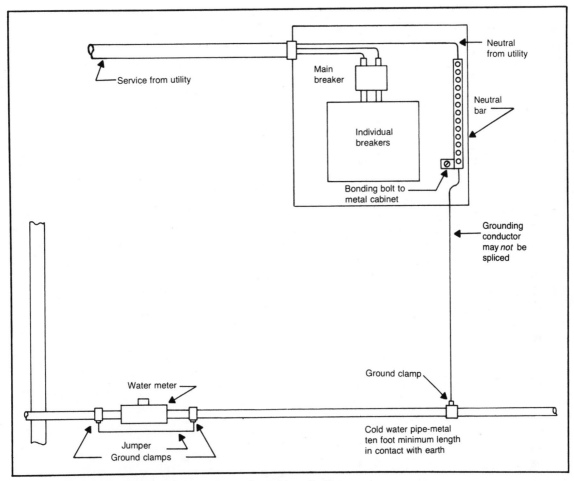

Fig. 1-5. Method of grounding service-entrance equipment in a dwelling.

required by the code. Even 150 amps is now common. The capacity of the service-entrance equipment is shown in the inside cover of the cabinet. The panel label will state Underwriters Laboratories, Inc. 'listed' and the amps capacity such as 120/240 volts, 125 amps.

THE LIGHTING AND POWER CIRCUITS

Lighting circuits are supplied with 115 volts. They are protected either by 15-amp fuses or 15-amp circuit breakers if the wire is No. 14 (14-2 w /gd.). If the wire is No. 12, it will be protected by either 20-amp fuses or breakers. Power circuits are supplied by 240 volts and they are protected by circuit breakers only, with a rating depending on their use, 30 A up to 60 A. The wire size used depends upon the appliance and corresponds to the rating of the circuit breaker.

REPAIRS

Items needing repair should be taken care of first so that the condition existing can be remedied as soon as possible. Faulty switches and worn electrical outlets are replaced easily. Everything is detailed fully in later chapters. Repair the cords on appliances and lamps by just replacing the attachment plug or by replacing the complete cord *and* plug. Do the same with extension cords. If the cord itself is damaged it should be replaced. If the damage is a bad cut in or near the center, the cord can be cut and two new connections can be put on the cut ends, making two cords.

ADDITIONS

Any number of additions can be suggested for the person who is ambitious. Some suggestions for additions are to:

■ Add a timer or photocell to control outdoor lighting.

■ Rewire a detached garage for lighting and power.

■ Wire a workshop in the basement.

■ Install a garage door operator. Include a pilot light to show that the door is open.

■ Add another pilot light to show that the garage light is on.

■ Consider an emergency power system if your area has many power outages.

OUTLETS, SWITCHES, AND RELATED DEVICES

Basic wiring devices consist of many varied types, styles, and uses. The basic item would be the socket used for lighting and signaling purposes in lamps and fixtures. Next are the switches for controlling lighting and various motors. Also needed are the outlets (receptacles) for all the uses we put them to.

WORK TO BE DONE

By now you will have made a list of work that appears to be necessary to take care of immediately (such as defects and worn devices). Second, you should list work that needs to be done during warm weather, such as outdoor work. Winter jobs might be basement work, such as in a recreation room, or wiring your shop for power equipment.

NOTE: Bear in mind that any major additions to the present wiring might overload the service entrance equipment and that equipment must have its capacity increased before adding an extra load.

MATERIAL SOURCES

Wiring materials can be obtained from many sources including discount stores, hardware stores, retail stores such as Montgomery Ward, Sears and their mail-order service departments. Certain devices such as range outlets, heavy-service-entrance cable, Greenfield, extra-large junction boxes and service-entrance equipment must be obtained from an electrical wholesale outlet.

THE ELECTRICAL INSPECTOR

Municipalities having ordinances regulating electrical installations within their borders will have an electrical inspection department as part of their building inspection department. There will be one or more electrical inspectors with the department. The department will require that you apply for a *homeowner's electrical permit.* Talk with the inspector for your area. If you explain to him your plans, he most likely will assist you by explaining things that you don't understand. He will also be helpful in many other ways. He might advise you to buy smaller-size wire for wiring special jobs such as a water heater, clothes dryer, or air conditioner. Smaller wire sizes will save you money and if the inspector approves that is fine. All inspectors are very knowledgeable about certain aspects of installations that many electricians are not familiar with. Ask him anything about wiring you don't know. He will be glad to advise you. All it costs you is the fee for the permit.

Chapter 2
Safety

THIS CHAPTER MIGHT WELL BE THE MOST IM-
portant chapter in this book. Safety is important in everything we do, but it is doubly important
in the wiring of a home. Read these pages carefully
and be guided by them.

THE NATURE OF ELECTRICITY

Electricity has been observed for many centuries.
The practical use of electricity developed during
the last hundred years has revolutionized our lives.

Electricity exists in two forms: *static* and *current*. When a person walks across a rug and touches
metal, they sometimes will receive a sharp pain and
will see a small spark. That is static electricity.
This form of electricity is harmless but unnerving.
The "poke" received is actually the jab of the spark
at the finger. To eliminate this, hold a coin in your
fingers and touch the metal. There will be no shock
but there might be a spark.

Current electricity is an entirely different
matter. This form of electricity has been portrayed
as an angry wolf with its fangs bared. This could be

the case when people come in contact with live
wires that appear to be installed correctly and
safely. Anyone who has considered wiring to be
safe and finds out differently by way of shock or
worse could come back to the original installer for
redress.

Current electricity can KILL. Because of this
danger, which is ever present, *all* installations of
electrical wiring must conform to the most recent
National Electrical Code. Currently, this is the 1981
issue. The 1984 National Electrical Code will be
out in mid-1983. If there is no local governing authority with jurisdiction, the wiring still must be
done according to the code.

The *National Electrical Code* is specific and
outlines the procedures by which electricity is
controlled and made safe and useful to us without
hazards and dangers. If after you have finished
reading this book you decide to do your own wiring,
keep these five Cs in mind: Care, Consideration,
Checkout, Confidence, and Caution.

Care. In any electrical work that you do, use

care in planning the installation and in doing the actual work. A workmanlike installation is more likely to be a safe installation.

Consideration. Consider the work you are doing and its use by other people and how they come in contact with your installation. Also make certain the devices and wiring materials are suitable for the use you are making of them. For instance, a dimmer switch for a fluorescent lamp installation will not work on an incandescent lamp installation. Now some *are* interchangeable. Also make sure that wiring of all devices is done according to recommended code practices. See Fig. 2-1.

Checkout. Check your work as you do it, after you have finished a certain section and before going on. When the job is completely finished, again check and re-check all of your work.

Confidence. Have confidence in the work you intend to do and the work you have completed. Have confidence in yourself. Then do it correctly, according to the code.

Caution. Remember to exercise caution at all times. Are there any bare wires exposed that will carry current? (This excludes *equipment grounding* wires). Are all connections tight? Are the correct wires attached to the correct terminals? Before starting work on electrical equipment of *any* kind, has it been de-energized? Check at least *twice* for voltage. Check and double check all work you have done before energizing the installation.

SAFETY PROVISIONS OF THE CODE

The first statement the code makes is that its purpose is to safeguard persons and property from the hazards of electricity. The provisions contained in the code do not necessarily provide an efficient, convenient, or adequate installation. As stated above, the installation will be safe as required by the code, but not correct as to what the job will require for its proper use.

The code limits the amount of current allowed in various wires by specifying the American Wire Gauge (AWG) size and also the type of insulation for an allowable current carrying capacity (ampacity). The fuse or circuit breaker (breaker) at the distribution center has a specified rating. In the event that the wire is overloaded, the fuse will blow or the breaker will trip to protect the wire from overheating and causing a fire.

Wiring methods and materials are also specified to eliminate substandard materials and poor installation and handling of those materials. A finished wiring job might appear to be perfectly installed even though it is faulty. This is the important reason to have the job inspected by the electrical inspector. The possibility of fire must always be considered. An electrical permit is the least expensive form of insurance you can buy.

AVOIDING SHOCK OR ELECTROCUTION

All wiring connected to a source of current *must* have a means to disconnect it from such a source, whether a private generating system or the public utility lines. Methods vary. There might be a lever handle switch on the service-entrance cabinet, pull-out fuse blocks, or a circuit breaker. Any of these can be operated to disconnect the wiring from any source of electricity. *Note:* The white or neutral wire *must not* be disconnected at any time, even when working on the wiring.

Before starting work on any wiring, after it has been disconnected, check for voltage with a tester. You *might* think that you have tripped the correct breaker or removed the correct fuse for that particular circuit. Errors *can* occur. You might have picked the wrong circuit to turn off. Check again. Remember the "C" for caution. During my work as a heating serviceman, I had occasion to replace many line-voltage (120 V) devices. My final no-voltage check was to short the terminals of the old control to its case with a screwdriver. One time there was a feed-back through another circuit and the screwdriver arced and blew the fuse. This way the tool rather than I received the shock. *Always use caution.* Sometimes the neutral and the hot (live) wire have been interchanged without anyone knowing about it. In this case, disconnecting the circuit would do no good and would do *you* harm.

I remember one instance where an oil burner motor was incorrectly wired. The switch for the burner disconnected the neutral wire instead of the hot wire, although it did stop the motor. On re-

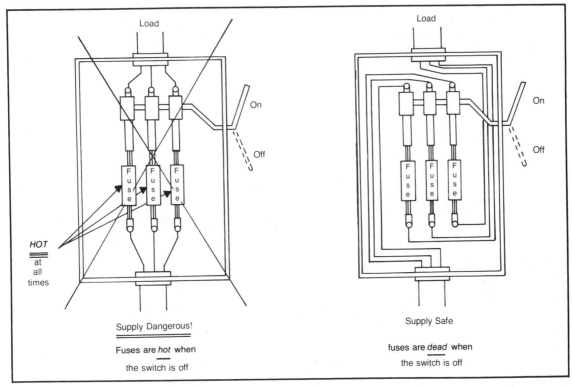

Fig. 2-1. An example of faulty wiring. Standard practices were not followed and the labeling on the terminals was not done. The left drawing shows *hot* fuses even though the switch is in off position. Because fuses are large, the wireman might tend to grip them with his hand and will get a severe shock!

moving the motor from the burner, it started up in my hands because it was wired wrong. The hot wire was still connected all this time even though the switch was off. This illustrates why wiring must be properly done. Remember the five Cs of safety.

Another hazardous condition shown in Fig. 2-1. A disconnect (switch) was wired so that it at least shut off current to the three-phase air conditioner it controlled. The hazardous condition existed because the wiring to the terminals of the disconnect was incorrect. The *line* (power supply) was connected to the bottom terminals. The conduit carrying the line voltage entered at the bottom. The load (wires to the equipment) was connected to the top terminals. This would disconnect the air conditioner, but it would leave the large fuses hot even though the switch was in the "Off" position.

The right-side drawing in Fig. 2-1 shows the *correct* method of wiring this disconnect for safety.

It is the *approved* method. Usually the top, always hot, terminals are covered with a fiber shield after wiring is completed. The hazardous condition encountered is that someone could turn off the disconnect and then grasp one of the large fuses to remove it and in so doing be grasping a *live part*. Be sure the equipment you are working on is DEAD so that you won't be DEAD.

WORKING WITH OR NEAR LIVE WIRES

If possible, do not work with or near live wires. In nearly all cases, the wiring can be disconnected before starting work. Many disconnects can be *locked* in the OFF position by a padlock to prevent accidental turn-on. Tag the switch to warn other people. As a last resort, it is possible to remove the electrical utility meter from its base. This kills everything.

As recommended in Chapter 1 use only one

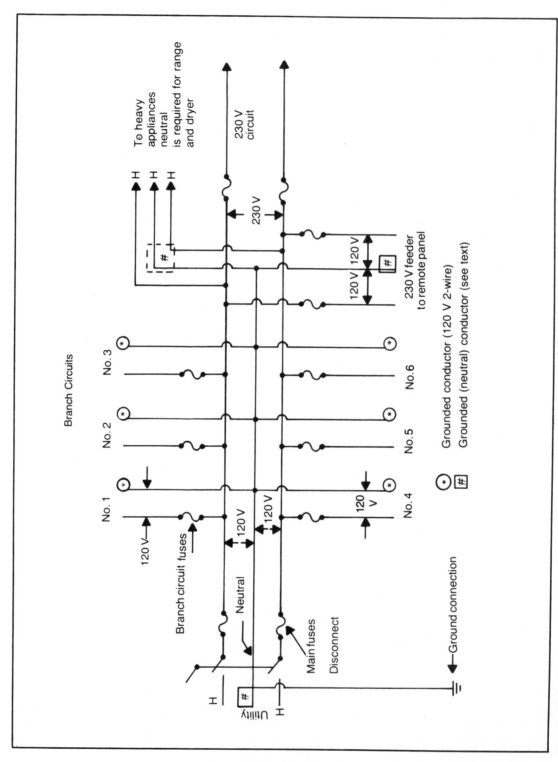

Fig. 2-2. Wiring layout for a residence.

Family Protection

A consumer guide to safer electrical living.

Fig. 2-3. *Family Protection* is a consumer guide to safer electrical living (courtesy General Electric Co.).

hand. Practice on a dead circuit until you can do this easily and with confidence. Only touch the part of the wire covered by insulation, not by the bare end. Rubber gloves are available at electrical supply houses. Do NOT use household rubber gloves.

Use only screwdrivers and nut drivers having good plastic (not wood) handles. No metal must show at the top of the handle. Some screwdriver blades go all the way through the handle and form the head for pounding on the screwdriver. The plastic handle must be large enough so that you cannot touch the metal shank. The shank can be wrapped in electrical tape for more protection. When connecting two small wires by means of a *wire nut*, the hot wire should be held in your left hand. Bring the dead wire alongside and cap the two wires together with the skirt of the nut. Tighten the wire nut and the job is done.

Avoid handling live wires. For the very few times that you might ever need to handle them, you might consider hiring a licensed electrician to make the final connection for you.

THE NEUTRAL AND GROUNDING WIRES

Power as supplied by the electric utility comes over three wires. Shown in Fig. 2-2 are two hot wires, A and B. The third wire is the neutral wire, N. Three wires are necessary to supply 240 volts for the range, electric water heater, and electric clothes dryer. If a central air conditioner is installed, this will also take 240 volts. The voltage between wires A and B is 240 volts. Between A and N it is 120 volts. Between B and N the voltage is also 120 volts. Circuits supplying 120 volts are used for lighting and portable appliances. The neutral wire must have white or natural gray color insulation. Wires A and B, the hot wires, may be black, red, or any other color except *white, green*, or *yellow*. The neutral wire, N, has no voltage to ground and will not give you a shock. Service-entrance cable neutral is usually bare.

Large-size wires do not come in white or gray, but they can be identified as the neutral by white tape or paint at their ends where they are attached to the terminals. The neutral is never interrupted by a fuse or circuit breaker, switch, or other method. The *only* exception to this rule is where all wires such as A, B, *and* N, are disconnected by a switch that will disconnect *all three* simultaneously.

THE GROUND WIRE VERSUS THE GROUNDING WIRE

The *grounding electrode conductor* is the wire running from the service entrance equipment to the *grounding electrode*. This grounding electrode may be a *cold water pipe*, a driven *ground rod* or a buried

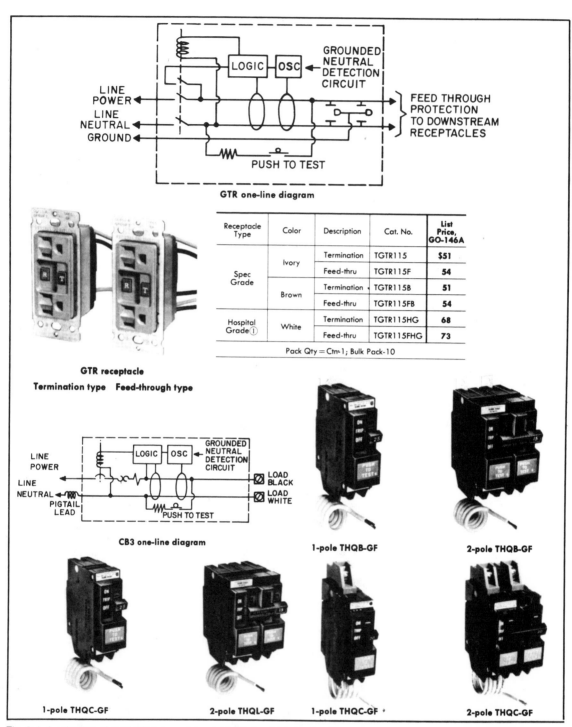

GTR one-line diagram

GTR receptacle

Termination type Feed-through type

Receptacle Type	Color	Description	Cat. No.	List Price, GO-146A
Spec Grade	Ivory	Termination	TGTR115	$51
		Feed-thru	TGTR115F	54
	Brown	Termination	TGTR115B	51
		Feed-thru	TGTR115FB	54
Hospital Grade①	White	Termination	TGTR115HG	68
		Feed-thru	TGTR115FHG	73
Pack Qty = Ctn-1; Bulk Pack-10				

CB3 one-line diagram

1-pole THQB-GF

2-pole THQB-GF

1-pole THQC-GF

2-pole THQL-GF

1-pole THQC-GF

2-pole THQC-GF

Fig. 2-4. A selection of available types of ground fault circuit interrupters for various requirements (courtesy General Electric Co.).

12

metal plate. The ground wire is mechanically and electrically bonded to the grounding electrode by a *ground clamp*. An *equipment* grounding conductor is the wire connected to frames of motors, washers, and all metal noncurrent carrying parts of the electrical system. The designation on the Romex cable and the carton holding the cable of "14-2 with ground" refers to this grounding wire. This grounding wire never carries any current *except* in case of a fault or short circuit somewhere. In this case, current would flow momentarily until the fuse blows or the breaker trips.

TESTING FOR HOT WIRES

Always test for voltage before doing any work on wiring. The only absolutely dead wire is when you can see both ends of the wire as well as the full length. First, test the circuit hot to test the tester. The tester might be defective and this test will show it to be defective. Now kill the circuit and test again. This time the tester will not register. Try the tester on another live circuit and then on the one to be worked on. *Be sure to tag the disconnect and lock it if possible. Be absolutely sure the circuit is dead before starting work.*

Figures 2-3 and 2-4 show the latest safety devices. The ground fault circuit interrupter in Fig. 2-4 should be in every place in the house where a person could receive a shock due to wet conditions (a bathroom) or from contacting a metal object.

Chapter 3
Tools

TOOLS ARE VERY IMPORTANT IN WORKING with electricity. Look for top quality and good design when you are buying your tools. Some well-known brands have inherently superior design as compared to other brands of as high quality. Top-quality tools, if properly used and cared for, will last a lifetime. The cheap ones will not. Some uncommon tools are illustrated in Figs. 3-1 through 3-5.

PLIERS

I prefer the nationally advertised brands and especially those made in the United States. These brands include Lufkin, Stanley, Crescent, Craftsman (excellent guarantee), Channellock, and Kliens, Proto, Snap On, Blue Point, and others. For certain hand tools I choose specific brands. Channellock groove joint pliers are of superior design even though others look identical. For electricians' linemans' pliers (sidecutters) and diagonals, Klien's are the best. This brand is usually only available at electrical wholesalers. They will readily sell you

tools. Also ask about buying wiring materials there. I have a pair of Crescent diagonal cutters at least 30 years old. They work like new and will cut bolts up to 3/16 of an inch in diameter. Never cut anything but copper wire with your lineman's side cutters (pliers).

SCREWDRIVERS

Screwdrivers are very important tools. To tighten screws properly, the screwdriver blade must fit the screw slot snugly. Too large or too small a blade will damage the slot and perhaps ruin the screw. For most terminal screws, use a ⅜-inch-wide blade that has a blade thickness to properly fit the screw slot. This is *very important*: Be sure the handle is made of solid plastic with no metal cap on the end or metal shaft through the handle. Some such as Crescent have a rubber sleeve over the plastic handle for gripping. This is good.

Screwdrivers for small screws need to be smaller in width and thickness to match the screw slots closely. Three sizes will do fine. For Phillips-

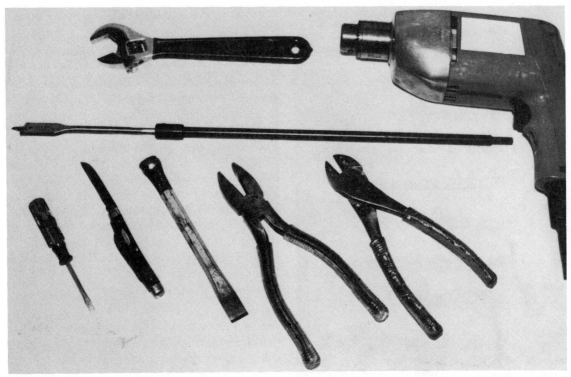

Fig. 3-1. Top: 8-inch adjustable wrench and drill motor. Center: 13/16-inch spade bit in bit extension. Bottom from left: pocket screwdriver, knife, cold chisel, electrician's side cutters (lineman's pliers), and diagonal cutters (dikes), that cut to end of blade.

type screwdrivers two or even one medium size may be all that's needed. These types of screws are not common on electrical equipment. Make sure of the plastic handle.

A very popular type of screw-holding screwdriver, called the *Quick-Wedge*, is used by electricians when working on live terminals. The screw can be started in the hole and tightened and then the screwdriver can be removed while at no time touching any live parts.

NUT DRIVERS

Although nut drivers appear similar to screwdrivers, the business end is a socket as in a socket set—except with a screwdriver handle, Some are part of a ¼-inch socket set that includes a ratchet handle. Others are individually complete with only one size socket on a handle. This type has a hollow handle to accommodate a long bolt that must have the nut run down quite a distance. Nuts are common

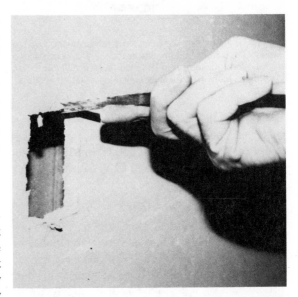

Fig. 3-2. A hacksaw blade can be used to cut an opening in drywall for a wallbox. The handle end on this hacksaw is taped.

15

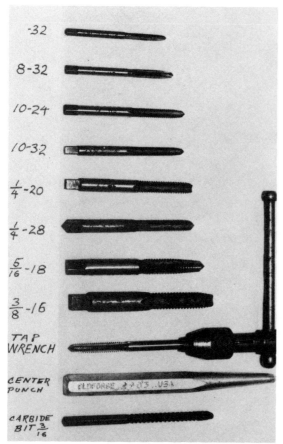

-32

8-32

10-24

10-32

¼-20

¼-28

5/16-18

3/8-16

TAP WRENCH

CENTER PUNCH

CARBIDE BIT 3/16

Fig. 3-3. Different size taps used in electrical work. The tap wrench (third from bottom) holds tap. The punch (second from bottom) makes an indentation to start drills in metal. Carbide bit (bottom) is used for concrete drilling for anchors.

on home appliances, service-entrance equipment, and distribution panels. One-quarter-inch drive-socket sets retail for about $10.00 to $15.00. Individual nut drivers cost from $1 to $2 each.

WRENCHES

Hex head nuts, bolts, and sheet-metal screws are tightened either with nut drivers or open end or adjustable wrenches. This is with *dead* equipment only. The larger sizes are used for types of conduit fittings (among other things). Sizes to buy are 6-inch, 8-inch, and 10-inch adjustable. Buy top quality.

HACKSAWS

The best tool for cutting metal is the hacksaw. They are made in many different styles. The common style is the frame hacksaw that takes a ½-inch by 10- or 12-inch long blade. Blades have three sizes of teeth with spacing of 18, 24, and 32 teeth to the inch. Buy the 32-teeth saw blade in high-speed steel. The cost is about $1 each, but they will last much longer than the less expensive ones. The teeth are hardened and the back is flexible. The less expensive ones will break in the middle. Most frame hacksaws are adjustable to take either 10- or 12-inch blades. Buy a medium-grade frame. There is also a small keyhole-type hacksaw useful for cutting drywall openings and for use in restricted areas. Another type of frame uses broken blades as the keyhole type uses its blade.

METAL SNIPS

Although most metal can be cut with the hacksaw, thin sheet metal must be cut with tin snips. Metal snips should be chosen with care. The best brand of snips are made by *Wiss*. They make every kind of hand shearing tool from heavy sheet-metal snips down to embroidery scissors. Aviation snips are not absolutely necessary, but they are extremely useful. If you have much sheet metalwork, "cuts right" and "cuts left" models are really necessary. Years ago I purchased a "non-Wiss" brand and I have been having trouble making them work right for me ever since. Keep in mind that no one brand is best in design for all tools.

BOLT TAPS AND DIES

All cabinets, wall boxes and junction boxes have tapped holes for mounting screws, as do many devices. These items when purchased usually have good threads tapped in them, but defects show up anyway. Wall boxes already mounted in place can be saved, if they have bad threads, by using the correct size tap. Taps cost from $.75 to over $1 each. All that are needed are 6-32, 8-32 and 10-32. Sometimes the 10-24 thread is needed. This is the common 3/16-inch bolt size. A tap wrench handle holds the tap so that it is entered into the hole

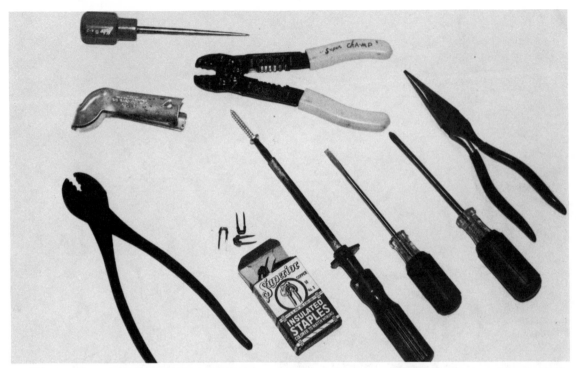

Fig. 3-4. Top: prick punch, crimping and wire skinning tool, Romex skinner (strips casing for removal), crimping tool for uninsulated terminals, low-voltage wire staples (insulated), screw holding screwdriver (may be used on "hot" wires because it only takes one hand; complete handle is insulated), rubber handle, 4-inch screwdriver, regular blade, rubber handle Phillips screwdriver (rubber handles are for comfort only), needlenose pliers. Plastic handles are for comfort only.

straight. These handles cost between $2 and $3. Dies with the accompanying die stock (handle) are used to thread bolts and machine screws. You would find occasional uses.

LOCKING (VISE) PLIERS

The very popular locking pliers are a great help. With no vise at hand, parts can be held for drilling holes in safely. Vise-Grip is the best brand. It is used almost exclusively by industry and is very reliable.

POWER TOOLS

The best time and labor savers have to be the portable power tools used in the home, building construction, repair shops, and industry. As in electric drill motors and hand-held power saws, price is an indicator of quality. The amperage listed on the name plate also is another good indication of

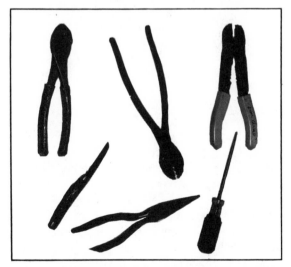

Fig. 3-5. Top, left to right: diagonal cutters (dikes), tools for crimping on terminals, and tool for crimping on insulated terminals. Bottom: pocket knife, needlenose side cutters, and rubber grip with 4-×-3/16-inch blade.

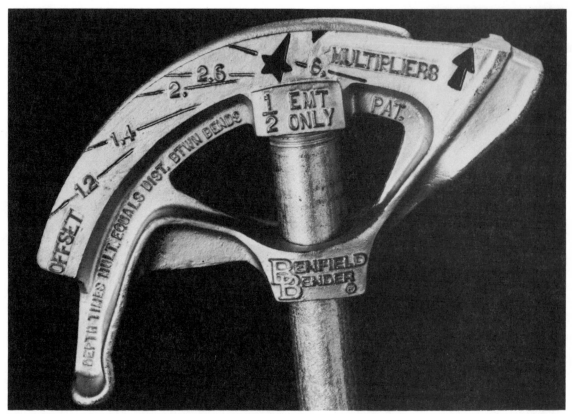

Fig. 3-6. Front view of Thinwall (EMT) bender by Benfield Co. (courtesy Jack Benfield, copyright holder and inventor.).

good quality. When buying an electric drill motor, select Black and Decker, Skilsaw, or Rockwell brand name motors. A ¼-inch or ⅜-inch capacity variable-speed drill motor is a good investment. Buy in the range of $35 and you need never buy another. Be sure not to lose it, though.

Electrically operated power tools *must* be maintained in first-class condition. Older models might have three wire cords with three-prong grounding plugs on them. They are supposed to have the metal housing connected to the grounding (green) wire that is in turn connected to the grounding prong of the plug (U shape). You can determine if this is the case by using a continuity tester. Put the probes of the tester (one on the metal housing and one on the U blade of the plug). A light indicates that the case is grounded properly. Now put one prod on the case and the other on one of the flat blades of the plug, then on the other flat

blade. A light in either of these last two tests indicates a ground to the housing. Dangerous! This defect *must* be repaired immediately before using the tool again.

A much older tool will have only a two-blade plug. This is not to be confused with the modern *double insulated* tools sold today. These new tools come with a *two*-prong plug and have a very good record of safety. Buy them with confidence. Three-prong grounded power tools are still available for purchase, but they are generally available in heavier usage types. The only way to be safe with this old two-wire tool is to rewire with three-wire cord and plug and ground the frame with the green grounding wire.

HAND TOOLS WITH PLASTIC-COATED HANDLES

Many hand tools such as pliers, wrenches, and tin snips are sold with plastic grips on the handles.

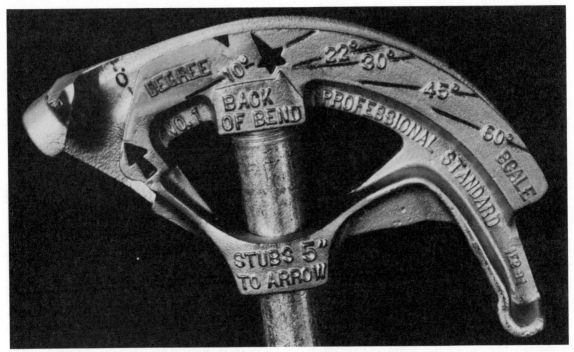

Fig. 3-7. Back view of Thinwall (EMT) bender (courtesy Jack Benfield, copyright holder and inventor.).

This plastic is put on by a dipping process. *Note*: These plastic grips are not to be considered as having any insulating value at all. They are merely a *comfort grip*. They will not provide insulation from electricity. This information is on the authority of the local electric utility (Detroit Edison). This is in the form of a notice posted in their repair shops for the information of their employees and others. They warn against using and depending on this so-called *insulation*. The only true source of true insulated grips is Sears. They sell them for self installation. The grips are softened in boiling water and then forced on the handles by tapping with a block of wood while still hot, They are sold as

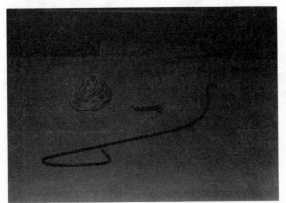

Fig. 3-8. Coil of chalkline with "mouse" attached. Tool for fishing chalkline out of wall made from coathanger wire. Shown bent to hook line from far side of hollow wall.

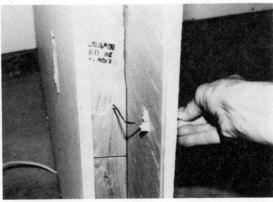

Fig. 3-9. Fishing tool bent to check for free area clearance for wallbox installation.

Fig. 3-10. Chalkline in place with "mouse" attached. Note it does not touch bottom.

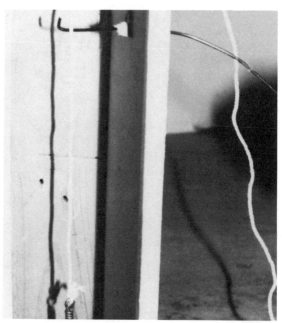

Fig. 3-11. Fishing tool about to hook line. If the "mouse" is laid on the bottom, the line will be slack and lie against the drywall and be hard to hook.

Fig. 3-12. Using a thinwall bender to make an offset (double bend) to allow thinwall to enter handy box and still remain flush to wall. Start of bend.

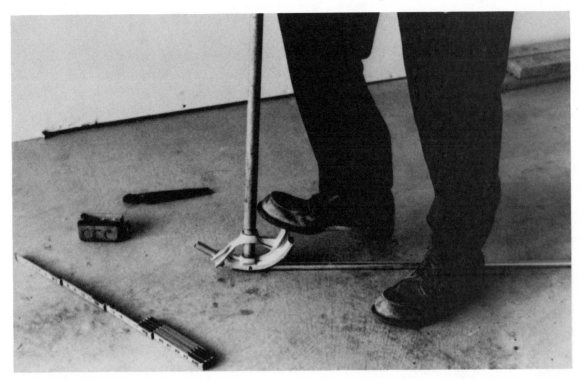

Fig. 3-13. First bend made.

Fig. 3-14. Second bend being made. Bender is upside down for convenience instead of looking for floor edge to let first bend hang over while second bend is made.

Fig. 3-15. Second bend completed. Your foot must be on the end of handle on concrete to prevent slipping.

Fig. 3-16. Completed offset.

Fig. 3-17. Box connector being tightened into knockout. Snug up inside locknut and tighten with groove joint pliers on the outside.

insulating grips. Their thickness is at least three times the thickness of the dipped grips and the plastic is a different material.

DRILL BITS

As with other tools, drill bits come in different grades and qualities. For drilling steel buy only *high-speed steel* bits. These can be used to drill all other materials except masonry. Carbide tipped drill bits, *masonry drills*, are the only drill bits that can be used for drilling all forms of masonry. The small sizes such as 3/16 inch, 1/4 inch, 5/16 inch, and 1/2 inch will be needed. Smaller sizes are for plastic inserts used with No. 10 sheet-metal screws to mount metal boxes. The ½-inch drill will accommodate ¼-20 lead anchors using plain ¼-inch bolts for heavier items. Also they will accommodate the insertion of toggle bolts in hollow tile and concrete blocks.

If you need to drill larger holes for conduit or cable, larger and longer carbide drills can be rented at rental businesses. Sometimes *hammer drills* are needed and they can also be rented there. Long lengths are up to 24 inches and larger-diameter drills are also available.

ELECTRICAL TESTERS

Testers that are used on live circuits are called *voltage testers* and are used to test for the presence of voltage (power) in equipment in use or having unidentified problems. Presence or absence of power is determined and is corrected or defective components are replaced. Electricians and service technicians use the testers constantly.

The commercial heavy-duty testers are on the market for about $20. They have long life and some have replaceable test leads available. A pocket tester costing under $2 is available in hardware stores. This tester is for testing circuits that are live (hot).

The *continuity* tester is *not* for use on live circuits! This tester is used on nonenergized circuits and certain controls to determine what problems are causing the trouble in equipment or wiring. One continuity tester is built into a flashlight. Brite Star manufactures such a tester. The flashlight has a radio jack in the end cap and is supplied with two test leads having a radio plug on one end that is plugged into the end cap. By turning on the flashlight switch, the tester is ready for use. The light will not go on even though the switch is pushed to "on." Touching the two test leads together or testing for continuity will cause the light to go on. Removing the plug will also cause the light to go on.

Fig. 3-18. Handy box with thinwall attached. Note the neatness of the finished assembly.

Fig. 3-19. Start of a "stub-up" 90-degree bend. Information on bender itself gives measurement instructions.

Turn the switch off when done using the tester. All continuity testers must have a current source (batteries).

Electricians use a homemade tester for testing wiring in an unfinished building that does not have the wiring connected to a source of power. In this way, all wiring is checked out before power is applied. This eliminates any defects that would show up as blown fuses or worse and might damage expensive equipment. This tester is made from a 6-volt lantern battery and buzzer or bell and long test leads.

Electronic buffs might use a volt-ohmmeter as a tester. This use will work but placing prods on connections and then watching the needle is difficult. The flashlight can be seen out of the corner of

Fig. 3-20. Finishing 90-degree bend.

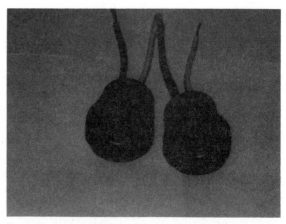

Fig. 3-21. Homemade 230-V tester. Two weatherproof rubber sockets wired in series. This will also test 115-V circuits. With the power on.

24

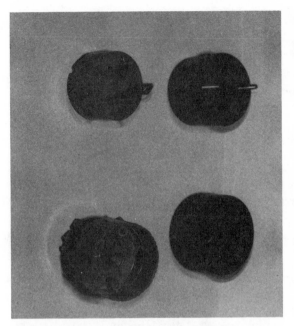

Fig. 3-22. Making your own extension cord (three-wire grounded cord and connectors). Attachment plug and connector shown disassembled. These are both "dead front" as required now.

Fig. 3-24. Cord end prepared for attachment. The extra "wire" is a shadow. There are only three wires.

Fig. 3-23. Wire end being stripped by stripper on tool. Outer covering had been removed.

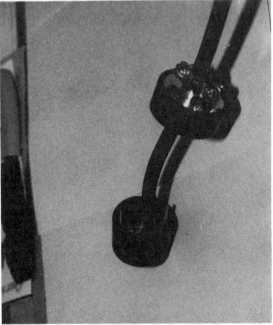

Fig. 3-25. Wires attached to terminals ready for assembly.

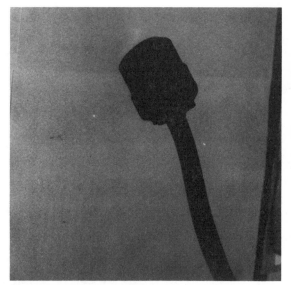

Fig. 3-26. Completed connector assembly.

Fig. 3-28. Assembled attachment plug.

the eye. You must look at the needle. Because this tester is used on only dead circuits, there must be a small voltage source—flashlight batteries.

A second type of tester is a vest pocket flashlight with one lead built in. This seems to me to be less handy because only one lead makes it more

Fig. 3-27. Wired attachment plug ready for assembly.

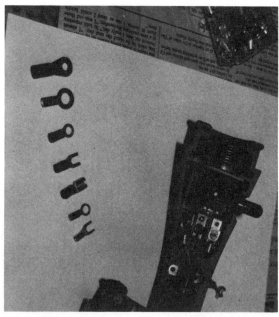

Fig. 3-29. Repaired (bad cord section cut away and new crimp-on terminals used) trouble light head. Crimp-on terminals show in lower left. Those with "fat" ends have them insulated so they do not touch each other.

Fig. 3-30. Two types of "live" circuit testers. The right one plugs directly into a receptacle. This for 115 V only. The other is for 230 V or 115 V. This must be handled with care because ends must touch "live" terminals.

awkward,. The case is used as the other lead. These cost about $4.

The type most used by electricians when testing new installations is homemade. A 6-volt lantern battery and a door buzzer plus leads are assembled by taping the buzzer to the battery and having 2-foot leads to handle greater spacing of the parts to be tested. The battery and buzzer might cost $6. The battery will last a long time but it is not so portable or handy as the Brite Star.

As electronic buffs usually have a volt-ohm-meter in their tool kit, this can also be used. It can be used as a voltage tester or as a continuity tester, the latter by using the ohmmeter scale. This tester is also awkward. I find I have to watch the needle while holding the prods on the wires or terminals being tested. With the flashlight type, the light will be seen out of the corner of the eye without taking the eye off the test area. This makes for an easier test procedure. You must make up your own mind.

The pocket tester has a neon bulb and short leads. The whole tester is the size of a large pencil. This tester has been known to give false readings

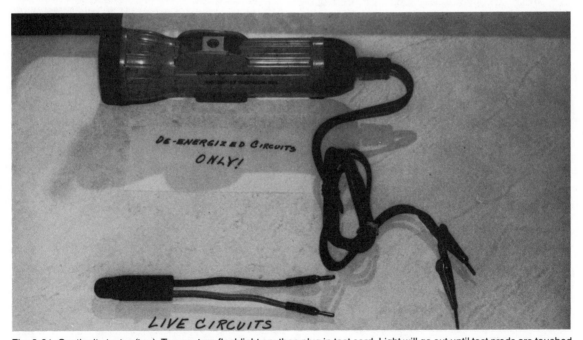

Fig. 3-31. Continuity tester (top). To use, turn flashlight on; then plug in test cord. Light will go out until test prods are touched together or continuous circuit is tested. Caution: Use only on dead circuits. Voltage tester (lower) 90 V to 600 V. Use on live circuits. Power on.

because of the neon bulb and the fact that a feedback can occur from other live circuits. Even though it is very low in cost, I do not recommend it.

EXTENSION CORDS

With the heavy usage that extension cords have to put up with, it is advisable to buy as good a cord as you can afford. A 50-foot, heavy-duty cord (16-3 or 14-3) should cost perhaps $15. The heavier wire is to prevent voltage drop on long runs. If you have all the current shut off you will need this long length. The three wires are the black, white, and green. The green is for grounding. Do not buy two-wire cords.

Some extension cords have a trouble light on the end of the cord and others do not. If the trouble light is a good one it will have an outlet or maybe two on the light handle. If the cord is three wire (with ground wire), it should have a three-slot grounded outlet. Check the lamp guard. It should be easy to change the bulb without having to dismantle everything to get at it.

When you buy a bulb or bulbs for the trouble light, be sure to get the *rough service* designated bulb. These bulbs cost more but last a very long time despite rough treatment. I have dropped them, in the guard, and they have just remained there on the ground burning as always.

CAUTIONS REGARDING POWER TOOLS

Power tools are great labor savers but they must be used with exceptional care. I have watched many workmen, amateurs and professionals, injure themselves or damage the item they were working on due to careless handling. I have also been injured or damaged something while using tools.

Drill motors are usually responsible for problems rather than a saw. The saw seems to command more respect in this regard. Large size holes drilled through the back or side of a junction box should be started by using a ⅛-inch pilot drill, then a ¼-inch drill, and finally a ⅜-inch or ½-inch drill. When a large drill breaks through the metal, it has a tendency to "hang up" (grab into the material). This can very easily spin an item like a 4-inch junction

box on the end of the drill letting it bang into your ankles.

To hold such an item, drive two nails through the holes in the back of the box into a length of 2 × 4. Stand on the 2 × 4 while drilling.

Important: When drilling anything overhead be sure to wear safety goggles. Eye protection is vitally important to preserve your eyesight. Safety regulations now recommend goggles at all times when working with tools. At least wear them whenever there is *any* danger of foreign material being thrown or dropped in your eyes. If you do get something in your eye, go immediately to the emergency room of the nearest hospital to have it removed. This is especially needed in case of metal in your eye. *Take no chances.*

TOOLS FOR CONDUIT WORK

Tools for conduit work are different in some ways from those used with Romex and BX. To bend conduit, it is necessary to purchase or rent a Thinwall bender. Thinwall tubing, which is the only type

Fig. 3-32. Duplex receptacle installed in handy box. Connecting bar broken off to separate the two outlets. One will be switch-controlled. The other hot all the time.

NEED MORE KITS?
USE THIS HANDY ORDER CARD.

"Tuck-A-Buck" SPECIAL

FOR
CONTRACTORS AND PROFESSIONAL ELECTRICIANS

THE FAMOUS BENFIELD® BETTER BENDING KIT . . . only $1.00 U.S. (Plus Postage)
(Works for any Bender made)

Each Kit Contains
- 3" x 6" Zip-Guide Label For Bender Handle
- Wallet Size Offset Reference Card
- 22 Page Manual "Bending The Benfield Way"

Tuck this card and one dollar plus 60¢ in stamps for each kit (to cover mailing costs) into an envelope and mail to:

Benfield Benders
P.O. Box 544
Ft. Lauderdale
Florida 33302

If by checks or M.O.
1-5 kits (ea.) $ 1.60
6 kits for $ 9.00
12 kits for $17.00
(We pay postage & Handling)

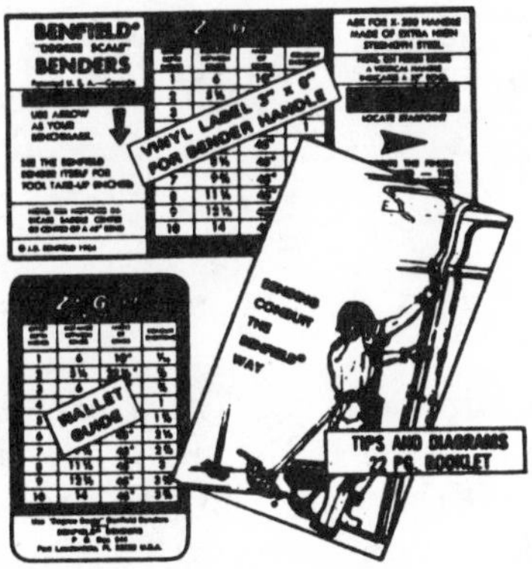

YOUR NAME ______________ (PLEASE PRINT)

ADDRESS ______________

CITY ______________

STATE ______________ ZIP ______________

BB-82-6

Send to: Benfield Benders
P.O. Box 544
Fort Lauderdale, Fla. 33302
(may be photocopied)

Fig. 3-33. Order form for "Famous Benfield Better Bending Kit." May be photocopied. Price for the unit is $1.60.

you ought to be using, must be bent with this special bender to prevent crushing the tubing. The bender costs about $14. Newer models of benders are able to bend both ½-inch and ¾-inch Thinwall. They also cost more. Benders come with directions in the form of an illustrated booklet giving complete directions. You might have to practice before becoming good at it.

The regular 90-degree bend is made with the bender hooked onto the conduit, in the right place, and pulled down by the handle. If the next bend is in the opposite direction, the bender is set on the floor handle end down and the conduit is inserted in the bender head which is up in the air. Then the conduit itself is used as the handle to bend itself down to the right angle. Your foot is on the handle end of the bender resting on the floor to keep it from slipping. This maneuver is tricky but it works. It took me quite a while to get the knack of it. Refer to Figs. 3-6 through 3-20 and Fig. 3-33.

The "hickey" is used for bending rigid conduit similar to water pipe. Never use water pipe for conduit. Rigid conduit is difficult to work with because it requires pipe dies, a pipe vise, and other related equipment. You will never need to use rigid conduit.

HOLE SAWS

If it is necessary to make large holes in metal, hole saws are very useful. Metal cutting saws are expensive but necessary to bore holes in metal. Uses would be for holes in cabinets to insert conduit or Romex where there is no knockout available. You will find other uses for them. Buy only high-speed saws.

TIPS ON TOOLS

In many cases, you will be able to purchase good hand tools and possibly power tools used at garage sales and the second-hand stores. Power tools should be inspected carefully before purchase to determine their condition. You might be able to find good bargains this way. Just be cautious because they might not be returnable.

Figures 3-21 through 3-32 show some tools and techniques.

Chapter 4

Service-Entrance Equipment

SERVICE-ENTRANCE EQUIPMENT, AS THE NAME implies, is the equipment and necessary cable or conduit and wires to bring electric service into a building. The meter and its connections, including the base, are included as components of the equipment. When the utility supplies service to this equipment, the wires might be overhead or underground depending on the utility's supply lines in the area. It also may be installed underground at the owner's option even though the service to the area is overhead on poles. You will have to pay for running the cable underground and up the utility pole. You might be able to do this work yourself paying only for the materials and trenching. See Figs. 4-1 through 4-26.

The service-entrance equipment is intended as a means of disconnecting the electrical supply to the premises. It consists of a circuit breaker or fuses and a switch (called a fused disconnect). This may be either inside or outside the building. The circuit breaker is used in many houses although fuses are still one of the best overcurrent protection devices available. The breaker is convenient and it can be reset. The fuse is very dependable.

The utility will make the connection to your service-entrance equipment when the installation has been approved by the local electrical inspector *and* the utility. Before starting any work on your system, visit the local offices of your utility and city inspection department. Have with you a simple plan showing the proposed location of the service equipment in relation to the utility's lines.

POWER SUPPLY

Power to modern houses is called the three-wire 115/230-V system. This system consists of three wires brought from the utility pole or underground to the house. If over head, the wires are twisted together to form a sort of cable. There will be two insulated wires and one bare wire. This is called a service drop. The bare wire serves as a messenger cable supporting the other two and is usually galvanized steel (stranded). This is the grounded neutral and it is attached to the building by a tension

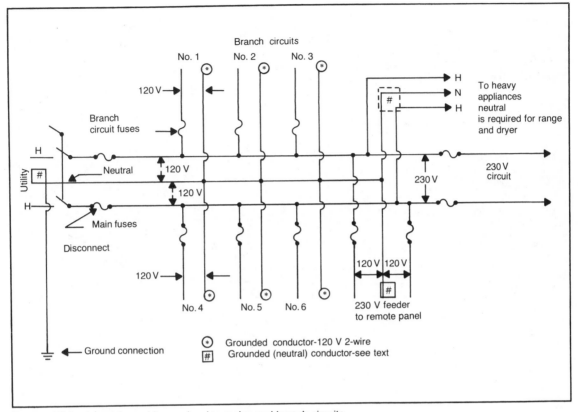

Fig. 4-1. Wiring layout for residence showing mains and branch circuits.

clamp and a bolt through the building framing. If underground, called service laterals, the wires are usually individual. This underground wire is called USE (underground service lateral). All three wires are insulated.

As shown in Fig. 4-1, the three wires provide either 115 V or 230 V depending on the connections between the wires. The two outer wires between them provide 230 V without a grounded wire (neutral); this is for water heaters and 230 V motors. Either one of the outside wires and the neutral provide 115 V for small appliances and lighting. For electric ranges and electric clothes dryers, the two outside wires plus the neutral (grounded) provide 230 V. The utility lines that supply power to the house, usually from the rear of the property, consist of two separate sets. The upper (higher on the pole) lines carry the high voltages, as much as 480 V or more. This is the transmission line from the utility

substation. At intervals, transformers are mounted on poles. These reduce the voltage to that supplied to the houses, (namely 115/230 V). One transformer supplies power to a group of houses (two or more). These low voltage wires are *below* those carrying the high voltage. Even lower on most electric utility poles are the telephone lines. Thus each different set of wires serves a different use and is always in its relative position on the utility pole.

Because of the characteristics of alternating current, the voltage can be lowered or raised by what is known as a transformer. This transformer consists of many turns of wire wound around soft iron laminations (plates). There are two separate windings known as primary, the voltage going *into* the transformer and secondary the voltage leaving the transformer. There is a ratio between the number of turns of wire in the primary and secondary windings. This ratio may be 10:1 (a voltage

Fig. 4-2A. Utility meter with tap taken off to feed an air conditioner outside condensing unit. It need not be fused as long as it is outside.

Fig. 4-2B. Utility meter with tap taken directly off load side of meter to feed an air conditioner outside condensing unit. This line need not be fused until just before connection to ac unit.

reducing transformer) or 1:10 (a voltage increasing transformer). The voltage reducing transformer is the one on the pole supplying power to your house. The high voltage from the higher (on the pole) wires, usually 2300 V, is led into the primary connection of the transformer and reduced to one-tenth emerging from the secondary connection as 230 V for use in your house. By making a center tap on the transformer, 115 V is provided for lighting and small appliances.

Storms greatly affect overhead open wiring on poles and cause power outages and downed wires (especially in the winter). The practice now is to run utility lines underground. This method is more expensive, but it eliminates a great deal of work during severe storms.

Reading an electric meter is comparatively easy. Start from the left and *always* read the number the hand has *passed*. All the dials are connected by gears between them. The gears are so proportioned that the hand on any dial rotates 10 times faster than the one to the left of that dial. Notice that one hand will rotate counterclockwise while the next one will rotate clockwise. Notice that when the *right* dial

hand moves just past "0" the reading of the meter will be for example 1880. The right dial hand continues and next records the reading as 1881, and so on. This arrangement is similar to the odometer on an automobile where each number wheel makes one revolution to move the next wheel only one number.

You can keep track of your electric usage by reading your meter at intervals. Subtract the last

Fig. 4-3. Electric watthour meter. This meter registers usage for an electric water heater. The meter reads 08217.

Fig. 4-4. Underground "service lateral" to a house in Michigan. Meter is outside. The main 100 A circuit breaker and distribution panel are inside.

reading from the present reading and you have the usage for that period. This is the usage in kilowatts (kW). The average family uses about 500 kW each month. If the water heater has a separate meter, you can monitor your hot water usage and perhaps use less hot water or lower the setting of the heater thermostat. Lowering the *set point* (temperature setting) is a simple procedure.

Shut off the power to the electric water heater before doing anything at the heater. Standard heaters usually have two stats, one upper and one lower. The stat is combined with the actual heating element that is immersed in the water of the tank. If you are sure the power is off, remove one of the stat cover plates. Figure 14-18 shows a stat and heater element exposed. The arrow points to the stat dial and pointer. The pointer is usually set at 140 degrees Fahrenheit to perhaps 150 degrees Fahrenheit. First try a set point of 130 degrees Fahrenheit. Then do the same to the other stat. Carefully replace both covers and turn the power back on. Try this setting of the stat for one week. You might be

Fig. 4-5. Overhead high tension lines in Michigan. The voltage is perhaps 175,000 V.

Fig. 4-6. Modern high tension tower in Michigan. The voltage is perhaps 175,000 V.

Fig. 4-7. Transformer substation and transmission lines in suburban Detroit. A highline tower is visible in right rear background.

Fig. 4-8. Meter box (base) as received from the utility. Notice the latch for accepting the utility's seal. This prevents tampering. Meter box is courtesy Detroit Edison Co.

able to reduce the set point even lower to 125 degrees Fahrenheit or less. Save money by doing this.

Some utilities might still control electric water heaters by means of a timer set up to power the heater only at low demand loads at the generating station. This means that the heater would be off for extended periods. With this arrangement, the heater size is understandably larger (80 gal.) and the water temperature is higher, 150 degrees Fahrenheit or more. The billing is a flat rate per month. For times when there is no more hot water there is another circuit that can be turned on, but which is *metered* through the regular meter at the high rate. This arrangement might still be used in some areas, but, it is not popular now.

SERVICEDROP AND SERVICE LATER

The overhead lines from the pole are called the *servicedrop*. This will consist of three twisted wires, one bare and two insulated. The bare wire, the stronger of the three, is the neutral and is used to support the cable by means of an adjustable *tension connector*. The point of attachment to the building must be a minimum of 10 feet above grade, in some areas higher, and 10 feet above the

sidewalk. Other clearances are 12 feet above a private drive and 18 feet above public highways. The utility will maintain these clearances on its own wires. Clearances over roofs must be a minimum of 8 feet. The building where the final attachment is to be made must have this attachment point high enough to give this 8-foot clearance. There are two exceptions to this. The first is where clearances over roofs range from 3 feet minimum where the voltage between the conductors does not exceed 300 volts and the roof has a slope of not less than 4 inches in 12 inches. The other clearance exception is where a service head extends through the overhang portion of a roof. This clearance minimum is 18 inches at the point of attachment to the mast. Clearance around building openings must be maintained a minimum of 36 inches away from the bottom and sides of door and window openings. Areas above such openings have no minimum clearance because they are considered out of reach.

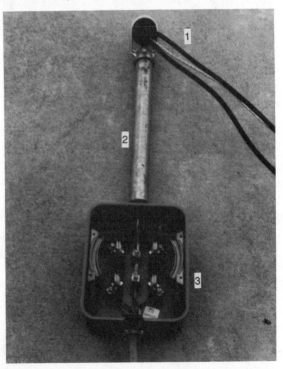

Fig. 4-9. Mock-up of 1) Service head; 2) Mast (the actual mast up at least 10 feet or more); 3) The meter box and the service-entrance cable. Notice the three wires going into the service head: two black insulated and one bare (neutral).

35

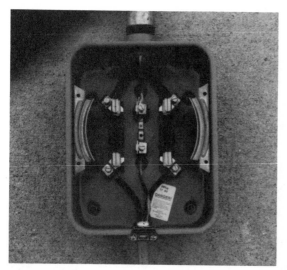

Fig. 4-10. Close-up view of meter box showing wiring. The two black insulated wires terminate at two connectors at the top and start again at two other connectors at the bottom. Between these two connectors are slots where the meter prongs plug in. The neutral (center) goes right on through without a break.

The underground lines from the utility connection to the premises are called *service laterals*. They are direct burial cable or three separate conductors. Raceways may also be used. These wires must be continuous. They may not have splices between the utility connection and the meter connection. Some utilities furnish and install the service lateral. You will be billed for this work. Raceways that may be used are duct, nonmetallic conduit, and galvanized rigid conduit. Galvanizing must be approved by the inspector to guard against corrosion. Otherwise a coating that is noncorrosive must be applied to the conduit. Cable or three separate wires must enter or leave conduit whose ends are capped with insulating bushings. This would be where they enter a building or leave the ground to enter a conduit that will go up a pole.

Because underground is classified as a *wet location*, the insulation must be one of the following types: RUW, RHW, USE, TW, THW, THWN, XHHW, and lead covered. The local inspector may require additional protection. Utility requirements are spelled out in Figs. 4-21 and 4-22.

METER AND SERVICE DISCONNECT

Usually only *one* servicedrop or service lateral is permitted per building. There are exceptions to this rule, but they do not apply to single dwellings. Figure 4-9 shows the mast, meter base, and conduit leading to the basement. The service disconnect will be on the first floor in cottages, and commercial buildings and dwellings with no basement. In this

Fig. 4-11. This mock-up of a 60-A, service-entrance panel shows wiring methods used. Top left is the service-entrance cable connected to the main terminals. Top right is service-entrance cable leaving to the range. Four branch circuits are shown wired and leaving the cabinet. The neutral bar is bottom center below the fuse holders. The wire nut lower right is tying together all the grounding wires from the "with ground" cables. Two large screws and one small screw at the top center are part of the neutral bar showing at the bottom center. These are to connect the service-entrance neutral, the neutral to the range, and the grounding conductor (wire) to the water pipe ground.

Fig. 4-12. Service-entrance cable at top center, range cable leaves right, grounding electrode (wire) from neutral terminal to copper water pipe clamp. This is a mock-up.

case, the cable may have to be brought out of the meter base and turned 180° and carried through the building wall to the service disconnect.

In other cases, the disconnect will be on the outside adjacent the meter. It can also be combined in one cabinet with the meter base. In cases where there is a roof overhang all around the building, the service mast and head must extend through the overhang at a location to allow the conduit to lie flush against the building exterior wall. The mast must be high enough to provide the 10-foot minimum clearance. If the mast is quite tall to provide this clearance, a guy wire *must* be installed to anchor the mast. This arrangement is needed to take the strain of high winds, snow, and ice on the servicedrop. The conduit must be at least 1¼-inch trade size. It must also be anchored securely to the building structure below the overhang. Commercial

buildings have specially formed galvanized angle iron masts with anchor bolts through the concrete block wall with 4-inch square plates on the inside under nuts and washers.

Conduit looks nice, but cable may be used below the meter through the wall and into the service-entrance panel. You may also use service-entrance cable *above* the meter from the service head to the meter base, provided there is enough height to maintain the 10-foot minimum of the servicedrop. The choice is up to you with the approval of the inspector.

The service disconnect must have enough capacity to handle the current draw of the system. If the system is designed for 100-amp, 125-amp, or 150-amp capacity, then the disconnect or circuit breaker *must have* that same capacity. In addition, the wires or cable serving the system must have

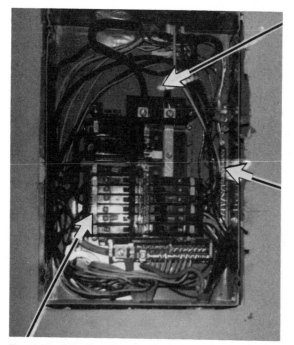

Fig. 4-13. Service-entrance panel showing 230-V mains upper right. The neutral is light gray connected to lower center terminal. The main breaker is outside with others because this is a condominium. The double breaker top left is for the range. Two more double breakers on the right are: furnace-ac and electric clothes dryer.

like capacity. Refer to the tables in the appendix giving the "ampacities" of wires and cables. Some *load centers* incorporate a *main breaker* and breakers for individual circuits. In areas where permitted, this assembly can be installed outside. Weatherproof panels are manufactured so individual circuit breaker panels are also installed outside.

The Service-Entrance Circuit Breaker (Main Circuit Breaker)

Overcurrent devices *must* be installed to disconnect the utility lines from the feeders for working on equipment beyond that point (the distribution panel, etc.). The other reason for the overcurrent device is to protect the wires between the main breaker and the distribution panel. These wires must be protected from currents in excess of their capacity that is determined by their size and type of insulation. The wires from the service head all the way to the distribution panel are thus protected from overcurrents.

The common form of overcurrent protection now used is the circuit breaker. Breakers have the advantage of being able to be reset instead of being replaced. Breakers are available in 15-amp to 50-amp sizes (in 5-amp increments) and from 50-amp to 100-amp (in 10-amp increments). Thereafter the ratings are 110, 125, 150, 175 and 200 amp. Service-entrance equipment is available in various capacities to meet the needs of the installation. For dwellings, the range is from 50 amp to 225 amp. They are also available with space for from two breakers to 42 breakers. See Figs. 4-17 and 4-18.

If the service-entrance equipment and the main breaker or fuses is at some distance from the distribution panel, the wires between these two panels are called *feeders*. This might be where the main service breaker or fuses are outside in the cabinet with electric meter. The main overcurrent devices will protect these wires. *Note*: The larger

Fig. 4-14. Service-entrance panel using nontamperable fuses (Fustats). One main pull-out, upper right; eight fustats, upper left; two spare fuseholders, lower left; ac and dryer fuse pull-outs, lower right. The neutral is bottom center and neutral bar is hidden on the right side behind all the white (grounded) wires. This is a 230 V service.

Fig. 4-15A. Condominium service entrance meter and disconnect assembly. Left: meters, power, right meters, water heaters. Four-unit building. Top left meter is for outside lighting (house lights). Top arrow points to photocell controlling outside lights. Lower arrow points to grounding electrode conductor going inside to cold water pipe.

sizes of wire used in these cases must be connected to the equipment using pressure type connectors. These connectors are those with an opening into which the bared wire end is inserted and a setscrew is tightened down on the wire, thus making a very secure connection. Soldering is prohibited.

In wiring houses the neutral wire is grounded. The ground is usually a cold-water pipe from a city water supply. This is a very good ground. If you use service-entrance cable for your installation, the neutral will be *bare*. The insulated wires are in the center and the bare neutral made of very fine wires is wrapped around the two insulated wires. When a connection is made at either end, this neutral is unwound from the other two wires and formed into a wire by twisting the strands tightly together. This and the other two are then inserted into their respective pressure-type connectors. The neutral

Fig. 4-15B. Condominium service entrance, meter, and disconnect assembly. Large center box is the building main disconnect. Left meter bank is lighting and power. Right meter bank is electric water heaters. This is a four-unit building. Top left meter is for outside perimeter lighting. Top center to the right of the small box is the photocell to control the outside lighting. Note the ground wire to the right of the large conduit at the bottom. This goes inside to a cold-water pipe ground.

Fig. 4-15C. Close-up of photocell. Cell "eye" faces to the right to not be influenced by car lights.

Fig. 4-16. Panel (in Fig. 4-13) with cover on. Main breaker is outside with meters.

able in sizes up to 125-amp capacity. Figure 1-4 illustrates a service-entrance panel of 125-amp capacity. Shown are pull-outs for the main, the range, and the air conditioner. Shown in use are eight circuits (four 15-amp and four 20-amp). The 15-amp "fustats" have hexagon windows to distinguish them as being 15-amp or less capacity. There are two spare circuits that are available for additions.

The disadvantages of the fuse type panel is that spare fuses (or fustats) must always be on hand (both 15-amp and 20-amp sizes) to prevent having to shop for fuses at such times as midnight, Sundays, or holidays. The fuses in the photo are the

wire, because it carries less amps than the two hot wires, may be *one* size smaller, provided they are larger than No. 6. In service-entrance cable, this is already taken care of by the manufacturer. The meter base is supplied by the utility and installed by the contractor or yourself. Go to the utility to obtain the meter *base*. This is part of the service assembly to be installed by you.

The Fused Service Entrance

The other type of overcurrent device is the fuse used in older installations. This older type of service-entrance panel consisted of a 60-amp enclosure and one or more "pull-out" fuse blocks. Larger-capacity panels had more pull-out blocks to accommodate an air conditioner or other heavily used appliances such as an electric water heater or clothes dryer. The main fuse block would have two 60-amp cartridge fuses that would protect the lighting circuits having plug fuses for protecting them. The fuse blocks for the range and other appliances would be directly supplied from the main bus bars and would not be fed through the main fuses.

This type of service-entrance panel is avail-

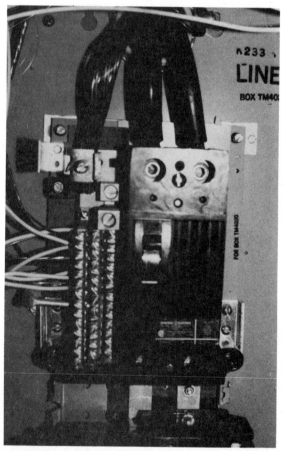

Fig. 4-17. Shows the main breaker in the center. Large neutral bar contains 42 spaces for 42 circuits. Building is under construction and wiring is not finished. Only a few circuits are used.

40

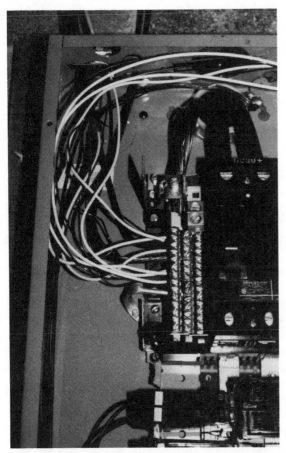

Fig. 4-18. View of white wires. Note last connection of neutral bar is jumper from cabinet itself to neutral bar, a code requirement.

slow lag type having a special thread on the base (type S fuse).

Fuses are hard to change and require caution when you do so. The cartridge fuses on the pull-out blocks are expensive. The 30-amp fuses cost about $.60 each and the 60-amp main fuses cost about $1.25 each. In all other respects, fused service-entrance panels and distribution panels are most satisfactory.

I must make it very clear that *any* wiring that is required to be protected by an overcurrent device *must* be protected by the correct size of fuse or circuit breaker. And vice versa, a circuit breaker or fuse of a designated rating must only have wiring of the correct size and insulation material connected

to it. Example: No. 14 wire may only be protected by a fuse or circuit breaker of 15-amp rating or less, not by a 20 A fuse or breaker. For more complete information refer to the 1981 Code, Article 230, Services, and Article 240.

Overcurrent Protection

When deciding on the size of the service-entrance equipment, allow for expansion of needs as the family grows and purchases additional appliances. Larger entrance and distribution equipment will cost more, it is true, but it will be only a fraction of the cost of its removal and the installation of larger equipment. Also the system would have to be de-energized to make the changeover.

INSTALLATION AND GROUNDING OF EQUIPMENT

All wiring systems *must* be grounded for the pro-

Fig. 4-19. Utility meter feeding service-entrance panel in large residence.

41

Fig. 4-20. Continuation of utility connections. Shows water-proof angle fitting to enter basement. Left conduit is the underground service lateral from the utility. Cable might be the phone line.

tection of persons coming in contact with any metal parts carrying current because of a fault when normally these parts would not be live. And to protect the wiring system itself from faults such as defective workmanship or materials, defects developing due to wear or age, and in case of lightning striking utility lines anywhere near the building causing melting of wiring and shorting through of switches and outlets on the premises.

Items To Be Grounded

Referring to Fig. 4-1 and Fig. 4-23, note that it is especially important to not only ground the metal parts not carrying current, but the neutral (grounded wire) at the service-entrance panel where it is connected to the neutral bar. If the

service entrance is combined with the distribution panel, the individual circuit neutral wires will also be connected to one neutral bar, a multiple connection point.

Methods Of Grounding

Referring to Fig. 4-23, notice that the *grounding* conductor must be carried from the service-entrance panel to a good earth ground. In the case of Fig. 4-1, the city underground water supply pipe is an excellent ground. Be sure to attach the ground clamp on the street side of the water meter. Otherwise a jumper wire with a ground clamp on the water pipe on each side of the water meter must be installed. This is necessary to maintain a proper ground for the system if the water meter were to be removed for replacement or repair by the city. If there were no ground jumper wire, with the water meter removed, the electrical system would be without a ground. This is exceptionally dangerous to persons.

If no water pipe is suitable nor available, a metal gas pipe *may* be used, but only with the approval of your local inspector *and* the gas utility. If you cannot use the gas pipe, you *may* use a well casing (metal) but not a drop pipe in a dug well. (The well may go dry and will not provide a ground in this case.) Any underground pipe of metal not having a corrosion-resistant coating may be used if more than 10 feet are underground and in direct contact with the earth. The metal building framework of a building may also be used.

Made Electrodes

If no suitable ground is available, you must use a *made electrode*. Approved ground electrodes are: 1. A rod driven 8 feet into the ground. If made of steel, it must be ⅝ of an inch diameter minimum. If made of nonferrous metal, it must be at least ½ of an inch in diameter. 2. Pipe or rigid conduit of ¾-inch trade size, either galvanized or metal coated, driven 8 feet into the ground. If the rod or pipe cannot be driven 8 feet into the ground, drive it in at a 45° angle. In all cases, the top of the electrode must be below or flush with ground level. 3. Plate electrodes having two square feet of surface exposed.

HAWAII ELECTRIC LIGHT COMPANY, INC.

74-5519 KAIWI STREET KAILUA-KONA, HI.96740

May 5, 1978

Mr. James L. Kittle
P. O. Box 338
Kailua-Kona, Hawaii   96740

Dear Mr. Kittle:

SUBJECT: Permanent Underground Service

This is in reply to your request concerning the proposed electrical
service installation to your new home on Lot 136 located at Kona
Palisades, North Kona.

Our Company will provide, install, and maintain single phase underground cables from our service laterals on Lihilihi Street to the
customer's meter loop.

The customer's contribution to our Company for this installation
is $41.00.

The cost quotation stated above does not include taxes relating to
the project which Hawaii Electric Light Company, Inc. may have to
pay. A ruling by the Internal Revenue Service in 1975 indicated
that non-refundable contributions will be taxable as ordinary income.
The utility industry will vigorously oppose the taxing of such
receipts before the U. S. Congress. However, if Congress concurs
with the IRS ruling, this quotation may be adjusted to reflect the
increased cost to HELCO. Accordingly, the cost quotation in this
proposal letter is subject to revision until the service orders
are issued for this project.

The customer is to provide and install the following:

1. Necessary meter loop.
2. One (1) 2" rigid galvanized or PVC conduit
   from the meter socket or splice can down the
   wall and into trench with a 2" standard bend.
3. Do all trenching and backfilling. Refer to
   our attached sheet, Page 26 of our Service
   Installation Manual for depth requirements.
4. Conduits shall contain a #12 AWG galvanized
   pulling wire or equivalent in each conduit.
5. Refer to our revised "Service Installation
   Manual" for specification.

Fig. 4-21. Specifications by Hawaii Electric Light Company, Inc. for residential service underground (service lateral). Notice the
requirements listed in the last paragraph.

SERVICE INSTALLATION MANUAL
Hawaiian Electric Co., Inc.
Hawaii Electric Light Co., Inc.
Maui Electric Co., Ltd.

Cancels Page No. 26
all previous issues

Page No. 26
Effective: June 1, 1977

RESIDENTIAL SERVICE

UNDERGROUND
(Continued)

B. TRENCHING AND BACKFILLING.

Except for the conditions listed below, service conductors shall be direct-buried in a trench or installed in a conduit provided by customer from meter location to the secondary connection point at the property line,* location of which point will be designated by the Company. Trench shall provide a minimum cover of 24" above direct-buried service conductors and shall be a minimum of 4" wide. As an alternate method, the cable may be installed in conduit (see Paragraph C.2 below) for which the minimum cover shall be 18".

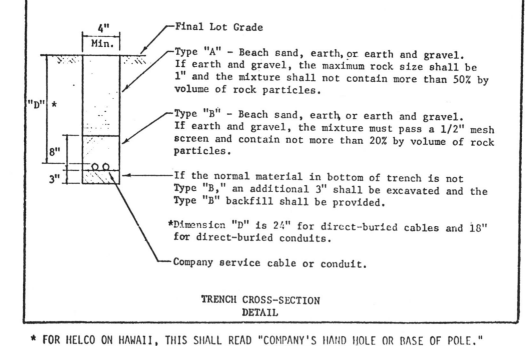

Final Lot Grade

Type "A" - Beach sand, earth, or earth and gravel. If earth and gravel, the maximum rock size shall be 1" and the mixture shall not contain more than 50% by volume of rock particles.

Type "B" - Beach sand, earth, or earth and gravel. If earth and gravel, the mixture must pass a 1/2" mesh screen and contain not more than 20% by volume of rock particles.

If the normal material in bottom of trench is not Type "B," an additional 3" shall be excavated and the Type "B" backfill shall be provided.

*Dimension "D" is 24" for direct-buried cables and 18" for direct-buried conduits.

Company service cable or conduit.

TRENCH CROSS-SECTION
DETAIL

* FOR HELCO ON HAWAII, THIS SHALL READ "COMPANY'S HAND HOLE OR BASE OF POLE."

Fig. 4-22. Excerpt from "Service Installation Manual" by Hawaii Electric Light Company, Inc. Shows their requirements for underground installation of wires from utility to house (service lateral).

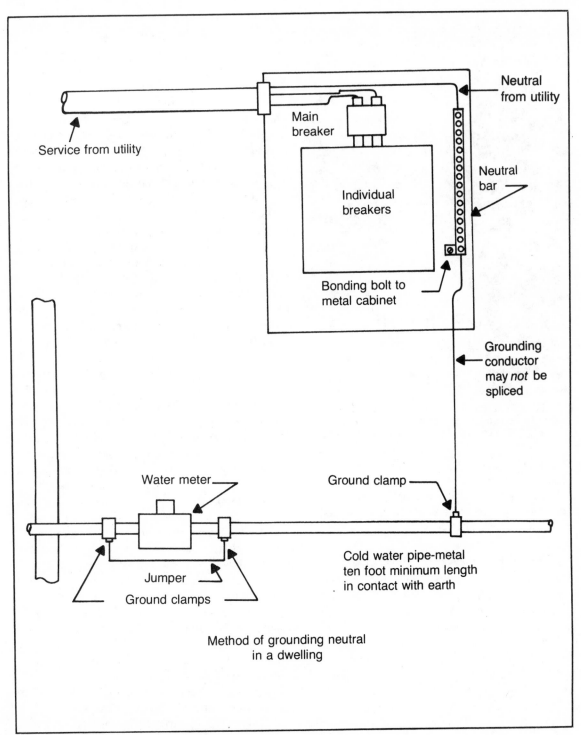

Neutral from utility

Main breaker

Individual breakers

Service from utility

Neutral bar

Bonding bolt to metal cabinet

Grounding conductor may *not* be spliced

Water meter

Ground clamp

Jumper

Ground clamps

Cold water pipe-metal ten foot minimum length in contact with earth

Method of grounding neutral in a dwelling

Fig. 4-23. Method of grounding neutral in a dwelling.

Fig. 4-24. Utility transformer in residential area. Top wires are 4800 V. Those wires directly below transformer are 115/120 V and 230/240 V. Lowest wires are telephone and cable TV.

Steel plates must be ¼ of an inch thick and nonferrous plates 0.06-inches thick. *Caution:* lightning rod grounds *shall* not be used as system grounds. The plate-type electrode shall be buried at least 18 inches below the surface.

The Ground Wire And The Grounding Wire

The grounding electrode conductor (grounding wire) shall have no splices. It shall be continuous for its entire length from the service-entrance panel neutral bar to the ground electrode (water pipe, rod, plate, etc.). This *grounding* wire may be of copper, aluminum, or copper clad aluminum. It must be at least No. 6, if stapled to the building. It may be insulated or bare or stranded or solid. Smaller size grounding wire may be used but it has to be in conduit and the requirements are stringent. It is easier and less expensive to use a minimum of No. 6 or No. 4 and staple it. Both the entrance enclosure and the ground clamp must have pressure-type connectors for the grounding wire connections.

Grounding Devices

There are various types of grounding methods because of the design of various devices requiring grounding. They are as follows: a clip to push onto the edge of a wall box, a machine screw inside the wall box, the ground clamp setscrew, and a *green* hex head screw on devices such as switches and outlets. Although not thought of as grounding devices, locknuts, grounding bushings, and grounding wedge lugs really are for grounding. Refer to Fig. 7-6 for grounding details. Another grounding device is the cord plug with the longer U-shaped third blade. This longer third blade makes a ground connection before the other two current-carrying blades make contact when inserted into the outlet. It is also the last to break contact when removed. *Never cut off the third blade.*

Some outlets and switches have a spring-type mounting strap-screw assembly that eliminates the need for a ground wire to the green hex screw on the device. This is used where the box is recessed in the wall and contact with the box is only by means of the mounting screw going through say an outlet mounting bracket. This is a very *loose* contact and it is not good enough. The device has plaster ears that maintain its position so that it is flush with the wall surface. That is why the outlet mounting bracket will not be against the metal wall box surface.

If you try to move such a device sideways it will be obvious that there is poor contact. This is why the strap-screw assembly is popular. Otherwise you must use the wire from the hex screw to the box grounding screw method. For obvious reasons nonmetallic boxes cannot be grounded. Be sure to ground all devices. Any grounding wire must be the same size as the current-carrying wires. Grounding of all equipment *must* be continuous from the last metal enclosure all the way back to the service-entrance enclosure. See Fig. 4-1.

No grounding wire may be disconnected by a switch unless *all* wires carrying current are simultaneously disconnected from the devices themselves. The metal boxes must be tied in by means of the green special hex head grounding screw that goes in the special tapped hole in the back of the box. Make sure the grounding is continuous back to the entrance panel.

UTILITY RULES AND RESTRICTIONS

Each individual utility has its own rules and will enforce them by withholding service to the property until you comply with the rules. For instance, no service will be supplied until a valid permit has been obtained by you from the governing body concerned. There are rules that govern overhead servicedrops and underground service laterals. The location of service equipment on the outside of the building will be determined by the nearest connection to the utility's lines. This will also depend on the type of area above which the wires will be installed. Any additional poles needed will be

charged to you. They are expensive. Sometimes underground service laterals can be routed around obstacles. Underground wiring may be charged to the homeowner.

Some states have passed laws prohibiting overhead wires and require that all utilities be underground. If you now have overhead service it will be allowed to stay if you are only upgrading your wiring. Check with the utility before relocating the meter location and distance from the original location. Figures 4-21 and 4-22 illustrate costs and requirements for an underground lateral service in Hawaii. See also Fig. 4-25.

ENTRANCE OF CONDUCTORS TO THE BUILDING

Underground conductors may come up out of the ground either through a long sweep conduit bend or may just enter the vertical conduit directly into the meter base. From there, they may go down and through the basement wall to the service-entrance

HAWAII ELECTRIC LIGHT COMPANY, INC.

1200 KILAUEA AVENUE
ELECTRIC LIGHT AND POWER

P. O. Box 1027
Hilo, Hawaii

Telephone 935-1171

DATE Feb. 27, 1978

SOLD TO Mr. James Kittle
P. O. Box 338
Kailua-Kona, HI 96740

Installation and removal of temporary single phase, three wire, 120/240 volt service for the construction of your new home on Lot 136, Lihilihi Place, Kona Palisades, North Kona $92.00

PERMANENT UNDERGROUND SERVICE INSTALLATION TO YOUR NEW HOME ON LOT 136 LOCATED AT KONA PALISADES, NORTH KONA $41.00

Fig. 4-25. Invoice from Hawaii Electric Light Company, Inc.

panel there. Overhead conductors will come down to meter through the service head and conduit to the meter base, and from there also down to the basement. In a dwelling with no basement, the service will enter the building near the meter base to a utility room or other room on the first floor to reach the service equipment.

The Service Head

Conduit or cable must have protection from the elements so that nothing gets into the conduit or cable (especially moisture). The service head is designed to do just that. The head is a curved cast fitting; one is used for conduit and another is used for cable. Still another for thinwall tubing. It is in gooseneck shape and the wire opening faces down at an angle (Fig. 4-9). This prevents moisture from entering. Each wire has a separate hole in the plastic insert. Although cable can be bent into a gooseneck, provided it is taped and painted and used without a service head, a better looking installation results and the top of the cable is anchored. Add one because they are very reasonable.

Drip Loops

Generally, the point of attachment of the service drop is below the service head. Some installations have the drop *above* the head. This might cause problems with water droplets finding their way into the cable or conduit. To overcome this condition, the service head wires *must* drop down lower than the service head by 6 to 8 inches, and then make a U-turn back up to the attachment point of the utility wires to the building. This lower loop allows water to drip off at bottom of the loop and not enter the service head or cable.

MOVING THE ELECTRIC METER OUTSIDE

Moving an electric meter outside might seem difficult to do. Actually it's quite simple. The time to do this work is when either updating or completely rewiring your house. If you can rough it for a day or two, borrow electricity from your neighbor using a heavy-duty electric cord. Our family did this without any trouble. Perhaps you could arrange to have a temporary power connection. If you don't run into problems, the work can be done in one day.

The actual changing of the service-entrance panel and accessories can be done without disrupting power until the changeover connections are made. At this point, you should make arrangements with the utility as to when you want the new service connected. In some very old houses, the service wires entered the second floor at ceiling level and the meter might be in a second floor hallway.

A new service-entrance/meter base assembly can be mounted close to the old conduit. As shown in Fig. 13-34, the old conduit is shown as ¾ of an inch. It has a gooseneck bend at the entrance through the wall into the basement. Special fittings to make a 90° turn were not available. There are now Condulet fittings that allow the conduit to lie flat against the building wall. The changeover should take no more than one day unless you run into problems. Consider all conditions you might run into and try to solve them before starting the work.

If you have an installation similar to the preceding situation, proceed as follows. Fully position a *wooden* ladder so that you can reach the connection of the entrance wires to the servicedrop wires (three or two depending on the old installation). *Be sure the ladder is made of wood.* Using side-cutting pliers having *approved* insulation on the handles, cut *each* wire separately between the service head and the servicedrop 6 inches from the clamp connector on the servicedrop wires. Figure 13-34 explains how to do this procedure. You will not receive a shock if you are careful to cut only *one* wire at a time.

Touch nothing but the wooden ladder (dry condition) and the *insulated* plier handles. Cut each wire in turn and bend them down out of the way of the servicedrop as you cut them loose. Do not touch the cut ends of the wires until all are disconnected from the servicedrop. Do *not* cut the wires from the pole to the house. Newer installations use the neutral wire as the support wire from the pole to the house wall. A large hook anchors this "support

Fig. 4-26. Electric meter. Reads either 01879 or 00879. Meter reader would check with last reading to see which was correct or would report a defective meter to the office.

wire" by means of a tension clamp. The other two (hot) wires are wrapped around the support wire. *Especially do not cut* the support wire.

When all the wires have been disconnected, you can remove the conduit. It is best to cut the conduit at the gooseneck. *Caution:* look up before

you start cutting to see if everything has been disconnected at the top. Now cut right through the conduit and wires. Use care in removing the assembly so that you do not hit the cutoff wires on the servicedrop. They are hot (live).

It is best to have help when removing the

assembly so as to avoid hitting the hot wires. The assembly might be heavier than you think. Everything inside can now be removed. Remove the meter so that you can turn it over to the utility when they come to make the changeover. The meter department will set a new meter and the line crew will connect the new service-entrance equipment.

After the old equipment has been removed, you can install the service head, mast meter base conduit assembly. If you continue below the meter with conduit, use an LB angle conduit fitting to make the turn to go through the wall into the basement. This whole assembly can be made up in advance and installed in one piece. You will really need help for this assembly.

Insert the nipple that is screwed into the LB through the house wall holding the assembly horizontally. Now rotate the assembly to vertical and anchor with suitable pipe straps. Be careful to avoid contacting the servicedrop wires. They are still *hot*. Use help.

Before mounting the assembly, you can install the wires from the service head down to the meter base. A 3-foot length of wire is needed extending from the service head for the utility to connect to the servicedrop. Tie these ends to the mast to prevent accidental contact with hot wires. Connect the other ends to the meter base terminals: red wire to left terminal, white wire to neutral terminal, black wire to right terminal. Figure 4-10 shows the meter base and wiring connections. Wires from the servicedrop to the meter base and from there down and inside to the entrance panel may be made of aluminum.

Refer to the 1981 Code, Table 310-16, Note 3. Three-Wire, Single-Phase Dwelling Services, 100 A ampacity for No. 2 aluminum wire and 100 A ampacity for No. 4 copper wire. This is for either cable or individual conductors at 90 degrees Celsius (194 degrees Fahrenheit) temperature rating. If you are using cable below the meter base and into the basement or utility room, you should mount the service head, conduit and meter base before continuing on into the house.

If you use conduit all the way, assemble everything before installing. The wires may be pulled in beyond the meter base later. If the meter was inside, all the wiring will be very old and outdated. In this case, you will be installing a new service-entrance disconnect/circuit breaker assembly. This can include the distribution panel with its breakers for the individual branch circuits needed. Because the new panel location may be different you may need more Condulets and conduit nipples to continue the conduit into the panel.

If all the old wiring is to be scrapped, remove the old fuse panel and separate disconnect, if there is one, so that you can mount the new service in place. When this equipment is installed and wired, and the utility has made the connection to its lines at the service mast, you *might* need to call for an inspection from the municipality. This depends on the inspection department. Check with the inspector.

If the entrance switch/breaker or fuse is separate from the distribution panel, connect them with a 2-inch nipple, locknuts, and insulating bushings. The more free area in the conduit, the easier it is to pull in the wires. It might be easier to use service-entrance cable if the distribution panel is some distance away from the service disconnect. Cable works easier if there are many turns.

The service disconnect *must* be directly inside the building. The code does *not* allow long runs of entrance cable inside a building without being protected by a fuse or breaker. This is very important. If it is necessary to mount the service disconnect some distance from the meter location, run the entrance cable on the *outside* of the building *then* go through the outside wall directly into the service disconnect. These back and forth references to conduit and cable are to show that both are accepted by the code. Check with the local inspector in advance. Conduit is *always* approved because there is no better raceway.

If the present wiring has been inspected by you and you feel it is in safe operating condition, you might need only to replace the service-entrance/distribution panel assembly. All *knob and tube* wiring, because it is very old, must be replaced. This type of wiring has rubber insulation covered with cotton fabric. In hot areas, the rubber deteriorates, cracks and falls off in pieces. Remove all of this wiring.

PROBLEMS WITH OLDER HOUSES

Older houses, and especially very old houses, will have knob and tube wiring and perhaps the meter will be upstairs. Prepare for a lot of hard dirty work. There will be probably two to six circuits. Much will depend on the size of the house and when it was wired. Many fuses in older houses were in open-faced fuseholders mounted on the basement ceiling or wall or on the second floor.

If there is old knob and tube wiring (open wiring on porcelain insulators) in the attic, if the insulation is in good condition and the wiring is strung tightly so that it does not sag and touch any flammable material, and if it is in use and is fused at 15 A, no more, then it may be used. All new wiring should be Romex or BX to comply with local codes.

Review your plan again and complete it to give you a more workable guide to follow when you start the actual work. You will need a plan for the first floor and basement. If there is a second floor, you will need an additional plan. Chapter 12 takes you through a complete rewiring on an existing building.

Chapter 5

The Fuse/Circuit Breaker Panel

T HE DISTRIBUTION PANEL, ALSO CALLED THE fuse panel or the circuit breaker panel, receives its current from the service-entrance panel. These two panels are often combined in one cabinet or enclosure. In single-family dwellings this is usually the case. The main breaker will be at the top of the panel with the individual breakers taking up the rest of the cabinet. A fused distribution panel will have a main fuse pull-out block and one or two other fuse blocks for a range, water heater, or dryer. Also there will be six to eight individual fuses for the various circuits supplied by them.

THE ENCLOSURE

The service-entrance panel with its circuit breaker or fuses may be mounted on the outside or inside the building. Many situations arise where the distribution panel cannot be adjacent the entrance panel. In this case, the service-entrance cable should be used to connect between the two panels. This cable must have the same ampacity as the cable feeding the entrance panel from the meter.

This cable must be *four*-wire cable having one black, one red (or black with red stripe), one white, and one ground. This ground is needed to provide grounding for the metal cabinets and other noncurrent-carrying parts.

Branch circuits are classified by type:

- Lighting circuits.
- Appliance circuits.
- Heavy appliance circuits (range or dryer).
- Laundry circuits.

The number of outlets on lighting and appliance circuits is not limited by the code; use six to 10 for each circuit. After you have decided on the number of circuits (both single- and two-pole) that you want, purchase a panel with space for 10 percent to 25 percent extra space. Later, an additional panel can be added beside the original. Figures 5-1 and 5-2 illustrate panels and service equipment.

OVERCURRENT AND SHORT-CIRCUIT PROTECTION

Modern residential installations tend to use circuit

Fig. 5-1. Old 60-A fuse panel. Cartridge fuses in center. Left is main; right is range. The four branch circuits are below. This is a mock-up to show details. Bare ground wire leads to copper water pipe at right and is clamped as shown.

breakers (breakers) instead of fuses. There is nothing wrong with using fuses. Just keep spare fuses on hand for when you need them. Breakers, once not ideal, have been improved so that they are now quite reliable.

Fuses

Fuses provide overcurrent protection in addition to short-circuit protection. The amperage (current flow) the wire can handle is limited by the wire size *and* the insulation type. Refer to Table 310-16 to 310-19, Note 3 of the Code lists Three-Wire, Single-Phase Dwelling Services, Conductor Sizes and Types, for both aluminum and copper wire. Most wire or cable has the designation printed or impressed on its surface at regular intervals, such as "14-2 w/grd." or "12-3 w/grd." along its full length. The safe operating voltage also determined by the insulation is also printed or embossed along

with the wire size and number. This designation might be "300 V or 600 V."

Plug Fuses

The standard plug fuse has an Edison base thread just like a regular light bulb. This fuse comes in the following amp rating sizes: 10, 15, 20, 25 and 30. It consists of a hollow porcelain or glass body with brass threads (like a light bulb) on the outside. On the top is a window of glass or mica so that you can see the *fusible link* inside. On the bottom is a contact that will touch the bottom screw in the fuse panel socket. The fusible link inside connects the bottom outside contact with the screw shell. When the fuse is screwed in place, the circuit is energized. Fuses up to and including 15-amp capacity have a hexagon-shaped window. Larger-capacity fuses have a round window. Plug fuses of special low amperage are used to protect motors sometimes being mounted directly on the motor itself. Other motors have an overload device built in. See Fig. 5-2.

Time Delay Fuses

Electric motors, when starting, will draw from three to six times their normal running amperage when running at normal speed. If a motor draws 6 amp when running, when starting it may draw 20 amp or more. This will blow a 15-amp fuse. For the two or three seconds for the motor to come up to full speed, there is no danger to the wires or their insulation. For just these situations the *time delay* fuse was developed. This type of fuse will carry a 200 percent overload for 12 seconds and a lesser overload for 30 seconds. They will blow immediately on short circuits. One trade name fuse previously called Fusetron is now called Tron. This is manufactured by Bussman Manufacturing Company.

Type S Nontamperable Fuses

To prevent the substitution of oversize fuses that defeats the purpose for which fuses are designed, a nontemperable fuse was developed. This fuse is different from the standard fuse. The threaded part is smaller and the threads are finer. This prevents a coin from being put behind the standard fuse and it also prevents bridging by means of foil of any kind. In addition, only 15-amp and smaller fuses will fit in a 15-amp adapter that is part of this fuse system.

Type S fuses are sold and manufactured by various companies and they all have the same features. They have the time lag feature in addition to being nontamperable. To fit in the standard Edison base fuse holder, they are provided with an adapter which is screwed *onto* the fuse base. Then this assembly is screwed *into* the fuse holder. The fuse may now be removed for replacement, but the adapter will not be able to be removed. It has a spur sticking out of the side of the Edison threads on its outside that will dig into the internal threads of the fuse holder—thereby preventing removal. The adapters match the fuses as to ampere capacity (through 15-amp one size, 20-amp, and through 30 amp another size). Be sure you insert the adapter

into the proper fuseholder. You have only one chance.

Cartridge Fuses

For conditions requiring fuses or time-delay fuses larger than 30 amp, cartridge fuses are used (Fig. 5-3 and 5-4). This fuse is a cylinder with brass end caps and a fiber center part. It somewhat resembles a rifle cartridge, hence the name. Inside is a fusible link and a dry powder to quench the arc when the fuse blows. To prevent overfusing, cartridge fuses are made in different sizes. Up through 30 amp they are 2 inches long by 9/16 of an inch in diameter. From 35 amp through 60 amp, they are 3 inches long by 13/16 of an inch in diameter.

All these are rated at 250 volts or less capacity. This means that they can be used on voltages up

Fig. 5-2. Four circuit auxiliary panel, four fuses. Two terminals from main panel shown at top. Neutral wire goes to neutral block at bottom. This is a mock-up.

Fig. 5-3. Auxiliary *fused* panel for furnace/air conditioner. Note *white* wires with black tape on them. This is a 230-V circuit. It also needs 115 V for furnace circuits.

Because the results are identical—protecting the wires in the circuit—either type of overcurrent device is very satisfactory.

PANEL REPLACEMENT IN AN OLDER HOME

The replacement of a distribution panel in an older home must depend on the capacity of the existing service-entrance equipment. If the service-entrance panel does not have sufficient capacity, then both panels must be replaced. In this case, buy a combination service-entrance/distribution panel. Using a combination panel will depend on the location of the meter in relation to the distribution panel inside. It is highly recommended that everything except the meter be located inside. Be sure to have the main breaker as close as possible to the point where the entrance cable enters.

Look the situation over and decide if the point where the service enters the building will have room inside (basement or other selected location) for the combination service-entrance/distribution

to 250 volts. Large amperage fuses have knife blade ends that fit between spring-loaded contact plates. Larger amperage and voltage fuses have larger dimensions. This is mainly to contain the arc that forms upon blowing. Normally, you will be buying a circuit breaker for your "main" disconnect rather than fuses. Do not be concerned with the larger size fuses. Service-entrance panels are available that have fuses as overcurrent protection for the mains. These are approved.

CIRCUIT BREAKERS

Because of the circuit breakers' reliability and permanent feature, they have become the preferred type of overcurrent devices used today. Circuit breakers are marked with a setting. This is calibrated at the factory and cannot be changed in the field. This setting represents the rating of a standard or time-delay fuse. See Figs. 5-5, 5-6, and 5-7.

Breakers are selected by their rating or the tripping value. Fuses are selected by rating only.

Fig. 5-4. Circuit breaker cabinet. The breaker was added later. Price shown is cabinet only.

55

Fig. 5-5. Breaker panel without breakers. Sold this way as breaker requirements differ.

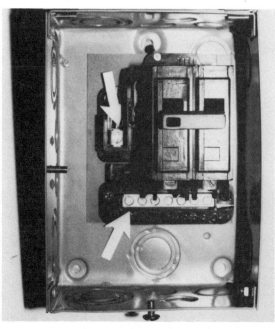

Fig. 5-6. Panel with breaker installed. Two pole breaker (double). This panel can house four ½-inch or two 1-inch breakers. This will accommodate different brands of breakers only as listed on the information inside cover.

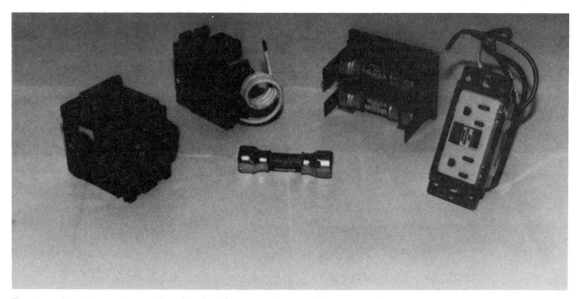

Fig. 5-7. Left to right: two pole "tie-bar" breaker. Ground fault circuit interrupter (GFCI) circuit breaker used in panel. Fuse block (pull-out) similar to those shown in Fig. 4-11. Block can accommodate 60-A fuses but these fuses are 35 A and need fuse "reducers." See fuse in front. Receptacle type GFCI. Used in bathrooms.

panel. If the location of the old fuse panel has ample room for the new combination panel, then install it there. The circuit leads from the old panel might have to be spliced or even go around to the other side of the new panel. Sometimes you will need a junction box (about 8 inches by 10 inches) with a cover to provide a neat workmanlike installation for extensions of these circuit leads. If your work is neat and shows care in the installation, the inspector will be favorably impressed. This will make a big difference in the inspector's attitude.

Start by removing the old panel after first disconnecting the circuit leads. Tie up the leads out of the way to make room to work. Hold the new panel up in place. It is usually empty except for the main breaker or fuse blocks. The circuit breakers are not supplied and neither are fuses in a fuse panel. Breakers or fuses are selected according to needs. Don't forget to install ground fault circuit interrupters (GFCI's) for all bathroom, outdoor, sauna, pool, and other hazardous locations.

If the enclosure is a combination be sure to allow room for the entrance cable to come into the enclosure back or side. Enclosures have knockouts in the back so that conduit or cable can be brought through the outside wall directly into the enclosure. Basement enclosure installations would generally have the cable or conduit brought in through the top of the enclosure because of the closeness to the top of the basement wall. The enclosure should be at eye level for inspection and servicing; don't mount it too high. A first-floor location can use a flush enclosure. This enclosure is designed to be mounted between studs.

If the basement wall is concrete, drill holes for anchors. The size anchors needed are ¼-20 A & J's. This means a lead anchor having a steel insert with a tapped hole in it having 20 threads per inch and accommodating a ¼-inch bolt. This anchor needs a ½-inch hole in the concrete for installation. Use a carbide drill bit and drill motor. Make the hole slightly deeper than the anchor. A star drill and hammer will work, but the carbide drill does not cost much and it saves time. Be sure to use goggles either way you drill. Hold the enclosure level and mark for the anchor holes. I have found a china

marker pencil best for such marking. The one I use has a crayon point and advances the point just like a mechanical. This pencil, having the brand name of Listo, is available in any stationery store for about $.50. Refills are also available.

When drilling with a carbide drill bit, be sure to guard against the bit wandering from the spot marked. Before starting to drill, mark over the original mark a vertical cross with china marker. That way you still will have a remnant of the original vertical cross even though the hole has removed the original mark at the center. If the drill does wander, try to angle the drill bit and motor to try to move the hole in the right direction. If the wall is hollow, use ¼-20 toggle bolts. These are 3-inch to 4-inch bolts with a nut having wings on it. They are squeezed together and inserted through the hole into the hollow part of the wall. The wings are spring loaded and will open out after they are in the hollow part of the wall.

Because the hole size needed to insert the wings is larger than the bolt shank, there is room for *some* adjustment if the hole is off its mark. Remember that the toggle bolt has to be put through the hole in the metal enclosure, then put through the hole in the wall, and then tightened. This is different than the A & J anchor, as the anchor is fixed permanently in the wall before the bolt is inserted. Therefore with the toggle bolt you have only one chance. If you insert the toggle bolt and for some reason need to remove it, you will *lose* the toggle part inside the wall.

Make all your work neat, plumb, and level. If you do this everything will look better, work better and the inspector will be pleased with your installation.

ACCESS TO THE PANEL

Easy, clear access to the electrical service equipment and distribution panel *must* be provided in case of emergency and for routine inspection and servicing. Code Section 110-16 requires this. While this section also requires lighting and head room for a large amperage installation, providing this for your residential installation makes good sense. If you have relocated the entrance of the cable or conduit into the dwelling, be sure to pick a suitable location for the equipment to be mounted inside. The service-entrance/main breaker panel should be installed *immediately* after the cable or conduit enters the building. This is because there is no overcurrent protection for the wires between the meter and the main circuit breaker. If necessary, the distribution panel may be some distance from the entrance panel. See Fig. 5-1 and refer to the section in Chapter 4 titled *Moving The Meter to The Outside.*

CAPACITY AND CALCULATIONS

In this section, I have made capacity calculations for a dwelling built in 1940 in a suburb of Detroit. The building is 28 feet wide and 26 feet deep, front to back. It is a one-story frame construction with a full basement. Refer to Figs. 12-8A, 12-8B, 12-9, and 12-10. This example starts with the wiring installed when the house was built. Note that there were few outlets and the service was 115 volts and possibly 60 amps. To completely update this dwelling, all the wiring might have to be replaced. At the time of construction, the outlets, fixtures, and switches were not required to be grounded. The 1981 code requires that a minimum of 100-amp service be provided. Older houses with 60-amp service may, under newer rulings, be able to use this service equipment, provided the ampacity is adequate for the calculated load.

To start, assume—for making the calculations—that this is a new house under construction and the wiring has not yet been installed. Also assume that power will not be needed for some time and that the house is not occupied. If when you actually rewire your own house, you might have to work on the wiring and live in the house at the same time. This can be done, but with some inconvenience. The work to be done first—in this case—is to change the service-entrance/breaker panel assembly and move the meter outside (if it is still inside). After that, you can rewire the rest at your convenience. In the above example, if you disconnect all power and need temporary power, either *buy* power from your neighbor or have a temporary service installed.

A note of warning is that if you get power from your neighbor, even if you are good friends or especially if you are just new in the neighborhood, be sure to insist on paying. I would suggest $1.00 per day. I have seen many cases of hard feelings over this. The neighbor thinks he is being taken advantage of and will become very angry. Ever after these hard feelings will persist.

ALTERNATE CALCULATION

Perhaps your dwelling has a floor area of 728 square feet (exclusive of unoccupied basement), no attic, and a small front stoop. Perhaps it has a 12-kW range, a 2.5-kW water heater, a 1.2-kW dishwasher, a 5-kW clothes dryer, and a 4.5-kW central air conditioner.

While I have listed in the computation an electric water heater and an electric clothes dryer, I highly recommend that these two appliances be gas fired. Electric resistance heating (red hot glowing coils) that also includes electric space heating, is the *most* expensive and also the *most* wasteful of energy. While this book is about electricity, I still advise buying gas appliances. If the above appliances are already installed, leave them. When replacements are needed, buy gas-fired types.

The dwelling represented by the calculations in Table 5-1 may be supplied by a 100-amp service. The code requires two small appliance circuits for kitchen and dining areas. It also requires one circuit for the laundry. These three circuits must be 20

Table 5-1. Computed Load.

	watts
General lighting 728 square feet @ 3 watts per foot	2184
Two 20-amp appliance circuits 1500 watts each	3000
One 20-amp laundry circuit	1500
Range circuit (at name plate rating)	12000
Water heater	2500
Clothes dryer	4500
Central air conditioning	4500
	30184
First 10,000 watts @ 100%	10000
Remainder @ 40% (20,184 watts × 40%)	8074
	18074
Calculated Load: 18,074 divided by 230 = 93 amps	

Circuit Breaker Technical Data

 A-120

 A2-130

 A-1515

 A-220

Plug-On Branch Circuit Breakers

Type A — 1/2" Per Pole — 120/240 Volt AC — 10,000 A.I.C.

Ampere Rating	1-Pole Side Clip	1-Pole Carton Qty.	1-Pole Carton Wt.	2-Single Poles Side Clip	2-Single Poles Center Clip	2-Single Poles Carton Qty.	2-Single Poles Carton Wt.	2-Pole, Common Trip Side Clip	2-Pole, Common Trip Carton Qty.	2-Pole, Common Trip Carton Wt.	Load Term Wire Range CU/AL
15	A-115	60	10	—	—	—	—	A-215	30	10	
15-15	—	—	—	—	A-1515	30	10	—	—	—	
15-20	—	—	—	—	A-1520	30	10	—	—	—	#14 THRU #4
20	A-120	60	10	—	—	—	—	A-220	30	10	
20-20	—	—	—	—	A-2020	30	10	—	—	—	
30	—	—	—	A2-130*	A-3020	30	10	A-230	30	10	
30-20	—	—	—	—	—	30	10	—	—	—	
40	—	—	—	A2-140*	—	30	10	A-240	30	10	
50	—	—	—	A2-150*	—	30	10	A-250	30	10	

*To be discontinued when present stock is depleted.

 C-120

 C-215

 C24-215

Plug-On Branch Circuit Breakers

Type C — 1" Per Pole — 120/240 Volt AC, 10,000 A.I.C.

Ampere Rating	1-Pole Carton Qty.	1-Pole Carton Wt.	2-Pole Common Trip	2-Pole Carton Qty.	2-Pole Carton Wt.	2-Pole[1] Common Trip	2-Pole Carton Qty.	2-Pole Carton Wt.	Load Term Wire Range CU/AL
15	C-115*	30	8	C-215	15	9	C24-215	15	10	
20	C-120*	30	8	C-220	15	9	C24-220	15	10	#14 THRU #4
30	C-130	30	8	C-230	15	9	C24-230	15	10	
40	C-140	30	8	C-240	15	9	C24-240	15	10	
50	C-150	30	8	C-250	15	9	C24-250	15	10	
60	—	—	—	C-260	15	9	C24-260	15	10	
70	—	—	—	C-270	15	9	C24-270	15	10	#4 THRU 1/0
90	—	—	—	C-290	15	9	C24-290	15	10	
100	—	—	—	C-2100	15	9	C24-2100	15	10	
125	—	—	—	C-2125	15	9	—	—	—	

[1]Rated 5,000 A.I.C. when used in 3 phase 3 wire grounded B phase system.
*SWD rated for switching duty.

 HAGF-15

Plug-On Branch Circuit Breakers/Special Application

Type C — 1" Per Pole, 120/240[2] Volt AC, 10,000 A.I.C.

Ampere Rating	Ground Fault Circuit Interrupter 1 Pole	Carton Qty.	Carton Wt.	Load Terminal Wire Range CU/AL
15	HAGF-15	12	6	#14-#4
20	HAGF-20	12	6	

Type C — 1" Per Pole, 120/240 Volt AC, 10,000 A.I.C.

Ampere Rating	Switching Neutral 2 Pole	Carton Qty.	Carton Wt.	Load Terminal Wire Range	Water Heater 2 Pole	Carton Qty.	Carton Wt.	Load Terminal Wire Range
15	C-215SN	12	10	#10-14 CU	C-215WH	15	10	#10-14 CU
20	C-220SN	15	10	#10-12 AL	C-220WH	15	10	#10-12 AL
30	C-230SN	15	10	# 6-10 CU # 4- 8 AL	C-230WH	15	10	# 6-10 CU # 4- 8 AL

[2]Ground Fault Circuit Interrupters are 120 Volt AC rated.

TYPE A CIRCUIT BREAKER INSTALLATION INSTRUCTIONS

SINGLE POLE BREAKERS

Two single pole breakers are packed in pairs for convenience. These breakers are alike except for the position of the plug-on clip which connects the breaker to the bus stab in the panel.

RIGHT HAND PLUG-ON CLIP

LEFT HAND PLUG-ON CLIP

LINE END   LOAD END

TO INSTALL:

Hook load end of breaker under the hold-down tab in the panel. Press line end of breaker down so that the plug-on clip slips over bus stab. Insert breakers by pairs for easier installation.

BUS STAB   HOLD-DOWN TAB
RIGHT HAND

LEFT HAND

When required, breakers may be installed between bus stabs as illustrated in drawing below.

BUS STABS   HOLD-DOWN TAB
LEFT HAND

RIGHT HAND

IMPORTANT NOTE:

These circuit breakers conform to Section 384-15 of the 1975 National Electric Code. Install only in panel positions having bus stabs with notch.

NOTCHED BUS STAB   UNNOTCHED BUS STAB

 C-215SN

C-215WH

Fig. 5-8. Various breakers (courtesy Sylvania Electrical Equipment).

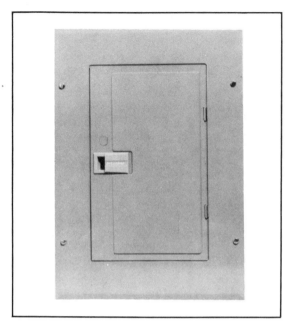

Fig. 5-9. Sylvania Loadcenter panel cover (courtesy Sylvania Electrical Equipment).

amp because of the heavy loads from toasters, toaster ovens and other heavy wattage appliances used in these areas. As shown in Table 5-1, the calculated load of 18,074 watts *must* be divided by 230 V rather than 240 V. This is required by the code.

GROUND FAULT CIRCUIT INTERRUPTER

Many times, faults occur in wiring that are not great enough to blow a fuse or trip a breaker. While these faults are not high, they *can* cause damage. Individuals could be injured and death could result under some circumstances. These are generally small current leakages that will give one a "tingle" but not the strong "wham" of the greater shock.

Many fires are caused by these same small current leakages where heating that results from the leak is not readily noticeable. For these reasons, the ground fault circuit interrupter (GFCI) was developed. The GFCI will interrupt a current of 5/1000 of an ampere almost instantaneously. As you can see, this is a very sensitive and fast-acting device.

Code Requirements

The code requires GFCIs in bathrooms, garages, and out of doors for pools, hot tubs, marinas, and any place where the danger of shock is very great. They are also required on new construction sites for connection of power tools, trouble lights and extension cords. Construction personnel are easily subject to shock because of defective equipment and wet or damp places where equipment has to be used.

Types of GFCIs

GFCI devices come in three types: the plug-in receptacle, the circuit breaker, and the portable. The receptacle type is usually installed in the bathroom, a very dangerous place. This type will protect its own receptacle only or can be so wired that it will protect other receptacles on the same circuit if they are beyond that point. In other words, if the bath is the first receptacle on that circuit it can protect any other receptacles *beyond* itself, away from the distribution panel. Be sure when installing a GFCI to connect the leads on it marked "line" to the wires coming *from* the panel and the leads marked "load" to the wires leaving the receptacle box and feeding

Fig. 5-10. Interior of entrance/breaker panel. All breakers have been installed (courtesy Sylvania Electrical Equipment).

the other receptacles "down the line." If the bath receptacle is second or third, it cannot protect "backwards" toward the distribution panel. When a "push-to-test" button is pushed, the reset button next to it will pop out. Push the reset button to restore service. Test the GFCI every two months.

The circuit breaker type is mounted in the breaker panel just as are standard breakers. It will have an additional white wire for grounding its internal mechanism to the panel neutral bar. This type will protect *all* outlets on its circuit because it is first "in line." Refer to Figs. 5-8, 5-9, and 5-10. You must go to the panel to reset this type of breaker. The breaker type is unsatisfactory for circuits having very long runs because voltage drop can cause the breaker type to trip. The portable type of breaker is intended primarily for construction sites. Portable power tools and extension cards can be plugged and they will protect the user. All types come rated 15 A or 20A.

Chapter 6
Branch Circuits

LIGHTING AND SMALL APPLIANCE CIRCUITS ARE used in homes for ceiling and wall fixtures and wall receptacles (outlets) used for vacuums, radios, television sets, and lamps. These circuits are rated at 15 amps or 20 amps at 115 volts. The 15-amp circuit *may* be wired with No. 14 *copper* wire. The 20-amp circuit *must* be wired with No. 12 *copper* wire. The 15-amp circuit may also be wired with No. 12 wire if you prefer.

Do *not* use aluminum wire *inside* the dwelling except to feed the main breaker and distribution panel. The branch circuits are also defined as "150 volts or less to ground" by the code. This means that the voltage between the *hot* wire and the equipment ground is 150 volts or less; in this case it would be 115 volts.

Even though a dwelling having 230-volt service will have no hot wire with a voltage more than 150 volts to ground, each wire will have voltage to ground of 115 to 120 volts. This comes within the definition stated above. See Figs. 6-1, 6-2, and 6-3, for details and to gain a better understanding of voltage to ground.

CLASSIFICATION OF CIRCUITS

Circuits are classified by the code according to the rating of the overcurrent protection, provided as follows: 15 A, 20 A, 30 A, 40 A, 50 A, and 60 A. These are general circuits *not* individual circuits. Even though the wire itself has a higher ampacity than the overcurrent device, the circuit still is designated by the rating of that device. An exceptionally long run from the distribution panel would require the next larger wire size to minimize the voltage drop and hold it to less than 5 percent. Refer to code Tables 310-16 through 310-19 for ampacities of various wire sizes and insulation types. The 15-amp and 20-amp circuits are commonly used in a dwelling as explained above. Circuits designated as 25, 30, 40, and 50 amp are designated as individual branch circuits for connection of large permanent equipment such as a range or clothes dryer.

Individual Branch Circuits

Such circuits are used for well pumps, sump pumps

Fig. 6-1. Two switches on the left duplex receptacle on the right. The counter space here is only 12 inches. Switches control patio outside light and over the sink light. Outlets are circuit one. This is a 20-A, small-appliance circuit.

and garage door operators. Other individual branch circuits are used for an electric water heater, a clothes dryer, central or window air conditioning, an electric range, and a furnace. Each of these circuits may supply only *one* piece of equipment and must be wired and protected by an overcurrent device appropriate for the ampere draw of such equipment.

Depending on the nameplate rating of the appliance served, the circuit will be rated and pro-

Fig. 6-2. The left receptacle is on circuit one. The switch is the garbage disposer. The right-hand receptacle is circuit two. These are quite close because the counter is short.

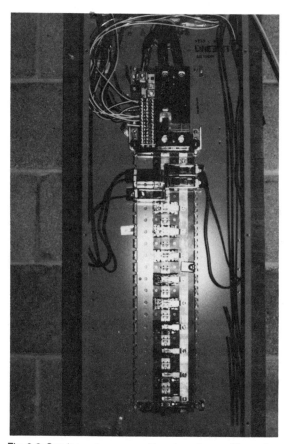

Fig. 6-3. Service-entrance panel for a large house. The mains are very large.

Air-conditioning systems are marked with the "minimum circuit ampacity" and the maximum fuse size. As an example: minimum circuit ampacity—21.2 A; maximum fuse size—30 A. For electric ranges, the code Table 220-19 gives for not over 12 kW rating the maximum demand of 8 kW. For ranges or cooktops and wall-mounted ovens over 12 kW through 27 kW combined ratings, the maximum demand shall be increased 5 percent for each kW or fraction thereof which exceeds 12 kW. Table 6-1 shows an example of the calculations.

Other individual branch circuits supplying appliances such as well pumps, sump pumps and garage door operators should be wired with No. 12 copper wire protected by 20 A breaker or fuse.

Buying a quantity of wire plus the service-entrance/distribution panel and the circuit breakers in one place might induce the supplier to give you a considerable discount. Try it. An order for 1000 feet of cable or BX, plus the other items, is different than buying only 25 feet of Romex. If you are buying service-entrance cable (because you will not need much over 25 feet), it is best to try a local hardware store or home improvement center. This cable runs up to $6.75 per foot. Try to purchase these items at an electrical wholesaler. They may sell to you and the price may even be lower. Shop around and try to save money.

To avoid buying too much of this cable, I take a cord, clothesline or any other line and actually run this as if it were the cable. Start at the outside where the cable would begin—at the service head above the meter location—and run it down and into the basement or other service-entrance location exactly as if the cord were the cable itself. After marking the length needed, you will be able to estimate the amount of cable to buy. Be sure to add

tected accordingly. Thus an electric clothes dryer rated at 4500 watts (4.5 kW) will require a 30-amp breaker and will be wired with No. 10 wire. Electric water heater circuits must be protected at 125 percent of the nameplate rating. Therefore, a water heater rated at 4500 W × 125% = 5625 W divided by 230 V = 24.5 A. Overcurrent protection of 30 A is required.

Table 6-1. Ampacity Calculations.

Cooktop	8 kW	5% × 7 = 35%
One wall mounted oven	6 kW	8 kW × 35% = 2.8 kW
One wall mounted oven	5 kW	8 kW + 2.8 kW = 10.8 kW
Total	19 kW	

10,800 ÷ 230 = 47.0A Use No. 8 copper wire or No. 6 Aluminum wire
Fuse for 50 A.

10 percent to 15 percent for bending the cable and for stripping the ends. The power company requires 3 feet at the service head for their tie-in. At the service-entrance panel, be sure to allow enough wire length to reach all terminals in the panel. Sometimes the *neutral* terminal is at the bottom of the panel and the neutral wire must reach down to that point. This will mean having excess length on the two hot wires. This occurs in many cases, but having a wire longer is better than having a wire too short.

Color Code for Branch Circuits

The *grounded* conductor is always white or a natural gray. The equipment *grounding* conductor always has green colored insulation or continuous green color with one or more yellow stripes—or it is bare. The *ungrounded* conductors may be any color *except* the above colors that are reserved for their special uses. This is *extremely* important and must be made very clear. The hot wires may be any other color, such as black, red, blue, brown, etc.

Because larger sizes of wire do not come in white, it is necessary to paint or tape (with white paint or tape) the ends of the wire where they can be seen in panels and other places so that this wire is recognized as the neutral or grounded conductor. The code requires this method.

Receptacles and Cord Connectors

All new receptacles installed on 15 A and 20 A circuits *must* be of the grounding type. If a means of grounding does not exist, an *ungrounded* type *may* be installed. *Caution:* Never install a replacement *grounding* type receptacle on a circuit that is *not* grounded. This gives a false sense of safety and it is dangerous if a defective grounded appliance or tool is plugged in to that receptacle. All tools and appliances that have attachment plugs must never have the grounding blade removed. This defeats the purpose of the whole grounding system and is very dangerous. In addition, the code *prohibits* this.

Ranges and clothes dryers may be wired with service-entrance cable, provided the cable starts at the service-entrance panel and is continuous all the way to the appliance receptacle. If the cable comes from a subpanel, it *must* be *four*-wire cable. One wire, the green or bare wire, is to ground the equipment. At each end, if the cable comes directly from the service-entrance panel, the neutral conductor (which is bare stranded and is wrapped around the two insulated wires) must be unwrapped from the other wires and twisted to make a conductor. For these two appliances *only*, the neutral may be used for both neutral and grounding purposes. This is the only exception to the rule of neutral and grounding wire being separate parts of the complete electrical system.

Wire Sizes and Ampacities

Wire sizes range from No. 18, used in lighting fixtures, to No. 3/0 and much larger for commercial and industrial installations. You can use wire sizes from No. 14 for individual circuits to, possibly, No. 3 which has ampacity of 110 amp for dwelling service. Any feeder wires or cable between the service-entrance enclosure and the distribution panel enclosure must be the same size as those of the service-entrance wires or cable from the servicedrop point of attachment. The code Table No. 310-16 lists the ampacities of various sizes of copper and aluminum wires by insulation. Note 3 to Tables 310-16 through 310-19 lists applicable ampacities for *single* dwelling units.

Types of Insulation

Code table 310-13 lists conductor application and insulation types. XHHW insulation is used in making service-entrance cable. This is a very popular construction now. Because it is rated for wet and dry locations, it can be used outside for the cable run from the servicedrop, to the meter base, and from there into the building to the service-entrance panel. In addition, it can be used for the feeder to the distribution panel, for the electric range, and for the electric clothes dryer.

Types TW and THHN are used in making Romex and BX and also for insulating single, solid, and stranded wire. Usually, the type available in the area is suitable and approved by the licensing authority.

ADEQUATE WIRING

A dwelling wired many years ago, and having sufficient capacity then, is surely not adequately wired for today. Even with energy conversation measures there still is a need to have adequate wiring. The minimum ampacity recommended for rewiring is 60 A. For a dwelling with a floor plan of 1500 to 2500 square feet, 100 amp is not too large.

The extra cost of 125 A service equipment, including the heavier wiring needed, will be nowhere near the expense and labor of removing almost new (five years old?) lower ampacity equipment and buying new larger equipment. In either case, the cost of *branch* circuit breakers will be the same (more might be needed) because 15-amp, 20-amp, 30-amp, 40-amp, and 50-amp breakers will still be used.

The main breaker, the enclosures, and the service-entrance cable or conduit and wires will be larger. The enclosure will be larger to accommodate the larger main breaker and provide space for more branch breakers.

Wire Sizes in Relation to Distance

The maximum voltage drop now allowed in a circuit is 5 percent a drop of more than 5 percent results in poor operation of such equipment as motors and electronic equipment. This can damage the equipment. If the voltage drop calculates at over 5 percent, use the next larger wire size. The basic formula for figuring the voltage drop in an alternating current circuit is shown in Table 6-2.

VD = 4.57 V; 4.57 V divided by 230 V = 0.0198% = 2% voltage drop means this voltage drop is satisfactory. This calculation will come in handy when figuring the size on farm wiring between buildings. There will be a chapter on farm wiring.

Noninterchangeable Outlets and Plugs

Receptacles that are on circuits having different voltages or special uses *must* have a configuration (arrangement of slots or blades on a plug) for accepting an attachment plug designed *only* for that voltage or special use. This prevents damage to appliances or other electrical equipment plugged in accidentally. I once plugged a percolator into a 230-volt outlet that had the same configuration as a 115-volt outlet. After that, the percolator did not perk.

Figures 6-4 and 6-5 show commonly used receptacle configurations. There are many special receptacles for radios, television antennas, public address systems, and many others. These configurations are not detailed in this book.

Table 6-2. Voltage Drop Formula.

$$VD = \frac{2 \times r \times L \times I}{\text{circular mills}}$$

VD = Voltage drop
r = Resistivity of conductor material (12 ohms per CM ft. for copper and 18 ohms per CM ft. for aluminum wire)
L = One way length of circuit in feet
I = Current in conductor in amperes

Example: 230-volt, 2-wire heating circuit. Load is 50 amp. Circuit size is No. 6 AWG THHN insulation. Wire copper and the one-way circuit is 100 ft.

Substituting in the formula, Circular mills = 26240 (Ch. 9, Table 8)

$$VD = \frac{2 \times 12 \times 100 \times 50}{26,240 \text{ (Table 8, Ch. 9)}} \qquad VD = \frac{120,000}{26,240}$$

TYPE	VOLTAGE		15 AMP	20 AMP	30 AMP	50 AMP	60 AMP
2-POLE 2-WIRE	125V	1	1-15R †A2				
	250V	2		2-20R A2			
2-POLE 3-WIRE GROUNDING	125V	5	5-15R A5-11, F3, G3	5-20R A17-21, F5, G5	5-30R A28	5-50R A29	
	250V	6	6-15R A12-15, G4	6-20R A23-26, G7	6-30R A28	6-50R A30	
	277VAC	7	7-15R A16	7-20R A27	7-30R A29	7-50R A30	
3-POLE 3-WIRE	125/250V	10		10-20R A31	10-30R A32	10-50R A33	
	250V 3φ	11	11-15R	11-20R	11-30R	11-50R	
3-POLE 4-WIRE GROUNDING	125/250V	14	14-15R	14-20R A34	14-30R A34	14-50R A35	14-60R A36
	250V 3φ	15	15-15R	15-20R A34	15-30R A35	15-50R A36	15-60R A36
4-POLE 4-WIRE	120/208V 3φY	18	18-15R	18-20R A37	18-30R	18-50R	18-60R A37

NOTE:
For quick reference purposes, this chart shows only the female configurations applicable to receptacles, connectors and flanged outlets. Mating configurations for plugs and flanged inlets are shown on catalog pages indicated.

†Plugs that comply to NEMA 1-15P are listed on page A2.

HOW TO USE THIS CHART:

NEMA configuration ⟶ 2-20R

Catalog page where product is listed ⟶ A2

Fig. 6-4. General-purpose, straight blade devices (receptacles) NEMA Configurations. (courtesy Leviton Mfg. Co.)

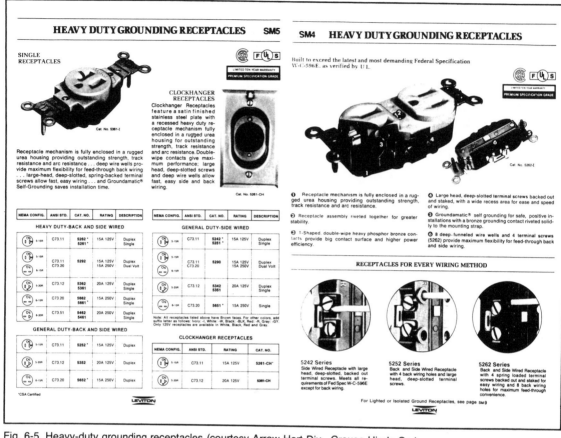

Fig. 6-5. Heavy-duty grounding receptacles (courtesy Arrow Hart Div., Crouse-Hinds Co.).

Lampholders

Lampholders (sockets) such as the kind used in ceiling and wall fixtures and portable lamps such as table lamps may only be connected to a maximum 20-amp circuit. This does not concern someone with a single dwelling although it is a code requirement. A single receptacle installed on a branch circuit must have an ampere rating at least that of the overcurrent protection. Example: A 30-amp circuit must be supplied with a 30-amp receptacle. Continuous loads must not exceed 80 percent of the rating of the branch circuit overcurrent protection. A load defined as continuous is one that is expected to continue for three hours or more.

FEEDERS

Installation requirements of feeders are determined by calculations made of the demand load to be carried by them. Feeder conductors for a dwelling unit need not be any larger than the service-entrance conductors. Example: If the service-entrance conductors have an ampacity of 55 amp or less, the feeder conductors must have the same ampacity. In practice, feeders should not be less than No. 10 copper wire. A feeder consisting of two hot wires and one neutral wire, furnishing 230 or 115 volts, can supply two or three sets of three-wire feeders. When run in a metal raceway, be sure that all the wires of a circuit (one or two hot wires and neutral) are in one raceway. *Raceway* is defined as an enclosed channel designed expressly for holding wires, cables, or busbars. It may be of metal or insulating material. Conduit and thinwall tubing are examples.

Branch Circuit Loads

General-use circuits of 15 A capacity may have eight to 10 outlets (receptacles or lighting fixtures) connected to them. Circuits of 20 A capacity may have 13 outlets. Loads for additions to dwellings or additional wiring in existing dwellings must be based on 3 watts per foot. Any one motor larger than ⅛ HP must be added to the load at 125 percent of the nameplate rating. In a dwelling, all general-use circuits should be divided so that, if one circuit is out, the area fed by that circuit will not be in complete darkness. In any event, the load on any circuit may not exceed a total determined by the overcurrent device and by the ampacity of the wires protected by such overcurrent device.

There must be *one* special appliance circuit for each of the following: laundry, furnace, pump, garage door operator, and air conditioning. If electric space heating is planned, its load is calculated at 125 percent of the full load current (nameplate rating). This is to protect the insulation from overheating during long periods of continuous usage. See Table 220-11 of the code.

Fixed Appliance Load

Clothes dryers must be added to the total load as 5 kW each or the actual nameplate rating if higher. Where heating and air conditioning are both installed in a dwelling, only the air-conditioning load needs to be considered. Both loads will never be connected at the same time. Be sure to add in the load of the furnace fan to the air-conditioning load if the fan also runs for the air conditioning.

On a 230-volt, three-wire system, the neutral in the feeder and service-entrance cable will carry only the *unbalance* current between the two hot legs on the 230-volt supply. This is illustrated in Fig. 4-1. For electric ranges and other permanent electric cooking units, the maximum unbalance load is considered as 70 percent of the load on the ungrounded (hot) conductors. Therefore, a range needing No. 8 conductors may use a No. 10 neutral. When you use service-entrance cable, this arrangement of wire sizes is used in its construction.

Balancing the load is accomplished by arranging the circuits so that both hot legs of the 230-volt service carry nearly equal loads. Example: If the 115-volt circuits are three at 15 amp and five at 20 amp, connect two 15-amp circuits and two 20-amp circuits to the *left* leg of the distribution panel and one 15-amp and two 20-amp circuits to the *right* leg of the panel. The neutral will carry an unbalance amperage of 15 amp. This is only an example. The named circuits will almost never be fully loaded. This balance is close enough because the neutral will have more than enough ampacity. Later you might want to add more circuits. When connecting the circuits, maintain the balance as closely as possible considering the arrangement of the original circuits.

Chapter 7
Concealed and Exposed Wiring

ELECTRICAL WIRING TAKES MANY FORMS but, because much of it is concealed, we don't notice it. Wiring is concealed mainly for aesthetic reasons. Other reasons for concealing wiring are protection of the wiring itself and protection of persons who might come in contact with the wiring. See Figs. 7-1 through 7-6. Vandalism is especially a concern in public buildings. Exposed wiring is so called because the wiring is visible and it is mounted on walls rather than inside walls. The wire itself is not "exposed." It is encased, first with insulation, then with either a sheath of tough material such as Romex has or a metal conduit protecting the wires. The old knob and tube wiring actually was exposed. It is now used in specialized areas and in industrial buildings.

CONCEALED WIRING

In a one-family dwelling, most wiring is inside walls supplying ceiling fixtures and wall boxes used for switches and receptacles. Exposed wiring can be seen in basements and attics. The exposed wiring in basements, unfinished garages, and outbuildings must be protected from damage. This means that the cable must be run through holes bored in the center of studs or joists, especially where these are exposed and fastened every 4½ feet and anchored within 12 inches of a junction box. For plastic wall boxes without a metal clamp inside, the cable must be anchored within 8 inches of the box. Less protection is needed in attics except around access openings to the attic where this area is considered exposed, and, the cable must be anchored and taken through bored holes where flooring might be laid.

Where buildings have hollow walls, wiring is easily concealed inside these hollow spaces. Concealed wiring is most easily installed during construction of the building and before the drywall or other material is installed. First the wall and ceiling boxes are mounted in place, then the cable is run after the holes are bored in the framing members. At this time, no devices are installed. When the cable is installed, be sure to leave 6 to 8 inches extending from the wall or ceiling box. Then coil

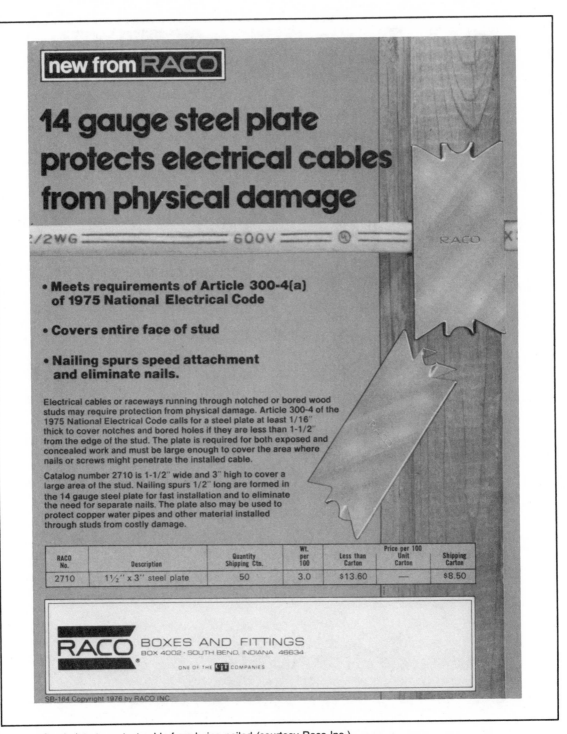

Fig. 7-1. Steel plate to protect cable from being nailed (courtesy Raco Inc.).

Fig. 7-2. Steel boxes used in electrical wiring. The "handy box" at the lower right is for exposed wiring. It is mounted by screws through the back on concrete, wood, or other wall surfaces. All other boxes are for concealed wiring (courtesy Raco Inc.).

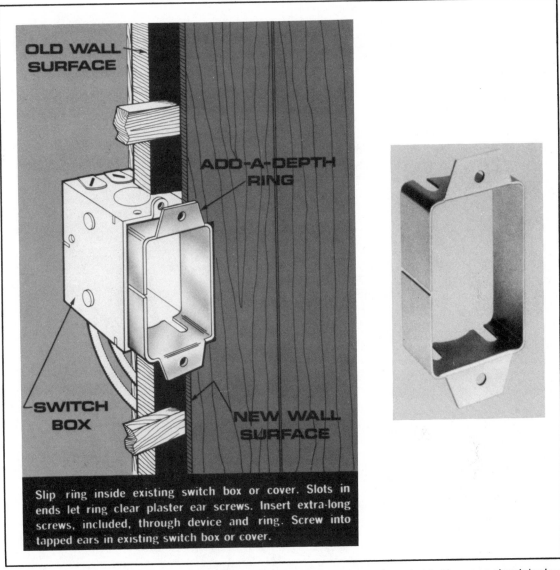

OLD WALL SURFACE

ADD-A-DEPTH RING

SWITCH BOX

NEW WALL SURFACE

Slip ring inside existing switch box or cover. Slots in ends let ring clear plaster ear screws. Insert extra-long screws, included, through device and ring. Screw into tapped ears in existing switch box or cover.

Fig. 7-3. Add-a-Depth ring. This is handy when paneling a basement or other area where electrical boxes are already in place (courtesy Raco Inc.).

this end up and push it back into the box so that it will not interfere with the application of the wall finish.

This "rough work" must now be inspected by the governing authority. If the work is approved or after the work is corrected to the inspector's satisfaction, then the wiring can be "closed in" or covered with the wall finish. No fixtures or other devices are installed until the wall surface is finished. At the time the rough work is being done, the service-entrance equipment and the service cable or conduit and meter base are installed. This type of construction is known as new work because the building is new or has not been finished on the inside. This type of installation is illustrated in Fig. 7-6.

If the building has the inside walls finished and wiring needs to be installed (such as an old farmhouse that never had electricity, it is considered old work. The adding or extending of circuits in a *new* finished building is also *old work*. The words *old* and *new* are not a definition of age but a definition of the type of wiring method used. Wiring or rewiring of an older building is very hard, dirty work, but it is rewarding. Old work, being harder to do, takes longer. More cable and sometimes different types of wall boxes need to be used. Runs cannot be as direct as new work. Old work entails lots of fishing and hole drilling. Try to save finish wood trim if you have to remove it.

Basement Areas

Open areas in basements such as ceilings require neat work. Support the cable every 4½ feet. Secure it so as to prevent damage to it. Many basement ceilings are of the suspended type so cable does not have to be run through bored holes in joists. The basement walls will need to have the cable run through bored holes in framing members. Just be sure to protect Romex from nail penetration. Cover it with 1/16-inch metal plates where it is exposed to possible nail penetration.

Now is the time to plan for lighting fixtures and receptacles in the basement. Shallow boxes can be used if 1-×-2 furring strips are used on the basement. It might be necessary to chip out behind the wall box slightly. Boxes are available that are about 1⅛-inches deep. NOTE: Only one Romex cable is allowed in these shallow boxes. Drywall, ½ of an inch thick combined with furring ¾ of an inch thick, will accommodate this box for a switch or receptacle. The box must be flush with the finished wall surface or slightly recessed. Any gaps must be patched with patching plaster so that there is no opening between the box and the drywall.

Attic Areas

Wiring is not subject to great damage in attic areas. Therefore, protection is only required within 6 feet of the attic access opening. If the attic is floored and used for storage, a light must be provided with a switch at the bottom of the stairs. The wiring must be protected just as in a basement area. Under the attic flooring, the cable must be run through holes in the joists. If a ladder must be used to gain access, the 6-foot rule applies. A light is not required, but it would be a good investment if the area is used for storage. I have one in my ladder access attic. It is

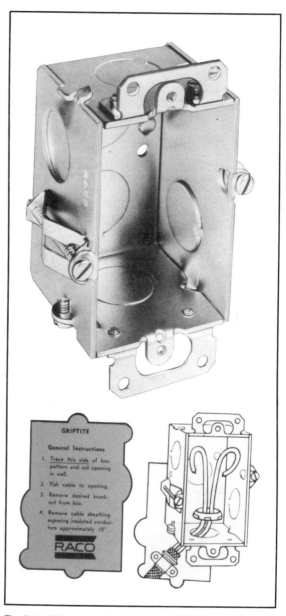

Fig. 7-4. Wall box designed with special pressure clamps to hold the box firmly in the wall (courtesy Raco Inc.).

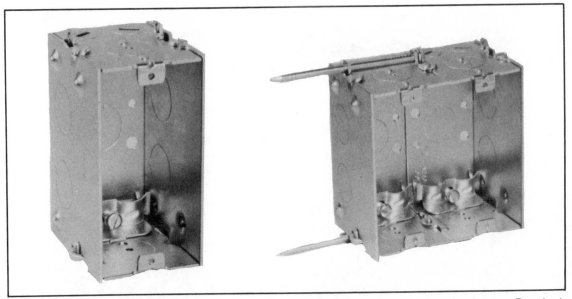

Fig. 7-5. Large-capacity wall boxes for drywall or even concrete block walls. Can be ganged together (courtesy Raco Inc.).

operated by a pull chain on the lamp holder, but it is also wired, as the garage ceiling light is, by means of the same toggle switch. This way the light can only be turned on when the garage light is on. Therefore a pilot light is not needed.

A garage is not required to have a disconnect: a toggle switch is sufficient. A toggle switch is approved for other residential outbuildings. Three-way switches are also approved. In one home I owned, I ran No. 10 wire to my garage and put a fuse panel in the garage. If a fuse blew, I would not have to go to the basement to replace it. My power tools were used in the garage. Figure 5-2 illustrates such a panel.

Overhead Installations

Overhead wiring is still used, but great care must be taken to have the overhead wires high enough to clear any vehicle driven underneath. They must be securely anchored with approved insulators. Taps must be taken off and led down through a service head into a conduit and then into the building. Consideration must be given to:

- The span.
- The strength of the wires.
- The "sag" in hot weather.

No. 10 wire is the smallest size permitted by the code for overhead spans. The longer the span, the larger the wire size. If the outdoor temp' rature is in the range of 90 to 100 degrees Fahrenhe.t when the wires are strung, be sure to leave slack in each span. Allow at least 1 inch for short spans and 2 to 3 inches for long spans.

Knob and Tube Wiring

Knob and tube wiring is generally not used in dwellings. It is prohibited by the code except in industrial and agricultural installations. Knob and tube wiring concealed within the hollow spaces of building walls is severely restricted by the code. I do not recommend adding on to or repairing old knob and tube wiring. It is better and safer to remove it and install new cable wiring in its place. When abandoning such wiring, make sure that there is no way that it can be reconnected to any new wiring. These old systems are a fire hazard. I have touched such old wiring and the insulation has fallen off in my hands. Any wiring consisting of *single* wires supported on porcelain knobs and going through porcelain tubes inserted through studs and joists is "knob and tube wiring" and should only be displayed in a museum.

Fig. 7-6. Thinwall tubing construction methods in metal partitions. A neat installation (courtesy Raco Inc.).

EXISTING SERVICE-ENTRANCE EQUIPMENT

Service-entrance equipment already in place in a dwelling to be rewired or having the wiring updated or added to will usually not be suitable for reuse. The equipment will have too small of a capacity and perhaps be outdated. The original equipment probably had only fuses and the contacts in the fuse sockets might be burned or otherwise damaged. Replacement parts *might* be available, but it is better and probably less expensive to buy all new equipment. The old equipment will have served its purpose and will have done the job for which it was installed. Remove it to make room for new, larger equipment. Quality equipment with extra capacity will last at least 20 years if it is properly installed and not overloaded.

If when you are rewiring only two to four new circuits are needed, an additional fuse or breaker panel and cabinet can be purchased and connected to the main panel cabinet by means of an offset nipple or a feeder (cable) if the panel must be some distance from the main panel. If adding these additional circuits—with their added loads—will overload the service-entrance conductors, then there is a question of having adequate capacity of the complete service-entrance equipment.

In such a case, figure the total connected load and buy new service-entrance equipment and cable or conduit and wire. New equipment will simplify the installation and make a neater job. Add-ons always *look* like add-ons. If necessary—because of basement remodeling work—the distribution panel can be installed remote from the service-entrance panel with its main breaker.

The code requires the main breaker to be as close as possible to the entry point of the service-entrance cable into the building. The cable on the street side of the main breaker has no overcurrent protection and should be on the outside of the building, except that portion necessary to enter and connect to the panel of the main breaker.

Equipment over five years old and newer equipment showing signs of arcing or burning should not be re-used. Panels using fuses sometimes show signs of deterioration of the fiber washer underneath the center contact of the fuseholder. If the panel is in a very damp location, these fiber washers become water soaked and will pass electricity (actually bypassing the fuse entirely). Other, old installations will have fuses in both wires (the live (hot) wire *and* the grounded wire). This is prohibited by the code. These prohibited conditions should be first priority in making repairs and changes as it is imperative that they be corrected.

SERVICE-ENTRANCE CABLE (SE)

Service-entrance cable is similar to Romex except that the wire is type XHHW (moisture- and heat-resistant insulation). There are *two* insulated wires (red and black). The neutral wire consists of many fine strands of tinned copper wire wrapped spirally around both insulated wires (see Fig. 14-38). This is then covered with a tough outer covering that is very damage resistant. There is no grounding wire as such. The neutral is also the ground wire. This cable brings power through the meter and into the building to the service-entrance equipment. The fine tinned strands of the neutral are bunched and twisted together and connected to the neutral bar and to the grounding wire in the panel and in the meter base.

Modern homes usually will need large service-entrance cable wire size such as No. 4, 3, 2, or 1 for 100-amp, 115-amp, or 130-amp capacity respectively. Service-entrance cable may be also used to wire ranges and clothes dryers using Nos. 6 and 8 respectively. Watertight cable connectors must be used in wet locations such as the top entrance to the meter base outdoors to prevent moisture entry. A special service head is used at the point where the servicedrop connects to the cable. You can purchase service-entrance cable by the foot at home improvement centers. Measure carefully to be sure that you don't run short. This cable is very expensive. Cable with aluminum wires is also satisfactory for ranges, dryers, and electric furnace uses.

CONDUITS

Conduits take different forms and they are made of different materials. The following sections describe them in the order that they were developed.

Rigid Metal Conduit. Rigid metal conduit has been in use almost as long as wiring has needed protection from damage. This conduit is similar to water pipe in appearance, but it is specially treated to make the insides smooth and to bend easily. It is threaded similar to water pipe, but it should be cut with a hacksaw rather than a pipe cutter. A cutter will raise a large burr on the inside and the burr must be completely removed with a reamer. Because this conduit requires a bender, vise, and pipe dies, the homeowner might not want to use it. It is readily available at electrical wholesalers. Fittings that eliminate threading are also available.

Electrical Metallic Tubing (EMT). This tubing, commonly known as Thinwall, is easy to bend and it can be cut with a hacksaw. It is bent with a *thinwall bender* that can be rented. The bender sells for under $15 and it will pay for itself if you plan to do much work with thinwall. This type of conduit is never threaded and it is connected to boxes with thinwall connectors and couplings. These fittings are made in various types:

■ Crimp-on that needs a large crimp-on tool.

■ Compression type using a nut and split ring to tighten onto the thinwall.

■ Setscrew type. The setscrew types are either steel or die cast. These have one or more setscrews depending on the size of the fitting.

■ For use with internally threaded hubs on cast boxes and meter hubs a thinwall "adapter" slips over the thinwall end and when tightened into the hub grips the thinwall tightly. See Figs. 3-6, 3-7 and 3-33.

Rigid Nonmetallic Tubing. This type of conduit is similar to plastic water pipe except that it is made especially for wiring use and can be used underground. Common sizes are of polyvinyl chloride. While metal thinwall needs supports only every 10 feet, the nonmetallic type needs support every 3 feet in the ½-inch to 1-inch sizes. It is more flexible. Because this conduit needs specialized equipment to bend it, the homeowner might find that it is not practical for home use.

Flexible Metal Conduit (Greenfield). This conduit appears to be the same as BX. The steel armor is the same, but the inside is empty. Greenfield is usually larger than BX. The ½-inch size is larger than ½-inch thinwall in outside diameter. For some areas, the ⅜-inch size is approved for lengths under 6 feet for connecting to light fixtures. BX connectors are used for ⅜-inch Greenfield conduit. Larger sizes use Greenfield connectors.

Liquidtight Flexible Conduit. This type of flexible conduit is used commercially for connections to motors, etc., where dampness is present. Special fittings are used to maintain the dampness resistance. The name Sealtite identifies the metallic type. Plastic types also are manufactured.

Chapter 8
Grounding: Theory and Importance

GROUNDING PLAYS A VERY IMPORTANT ROLE in the safety of any electrical system—whether it is in a garage or a skyscraper. A listing of terms used in this chapter follows. I refer to them throughout this chapter.

Continuous ground—All circuits *must* have a grounding wire connecting all metal (noncurrent carrying) parts, cabinets, wall and ceiling boxes, fixture canopies, and mounting brackets holding toggle switches and receptacles in their respective wall boxes. This system, if carefully installed, is a direct connection to ground for each device bracket, fixture, box, and cabinet.

green wire—Extension cords, portable saw and drill cords and other cords having three wires and having a three-blade attachment plug are called grounding cords. The cord is made up of a rubber covering (or plastic), jute fillers to make a round cord and *three* wires—one black wire (hot), one white (neutral) and one green. This green wire is more important than the other two

wires. It is the *safety* wire. Without this wire any tool or appliance would be a potential hazard to the user. *Never* cut off the third grounding prong from a three-wire attachment plug, *never*.

ground—(Code designation *grounding electrode*). The pipe of an underground metal water system. A driven pipe or ground rod used where there is no underground piping system.

ground, to—Connecting a wire (ground wire) from the metal parts (that are noncurrent carrying) such as cabinets or neutral wire to the ground.

grounded neutral wire—This is the white or natural gray color wire coming in to the service-entrance panel. If service entrance *cable* is used, the neutral wire will be bare strands twisted to make a wire shape.

grounding wire—This wire does not normally carry current. It can be bare or have green-colored insulation. It is connected to the metal parts of the system such as cabinets and frames of home appliances, fuse, and breaker enclosures. The *only* time current flows in this wire is when a fault occurs in the current-carrying parts of the equipment. This grounding wire must be installed and maintained in tiptop condition with low resistance so that the flow of fault current will be great enough to blow the fuse or trip the breaker promptly.

ground wire—(Code designation *grounding electrode conductor*). A wire connected to the neutral terminal bar in the service-entrance panel and also to the metal cabinet itself, plus the conduit or BX or the ground wire in Romex cable.

insulation—The neutral wire *must* be insulated (except in service-entrance cable) and treated the same as a hot wire. This is a code requirement.

neutral integrity—The neutral wire must never be disconnected by a fuse breaker, switch, or other device. If such a device can break the hot wire *and* the neutral *simultaneously*, it may be used. This is extremely important. The neutral wire must *run without a break* from the service-entrance panel to the place where the current is consumed. For 120-volt circuits there are *no* exceptions.

nonuse of neutral—Appliances rated at 230 volts and 230 volt motors do not need a neutral wire. A separate grounding wire is used for equipment grounding unless conduit runs to the equipment. Conduit acts as the grounding wire.

white neutral wire—Large-size insulated wires do not come in white. In this case, *both* ends that are visible are painted white or taped with white tape so that all of the wire showing is white. This is then the neutral wire.

ADVANTAGES OF GROUNDING

While grounding is required by the code, it is very much to your and other people's advantage to maintain a properly installed ground at all times. See Figs. 8-1 through 8-7. If a high voltage line of say 4800 volts should fall across your 120/240 volt service in a storm, a serious condition would exist. This and lightning strikes are very greatly min-

imized by a good solid ground wire connected to a proper ground.

Assume a motor has an internal fault (a bare hot wire inside the motor housing touches the housing). If the motor housing is grounded, the fuse will blow or the breaker will trip. If the housing is *not* grounded, you will get a shock if you touched the housing. This is especially crucial when using power tools outdoors. Be sure they are grounded properly.

Even though grounding is done, but not done properly, fuse in the neutral instead of the hot wire, or fuses in both hot and neutral wires, severe shock or even death could occur. In some installations, the disconnect switch opens the neutral leaving the hot wire connected. In this case, the equipment is still hot even though it is not operating. As with all electrical work, attention to detail and exactness in following the code and checking the completed work for defects and mistakes is the ultimate goal of the good electrician.

OUTBUILDINGS

Outbuildings supplied from a main building must have their own service-entrance equipment provided with a separate grounding electrode with a grounding conductor. There are exceptions to this rule, but for farm buildings I would advise that each outbuilding entrance panel be grounded. The cost is small when done as the building is being wired. The *grounding electrode* must be as near as possible and in the same area as the *grounding conductor* from the system. Grounding electrodes shall be:

■ The nearest available effectively grounded steel structural member of the building

■ Or the nearest available effectively grounded metal cold water pipe (the water pipe must be buried in the earth for at least 10 feet).

■ Or other electrodes specified by the code, Sections 250-81 and 250-83 where the first two electrodes are not available. The *made* electrode described in code Section 250-83 is used on farms and cottages where other electrodes are not available.

Rod or pipe electrodes are commonly used. They are to be driven vertically 8 feet into the

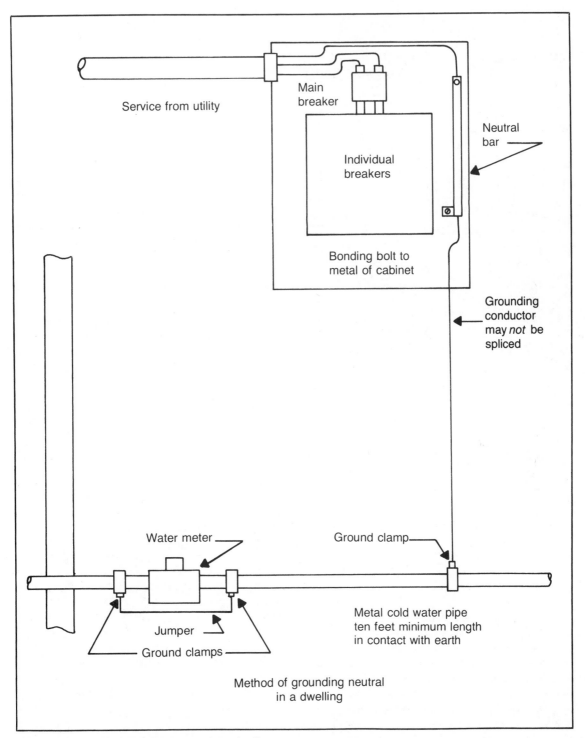

Fig. 8-1. Layout of the grounding system for a dwelling.

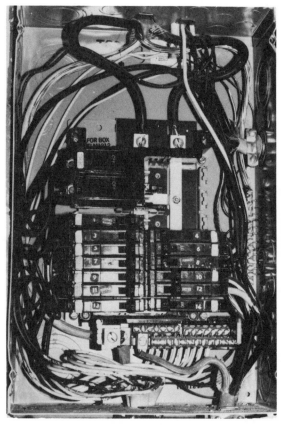

Fig. 8-2. View of service-entrance panel in a condo unit. Because the main breaker is on the outside of the building, cable from it has four wires: two black, one gray (neutral), and one bare (equipment ground). The gray wire is attached to a large slotted screw below the left bank of breakers. This is the neutral bar. The equipment grounding bar is on the extreme right-hand side and connects to the bare wire from the SE cable, as are all Romex ground wires.

ground. If rock is encountered, they may be driven at an angle. Eight feet is the *minimum*. Sometimes the driven ground is required to be driven more than the 8 feet so that the upper end is recessed below the normal ground level. The grounding conductor is then clamped to the top of the electrode with the grounding clamp. After inspection the electrode is then covered with earth for protection.

Plate electrodes must be at least two square feet in area. Ferrous plates must be ¼-inch thick; nonferrous plates must be a minimum of 0.06-inches thick. I recommend a greater thickness of the nonferrous plates because parts of such a thin

plate could break off and reduce the effective surface area and impairing the grounding system.

The code Table 250-94 lists grounding electrode conductors sized for the largest wire in the entrance cable. For dwellings, the maximum is No. 6. The grounding conductor *must* be one continuous length. Splices are never permitted. The conductor may be of copper, aluminum, or copper-clad aluminum. This can be run exposed if it is not liable to be damaged. Staple it to wood or use clips with anchors on concrete. It is not recommended that it be run inside conduit or Greenfield because of special conditions causing stray eddy currents to be present because of having the wire inside metal conduit. Nonmetallic could be used for protection in exposed places. There are special ground clamps available to accommodate conduit and Greenfield, plus the grounding electrode conductor. For the home and farm, you will very seldom have need for mechanical protection. If you do need protection, consult an electrical inspector before using metal conduit.

Equipment grounding conductors may be of copper, aluminum or other corrosion-resistant metal that is stranded, solid, insulated or bare. Conduit may be used as the grounding conductor. The bare ground wire in Romex, BX, and the green conductor are to be used as grounding conductors. The correct installation of the equipment grounding conductor is very important.

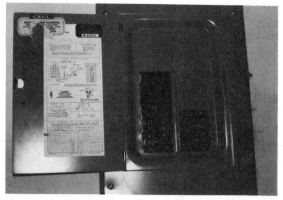

Fig. 8-3. There are spaces for 24 ½-inch breakers or 12 1-inch breakers. Double breakers (two-pole) take twice the space (whether ½-inch or 1-inch). The main breaker is outside the building.

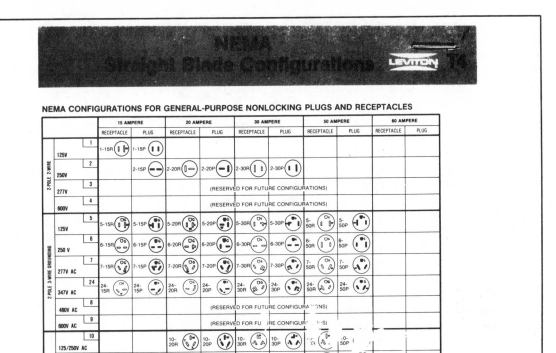

Fig. 8-4. The commonly used configurations. These female configurations are found on receptacles, cord connectors, and flanged outlets. The two-pole, two-wire receptacles shown are obsolete and may not be used for "new work." All current-carrying devices must be grounded to comply with code requirements. Courtesy Leviton.

Every connection of the equipment grounding system must be mechanically and electrically tight (this means that an electrical fault *must* be able to travel all the way back to the service-entrance panel and then to the ground electrode with very low resistance so that the fuse or breaker opens). High resistance may not allow the overcurrent protection to operate to disconnect the equipment (or person) from the hot wire. This means that the metal housing of the electric drill motor is directly connected to the water pipe or other ground. This protects you from shock providing the cord and plug are in perfect condition and the receptacle is properly grounded. This is why you are warned *never* to cut off the grounding blade on the attachment plug.

Electric clothes dryers and electric ranges are permitted to have the noncurrent-carrying parts (stove-top over door and sides) grounded by the system *neutral*. Service-entrance cable may be used and the neutral may be bare *only* if the cable originates at the service-entrance equipment panel. The code Section 250-60 in its entirety and Section 250-61, Exception No. 1. detail this requirement.

Duplex receptacles of the grounding type must have solid metal-to-metal contact with the metal box in which they are mounted. Surface mounted boxes such as "handy" boxes give tight contact. Wall boxes sometimes are recessed below the finished wall surface and do not have tight contact. The plaster ears holding the box flush with the wall prevent this. Code Section 250-74, Exception 2, allows a special type of yoke "Underwriters listed" to be used. A special spring holds the screw tightly. All devices do not have this; if not use a jumper wire from the device green ground screw to the metal box *and* the grounding conductor in the cable or BX. Don't forget to make this connection.

Where an *ungrounded* receptacle is to be replaced by a *grounded* receptacle, the green grounding screw *must* be connected to the *metal* wall box with a green hex head grounding screw. If this metal box is *not grounded* (check with your voltage tester), the green screw *must* be connected to a cold-water pipe. If this is impossible, a new *ungrounded* receptacle *must* be used (one that will accept *only* two-prong plugs). A grounded type receptacle that is not grounded will give a false sense of safety and lead to serious consequences!

Short sections of raceway (conduit, etc.) must be grounded. This might be where Romex is brought down a concrete basement wall for an outlet or switch. As the Romex will have the grounding conductor at the point of attachment to the device, merely attach the grounding conductor to the green box grounding screw. Screw the device mounting

bracket to the handy box ears and the device is effectively grounded.

THREE-TO-TWO PLUG-IN ADAPTERS

Plug-in adapters are sold everywhere and they are used to supposedly convert the two-slot receptacle for use of the three-blade attachment plugs found on grounded power tools and appliances. They either have a spade terminal on a short pigtail or an eyelet. Either connection is fastened under the center plate screw on a duplex receptacle cover. Unless it is determined that this center screw is in fact providing a good positive ground all the way back to the system ground, there is no assurance of safety. Rewire everything from the service-entrance panel throughout the dwelling.

BONDING TO OTHER SYSTEMS

There are many reasons for bonding other grounded systems to the dwelling electrical ground. Interconnection is required for lightning rod systems, communications systems, and cable TV systems. Lack of interconnection may cause severe shock and fire hazard. Cable TV cables have a metal casing and lightning striking the cable can be led directly into the dwelling through the cable connec-

Fig. 8-5. Mock-up of 60-A, service-entrance panel. Service cable comes in as shown in the top center. Range cable leaves as shown at the top right side. Notice the bare ground wire across to the ground clamp on the copper water pipe. Normally the pipe would not be so close, but this is only a mock-up to show methods.

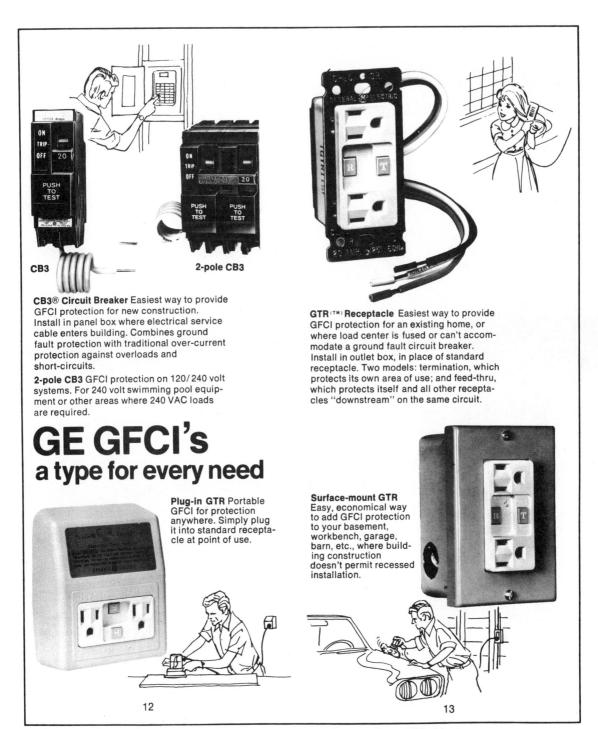

CB3® Circuit Breaker Easiest way to provide GFCI protection for new construction. Install in panel box where electrical service cable enters building. Combines ground fault protection with traditional over-current protection against overloads and short-circuits.

2-pole CB3 GFCI protection on 120/240 volt systems. For 240 volt swimming pool equipment or other areas where 240 VAC loads are required.

CB3

2-pole CB3

GTR⁽™⁾ **Receptacle** Easiest way to provide GFCI protection for an existing home, or where load center is fused or can't accommodate a ground fault circuit breaker. Install in outlet box, in place of standard receptacle. Two models: termination, which protects its own area of use; and feed-thru, which protects itself and all other receptacles "downstream" on the same circuit.

GE GFCI's
a type for every need

Plug-in GTR Portable GFCI for protection anywhere. Simply plug it into standard receptacle at point of use.

Surface-mount GTR Easy, economical way to add GFCI protection to your basement, workbench, garage, barn, etc., where building construction doesn't permit recessed installation.

12

13

Fig. 8-6. Various types of ground fault circuit interrupters (GFCI). Courtesy General Electric.

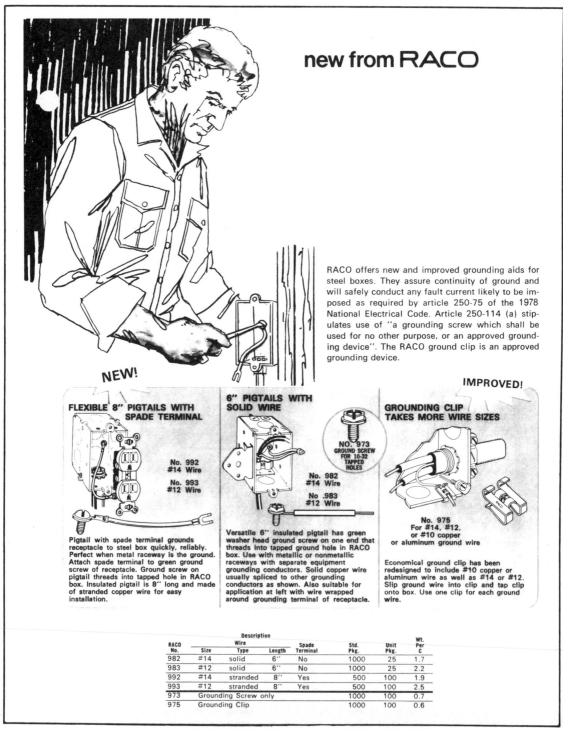

new from RACO

RACO offers new and improved grounding aids for steel boxes. They assure continuity of ground and will safely conduct any fault current likely to be imposed as required by article 250-75 of the 1978 National Electrical Code. Article 250-114 (a) stipulates use of "a grounding screw which shall be used for no other purpose, or an approved grounding device". The RACO ground clip is an approved grounding device.

NEW!

IMPROVED!

FLEXIBLE 8" PIGTAILS WITH SPADE TERMINAL

No. 992
#14 Wire

No. 993
#12 Wire

Pigtail with spade terminal grounds receptacle to steel box quickly, reliably. Perfect when metal raceway is the ground. Attach spade terminal to green ground screw of receptacle. Ground screw on pigtail threads into tapped hole in RACO box. Insulated pigtail is 8" long and made of stranded copper wire for easy installation.

6" PIGTAILS WITH SOLID WIRE

NO. 973
GROUND SCREW
FOR 10-32
TAPPED
HOLES

No. 982
#14 Wire

No .983
#12 Wire

Versatile 6" insulated pigtail has green washer head ground screw on one end that threads into tapped ground hole in RACO box. Use with metallic or nonmetallic raceways with separate equipment grounding conductors. Solid copper wire usually spliced to other grounding conductors as shown. Also suitable for application at left with wire wrapped around grounding terminal of receptacle.

GROUNDING CLIP TAKES MORE WIRE SIZES

No. 975
For #14, #12,
or #10 copper
or aluminum ground wire

Economical ground clip has been redesigned to include #10 copper or aluminum wire as well as #14 or #12. Slip ground wire into clip and tap clip onto box. Use one clip for each ground wire.

RACO No.	Description				Std. Pkg.	Unit Pkg.	Wt. Per C
	Wire			Spade Terminal			
	Size	Type	Length				
982	#14	solid	6"	No	1000	25	1.7
983	#12	solid	6"	No	1000	25	2.2
992	#14	stranded	8"	Yes	500	100	1.9
993	#12	stranded	8"	Yes	500	100	2.5
973	Grounding Screw only				1000	100	0.7
975	Grounding Clip				1000	100	0.6

Fig. 8-7. Grounding devices to provide continuity of ground and ensure safety. Courtesy Raco, Inc.

tion at the TV set. Many times there is so much plastic plumbing in a dwelling that it is hard to locate a true system ground. New installations are now providing externally mounted pressure type connectors on the service-entrance equipment cabinet just for this interconnection.

METHODS OF BONDING SERVICE EQUIPMENT

Pressure type connectors have a hole to put a screw in order to anchor it to the metal cabinet. At the other end is an opening for insertion of the solid or stranded grounding conductor. A setscrew tightens down on this wire and makes an excellent bond. See Figs. 4-17 and 4-18.

All of these methods are used to effectively ground the service cabinets and the service neutral on the *incoming* of the service. One type is a grounding bushing to bond the conduit. There is a pressure connector to accept the wire and in addition there are two setscrews that go through the bushing and bite into the metal of the cabinet wall. Grounding wedges provide a clamping action and also have setscrews to bite into the bushing inside the cabinet, at the same time pulling up against the conduit threads. Rigid conduit screwed into the threaded boss of, say, a meterbase must be "wrench tight" so as to make a positive ground through the threads.

GROUNDING ELECTRODE SYSTEM

To form a grounding electrode system, the following items must be bonded together (if they are present):

■ Metal underground water pipe.
■ Metal frame of building if it is effectively grounded.

These must be bonded together with No. 6 copper wire the same as the grounding conductor. Solderless pressure connectors must be used to connect the grounding electrodes. Soldering is not allowed. The reason for this elaborate grounding electrode system is that metal water pipes are sometimes replaced with plastic pipes, thus losing the continuity of grounding. Other building alterations are made that can loosen or disconnect the grounding conductor. This is a dangerous condition. One used home I purchased had *no grounding electrode conductor* of any kind. I installed one very soon after buying the house.

When installing switches or receptacles in wall boxes—if there are two or more grounding wires entering the box—they must be twisted together, *plus* a short pigtail and a wire nut are screwed on. The pigtail is to go to the device to be mounted in the box. In thus manner, if the device is ever removed for any reason, there will be a continuation of grounding. See Fig. 7-6.

Metal wall boxes also must be grounded by the ground wire. Fit a green grounding hex-head screw in the tapped hole in the box and clamp the ground wire underneath it. Nonmetallic boxes cannot be so grounded. Be sure to attach the cable ground wire to the green device screw. Approved ground clamps must be used to connect the grounding *conductor* to the grounding *electrode* (water or other pipe).

Many different clamps are available for the various electrodes used. The surface of the electrode must be absolutely clean (use emery cloth to shine it). It must have no paint or corrosion to prevent good contact. Watch for aluminum or silver paint on galvanized pipe at the point of clamping. Scrape this off as the pipe has to be absolutely bare.

Chapter 9

Special Wiring Methods and Techniques

O VER THE YEARS ELECTRICIANS HAVE DE-veloped certain construction methods and techniques that enable them to do better work faster and more accurately. These methods are passed on to apprentices and helpers in training programs in the industry and by journeymen providing help and advice on the job. See Figs. 9-1 through 9-21.

EXTENDING WIRING IN BUILDINGS

When an additional receptacle is needed, many times power for it can be obtained from a nearby receptacle, provided that the circuit supplying that receptacle is not overloaded. If that circuit is carrying its full load, another circuit must be used or a new one can be provided by adding another breaker or fuse to the panel.

Assuming that you have made this determination and that the circuit can handle the extra load, this circuit can be extended. If you have located a junction box or light in the basement or have a nearby receptacle, proceed from this point. The basement light must not be switch controlled. A pull-chain fixture is satisfactory. Connecting to a switch controlled circuit would shut off your new receptacle.

When you have decided on the location for the new receptacle, remove the base shoe molding and drill a ¼-inch hole down at an angle through the corner between the floor and the baseboard. This will locate the exact point for drilling up from the basement—directly into the hollow wall space. Figure 9-16 illustrates this. Use a ⅝-inch or ¾-inch spade bit for this (using an electric drill motor). If you plan to do much of this type of work, it would pay you to buy an electricians' 18-inch ¼-inch or ⅜-inch size wood bit for drilling pilot and test holes.

This preliminary work is to find out if the wall space is hollow and will accept a wall box. Many electricians use a long spike to drive down at an angle without removing the base molding. If you first cut an opening in the drywall or plaster and then find that you cannot get cable to that location or that interference in the hollow wall prevents a box from being installed, you have damaged the wall. Check things out first.

Fig. 9-1. Plastic wall box with saddle ears on front to hold box flush. Clamp in back anchor box.

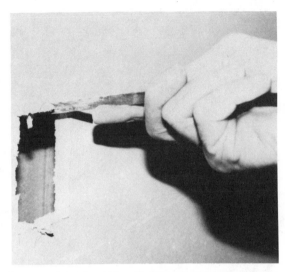

Fig. 9-3. Trimming hole with hacksaw for mounting ears clearance.

Straighten a wire coat hanger. Loop one end for a handle and probe up inside the hollow space beyond the height of the proposed box location. For switch box locations, two coat hangers must be spliced together or another stiff wire can be used. Switch box heights are standard at 48 inches. If you find that the wall will accept the box and cable, hold the box *face* up to the wall at the proper place and mark around all four sides.

Trace around any edge projections on the box. Using a small screwdriver, punch a small hole in the center of the outline. Then wiggle the screwdriver sideways to see if there is a stud in the way of the box. To cut out the opening, use a keyhole saw. You can also use a hacksaw blade with one end wrapped with tape to protect your hands. Coarse tooth blades are best. Gently start sawing at one corner while holding the blade almost parallel to the wall.

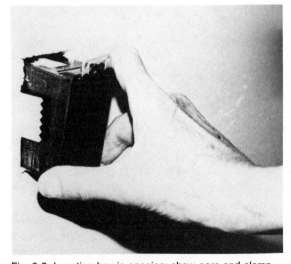

Fig. 9-2. Inserting box in opening; show ears and clamp.

Fig. 9-4. Plastic box held in place with Madison brand supports. Shows ears bent into box.

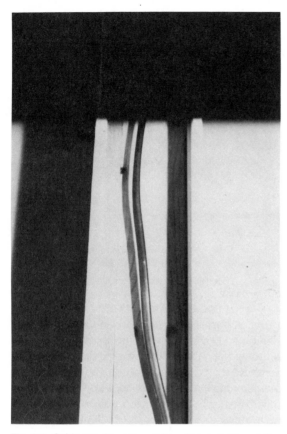

Fig. 9-5. Cable run down to wall box. This is "old work."

and bracket are pushed into the wall opening, the bracket spreads. When the screw is tightened, it bites into the back side of the drywall, again like a toggle bolt. The last type is sheet metal in the shape of the Greek letter Pi, having one long arm with two short legs at right angles near the center. See Fig. 9-4. The long arm is inserted into the wall opening vertically if the opening is vertical and the short arms are bent slightly to the side. One bracket is needed for each side of the box. The box is then inserted into the opening. After the box is aligned, the short arms are bent around and into each side of the interior and tightened against the box sides out of the way of any device to be installed in the box. See Fig. 13-38.

When extending a circuit, it is best to install the new wiring backwards from the far end of the extension and make the final tie-in last. This

This way you will be able to go through the drywall without first making a starting hole. Saw all four sides *almost* all the way. Leave a little on each side. This will prevent breaking the drywall in the wrong places. Then finish sawing each side.

When the opening is finished, try the box. Some trimming might be needed. Trim carefully around the box projections so as not to enlarge the hole too much. If the hole is too big, you must plaster around it to seal the box. This is a code requirement.

Depending on the method of support for the box, you will need to provide clearance for these supports. Some boxes have screws inside which, when tightened, spread arms out behind the drywall like toggle bolts to hold the box. Others have a U-shaped bracket that fits around the box and it is held by a screw through the box back. When the box

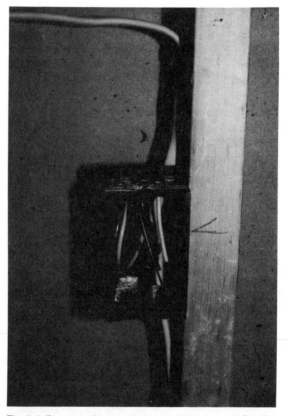

Fig. 9-6. Plastic wall box nailed to stud as new work. See Fig. 9-8.

Fig. 9-7. Wiring has been run to mounted box (old work).

method eliminates shutting off the power for a long time while you are doing all of the new wiring installation.

With the box opening cut in the wall and the hole bored up through the bottom or down from the top of the hollow wall, it is easy to shove the cable into the wall space and bring it out the opening. When buying a metal wall box, try to get one that has the two rear corners made at an angle. This will make the box easier to insert into the wall opening after the cable has been inserted into the box. See Fig. 9-2.

If the hole into the basement is large enough, the cable will slide back down when you insert the box into the drywall opening. Depending on the box anchoring device you are using, secure the box in the drywall. When you prepare the BX cable, remove 6 to 8 inches of armor from the end. Do the same if you are using Romex. It is best to bend the wires so that they do not drop out of the box after the box is secured. If more than one receptacle is being installed, two knockouts must be removed (knocked out). In addition, two holes are needed through into the basement unless the one is large enough for two cables. Instructions for working with BX and Romex are given in Chapter 14.

If two receptacles are to be installed back to back, do not place them *exactly* back to back because the wall thickness might not be enough to accommodate them in this position. Try to leave 6 inches of space between the boxes where their backs are adjacent inside the wall. When there is a stud, a hole can be bored through it and a cable can be shoved through. Another receptacle can be installed farther along the wall on the other side if necessary. Probe this next hollow wall space before cutting into the drywall. Figures 3-8 and 3-9 illustrate these techniques.

If you are wiring a switch or other wall-mounted device, you might need to shove a long piece of stiff wire up inside the wall space (or two straightened coat hangers) to reach up to the wall box opening. Working down from an unfinished attic is more difficult because you must be careful not to step on the plaster ceiling. Step only on the joists or boards laid across them.

Sometimes measurement is the only way to find access to the desired hollow wall space. Measure *very* carefully. I have made errors in measurement and drilled through ceilings instead of into the top of the hollow wall space. Find a reference point

Fig. 9-8. Mock-up wall panel showing boxes installed.

Fig. 9-9. Box and wiring installed. Voids around such a box must be plastered as a code requirement.

that shows on the room ceiling and in the attic. A light fixture will show in both places. When you measure, be sure to take the *center* of both the fixture *and* the box in the attic because an error of even 2 inches will bring the drilling into the room ceiling rather than in the hollow wall space. When going into the attic, keep your bearings so that you don't measure in the wrong direction.

Many metal wall boxes are made with removable sides so that two or more can be "ganged" together to accommodate more devices. Not all boxes are made this way. Plastic boxes are now made in two and more gang style. The interchangeable line of wiring devices (of various manufacturers) can be installed so that up to three devices—such as switches, pilot lights and outlets—will fit in a one-gang wall box. I would rather not use these devices because of the crowding of wires in a one- or two-gang box and the closeness of the terminal screws in the assemblies. They are approved, but use them only when necessary.

Sometimes measurement is the only way to determine how to gain access to the hollow wall space desired. Measure *very* carefully. I have made mistakes in measurements and drilled through a ceiling (only once) and not down into the hollow partition. Usually there will be a reference point that shows on the room ceiling and in the attic. A light fixture location will show in the room *and* in the attic; the fixture and the ceiling box in the attic

are in the same relative location. Be sure to measure from the exact center of both parts of the reference point, whatever it is, because an error of only 2 inches might bring the hole into the room ceiling. When stepping into the attic, keep your bearings (direction) because measurement in the wrong direction will throw you off.

Second floor finished rooms become a greater problem when adding wiring circuits. It might be possible to go toward the eaves through storage-space entrances. A flashlight aimed between joist spaces should provide clues to ways of running wiring underneath finished second-story flooring. See Fig. 9-21.

Where it is absolutely necessary to go all the way to the eaves and down an outside wall with cable, it might be simpler to notch the top wall plate after cutting through the plaster corner at the junction of the wall with the ceiling. When flooring has

Fig. 9-10. Showing method of using toggle bolts to mount 4-inch box as exposed work (on the surface).

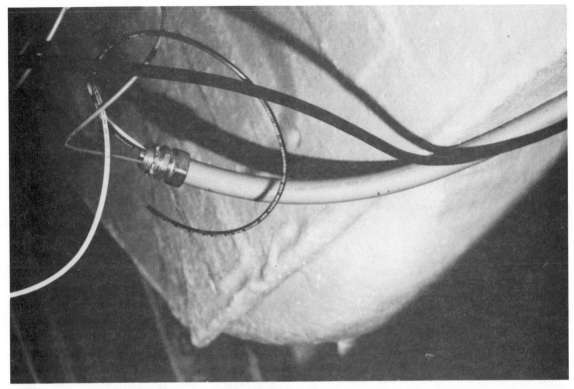

Fig. 9-11 Jacuzzi tub. Wiring is Sealtite flexible moisture-proof cable. Notice the special Sealtite fitting used and the two insulated black and white wires. A green wire is for grounding purposes.

to be removed on the second floor, it is a painstaking process.

If the boards are tongue and groove one board must have the tongue split off so that board can be pried up and removed. Use a sharp stiff putty knife as a chisel. Saw the board at each end, using a keyhole saw, after drilling a series of ⅛-inch holes to allow the saw blade to be started. The board should span *three* joists instead of two for better strength after replacement. When you are using the putty knife to split off the tongue, you will be able to locate the joists. If you use a power circular saw, set the blade to just cut through the floorboard thickness and center the cut on the center of the joist. This will eliminate nailing support cleats on the sides of the joists to support the ends of the removed flooring boards.

Save the sawdust to make a matching filler for the saw cuts after replacing the flooring. Mix with glue to make the filler putty. If hardwood flooring has to be removed to run the cable, try to remove flooring in an inconspicuous area such as a closet rather than in an open hallway.

Figure 9-16 shows how a baseboard can be removed and cable run behind it where there is no other route. This method runs the cable in notches cut in the studs. When using nonmetallic cable (Romex), protection must be provided to guard against driving nails through the cable when nailing back the baseboard. Two methods are approved:

■ Nonmetallic cable protectors, 16-gauge metal plates with prongs for pounding over the cable notches after the cable is run.

■ Thinwall tubing (EMT) is set in notches cut in the studs and having the cable run through for protection. The ½-inch size is usually large enough for 14-2 and 12-2 cable.

Many older houses have lath and plaster rather

than the typical drywall. When cutting out for wall boxes, be sure to locate the box so that it is centered on one lath. This leaves a part of the top and bottom lath to screw the box ears in place.

Mark the box outline on the plaster. Remove all plaster from the laths inside the box outline. Be careful not to loosen the lath from the back side of the plaster. Cut the laths by using a hacksaw blade backwards. This creates a pull instead of push on the lath. Saw up to the top on both sides. Insert a screwdriver in the saw slot and twist, breaking this half piece off. Use a pocketknife to trim if necessary. Do the same with the bottom lath. Now you have room to stick your forefinger in and hook the center lath. This is to prevent the lath from moving when sawing. Sawing might break the lath away from the plaster "key" (the part of the plaster that oozes through between the laths and down the back a little forming a hook).

If the lath breaks away from the plaster, the plaster is weakened and might crack or break away. This is why you must support the lath while sawing. Make sure you have the blade backwards. Most metal wall boxes have *reversible* mounting brackets. You might want to use this method.

Chip out the plaster so that the reversed brackets contact the lath itself. Half-inch #6 screws are all that is needed and the box is more secure. Patch the areas over the brackets and around the box if needed. This is required by the code.

Removing Existing Box

If a switch or receptacle box must be removed from its location in a finished wall to make additions or changes, it can be done with not much trouble. Plastic wall boxes are fastened to a stud by two nails driven through nail guides cast into the top and bottom *outside* of the box. These nails can be cut off using a hacksaw blade (the blade only, no frame).

Insert the blade near the top and bottom corners of the box opening in the drywall (not inside the box). Sometimes a screwdriver is needed to make a hole to start the blade. You will saw at a position just above and below the corner of the box so angle the blade in that direction. You will feel and

hear the blade contacting the nail. After both nails have been cut, run a pocketknife around the box and you will be able to remove it easily.

To replace the box, drill two holes—3/16 of an inch in diameter—about an inch inside the stud side and about 2 inches apart. Use #8 roundhead screws to fasten the box to the stud. Try a screwdriver angled into the box where the screws would be before drilling the holes to make sure you are able to tighten the screws. Avoid any closeness of the device in the box to the screws.

Finding the Center of a Ceiling

Assume, as an example, that the room you want to find the center for is 12 × 14 feet. Set a stepladder

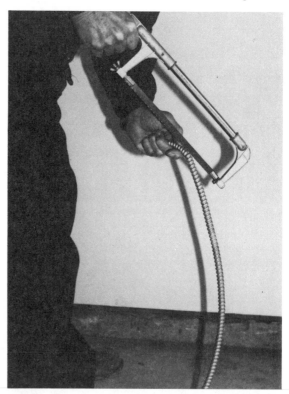

Fig. 9-12. Method of holding BX for cutting with a hacksaw. Foot-holding end of BX coming from roll. This method will work for cutting armor from the end already installed in a ceiling, basement, or elsewhere. Notice the length is quite taut and the end is bent at the contact point. This bend perhaps pulls the wires inside, down and away from inside of armor.

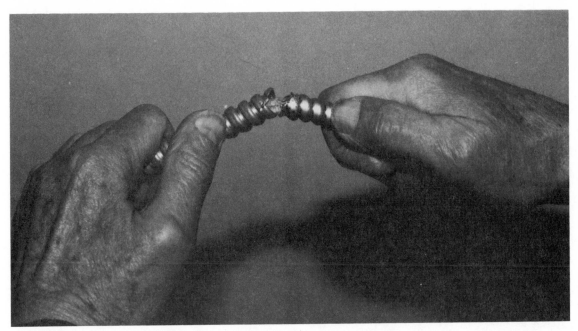

Fig. 9-13. Bending cut armor to snap each end of the cut.

near the room center. Find a piece of 1- × -2 wood to use as a measuring device. Go up the ladder so that you can hold the stick with one end at the wall and ceiling juncture near the center of that wall. Mark the other end, that is over your head, with a pencil mark on the ceiling. Now put the stick against the other wall-to-ceiling juncture and make another mark on the ceiling at its end. You now have two marks about one or two feet apart. Whether the stick was *more* or *less* than half the span does not matter. With your rule, measure that span and divide the figure in half. Half of 11½ inches is 5¾ inches; half of 19 inches is 9½ inches. Be sure to designate this mark as the center of that span. Circle the mark.

Do the same with the other two walls to find the center in that direction also. Make your marks near the first *circled* center mark. This second center mark may have to be moved slightly one way or the other so as to coincide with the other mark. This method can also be used with new work. The first marking should be the bottom of a joist the same as on a finished ceiling. Determine which joist

space is nearest to the room center. Locate the room center in the other direction on *this* joist.

Temporarily *tack* up a sliding bar box support at the approximate center in the crosswise direction to the joists. Now by a skillful handling of the stick (1 × 2) and your rule, find the center in this direction. This is easier *done* than *said*. I hope Fig. 9-20 will make this method clearer. This whole layout takes no more than five minutes to do.

Because off-center fixtures are an eyesore, it is important to locate them accurately. If the center falls on a joist, buy a half-inch deep ceiling box. Any ceiling finish that is thinner than one-half inch will make it necessary to notch the joist slightly. The box must be flush with the finished ceiling. Be sure to allow knockouts to be available for insertion of necessary cables into the box. For old work conditions where the box comes *between* joists, use either a spring out U-support or the bar hanger. If the fixture is heavy, it is safer to use the bar support. For heavy fixtures, the code makes it mandatory to support it from the building framing members.

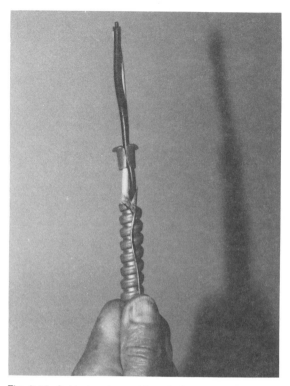

Fig. 9-14. Cable has been stripped of armor and antishort bushing is in place. Bonding wire has been bent back; it can go over the antishort bushing back along the cable, or before the bushing and back along the cable. Alternately, the bonding wire can be wrapped spirally around the cable. In any case, the box connector clamp will establish a proper ground continuity.

Mounting Boxes on Masonry Walls

Boxes mounted on masonry walls usually are found in basements of homes or in commercial and industrial buildings. Such boxes must, of necessity and code rules, have conduit brought to them from overhead (in home basements) or they form part of a complete raceway (conduit) system in a commercial building. Anchoring methods have many forms such as plastic inserts, fiber inserts, toggle bolts (for hollow block walls), and hardened steel drive-pins. Drive pins are driven either by a manual pin holder and hit with a hammer or by a *powder* actuated special tool (they are actually shot into the concrete).

Boxes used on masonry walls are usually the "handy box" type having rounded corners. There are two holes in the back of the box in a staggered arrangement for stability in case the wall is not level. Hold the box plumb and mark the hole locations through each hole with a Listo pencil. The Listo pencil is similar to a mechanical pencil except the marking point is 1/8 of an inch in diameter and is soft like a crayon. They are very good for rough work. Buy one in an office supply store. They cost about $.50. Buy several refills.

Before drilling the holes, mark a large cross with its lines intersecting on the mark you made through the box holes. For drilling, use a 3/16-inch carbide drill and drill a little deeper than the insert. Plastic inserts work fine for this lightweight box. A popular brand made by Rawl is Bantam Plugs Size #8-10 × 7/8 of an inch. A 3/16-inch carbide drill is used. Use #10 sheet-metal screws (3/4 of an inch long) for fasteners. You will be bringing 1/2-inch or 3/4-inch conduit down the wall and into the box, usually from the basement ceiling.

To have the conduit enter the box properly, the conduit must have an offset at the end where it enters the box. An alternative is to buy a conduit offset connector that makes forming an offset unnecessary. Secure the conduit with *one-hole* straps. These are a little more expensive, but they eliminate drilling two holes for each strap.

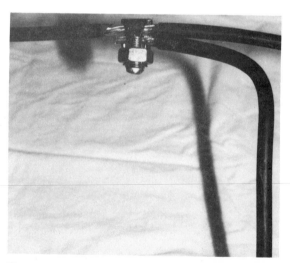

Fig. 9-15. Split connector for large-size wires. Used mainly on power lines at the pole. During cold weather, these connectors might split and drop off, causing power outage.

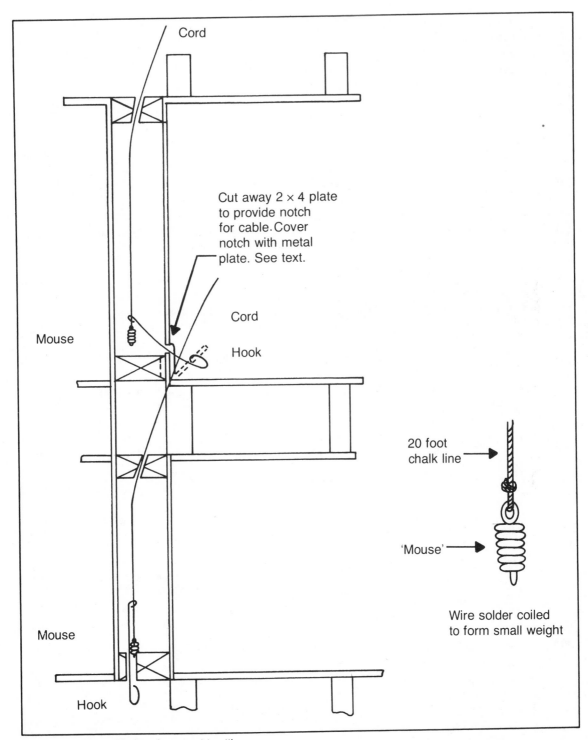

Cord

Cut away 2 × 4 plate
to provide notch
for cable. Cover
notch with metal
plate. See text.

Cord

Mouse

Hook

Mouse

Hook

20 foot
chalk line

'Mouse'

Wire solder coiled
to form small weight

Fig. 9-16. Fishing cable from basement to attic.

ANCHORING DEVICES AND FASTENING METHODS

Devices, boxes, cabinets, cables, and wires need some means of being secured to a supporting member. Anchoring devices described in Table 9-1 include many items for many differing support conditions.

Drive pins can be used with a drive-pin holder and a small sledge or used with a *powder* actuated (explosive charge in a .22-caliber shell) gun-type tool. These pins are hard to use. Some types of concrete in certain parts of the country are almost impossible to drive pins into. In my area, the concrete has extra hard stones that divert the pin, bending it and causing it to chip out a piece of the concrete. On one job, I tried five times to shoot a pin into the concrete, losing both the pin and the powder charge each time. I ended up using a lead anchor and machine screw. One pin shot costs about $.40. Two dollars plus my time reloading, holding the box and shooting was wasted. I had the lead anchor in the wall and the box mounted in about two minutes.

Lead anchors might be prohibited by local fire codes because in a fire the lead will melt and release whatever it was supporting. In such locations, steel anchors must be used. These work the same way as the lead anchors, but they are all steel. Local codes might only require steel in commercial buildings.

Lead anchors, steel anchors and hollow-wall anchors all use machine screws that are not supplied with the anchors, with the exception of hollow wall fasteners. All these anchors are available in various sizes to suit the job at hand. Lead anchors are commonly known as A & J's because they were developed by the Ackerman-Johnson Company. Lead anchors need a "setter" to pound them into place. One is furnished with a full box. Because the setter costs about $.75, a satisfactory substitute is a ¼- × -4 inch long pipe nipple of steel, not brass. If you don't have a carbide drill, a substitute is a ½-inch star drill and a heavy hammer. In an emergency, you can use a ½-inch wide cold chisel. Both the star drill and the cold chisel must be rotated when pounding on them.

For mounting boxes and devices on sheet metal, use sheet-metal screws. These screws are very hard and tend to chew up screwdriver blades. Use a screwdriver that fits the screw slot snugly. This will help prevent blade wear. Phillips type screws are unsatisfactory because the screwdriver tends to slip out of the cross slot when trying to start such a screw while using great pressure. For standard slotted screws in the "pan" head style, boxes of 100 are less expensive by the piece than those in bubble packs of 10 or so. If you can use that many, buy the larger quantity. These screws have

Table 9-1. Fastening Devices and Uses.

Item	Uses
Wood Screws	Mounting cabinets and boxes on wood or composition surfaces.
Sheet-metal screws	Mounting cabinets and boxes on wood sheet metal or composition surfaces.
Concrete anchors	Mounting cabinets on concrete surfaces.
Drive pins	Mounting cabinets and boxes on concrete surfaces.
Toggle bolts	Mounting cabinets and boxes on concrete block walls and drywall.
Plastic plugs and Fiber plugs	Mounting lightweight boxes on concrete or drywall.
Lead anchors and Steel anchors	Mounting heavy cabinets on concrete.
Wood plugs	Prohibited in electrical work.
Hollow wall anchors	Mounting cabinets on hollow walls such as concrete block drywall and paneling.
Beam clamps	Mounting equipment on steel beams.

many uses in other work. Plastic and fiber plugs require sheet-metal screws.

When drilling for plastic or fiber plugs, and you have made an error in placement of the hole and have inserted the plug, it can be removed. Start a screw in the plug about halfway; grip the screw with electrician's side cutters as if you were going to cut the screw head off. Now lift the handles of the cutters and most of the plug will come out with the screw. The hole can now be patched. Plan carefully and you won't miss often.

Fiber plugs (Rawl Plugs is one brand) have a fiber shell with a lead lining. The plug, screw, and drill should be all the same size. As the screw is driven in, the tightness is very considerable. If the conditions are all not right, the plug might, in plaster or drywall, start turning. The screw then cannot enter and expand to make a tight fit. Some plastic plugs have fins on the sides and a flange on the top to help with the installation and to prevent turning.

Boxes for masonry walls are usually handy box style with rounded corners. There are two holes in a staggered arrangement in the box back. This will make the box more stable when it is mounted. Concrete walls are not always level. Hold the box plumb and level and mark the location of the two holes. Using a 3/16-inch masonry drill, drill a 1-inch hole at both marks. Masonry drills tend to wander from the mark. Make a cross over the original mark using a Listo china marker pencil. This type of pencil is available at office supply stores. Make the legs of the cross 1-inch long. If the original mark is gone, the intersection of the cross lines will locate it again. Try to guide the drill back to center by angling it slightly (not too much or it will skid away entirely). The Listo pencil is like a mechanical lead pencil except that its lead is ⅛ of an inch in diameter and is soft like a crayon. It is fine for marking on rough surfaces such as concrete and for marking pipe and conduit.

Toggle bolts fit in holes in hollow walls such as drywall and concrete blocks. The wings of the toggle bolt are larger than the shank of the bolt so a larger hole must be made to insert them. Thus the bolt is a sloppy fit in the hole and it must be tightened very tightly to prevent movement of the object being mounted on the wall. The toggle bolt assembly cannot be recovered if the item is removed. The toggle wings fall down inside the wall.

Hollow-wall fasteners are sometimes better than toggles because they fit tightly in the hole and allow no lateral movement of the cabinet or box, and cabinets, shelves, or other items can be removed from the wall and later replaced when decorating. The hollow-wall fastener has a hollow cage arrangement consisting of four metal strips slightly bent out at the center and connected at the top and bottom. The top has a flange wider than the cage and the bottom has a round nut with internal threads. The hole is drilled and the anchor is tapped into the hole. Then the screw is inserted and tightened until the four strips behind the wall start to bend outward. Further tightening pulls the nut up tight on the back side of the wall, thus forming a solid anchor similar in appearance to a toggle bolt viewed from the rear.

When using a toggle, sometimes a part is left off the bolt and the toggle is tightened to the wall. To remove the toggle results in the loss of the wings inside the wall.

Bending Thinwall Conduit (EMT)

The bending of thinwall is somewhat of an art because it takes forethought, accurate measurement, and an even temper. Once a bend has been made, there is no rebending or correction of the bend possible. Slight adjustments may be possible, but beyond that the piece is best set aside for possible use in another location.

If you plan to do much thinwall work, it will pay you to get an instruction booklet for the make of bender you will be using. See Fig. 3-33. Benders cost about $15 or they can be rented in many areas. The rental agency might have a book or they will show you how to use the bender. The two basic operations are making the 45-degree or 90-degree bend and making the offset and saddle bends.

The offset bend is made to raise the end of the thinwall off the wall so that it can be entered into the box or cabinet knockout. The saddle bend is a neatly formed "hump" to allow the thinwall to be run over another pipe or other type of obstruction. For the

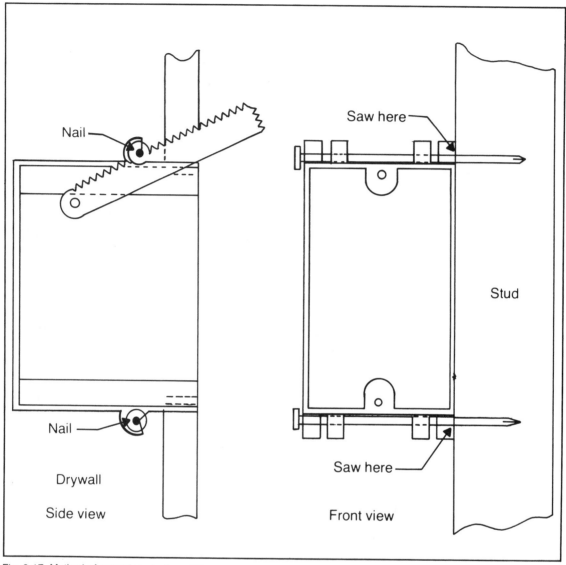

Fig. 9-17. Method of removing plastic wall box.

offset, there are offset box connectors made which will eliminate the need for a job-made offset. These connectors are for the standard offset and will not work if the distance is more than about ⅜ of an inch. The job-made offset looks the best, but it takes time.

To make a 90-degree stub bend 12 inches high, make a mark on the thinwall 7 inches from the end. The bender takes up the other 5 inches. This is for ½-inch thinwall benders. The arrow on the bender is then set on this mark with the bender hook around the thinwall itself. Put your foot on the bender foot pad. Use either foot depending on your convenience and whether you are right-handed or left-handed.

Now pull down on the bender handle until the handle is at a 45-degree angle. This will complete the bend and the stub will be vertical. The second bend on the same piece will be more tricky because the two bends must be in correct relation to each other. If the second bend is not made in the right direction, the piece will not fit. This can be corrected by cutting the thinwall between the two bends and using a coupling. The second bend can then be pointed in the right direction. Figures 3-12 through 3-16 illustrate the 90-degree bend and the offset bend methods.

To make an offset bend to enter a cabinet or box, hook the bender *near* the thinwall end, but not on the end because the hook will distort the end itself. To avoid this, attach a box connector on the end tightly. Then the bender hook can be hooked on just behind this connector. As before, set the bender on and bend. The idea is to make a 45-degree bend, almost. Now "upend" the bender with the handle end on the floor and bender in the air. Put the thinwall back in the bender so that the opposite direction bend will be made. See Fig. 3-14.

Sometimes it is advantageous to slip a larger

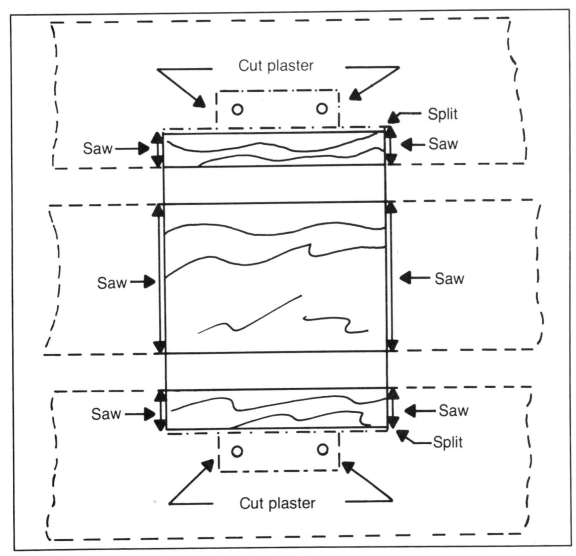

Fig. 9-18. Method of cutting wall box opening in lath and plaster.

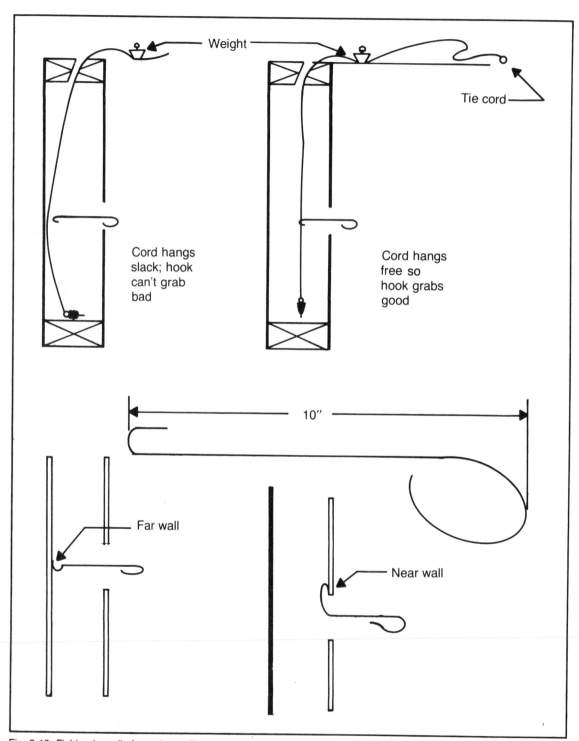

Fig. 9-19. Fishing in walls from above. Fishing tool and its uses.

pipe over the conduit being bent so that the bend will not form *away* from the bender itself rather than in the bender groove. This pipe is called a *slip pipe*. A saddle is two offsets back to back, one to raise the thinwall run over an obstruction (pipe, beam, etc.) and another offset to return the run to the previous level. Thinwall bending takes some skill and practice to accomplish the proper bends. Once you get the hang of it, you will have little trouble. Expect to spoil one or two lengths practicing, but this will cost much less than hiring an electrician.

When bending, use a slow, even pull on the bender handle. Do not jerk on the handle because you could kink the conduit. Keep the conduit flat on the floor and your free foot on the bender foot pad. If the conduit raises up from the floor, it might kink just behind the bender itself instead of bending in the bender groove. Kinks cannot be repaired because the inside wall is damaged and it will damage the wires when they are pulled through. An inspector will turn down damaged conduit. Slow and easy does it! You *will* have failures at first. Be patient.

Bending Rigid Conduit

Rigid conduit is entirely different than thinwall conduit. A special bender called a *hickey* is used. Because the hickey is much shorter than a thinwall bender, the bend must be made in short bends or bites of the hickey on the conduit rather than one full sweep as in thinwall. The use of rigid conduit is discouraged because of the additional work and tools needed for its installation. To use rigid conduit, you would need a pipe vise, threading dies, cutting oil and an oil can, and a pipe reamer. The homeowner generally has no need to install rigid conduit unless special conditions cause the local inspector to require it.

Bending instructions are much the same as for thinwall except for allowances for threads going through the walls of boxes and cabinets (to take the place of box connectors on thinwall). Larger sweeps can be made with the hickey than with thinwall because there is no set radius for bends. Both conduits restrict the number of bends in one run to four 90-degree bends or the equivalent. The number of wires allowed in each size conduit is restricted by code Tables 3A, 3B, and 3C. Three tables are necessary to allow for the different physical diameters of the same size wire due to different types and thicknesses on them.

Rigid conduit is threaded similar to plumbing pipe. Plumbing threads have a certain taper to the threads, while electrical rigid conduit threads have less taper than the plumbing pipe threads.

Different styles of pipe dies are available. Examples are:

■ Two handled (die in the center and a handle on each side).

■ Ratchet type (one handle worked like an automotive ratchet wrench). This is ratcheted on to cut the thread by pushing down on the handle and lifting up and then down again. The direction dog is reversed and the die and handle are spun off backwards, counterclockwise.

■ This type is ratcheted on and after the thread is cut the die is opened and the whole tool is then lifted off the conduit.

■ The last is a power-operated pipe-threading machine that costs about 3 thousand dollars.

In all types, the die is run on the conduit until one or two threads show beyond the die edge or face. Cutting oil *must* be used or the die will become overheated and lose its edge, and it will need to be replaced. This is extremely important in the case of the power threading machine. In certain cases, underground wiring needs to be run in rigid conduit, such as for swimming pools and similar installations.

Intermediate Metal Conduit

This type of conduit was developed as an excellent substitute for heavy and heavy-walled rigid conduit. It has been approved for any and all uses for which rigid conduit is approved. It is easy to handle and work. Although standard threaded fittings are used, the metal wall is thinner, thus saving in cost as well as saving of steel. The conduit is galvanized and can be buried in concrete. Threadless fittings can be used that are similar to those used with thinwall tubing. This is a very satisfactory conduit. Nevertheless, a homeonwer might never have occasion to use it.

Armored Cable (Type AC)

Armored cable, commonly known as BX, is similar to conduit except that it is flexible. It is approved for all residential uses in nearly all areas. Installation in damp or wet locations is prohibited unless type ACL (lead covering inside outer armor) is used. The steel covering consists of a spiral steel strip with interlocking edges wrapped around to form a continuous covering for the wires inside. The armored covering itself, with no wires inside, is known as Greenfield. BX is sold in sizes from #14 to #1, having two and three wires in the cable.

Where BX is run through studs and floor and ceiling joists, holes must be bored through the members in the center of the face to prevent nails

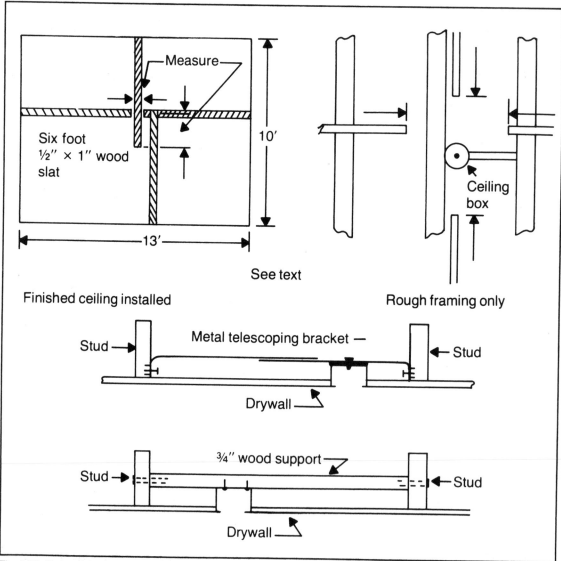

Fig. 9-20. Determining the center of a room. Mounting ceiling boxes. Top row of drawings is looking up at ceiling.

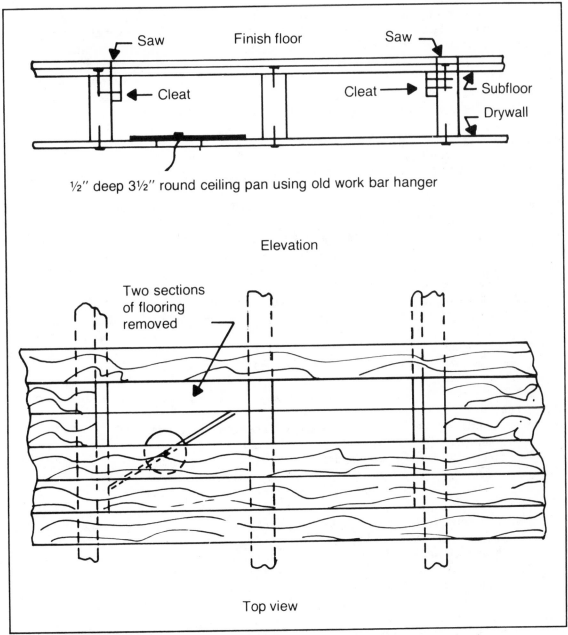

Saw — Finish floor — Saw

Cleat ← → Cleat → Subfloor

Drywall

½″ deep 3½″ round ceiling pan using old work bar hanger

Elevation

Two sections of flooring removed

Top view

Fig. 9-21. Mounting ceiling boxes where there is a finished floor above. How to remove floor and replace.

from being driven through the cables. When cable is run in notches cut in the edge of the framing, metal plates must be put over the cable and notch. Commercial faceplates are made with points to be driven in the wood to hold the plate in place. These plates are mandatory for nonmetallic cable and optional for BX.

When BX is cut and the armored covering is removed, a fiber bushing *must* be inserted between the cut edge of the armor and the insulated wires

105

inside. If the bushing is not put in place, the rough edge of the armor will damage the insulation. Because the bushing is red, it can easily be seen through holes in the BX connectors and BX style clamps (different than Romex clamps) in the boxes and cabinets. *Always* insert the bushing.

To cut BX, use a hacksaw blade with 32 teeth per inch. Coarse tooth blades will cut too fast and cut into the wires inside. Figures 9-12 and 9-13 show procedures for cutting BX cable. A BX cable to be cut will either come from a cable already installed and ready to be cut off to the correct length or from a roll being used on the job.

To cut off an installed length from a coil, be sure the part already in place is secured. Make a mark with a Listo pencil for the length. Grasp the BX 6 to 8 inches beyond the mark on coil side; use your left hand. Pull the cable tight. Then cock your hand up at the wrist back toward your body to put a "hump" in the cable at the pencil mark. Carefully start sawing at the mark. Make sure to saw at right angles to the spiral but *not* at right angles to the run of the cable. Saw the highest part of the spiral almost through, leaving just the lower parts not sawed. Take the cable in both hands and bend it back and forth at the cut until the strip snaps free. By twisting the two cut ends counterclockwise a separation is formed and the wires can either be cut with diagonal cutters or sawed in two. From the coil on the floor you must put your foot on the wire at the floor so as to be able to make the cable tight, then proceed as above.

To strip the armor in preparation for inserting it into the box or cabinet, mark 8 inches back from the end. Now *very carefully* saw through the armor only. Bend the cut back and forth until the armor breaks. Do not bend too sharply because that might cut into the insulation at this point. If the insulation is damaged here, you must cut the damaged part off and start again. The internal bonding strip should be bent back over the armor before putting on the box connector.

Tighten the connector (binding all parts together). The best way to tighten the connector to the box is to run the locknut up tight on the threads and then, using Channellocks, tighten the outside part of the connector. Adjust the locknut so that the connector setscrew ends up on the topside. Then insert the BX with its bonding strip bent back. Finally, tighten the connector setscrew. There are cutters for stripping the armor from the BX in preparation for inserting into the box or cabinet, but they are expensive. The hacksaw has worked fine for many years; just be careful.

Nonmetallic Sheathed Cable (Romex)

Nonmetallic sheathed cable is commonly known as Romex. Romex was developed by Rome Cable Co., Rome, New York. It was originally called Rome-X. Both Romex and BX have many characteristics in common. BX was the forerunner and Romex was probably developed from BX. Both cables have two or three insulated wires as required for use in various circuits. The two-wire type has one black and one white wire (the white wire in any circuit is called the grounded wire *not* the neutral.

The three-wire cable has one black wire, one red wire and one white wire. BX has, in addition, the flat aluminum continuity strip for grounding of the outside armor to provide a continuous *equipment* ground system. As BX has the aluminum strip, so Romex has the *copper* ground wire. Never buy Romex that does not say "with ground." This type of cable is illegal in most areas.

The uses for both cables are the same: residential and light commercial. Some local codes prohibit Romex; Chicago is one.

There are tools for stripping the Romex sheath. At one time, I was using a seamstress' seam ripper, but the outer covering on NMC type cable is thicker and tougher, and the seam ripper was not strong enough to do the job. One cable stripper on the market sells for under $2 and it works well. I had to sharpen the cutter blade on mine before it would work properly. I now have, in addition, a utility knife with a hook blade. This hooked blade is dug into the center of the flat of the cable and pulled along, cutting the covering but not the insulation. Be careful and practice some before using it.

Strip about 8 inches of covering from Romex when you are ready to insert it into a box or cabinet. Make sure ¼ inch of covering shows inside the box clamp. Cable must be supported (stapled) every 4½ feet and within 12 inches of the box or cabinet. If the plastic box has no clamps, Romex must be stapled within 8 inches of the box. There are now Romex staples consisting of a plastic top bar with a nail in each end. These are better than the all-metal staple that is hard to drive straight and is liable to damage the cable covering. The new plastic-top staple will give some and prevent cable damage. Each nail can be driven separately. With either staple, do not drive tightly!

Romex must be protected from damage. If it is carried in notches in framing members, it *must* be protected by a metal plate, 1/16 of an inch thick, fastened over the cable and notch to protect the cable from nails. If Romex is threaded through holes bored in framing members, the holes must be at least 1¼ inches from the front edge framing member. In this case, a metal sleeve 1/16 of an inch thick (use ½-inch thinwall about 2-inches long) driven into the bored hole. Ream *both* ends of the sleeve.

Running cable in "old work" is easier and faster when two people work together. When two people are not available, weight a drop cord from a switch or receptacle box to the bottom of the hollow partition. A bent coat hanger wire, when bent properly, will hook the cord and pull it down through the hole in the base plate of the hollow partition. Because old work is concealed and cannot be stapled, boxes should have cable clamps. The boxes with diagonal back corners should be used if available. This makes it easier to insert the box in the wall with two or three cables clamped in it. Be sure the cable sheath shows inside the box clamp. This is a code requirement.

When you are ready to attach the wires to the device, allow 6 inches from the point where the wires enter the box to where they end. This will give enough slack to allow the wires to be bent, S-curve shape, back into the box after attaching the wires to the device. You can form the wires into loops with needle-nose or side-cutter pliers. The loops *must* go around the screws *clockwise* to prevent opening the loop when the screw is tightened. If the device has push-in connections, strip ⅝ of an inch. If it has screw connections, strip ¾ of an inch.

Wire Identification

When it is necessary to disconnect wiring—such as on motors, heating and cooling equipment and loose wires in junction boxes—each wire must be marked to identify it for reconnection. Various methods of identification are used; examples are paper covered with clear tape, tags, and bending each wire end into a distinctive shape. Each of these methods sometimes results in the loss of the identifying marker.

Permanent marking materials are available that consist of printed numbers, letters and words with pressure-sensitive backing. The material is a clothlike substance packaged in different forms. Pocket booklets have numbers 1 to 25 or 1 to 50. Other *cards* consist of individual numbers, each card having only one number such as 3 or 47. Electrical supply houses sell these numbers and they will usually sell to individuals. Some electronic stores might also have these numbers.

Whether you make your own or buy your identification tags, be sure to identify wires for reconnection. If you don't, you are in trouble. Even two wires, if they are part of control circuits, should be identified. The stick-on numbers really stay in place on the insulation of the wire. Just make sure the wire is not greasy. Even though the stick-on number is overlapped on itself, it may slide off from a greasy surface.

Chapter 10
Permits and Inspections

AS WITH ANY ALTERATIONS OR ADDITIONS, A permit is needed and required to legally do this work. Permits are obtained from the governing authority having jurisdiction in the area. Aside from the legal aspects of obtaining a permit, there is the satisfaction of having the work inspected and approved.

PROCEDURE FOR OBTAINING PERMITS

To apply for a permit to do electrical wiring, visit the building inspection department of the local governing body. This will usually be city hall or the local township offices. Most, but not all, governing authorities will issue what is known as a homeowner's electrical wiring permit. There might be variations in the title of the permit, but the purpose is the same. This permit allows you to do electrical wiring only in your own residence. This excludes rental property which you may own. Ordinances are very strict about this.

Some areas will not permit persons who are not licensed electricians to do electrical, plumbing,

or heating and air conditioning work. Hawaii is one state that has this restriction statewide. In such areas, it might be possible to take an examination and thus obtain your own license (if you pass the exam). You can then get a regular permit to do the work.

Permits are necessary for two reasons.

■ To protect your insurance coverage. If the house burns down and the insurance company finds that the wiring was done without the proper permits being obtained, it could void the insurance coverage and you will not be covered for the fire damage.

■ The inspector will have inspected the work at least once (usually twice), and will approve or not approve of the work. If the inspector does not approve the work, he will usually tell you what is wrong and how to correct the work.

When you apply for a homeowner's electrical permit, you will have to swear that you will do all the work yourself and not contract out any of the work. You *must* do the work yourself. No officials will complain, however, if you have one of your children or your spouse give you a helping hand now and then.

If the wiring is extensive or in a new building, you will be required to provide an outline and perhaps rough drawings of the proposed wiring layout to the building department. This would not be a detailed wiring diagram, but just a layout showing receptacles, switches, range and dryer receptacles and the service entrance location and capacity. Most always the inspector will help you with wire sizes and types and will clue you in on any variations of the local code from the national Electrical Code.

Forms (Figs. 10-1, 10-2 and 10-3) from two cities in different states show types of permits issued by municipalities for homeowners to do their own electrical wiring. The permit form (actually called the homeowner affidavit) from the city of Troy, Michigan, outlines the rules and regulations and is restricted to a *single family residence*. I have underlined the statement of the owner agreeing to do all the work and not to sub-contract any work listed on the permit to another person.

The second permit—from the city of Zion, Illinois—assumes that the applicant is a licensed electrician. Conversation with the chief inspector confirms that a permit may be obtained by a homeowner. The permit contains a statement that the installation will conform to all applicable codes, including the National Electrical Code. If not mentioned, the code is assumed to be the latest and current edition. Note that there is a list of fees for various inspection permits. See Figs. 10-2.

The inspector will be required to make at least two and perhaps more inspections. The first inspection will be made before the wall finish (such as drywall) is applied. This is so that the roughed-

---

CITY OF TROY

500 W. Big Beaver ~~689-4900~~ 524-3344

HOME OWNER AFFIDAVIT

LOCATION_____ DATE_____

As the bona fide owner of the above mentioned property which is a single residence, and which is, or will be on completion my place of residence and no part of which is used for rental or commercial purposes nor is now contemplated for such purpose, I hereby make application for an owner's permit to install_____ as listed on the permit application.

I certify that I am familiar with the provisions of the applicable Ordinance and the rules governing the type of installation which is contemplated at the above mentioned location and hereby agree to make the installation in conformance with the Ordinance.

In making this application, I realize I am assuming the responsibility of a licensed contractor for the installation of the work mentioned in the permit application and for putting the equipment in operation. I further agree that I shall neither hire any other person for the purpose of installing any portion of the_____or related equipment at the above premises, nor sub-contract to any other person, firm or corporation the installation of any portion of the above equipment.

I agree to notify the Inspection Department within seventy-two (72) hours after the installation is completed and is ready for service so that the Department may make its required inspection. I further agree to keep all parts of the installation exposed until the installation is accepted as being in compliance with Ordinance requirements.

I further agree to correct within two weeks time any violations on the work installed and to provide access to the premises between the hours of 8 a.m. and 5 p.m., Monday through Friday for the necessary inspection or inspections. Failure to correct violations or to provide access will subject the permit to cancellation in which case a licensed contractor must be employed to complete the work.

APPLICATION: ☐ ACCEPTABLE ☐ NOT ACCEPTABLE _____

White copy to applicant.
Yellow copy retained in office.

Department Representative

If not acceptable, list reason_____

Subscribed and sworn to before me this

_____day of_____, 19___.

Notary Public,_____County, Michigan.

My commission expires_____.

Owner

Present Address

Telephone Number

Fig. 10-1. Home owner affidavit, City of Troy, Michigan. This type of permit is also used for other types of work, such as plumbing and air conditioning (courtesy City of Troy, Michigan).

Sec. 7-48. Regulations of electrical utility adopted.

The rules and regulations regarding the installation, alteration and use of electrical equipment as last adopted by the electricity supply company supplying the city as last published, and filed with the Illinois Commerce Commission and as approved by the electrical commission of the city are hereby adopted. (Code 1953, § 21-501; Ord. No. 54-0-68, § 1, 10-6-64)

Sec. 7-49. Filing, incorporation of code and regulations.

A copy of the code and rules and regulations adopted by this article are on file in the office of the chief electrical inspector and the provisions of said code and said rules and regulations are hereby made a part of this Code. (Code 1953: § 21-501; Ord. No. 64-0-68, § 1, 10-6-64)

Sec. 7-50. Exceptions, modifications in code and regulations.

The following exceptions and modifications not clearly indicated in the National Electrical Code or in the rules and regulations of the electricity supply company are found necessary to meet conditions, and shall prevail in case of conflict thereof with any other provisions of this chapter or other ordinances of the city.

(1)

Section 348-1 of the National Electrical Code is amended to read as follows: "1. All electrical wiring shall be in electrical metallic tubing as specified in article 348 of the latest edition of the National Electrical Code as amended, or rigid metal conduit as specified in article 346 of the National Electrical Code, except that other types of conduit or wiring protection may be permitted by the electrical inspection department for portions of the wiring where use of electrical metallic tubing or rigid conduit is impractical. 2. Electrical metallic tubing may be used for both exposed and concealed work, except as follows: Electrical metallic tubing protected from corrosion solely by enamel shall not be used. Electrical metallic tubing shall not be used—where, during installation or afterward, it will be subject to severe physical damage, and shall not be used in or under concrete or slab or grade

construction. Only rigid steel conduit is to be used under concrete in slab or grade construction and not rigid aluminum conduit.

"In permitted closed wall construction a minimum one-half inch Greenfield flexible metallic conduit with appropriate size copper wire pulled and all metal, connectors and boxes may be installed. Ninety (90) degree els are not allowed. Thin wall or rigid conduit shall be installed where such work is open and accessible.

"In all existing buildings additional wiring may be installed in rigid or thin wall conduit, B.X. flexible metallic conduit, approved flexible metallic conduit or approved metal moulding except that where exposed to moisture or weather rigid conduit or thin wall conduit shall be used. Where flexible metallic conduit or B.X. is used, it shall terminate in a box in the basement to be located not more than three (3) feet from where the conduit or B.X. enters the basement. All electrical materials and fixtures are to carry the underwriter's label."

(2)

All service shall be in rigid or thin wall metal conduit on the outside of the building and firmly fastened to the building, installed according to the national code.

All underground services under streets, alleys or public ways must be enclosed in rigid metal conduit and must be installed at least thirty (30) inches below the lowest level in said street, alley or public way at the point where said service crosses them.

(3)

All wiring for gasoline station pumps, outside lighting and signs installed in rigid steel conduit with conductors of gasoline and oil resistant type wire as approved for such installations and as of article 514 of the latest edition of the National Electrical Code.

(4)

No entrance service shall be smaller than 100 Amp. capacity. Minimum size wire to be No. 3RH copper.

Fig. 10-2. Excerpts from amendments to the National Electric Code that have been made part of the City of Zion, IL building code (courtesy City of Zion, IL).

in wiring can be checked for correctness and conformity to code requirements. The inspector will check on support of the cable and proper mounting of switch/receptacle/junction boxes. Protection for cable where it is run through 2-×-4 studs or 2-×-6 and 2-×-8 joists to make sure no nails can penetrate the cable (especially Romex) will be inspected.

The arrangement of the service entrance/distribution equipment and the proper mounting and anchoring of the cabinets and the securing of the entrance cable along the outside of the building will

be checked. The inspector will check to make sure the entrance head at the top of the cable is *above* the point of attachment of the service drop to the building wall. Many other items will be checked. I have only named the major ones. Call for this first inspection well in advance because the inspector might be busy and might not be able to come when you request. If the inspector makes an unnecessary trip you might be charged additional fees.

The second inspection will check receptacles, switches, circuit breakers (the right size?) and all distribution and supply wiring (also for correct size). If you have learned and followed the code, you should have no trouble getting approval. If your work is *not* approved, listen to the inspector because he will usually give you suggestions as to how to correct your installation. It would help if, on the first inspection, you would ask if there is anything that could be corrected or made better. Most inspectors will advise of changes during the rough-in (first) inspection, but it would not hurt to ask, "Is there any way that the job could be improved over the way it is now?"

A page from installation instructions of the Hawaiian Electric Light Company, Inc., for the in-

---

APPLICATION FOR ELECTRICAL INSTALLATION PERMIT

Building Permit No. _____ Electrical Application No. _____

Date of Inspection _____ 19 _____ Application checked by _____

CITY OF ZION

Phone: 872-4546   Date _____ 19 _____

APPLICATION is hereby made for the approval of the plans and specifications hereby submitted, and made a part hereof for the construction or alteration, as appears in specification sheet attached hereto, of electrical installations in the building on premises described below:

APPLICANT agrees to comply with all provisions of the Municipal Code of the City of Zion with reference to electrical installations and such other laws relating to erection and alteration of buildings in effect at this date.

APPLICANT agrees to post the Electrical permit on the premises before work is started and notify the Electrical Inspection Department when ready for inspections, as provided by the electrical ordinance.

Location: Street and Number_____ Lot _____ Block _____ Sec. _____

Contractor_____ Address _____

Owner_____ Address _____

For Initial Installation of Electrical Service: Fees   PAID

  (a) Single Family Residence or Bungalows (New construction):
      Without electric heat_____ $ 7.50   _____
      With electric heat_____ 10.50   _____
      (plus 15¢ per kilowatt over 600 watts)
  (b) Multi-Family or Apartments:
      First Apartment (new construction)
      Without electric heat_____ 7.50   _____
      With electric heat_____ 10.50   _____
      (plus 15¢ per kilowatt over 600 watts)
      Each additional apartment:
      Without electric heat_____ 6.00   _____
      With electric heat_____ 9.00   _____
      (plus 15¢ per kilowatt over 600 watts)
  (c) Commercial or Industrial:
      The fee for commercial or industrial wiring
      shall be $5.00 per thousand valuation.
      Minimum charge to be _____ 7.50   _____
  (d) Electrical Neon Signs_____ 3.00   _____
  (e) Swimming Pool Fee_____ 12.00   _____
      (subject to Article 680 of the National Electrical Code)

Revisions - Additions:
  (a) Incidental Units:
      Air Conditioning Units (1 ton or more), Water Heaters, etc.
      First Unit _____ $ 3.00   _____
      Each additional unit _____ 1.50   _____
  (b) Up to five outlets, not included in (a) or (b) as shown in Section 1.
      Minimum charge _____ $ 3.00   _____
  (c) Entrance services _____ 3.00   _____
  (d) Electric space heating:
      The basic fee will be $3.00 plus 15¢ per kilowatt over 600 watts.   _____

Plan filed _____ 19 _____   TOTAL _____

I hereby certify that I have read the Electrical Sections of the Municipal Code and know the contents thereof.

Applicant _____ Address _____
      Licensed Electrician

Applicant's Phone No. _____ License No. _____

Fig. 10-3. Application for Electrical Installation Permit, City of Zion, IL. (courtesy City of Zion, IL).

stallation of underground cable from their lines to the customer's meter, gives their requirements for underground cable installation. See Fig. 4-22.

THE INSPECTOR

The local inspector is usually a former electrical contractor who has retired from contracting and has been appointed to the position of electrical inspector. Many inspectors have had extensive education both in the practical application and the theoretical knowledge of electricity. One inspector in my area is on the board of the National Electrical Code. Almost all inspectors have worked with tools and have intimate knowledge of all phases of electrical construction and design. The position of inspector is usually political and appointive.

Inspector will be very helpful to those who do not have extensive knowledge of wiring practices. A few words from him might, in the long run, save you time and money as he knows the best and most economical methods of wiring. Listen and talk to him every chance you get. Be informed of *local* regulations that differ from the National Electrical Code. Be sure to follow all rules and regulations.

Be sure to follow code practices and regulations. The code is not difficult to follow. In the code handbook for 1981, as in previous editions, there are many explanations and illustrations (neither of which are in the less expensive "code text only" edition). It may be advisable and to your advantage to purchase this edition at $22.50 postpaid. Important information for the do-it-yourself electrician is covered in my book, with emphasis on safety, adherence to Code practices, proper installation methods, and good workmanship. In most, if not all cases, this book will suffice. Use top quality materials and devices in all your work. To match that quality, do quality work neatly and properly.

Almost all electrical wiring materials and devices sold carry the Underwriter Laboratories, Inc., mark denoting that the product is suitable for the use intended. Watch for the UL label.

Chapter 11
The National Electrical Code

T HE FIRST ELECTRICAL CODE WAS PUBLISHED in 1895 by the National Board of Fire Underwriters. This same Board continued to publish the National Electrical Code until 1962. The code continues to be published every three years, each time being revised and updated as necessary to keep up with new developments in the field of electricity. The National Electrical Code continues to be the most widely adopted code of standard practices in the United States and the world. See Figs. 11-1 through 11-5.

While the code itself is only advisory, it *may* be adopted by reference aand become law by reason of it's adoption by a municipality or other governing body. Every governing body establishes a building inspection department for the purpose of inspection to determine the safety and reliability of all building construction. This department is usually divided into many individual sections. One of them usually will be an electrical inspection section that enforces the National Electrical Code and local jurisdictional codes.

LOCAL CODES

Special codes developed by groups of municipalities are enforced by the governing bodies, in addition to the National Electrical Code. In the Detroit area, there are 118 cities and villages that have formed the Reciprocal Electrical Council. This council has published supplementary rules consisting of 13 pages of amendments to the code. These amendments are minor, but they must be considered when doing wiring.

AVAILABILITY OF THE CODE TEXTS

Copies of the current codes can be obtained from city electrical inspection departments. Local public utilities might have copies for sale. The best source is directly by mail from the publisher but electrical suppliers usually have it.

The *Electrical Code for One- and Two-Family* dwellings should be purchased and referred to when there is any question about a wiring installation. This abridged edition is a must for the homeowner.

Electrical Code

for

One- and Two-Family Dwellings

NFPA 70A - 1981

Excerpted from the 1981 *National Electrical Code*©

NFPA 70 - 1981

Explanation of this Code

This Electrical Code for One- and Two-Family Dwellings (NFPA 70A-1981) covers those wiring methods and materials most commonly encountered in the construction of new one- and two-family dwellings. Other wiring methods, materials and subject matter covered in the 1981 *National Electrical Code* (NFPA 70-1981) are also recognized by this Code. (See Preface for further information.)

The development of this Code was first undertaken in 1968 to meet the expressed need for an electrical code applicable only to dwellings as a convenience to those whose interests are so oriented. With the approval of the Correlating Committee of the National Electrical Code Committee, an Ad Hoc Committee was established of those primarily concerned to guide this project to completion. Those asked to serve on the Ad Hoc Committee included representatives of the following organizations: American Insurance Association, Building Officials and Code Administrators International, Inc., Department of Housing and Urban Development, Edison Electric Institute, International Association of Electrical Inspectors, International Brotherhood of Electrical Workers, International Conference of Building Officials, National Association of Home Builders, the National Electrical Contractors Association, and Underwriters Laboratories Inc.

It was decided that the Electrical Code for One- and Two-Family Dwellings should consist of excerpts from the complete current *National Electrical Code* without any modification of intent and with minimum editorial change. Article and Section numbers have been retained to permit close correlation.

Following decisions made by the Correlating Committee and by the Technical Subcommittee as to format and content, the excerpted material containing editorial revision was formally submitted to members of the Technical Subcommittee and the Correlating Committee for letter ballot to determine if the editorial changes accomplished had been achieved without altering the intent of the complete Code.

Fig. 11-1. Explanation of Electrical Code for One- and Two-Family dwellings, NFPA 70A-1981. Reprinted with permission from NFPA 70A-1981, Electrical Code for One- and Two-Family Dwellings, Copyright© 1981, National Fire Protection Association, Quincy, Massachusetts 02269. This reprinted material is not the complete and official position of the NFPA on the referenced subject, which is represented only by the standard in its entirety.

**Table 220-19.   Demand Loads for Household Electric Ranges,
Wall-Mounted Ovens, Counter-Mounted Cooking Units, and
Other Household Cooking Appliances over 1¾ kW Rating.
Column A to be used in all cases except as otherwise
permitted in Note 3 below.**

NUMBER OF APPLIANCES	Maximum Demand (See Notes)	Demand Factors Percent (See Note 3)	
	COLUMN A (Not over 12 kW Rating)	COLUMN B (Less than 3½ kW Rating)	COLUMN C (3½ kW to 8¾ kW Rating)
1	8 kW	80%	80%
2	11 kW	75%	65%
3	14 kW	70%	55%
4	17 kW	66%	50%
5	20 kW	62%	45%
6	21 kW	59%	43%

Note 1. Over 12 kW through 27 kW ranges all of same rating.   For ranges individually rated more than 12 kW but not more than 27 kW, the maximum demand in Column A shall be increased 5 percent for each additional kW of rating or major fraction thereof by which the rating of individual ranges exceeds 12 kW.

Note 2. Over 12 kW through 27 kW ranges of unequal ratings.   For ranges individually rated more than 12 kW and of different ratings but none exceeding 27 kW, an average value of rating shall be computed by adding together the ratings of all ranges to obtain the total connected load (using 12 kW for any range rated less than 12 kW) and dividing by the total number of ranges; and then the maximum demand in Column A shall be increased 5 percent for each kW or major fraction thereof by which this average value exceeds 12 kW.

Note 3. Over 1¾ kW through 8¾ kW.   In lieu of the method provided in Column A, it shall be permissible to add the nameplate ratings of all ranges rated more than 1¾ kW but not more than 8¾ kW and multiply the sum by the demand factors specified in Column B or C for the given number of appliances.

Note 4. Branch-Circuit Load.   It shall be permissible to compute the branch-circuit load for one range in accordance with Table 220-19. The branch-circuit load for one wall-mounted oven or one counter-mounted cooking unit shall be the nameplate rating of the appliance. The branch-circuit load for a counter-mounted cooking unit and not more than two wall-mounted ovens, all supplied from a single branch circuit and located in the same room, shall be computed by adding the nameplate rating of the individual appliances and treating this total as equivalent to one range.

220-21. Noncoincident Loads.   Where it is unlikely that two dissimilar loads will be in use simultaneously, it shall be permissible to omit the smaller of the two in computing the total load of a feeder.

Fig. 11-2. Table 220-19 (part of Article 220) with Notes 1, 2, 3, and 4. Demand Loads for Household Electric Ranges, etc. excerpted from the 1981 National Electrical Code, NFPA 7 0A-1981. Reprinted with permission from NFPA 70A-1981, Electrical Code for One-and-Two Family Dwellings, Copyright© 1981, National Fire Protection Association, Quincy, Massachusetts 02269. This reprinted material is not the complete and official position of the NFPA on the referenced subject, which is represented only by the standard in its entirety.

220-22. Feeder Neutral Load. The feeder neutral load shall be the maximum unbalance of the load determined by this article. The maximum unbalanced load shall be the maximum connected load between the neutral and any one ungrounded conductor, except that the load thus obtained shall be multiplied by 140 percent for 5-wire, 2-phase systems. For a feeder supplying household electric ranges, wall-mounted ovens, and counter-mounted cooking units, the maximum unbalanced load shall be considered as 70 percent of the load on the ungrounded conductors, as determined in accordance with Table 220-19. For 3-wire dc or single-phase ac, 4-wire, 3-phase, and 5-wire, 2-phase systems, a further demand factor of 70 percent shall be permitted for that portion of the unbalanced load in excess of 200 amperes. There shall be no reduction of the neutral capacity for that portion of the load which consists of electric-discharge lighting.

See Examples 1, 1(a), 1(b), 1(c), and 1(d) in Tables and Examples.

C. Optional Calculations for Computing Feeder and Service Loads

220-30. Optional Calculation — Dwelling Unit.

(a) Feeder and Service Load. For a dwelling unit having the total connected load served by a single 3-wire, 120/240-volt or 208Y/120-volt set of service-entrance or feeder conductors with an ampacity of 100 or greater, it shall be permissible to compute the feeder and service loads in accordance with Table 220-30 instead of the method specified in Part B of this article. Feeder and service-entrance conductors whose demand load is determined by this optional calculation shall be permitted to have the neutral load determined by Section 220-22.

(b) Loads. The loads identified in Table 220-30 as "other load" and as "remainder of other load" shall include the following:

(1) 1500 watts for each 2-wire, 20-ampere small appliance branch circuit and each laundry branch circuit specified in Section 220-16.

(2) 3 watts per square foot (0.093 sq m) for general lighting and general-use receptacles.

(3) The nameplate rating of all fixed appliances, ranges, wall-mounted ovens, counter-mounted cooking units, and including four or more separately controlled space heating units.

Table 220-30
Optional Calculation for Dwelling Unit

Load (in kW or kVA)	Demand Factor Percent
Largest of [see Section 220-30(c)]	
Air conditioning and cooling, including heat pump compressors	100
Central electric space heating including integral supplemental heating in heat pumps	65
Less than four separately controlled electric space heating units	65
Plus:	
First 10 kW of all other load	100
Remainder of other load	40

Fig. 11-3. Table 220-30 Optional Calculation for Dwelling Unit (part of Article 220). Article 220-31 Optional Calculation for Additional Loads in Existing Dwelling. Complete. Both excerpted from the 1981 National Electrical Code NFPA 70A-1981. Reprinted with permission from NFPA 70A-1981, Electrical Code for One-and-Two Family Dwellings, Copyright© 1981, National Fire Protection Association, Quincy, Massachusetts 02269. This reprinted material is not the complete and official position of the NFPA on the referenced subject, which is represented only by the standard in its entirety.

(4) The nameplate ampere or kVA rating of all motors and of all low-power-factor loads.

(c) Largest Load. When applying Section 220-21 to Table 220-30 use the largest of the following:

(1) Air-conditioning load.

(2) The 65 percent diversified demand of the central electric space heating load including integral supplemental heating in heat pumps.

(3) The 65 percent diversified demand of the load of less than four separately controlled electric space heating units.

(4) The connected load of four or more separately controlled electric space heating units.

220-31. Optional Calculation for Additional Loads in Existing Dwelling Unit.   For an existing dwelling unit presently being served by an existing 120/240 volt or 208Y/120, 3-wire, 60-ampere service, it shall be permissible to compute load calculations as follows:

Load (in kW or kVA)	Percent of Load
First 8 kW of load at	100%
Remainder of load at	40%

Load calculation shall include lighting at 3 watts per square foot (0.093 sq m): 1500 watts for each 20-ampere appliance circuit, range or wall-mounted oven and counter-mounted cooking unit and other appliances that are permanently connected or fastened in place at nameplate rating.

If air-conditioning equipment or electric space heating equipment is to be installed the following formula shall be applied to determine if the existing service is of sufficient size.

Air-conditioning equipment*	100%
Central electric space heating*	100%
Less than four separately controlled space heating units*	100%
First 8 kW of all other load	100%
Remainder of all other load	40%

Other loads shall include:

1500 watts for each 20-ampere appliance circuit.

Lighting and portable appliances at 3 watts per square foot (0.093 sq m)

Household range or wall-mounted oven and counter-mounted cooking unit.

All other appliances fastened in place, including four or more separately controlled space heating units, at nameplate rating.

* Use larger connected load of air conditioning and space heating, but not both.

3. Three-Wire, Single-Phase Dwelling Services. In dwelling units, conductors, as listed below, shall be permitted to be utilized as three-wire, single-phase, service-entrance conductors and the three-wire, single-phase feeder that carries the total current supplied by that service.

Conductor Types and Sizes
RH-RHH-RHW-THW-THWN-THHN-XHHW

Copper	Aluminum and Copper-Clad AL	Service Rating in Amps
AWG	AWG	
4	2	100
3	1	110
2	1/0	125
1	2/0	150
1/0	3/0	175
2/0	4/0	200

Fig. 11-4. Note 3 Three-Wire, Single-Phase Dwelling Services, to Table 310-16, including the table listing Conductor Types and Sizes—RH-RHH-THW-THWN-THHN-XHHW. Reprinted with permission from NFPA 70A-1981, Electrical Code for One-and-Two Family Dwellings, Copyright© 1981, National Fire Protection Association, Quincy, Massachusetts 02269. This reprinted material is not the complete and official position of the NFPA on the referenced subject, which is represented only by the standard in its entirety.

Secs. 7-35—7-45. Reserved.

ARTICLE III. STANDARDS*

Sec. 7-46. Adoption generally.

Pursuant to the recommendation of the electrical commission of the city the following are hereby adopted as the safe and practical standards for the installation, alteration, and use of electrical equipment in the city. (Code 1953, § 21-501; Ord. No. 64-0-68, § 1, 10-6-64)

Sec. 7-47. Code adopted.

The 1978 edition of the rules and regulations of the National Fire Protection Association for electrical wiring and apparatus contained in the code known as the National Electrical Code approved by the American Insurance Association, except as modified hereinbelow, are hereby adopted and incorporated as fully as if set out at length herein. (Code 1953, § 21-102; Ord. No. 64-0-68, § 1, 10-6-64; Ord. No. 76-0-11, § 1, 2-17-76; Ord. No. 79-0-37, § 1, 8-21-79)

*State law reference—Authority to provide standards, Ill. Rev. Stats., Ch. 24, § 11-87-3.

Supp. No. 34

Fig. 11-5. Excerpts from "Amendments to the National Electrical Code" formulated by the City of Troy, Michigan (courtesy City of Troy, Michigan).

or equivalent and 1 No. 5. Minimum of 1 240 volt circuit and 8 120 volt lighting circuits, all branch circuits to be protected by automatic circuit breaker or fusestat.

(5) Services for commercial buildings using 4,000 watts or more shall not be smaller than three No. 3 wires and 100 ampere service switch. All circuit wiring in commercial buildings shall not be less than No. 12RC wire and shall be either RC or TW Type T. Overload protection or limiting fuses shall be installed in installations over 4,000 watts. House wiring or installations under 4,000 watts will be fused according to NEC standards.

(6) #14 wire in all areas, except kitchen, utility, and dinette which will be #12 wire. Kitchen area, 2 #12 circuits to receptacles. In areas where #14 wire is used, maximum outlets allowed is 10, 1,000 watts maximum per circuit. Separate circuit to heating system with fused disconnecting means within the reach of heating system fused properly.

(7) All underground wiring if not approved direct burial cable must be protected with metal or fiber covering placed at least 30 inches below grade. Lead covering will not be considered sufficient protection.

(8) All motors permanently installed shall be wired on a separate circuit with externally operated fused switch as near to the motor as within 5 feet.

(9) All transformers used for neon inside window signs or borders shall be indoor type and shall be enclosed in a grounded metal box. Outside neon signs or borders shall be installed with outside type transformers, weatherproof type.

All leads from such metal boxes shall be brought on through porcelain-glass or other bushings of equal dielectric strength. All high tension wiring for the electric service shall meet the requirements as covered in this chapter; except not to exceed three feet of Greenfield flexible conduit may be used in making connections to transformers. All high tension con-

Supp. No. 34

Fig. 11-5. Excerpts from "Amendments to the National Electrical Code" formulated by the City of Troy, Michigan (courtesy City of Troy, Michigan). (Continued from page 118.)

nections for window signs and borders shall be installed on glass insulators not less than 1½ inches long and securely fastened to the window frame, except where wires are hanging free in air and of necessity across the window. All connections from high tension cables to sign shall be covered with glass insulators of equal dielectric properties and strength.

(10) System or common grounding conductors shall be attached to the street side of water meters, using not less than No. 4 wire firmly stapled to beams, joists or supporting walls from box to connection of ground A driven ground may be used inside or outside the building but directly below the service switch or meter box if no other means of grounding is available. When clamping ground conductor to driven ground or water pipe an approved ground clamp must be used which provides both mechanical and electrical connection.

(11) Electric space heating equipment: Fixed indoor electrical space heating equipment to be listed by the Underwriter's Laboratories, Inc., and have affixed labels of the Underwriter's Laboratories, Inc., as having been tested and approved for such installations. All fixed indoor electrical space heating equipment and installations to comply with Article 422-40 of the latest edition of the National Electrical Code.

(12) Swimming pools: Shall comply with Article 680 of the National Electrical Code of 1978 for all electrical installations and equipment for swimming pools. All underwater lights to be 24 volts or less. (Code 1953, § 21-501; Ord. No. 64-0-68, § 1, 10-6-64; Ord. No. 77-0-9, § 2, 2-15-77; Ord. No. 79-0-37, §§ 2, 3, 8-21-79)

Secs. 7-51—7-60. Reserved.

Fig. 11-5. Excerpts from "Amendments to the National Electrical Code" formulated by the City of Troy, Michigan (courtesy City of Troy, Michigan). (Continued from page 119.)

The designation is NFPA No. 70-A. The current edition, 1981, costs $8.25 postpaid. The complete code only (no handbook text) is NFPA No. 70-81 at a cost of $10.25 postpaid. The *National Electrical Code Handbook* NFPA No. SPP-6C-81 costs $22.50 postpaid. This is a hardcover book containing the complete code text. In addition, it has explanations for nearly all code sections (with many drawings and illustrations). This is a great buy. Most public libraries have the code handbook in the older editions. Look through these older handbooks to see if you would like to own the current edition. Early in the publication year, there is a reduced price for early purchase. I missed getting the $16.00 price and paid the $22.50 price. If you order, ask for the special reduced price for early orders.

To purchase direct from the publisher, write to National Fire Protection Association, Batterymarch Place, Quincy, Mass. 02269 for their *current* price list. Ask about their special reduced price for early orders.

PURPOSE OF THE CODE AND THIS BOOK

With this book, I am attempting to teach you how to complete an electrical installation as follows.

■ Using correct methods and practices.

■ Using the proper tools safely and efficiently.

■ Understanding the *why* of the how-to instructions given.

■ The calculation of wire sizes and ampacities for the expected load on the system.

■ Finally and most importantly, installing a completely safe wiring job in accordance with the applicable electrical codes.

The installation of electrical wiring, while not difficult, must be done very carefully and accurately. One wire misplaced or improperly attached can blow up in your face. If you are not prepared to follow rules and instructions to the letter, you had best employ a licensed electrician to do your wiring.

In *almost* every instance wiring *can* be done with all power *off*. If you are hesitant about making a final connection to hot (live) terminals, employ a licensed electrician to make this connection. Before calling the electrician, make sure all your work has been carefully double checked.

UNDERWRITERS LABORATORIES

Underwriters Laboratories, Inc. is a testing facility devoted to testing nearly all manufactured products that have any connection with Electricity, Burglar Protection, Casualty and Chemical Hazard, Fire Protection, Hazardous Locations, Heating, Air Conditioning and Refrigeration and Marine applications. Any material or product that has anything to do with personal safety will have the familiar UL label prominently displayed on the material. This is a pledge of safety of product or material. Look for this symbol when buying any electrical materials and devices.

Inquires to Underwriters Laboratories, Inc. may be addressed to 333 Phingston Road, Northbrook, Illinois 60062, telephone 312/272-8880.

Chapter 12

Troubleshooting

THE PROCESS OF TROUBLESHOOTING IS MUCH like playing detective. You must ferret out the source of trouble. A blown fuse can be caused by many different conditions. These faults can be localized or affect many other homes besides your own. See Figs. 12-1 through 12-10.

NO POWER

A condition of no power might affect only your home or the whole area. Determine this by going outdoors or at night by looking out the window at neighbors homes. If the trouble is general, call the utility. Heavy storms will cause power failures. Utility equipment failure happens occasionally, but it can in some cases be automatically bypassed. The lights will come on again soon.

If your house has no power at all, there are two causes:

■ Your main breaker has tripped or the main fuses have blown.

■ There are open lines between your meter and the utility connection either at the pole or at the

servicedrop where it is attached to your house outside wall. Using a flashlight check the position of your breaker handle. Some breakers have three positions: ON—TRIPPED—OFF in that order. The tripped position is halfway between ON and OFF. The other type breaker is either ON or OFF. The tripped position is also the OFF position.

If the breaker has tripped, reset it to ON. If the breaker has the center "tripped" position, it must be pushed to the OFF position and then pushed to the ON position. If the handle stays in the ON position, the problem is usually a low voltage condition caused by the utility. The breaker tripped because a low voltage causes an increase in amperage draw. The breaker senses this and trips. This condition might not happen again. If the breaker will not stay in the ON position, there is fault on your premises.

If the breaker stays in the ON position but there is still no power, test for power with the homemade series double-socket tester assembly. The breaker panel cover will have to be removed to

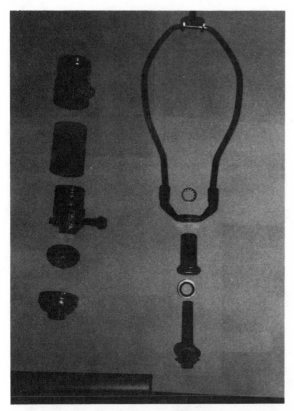

Fig. 12-1. Table lamp was disassembled for replacement of socket. Parts on the left are, from the top: shell, fiber insulator, three-way socket, lower fiber insulator, shell bottom (has ⅛-inch internal pipe thread). On the right are: harp, lock washer, spacer, washer, ⅛-inch running thread nipple, felt washer and jamb nut for tightening the complete assembly.

utility. In daylight, you can look up at the pole and see the wires dangling free. I have had only one of these wires come loose and cut off half the lights in a house. Again some connectors just work loose and allow the wind to make and break the connection, causing the lights to go on and off. These problems are few but they do happen.

IN-HOUSE FAULTS

Problems encountered in the house are faulty appliance cords and overloaded circuits. Most overloaded circuits are caused by too many current draw appliances being plugged in to an already *nearly* overloaded circuit. With a fused panel, it is possible to have installed an undersized fuse. This is *very* unlikely, but check it out.

Circuits using #12 copper wire are to be fused at 20 A or be protected by a 20 A breaker. Overloaded circuits can be relieved by moving some heavy appliances to other circuits. It may be that a new circuit needs to be installed. The service equipment must be large enough to handle this new addition. Kitchen appliances now are drawing more current as new models are designed having higher

test for power. Be *very* careful when removing the cover that you do not poke a corner of the cover inside the panel. Test on both sides of the breaker. Get help to hold a flashlight if it is dark in the area and to guide the cover.

There is a possibility that the breaker is faulty or wires might have come loose in the panel. Test first where the power enters the panel (usually the top). If you have no power at any place in the panel, then power is not getting to the service entrance equipment and the utility should be called. Your servicedrop wires are connected to the wires on the pole by a split connector. These clamps sometimes break when they are old, and this will let your supply wires hang loose. This is the problem of the

Fig. 12-2. Start of disassembly of socket. Shell is being pried from bottom section. Sometimes finger pressure is not enough.

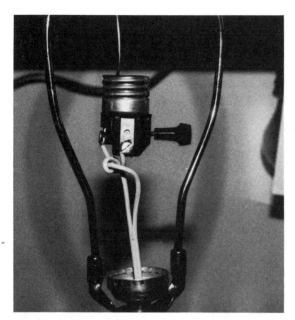

Fig. 12-3. Shell removed from defective socket that is ready for replacement. Note "Underwriter's knot" in place to prevent strain on the wires at the screw terminals.

wattage than last year's models. New percolators now draw 1000 watts.

If you plug in an appliance and the plug sparks or the cord flames up, the problem is obvious. This type of fault will show in the fuse as a blackened window in the fuse. An overload will not show this, but the fuse link that shows in the window will have disappeared (it melted and fell down inside the fuse body). With a short-circuit, the fuse really "blows."

With branch circuit fuses and breakers, if the fuse blows again or the breaker will not stay ON, unplug all plug-in appliances. Then reset the breaker or replace the fuse. If either holds, one of the unplugged appliances might be at fault. Carefully plug in each appliance *in turn*. Plug in only *one* appliance at a time. At each plug-in, if the breaker holds or the fuse holds, unplug that appliance. Do this for each appliance in turn. If *no* appliance opens the circuit then the appliances are OK.

It may be that the total load of all appliances together on the circuit is causing an overload. Two appliances at 1000 W will draw 17.4 A; that is more than a 15 A circuit will handle. A modern kitchen circuit installed correctly will carry a load of 20 A.

This should not be for a long time as circuits are derated to further protect the wire and insulation.

DEVICE FAILURES

Devices such as switches and receptacles wear out from daily use. Switches get high usage. Receptacles get hard usage and especially in the kitchen or where vacuum cleaners are plugged. Long cords are stretched and pulled on the receptacle contacts, as do those cords on portable electric tools. This strain does wear out and break receptacles. Because these devices are reasonable in cost, buy the best you can afford. Better-quality devices last longer and give better service.

Always turn off the power when replacing any electrical device. Remove the fuse that controls the circuit feeding the device to be replaced. Put the removed fuse in your pocket to prevent others from replacing it unknown to you. The cardinal rule when working with electricity is to treat every wire as hot (live) unless you can see both ends and the full length between them. Just be *careful!* Turning a

Fig. 12-4. Motor having an internal centrifugal switch made ready for disassembly. Punch marks have been made on endbells and directly opposite on center housing. Note through bolt partially removed in lower right corner.

Fig. 12-5. Endbell having the centrifugal switch removed. Arrow points to switch contacts. Barb of arrow touches pressure point (other pressure point is opposite). Centrifugal mechanism is still on shaft. This is the square part showing just above the windings near the bottom of the photograph.

breaker OFF poses some risk after you start to remove the device. As a precaution, post a large sign covering the whole breaker panel to alert others to: "DO NOT TOUCH! WORKING ON THE WIRING".

REPAIRING THE DEFECTIVE APPLIANCE

Appliances, including lamps and power tools, blow fuses and trip breakers usually because of cord defects. Constant use flexes and wears the cord and the attachment plug on the end. Cords can be repaired up to a point. *Do not splice a cord*. The splice is unsatisfactory and the tape never stays well. It is less expensive and faster to replace the whole cord. Worn cord ends can be cut off and the cord can be reattached to the appliance. Do the same with the plug end by putting on a new attachment plug.

Buy good-quality cords and accessories. Cords are available in various lengths with the attachment plug molded on. Lightweight cords are good for

table and floor lamps. Toasters and similar high-wattage appliances require heavy-duty cord with No. 16 wire such as the SPT-2 type. These heavy-duty cords are available with molded-on plugs. This heavy cord can be used for all heavy-wattage kitchen appliances. SV cord is a special type made only for vacuum cleaner use.

Newer, light-duty attachment plugs are made with no exposed screw terminals to contact metal receptacle cover plates and arc. These plugs open to expose the terminals inside for connecting the cord wires. There are heavier-duty plugs for use on power tools and extension cords. Because these cords are larger diameter, larger-size plug bodies are required to accept this heavier cord.

BALANCING THE LOAD BETWEEN CIRCUITS

Modern houses have 240 V service. This consists of *two* hot (live) wires, one red and one black or sometimes two black and one neutral. The neutral wire can be either bare or insulated. Service-entrance cable will have a bare neutral wrapped around the two insulated wires. Wires in conduit will have *three* insulated wires. The two hot wires will have a

Fig. 12-6. Arrow points to motor overload that is self resetting. Sometimes these fail and have to be replaced.

125

Fig. 12-7. Service-entrance cable and meter. Note the individual servicedrop wires.

voltage to ground of 120 V. They will also have a voltage to the neutral wire of 120 V. *Between* the two hot wires there is a voltage of 240 V. This 240 V supplies such fixed appliances as electric ranges or cooktops and wall-mounted ovens, electric dryers, and electric water heaters. Motors running on 240 V also are fed by these two hot wires *only*; they do not need the neutral wire.

Because lights, small portable appliances, vacuums, and many power tools run on 120 V minimal voltage, the neutral is needed in the distribution panel to provide the necessary 120 V. As an example, if a toaster is connected to one side of the 240-V wiring through a receptacle, one wire will go to the neutral wire in the panel (through the house wiring) and the other wire will go to *one* hot wire. In this case, there will be a current flow in the *panel* neutral. This is what the neutral is for. A large

current flow in the neutral is undesirable and should be minimized. This requires that you arrange to equalize the current draw on both sides of the panel. Then there will be a minimum of current flowing in the neutral. The ideal condition would be for no current flow in the neutral, but this will never be attained—thus the neutral.

Add up all the loads expected in each circuit and try to balance current flow on both sides. Some circuits might have to be moved to the other side, but exact balance is not necessary.

ADDING TO PRESENT WIRING

Houses built in the last 20 years will usually have enough electrical capacity for your present needs. Quite small, older houses might not be wired for 240 V because in former years heavy-current-usage appliances were only provided with 60 A service-entrance equipment because that capacity was enough. The major load might have been an electric range (instead, perhaps a gas range) a radio, toaster and an iron.

At one time, many utilities supplied the electric water heater directly for a set monthly fee based on the heater size. In such a case, the electric heater was supplied independently of the main service-entrance equipment. Therefore, the service-entrance cable did not take into account this additional load.

The National Electrical Code now requires 100 A service entrance conductors *and* equipment for any net computed load over 10 kW. Existing dwellings can continue to use 60 A service.

As an example of load calculations, assume the following. A dwelling has a floor area of 900 square feet exclusive of basement and attic (unusable). See Table 12-1.

Because the net computed load exceeds 10 kW (10,000 watts), you must have an ampacity of 100 A. No. 3 AWG cable may be used. The neutral size is computed at 70 percent of the *ungrounded* wires' ampacity. Service-entrance cable will have the correct ratio of grounded wire size to the two ungrounded wire sizes. If you are using conduit from the service head down to the meter, buy enough *single* wire for the two wires needed. For the neutral wire, buy one length. For 100 A service, the hot wires should be No. 3: the neutral should be No. 4. There is no No. 5. The inspector may approve No. 6 for the neutral. Ask him.

All three wires may be the same size if you wish. Be sure to paint both ends of the neutral white. White tape may be used instead. The utility requires that three or four feet of each of the three wires extend from the service head for connection to their servicedrop at the building wall. Service-entrance cable *may* be used instead of conduit above the meter. I recommend a service head on the cable. It looks much better.

In Fig. 12-8, original wiring is shown from a 1942 house. The wiring is the minimum required by the FHA at that time. Each room had two receptacles and a switch-controlled ceiling fixture.

There was no automatic heating system, only a coal-fired gravity furnace. We had a refrigerator, iron, toaster, radio, and, later, a power saw in the basement. The basement plan shows four 15-A circuits originating at the 60-A service-entrance panel. The basement lights were four pull-chain porcelain sockets. There was a light at the foot of the basement stairs controlled by a switch at the first floor level. The laundry had an outlet on the pull-chain porcelain socket. These are still available, only the outlet is *grounded* now. No convenience receptacles were provided in the basement. See Figs. 12-8A and 12-8B.

Refer to the modernized wiring plan shown in Fig. 12-9. Notice that the service is increased to 125 A. Perhaps 100 A would be sufficient also. Receptacles in the rooms are installed to conform to the present code. The wiring is all completely new because the original Romex was *ungrounded* and provided no grounding for the metal frames of appliances, etc.

In the kitchen there are two small appliance circuits and the range circuits are designated as D and R. There were four new circuits added: workshop, range, heating/ac, and laundry. This shows on the *new* basement plan (Fig. 12-10). The original three other circuits were kept, but rewired with new cable. All of the wiring is new.

This type of project is a large undertaking and will take a great deal of time. Make a wiring layout to take to the city inspector and ask his help in guiding and advising you. With the help of the *Electrical Code for One- and Two-Family Dwellings*, you

Table 12-1. Computed Load.

General Lighting Load	
900 sq.ft. @ 3W per foot.	2700W
Minimum number of branch circuits required	
General Lighting Load	
2700 ÷ 115 = 23.5 or two—15A 2-wire circuits or	
two—20A 2-wire circuits	
Small Appliance Load: two 20A 2–wire circuits	
one 20A 2—wire circuit	
Minimum Size Feeders Required	
Computer Load	
General Lighting	2700W
Small Appliance Load	3000W
Laundry Load	1500W
Total (less Electric Range)	7200W
3000W 100%	3000W
7200W — 3000W — 4200 @ 35%	1470W
Net Computed Load (less range)	4470W
Range Load	8000W
Net Computed Load, with Range	12,470W

For 115/230 V 3-wire system feeders: 12,470 ÷ 230 = 54.2A

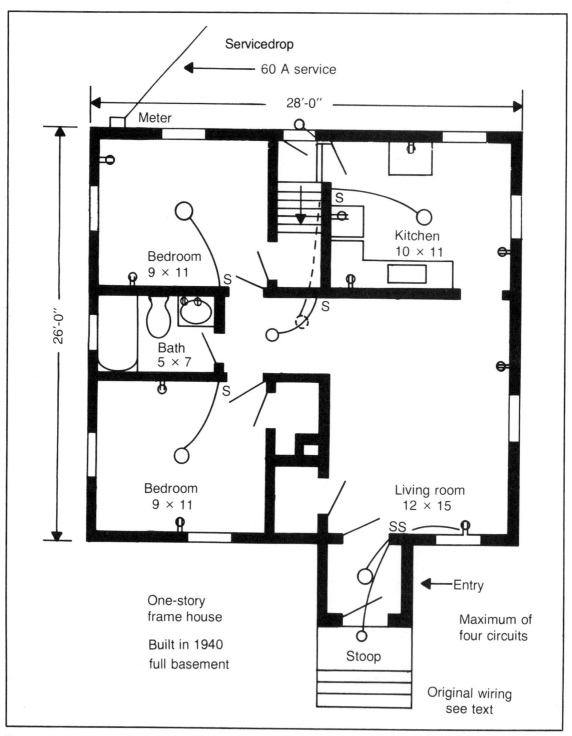

Fig. 12-8A. Original layout of wiring in 1940 house.

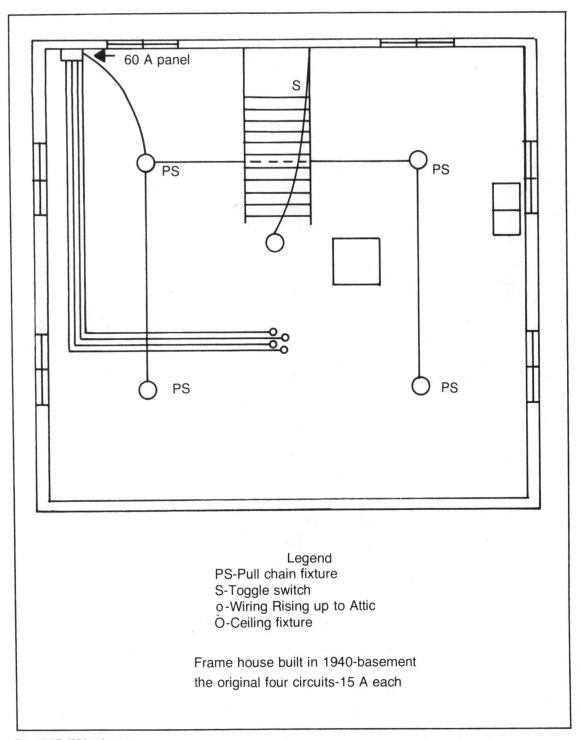

60 A panel

S

PS

PS

PS

PS

Legend
PS-Pull chain fixture
S-Toggle switch
o-Wiring Rising up to Attic
Ō-Ceiling fixture

Frame house built in 1940-basement
the original four circuits-15 A each

Fig. 12-8B. Wiring layout.

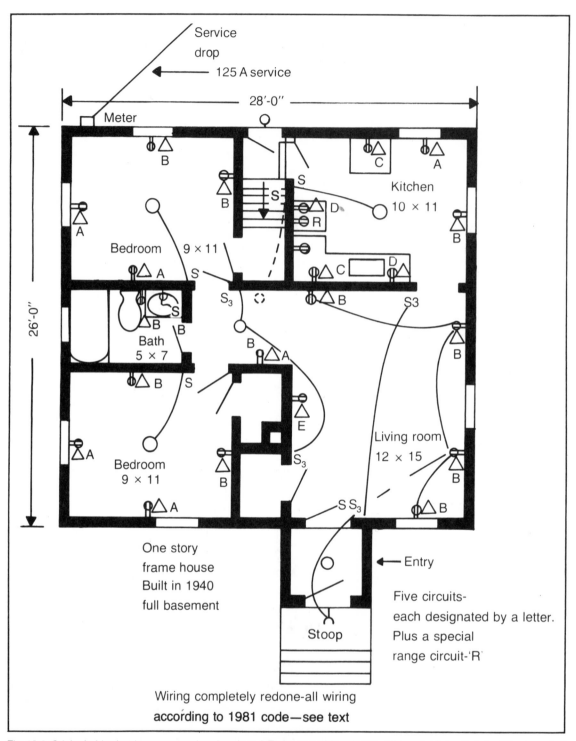

Service drop

125 A service

Meter

28'-0"

26'-0"

B

B

A

B

Bedroom 9 × 11

A

S

S₃

B

A

S

Bath 5 × 7

S

B

B

B

S

A

Bedroom 9 × 11

A

B

E

S₃

Kitchen 10 × 11

C

A

S

D

R

C

D

B

S3

B

B

S S₃

Living room 12 × 15

B

B

One story frame house
Built in 1940
full basement

Entry

Stoop

Five circuits-
each designated by a letter.
Plus a special
range circuit-'R'

Wiring completely redone-all wiring
according to 1981 code—see text

Fig. 12-9. Original wiring has been removed or abandoned. Entire new wiring plan has been established to bring it "up to code."

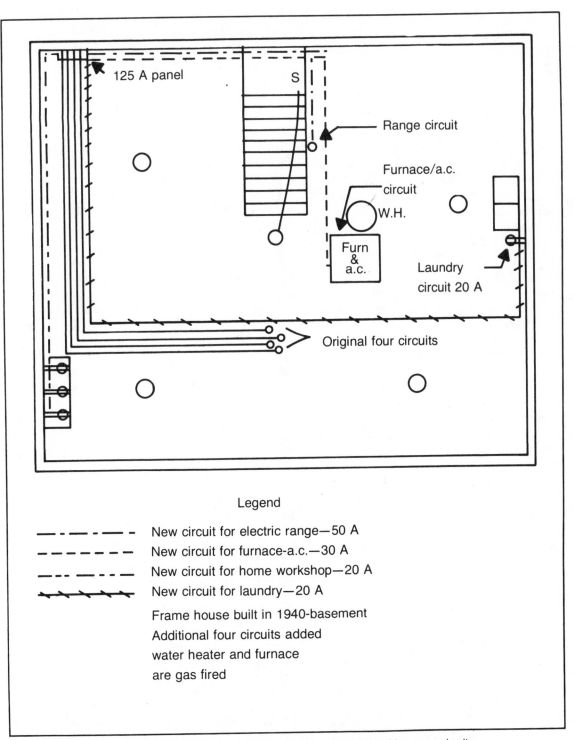

Fig. 12-10. Basement plan showing increased entrance equipment and addition of four more circuits.

can do a fine job. If you now live in the house, do the job piecemeal. If the house is vacant, start with the service-entrance equipment and do the whole job at your convenience. Borrow power or install a temporary power setup.

SMALL APPLIANCE REPAIR

Start with easy repairs and you will learn how to do them properly and accurately. A simple repair is the replacement of the socket and cord on a table or floor lamp. Generally, if the socket is defective, the cord also will be worn and should be replaced. Two common places of wear are where the cord enters the lamp base and at the connection to the attachment plug. It is best to replace the whole electrical assembly at one time. Cord is sold by the foot and as an assembly of cord and plug. If the plug looks sturdy, buy the assembly available in different lengths. Do not buy too long a length. Excess cord length gets stepped on and damaged; buy a suitable length.

To repair the lamp see Figs. 12-1, 12-2 and 12-3. Unplug the cord (this eliminates the sparks) and remove the shade. The top part of the *harp*, the metal loop that supports the shade, on some lamps is able to be removed because its lower ends fit into two sockets. On others, the complete harp is in one piece.

If the harp is not removable, proceed to dismantle the socket. Unscrew the bulb. Next to the switch on the socket (whether it is pushbutton or turn knob) is the word *push*. Push on this word while trying to tilt the socket shell away from you slightly. At this point, the socket shell will part from the socket base. If the shell does not separate from the base readily, insert a *small* pocket screwdriver and gently place it between the shell and the base. By prying outward on the screwdriver handle, you will actually be "pushing" on the shell. This will release it from the base. It's simple to do, but complicated to describe.

Now push some of the cord back into the lamp base for enough slack to lift out the socket far enough to disconnect the wires from it. If you go this far, it is best to replace everything—cord, plug and socket. About $3 should do it. The socket base

(the bottom half of the shell) is threaded onto a ⅛-inch pipe nipple. There might be a small setscrew in the side of the threaded part keeping the base from turning. This base also secures the harp. Buy the complete socket. Match the operating type—pushbutton, on-off switch, or three-way (for three-way light bulb). Any of these three types of sockets will work on most lamps. As a precaution, take the old socket shell to compare the threads (just to make sure). Wasted trips are wasted money.

To replace the attachment plug on a lamp cord, extension cord, or power tool is simple to do, but it *must* be done right. The plug is usually broken and the cord is frayed at the plug end. Old plugs that have seen much use should be replaced. The new type of attachment plugs are designed so that no bare wire ends and no screws are exposed to contact a metal receptacle cover plate. This is called a *dead front* type of plug. The 1981 Code, Section 410-56(d) requires this type. This new design costs about $1.50. This is a safeguard to prevent fires.

I have seen many metal receptacle cover plates with burns on them just from this cause. The exposed terminal plugs were supposed to have a fiber washer fitted over these exposed terminals, but usually the washer will be missing just when needed. It is common for receptacles to have metal plates; they are even used in homes instead of plastic ones. Perhaps this is the reason for the new design attachment plugs.

Shop clearance counters at hardware and home improvement centers. They often have astounding bargains in electrical supplies there. If the items *are* reduced in price, check other stores before buying. Also check the items for perfect condition and the privilege of return if defective in any way. For cord repair, see Figs. 3-22 through 3-26.

Don't buy just because items are reduced. Bargains are to be found in cable reel ends or for other reasons. Just make sure the lengths are long enough for your needs. Too short a length will do you no good. When measuring for length, allow for the 3 feet at the service-entrance head and at least 2 feet at the panel end for service-entrance cable and other expensive cable that you will need.

Different types of attachment plugs require different connection methods. Some plugs for use with "rip" cord (the common lamp and household extension cord type) just need to have the square cut end inserted into the side of the plug body and the lever pushed down to make contact. These plugs are not very satisfactory because of the poor contact made between the cord and plug prongs (points puncture the cord insulation and "sort of make contact"). Buy the new dead front type; it's worth it. Illustrations in this chapter show connections being made to various plugs and cord connectors and a trouble light is wired to a cord. All of these wiring methods are shown using *three-wire* cord.

Cords on power tools are replaced in a similar manner. Also illustrated is the repairing of the connection to a trouble light head (McGill Manufacturing Co. is a top-quality brand). Although not necessary, crimp-on terminals have been put on the wire ends of the cord itself. This is not necessary but desirable. Stranded wire tends to spread when tightened under terminal screws. Crimp-on terminals eliminate this. The heavy-duty cord is similar to cord used on power tools. Black, white, and green wires are attached to the brass, silver and green terminal screws. There are plastic ribs between the terminal screws (barriers). This prevents stray strands of wire shorting over to the adjacent terminal. The crimp-on terminals are bare. There are also those with a plastic sleeve over the crimp-on part. These are crimped directly over the plastic using a special crimping tool.

The cords on the new *double-insulated* power tools should be replaced only by the service center for that tool. This is because special equipment might be used to maintain the integrity of the insulation system.

LOCATING THE CAUSE OF POWER FAILURES

If a fuse blows or a breaker trips and you are using a power tool or appliance, immediately disconnect the item you were using. Also disconnect any lamps and turn off any ceiling lights. Now go to the panel and inspect it. A *fused* panel (having fuses) will give you a clue. A simple overload will show a "missing" fuse link that normally shows in the fuse window. A short circuit will show a *darkened* window caused by an arc. *Arc*, as in arc welding, is an actual flame that will carbonize the fuse link, making the dark colored window. In this manner, you can look for trouble more easily. Circuit breakers do not tell you anything except that the circuit has been protected as required.

If many appliances were being used on the circuit, then removing one or more and plugging them in on another circuit might solve the problem. Check all cords on anything used on this circuit. Any cord fault might cause the trouble. I have a toaster that pulls (uses) 10.5 A and a vegetable juicer that pulls 6.7 A. This totals 17.2 A. Because these both are on a 20-A circuit, this is allowable. No single portable appliance over 16 A (1840 W) may be plugged into this circuit. So my two heavy-amperage appliances are OK to use on this circuit.

In a modern house, it is unlikely that the building wiring is defective, but it is still a distinct possibility to be considered. At this point, with everything *unplugged*, reset the breaker *once*. If the breaker will not stay ON, take your light bulb adapter (socket-to-prongs, explained in Chapter 3) and try all the receptacles for power. Something might still be plugged in. Many times whatever caused the fault will have flashed to alert you (though not always). If now the breaker stays on, plug in *one* appliance at a time.

If the breaker holds (stays on) remove the item. Now do the same with each item *in turn*, each time removing it and noting that it was not the cause before you plug in another item. If you have help, let the person stand near the panel to call out if the breaker trips. If the breaker holds for each item in turn, add up the combined amperage (watts × 120 V = amperes). You may have a borderline overload circuit.

If you have a low voltage condition from the utility, the appliances and other items will draw more amperes and thus overload the affected circuit. This entire procedure explained above is exactly the same for a panel using fuses. The difference is that spare fuses must be on hand to replace the blown fuse instead of resetting the breaker.

Spare fuses should always be on hand in any case.

Another possible cause of trouble might be defective or worn devices. Switches or receptacles that have heavy usage can cause a fault current. This will cause the breaker to trip or the fuse to blow. Feel cover plates at switches, receptacles and junction boxes. Sometimes this will alert you to trouble spots. Now remove the plates and inspect the inside with a flashlight *and* your nose. Not too close with the nose! It is easy to detect burned odors by the smell. Just don't get too close that you would get a shock; keep 4 to 6 inches back.

Other areas of trouble might be in junction boxes in the basement or attic. Loose wire nuts or defective soldered wire connections can heat up. The soldering of electric wires is an art that has to be practiced to become good at.

Be sure to check wire nuts and soldered connections with the power *off*! As described in Chapter 1, check and tighten all terminal screws found in the service entrance/distribution panel. Any sustained current passing through wires and terminals causes some heating. This sustained heating eventually loosens connections. This is why all terminal screws *must* be kept tight. Hazardous conditions such as these cause many house fires every year.

Even though you have eliminated the condition causing the breaker to trip or the fuse to blow, it is wise to tighten all terminal screws on switches and receptacles. This is especially true if the house is old. It takes only a few minutes to check each device. First turn off the power to the circuit you will work on. *Check for voltage*. Then remove the cover plate and the two screws holding the device. Pull the device out far enough to reach the screws and tighten them. Replace the device and go on to the next one. Do all devices on one circuit, but be sure to *check for voltage* before you touch any terminals.

Most circuit faults are not in the wiring itself. Look at the appliances first before disconnecting any wiring. Many split-phase motors on furnace blowers and oil burners have an *internal* switch *inside* the motor housing. This switch becomes covered with an oil film from oil in the bearings.

Because oil attracts dust, these contacts tend to become dirty and in some cases do not make contact with each other. In such a case, the motor will not start, but it will keep trying until it trips its own overload protection. If this overload does not shut off the motor circuit, the fuse or breaker in the distribution panel will operate and kill the circuit. Furnaces are supposed to be on a separate circuit, but other equipment might have been connected to this same circuit. This will cause a localized power outage. Many of these motors have an automatic overload that will reconnect the motor. This has the effect of letting the motor try to start many times (eventually blowing the fuse or tripping the breaker).

These motors have two separate windings (wire coils) inside, the *start* winding and the *run* winding. Both windings are ready to go when the motor is at rest. When the motor receives power, both windings combine forces to turn whatever load is connected—pump, fan or whatever. If the centrifugal switch sends power to the *start* winding to help the *run* winding get the motor turning, that is fine.

If the switch contacts are dirty, the *start* winding cannot help. The motor then tries but cannot make it alone. In this case, the motor will try many times, finally tripping its overload protector and stopping. This will blow the fuse or trip the breaker and cause a localized power failure. Under normal conditions, the run winding helps to start the motor. When the motor gets up to speed (1825 rpm), the centrifugal levers on the motor shaft operate to open the switch and disconnect the *start* winding. The motor then runs on the *run* winding only.

Other loads might be on this same circuit and will be without power. This is a violation of the code. Furnace and air conditioning circuits may have no other loads connected to them. In your preliminary inspection, you should have noted this and planned to separate other loads from this circuit. This drawn-out description of motor problems will apply to any residential motor except air conditioning compressor motors (a special case). Motors can be oil burner, fan water pump, sump pump and the air conditioner fan motor. See Figs. 12-4, 12-5 and 12-6.

Faulty centrifugal switches can be cleaned, if the points are not burned, by taking the motor end bell off. This is the end having the connections to the power supply. These terminals have a cover plate over them to be removed if you have to disconnect the motor to work on it. The centrifugal switch is mounted on this end bell. The illustration of the dismantled motor shows this switch with an arrow pointing to it. The part on the shaft operates the switch by centrifugal force. These switches can be replaced if necessary. When buying take the old part with you for exact replacement. Repair centers and motor repair shops will have parts. Better take the motor with you or at least copy the nameplate information to have with you.

Motors are assembled with four "through bolts" that go through the complete motor housing, holding the two end bells to the center section. Before dismantling the motor mark the end bells so that they can be replaced exactly as they were before. Do this by using a prick punch to mark each end bell *and* its housing end with adjacent punch marks on housing and end bell.

Each end bell should have different marks: one end to have only one mark each on end bell and center housing, the other end to have *two* marks each on its end bell and center housing. These end bells fit snugly to assure alignment of the bearings.

After removing the through bolts, tap the end bell free using a screwdriver and hammer. At some place, the end bell will be slightly raised along its edge. Tap with the screwdriver at this point. Tap all around the circumference to remove the end bell; do not pry on one side only as you might break it. Remove only the end bell with the centrifugal switch. When reassembling, align the punch marks and tap the end bell all around the edge. Be careful and tap gently because the end bell is a casting and will break. Insert the through bolts before completely seating the end bell. After assembly, try to turn the shaft to make sure it turns free. Double check everything thoroughly before you reconnect the motor.

Special heavy-duty motors such as those used on water pumps and other uses where the motor must start under a load, require what is known as a capacitor type motor. This motor will have one or two cylindrical cases mounted on the outside of the motor housing that contain the capacitor (condenser). This device gives the motor a much stronger torque to overcome the heavy load imposed by the pump or large fan that it has to start.

These capacitors sometimes short out and fail. This will blow a fuse or trip a breaker. Unscrew the capacitor case and check and smell the capacitor. You may have to unsolder it from its leads and take it to a motor repair shop to have the capacitor checked. The rating of the capacitor is printed on its metal or plastic case. Be sure after doing any repairs to recheck everything you have done before using the equipment. Be safe!

BUILDING A BATTERY-POWERED TESTER

A simple battery-powered tester can be made by using a 6-volt lantern battery and a door buzzer. Two wires are attached to the battery terminals (you may have to solder them). A length of lamp cord is good. One wire of the cord goes to one battery terminal, the other wire goes to one terminal of the buzzer. A short, single wire goes from the second battery terminal to the second buzzer terminal. The cord should be about 5 or 6 feet long.

At the free end of this cord separate the two wires for about 2 feet to form test leads. Strip each end for 1 inch to form test prods. You might want to solder these ends to make them stiffer. As the voltage is only 6 volts it is not important, but it might be handier to them if they are stiff.

Touching the two ends together will make the buzzer sound. This enables you to check out any dead circuit (deenergized). This tester cannot be used on hot (live) circuits under *any* circumstances.

Using The Battery Operated (Continuity) Tester

Suppose you suspect a length of Romex has a defect or break in it or the three wires might have been shorted out due to the cable being crushed at some point. At each end of the length of cable, strip the wires so that you can test them individually. Using your handmade tester, touch one test probe to the black wire; then touch the other probe to the far end of the same black wire. A "buzz" shows that the black wire is OK.

Now remove the second probe from the far end of the black and touch either end of the white wire. A buzz shows a "dead short" between the black *and* white wires.

Now check the white wire as you first tested the black wire. The white wire may be broken or touching the black wire at a defect area of the cable. Also check the black wire to the ground wire. A buzz here shows a serious defect in the cable length. You will have to visually check the outside of the cable inch by inch to detect any obvious damage. Some object has crushed the cable even though it does not show. If the defect cannot be found, the cable must be discarded.

If you cut the cable in two, one-half might test OK. You can use this half if you are sure you have tested properly. If you are careful when installing cable and do not pound the staples too tightly, you should have no trouble with new cable. Diagrams included with this chapter show how to do this testing properly.

Using The Line Voltage Tester

To test hot (live) wires a line voltage tester is needed. This can be a $1.49 pocket tester or the professional $25 one. Either will work fine. Just be certain that your fingers do not contact any hot wires. They will really *feel* hot. Work carefully and slowly when testing hot wires.

A homemade tester for 230 V *and* 115 V is easily made from two rubber pigtail sockets with 6-inch leads with ends bared ½ of an inch. One lead from one socket and one lead from the other socket are spliced together with a wire nut. This makes the two sockets in series with each other and allows bulbs used on 120 volts to be used to test 230-V circuits. Make this tester carefully and properly use it and it will serve you well.

Line voltage testers are used to find out if voltage is present. A homemade tester will tell you if the voltage is 115 V or 230 V. When testing for 115 V, the bulbs will burn at one-half brightness. When testing for 230 V, the bulb will burn at full brightness.

Line voltage testers can test for open circuits. They can test both fuses and breakers in place (continuity testers will test fuses *not* in place, meaning on the workbench or in your hand) and test for voltage at outlets and fixtures. There are also *low voltage* testers for testing 6 to 50 volts. You can test door bells and furnace and air conditioning controls with them.

Chapter 13
Wiring Materials and Standard Wiring Methods

W HEN DOING ELECTRICAL WIRING, IT IS NEC-
essary to use wire, wiring devices, conduit,
cabinets and fastening devices to complete the installation. Examples are shown in Figs. 13-1
through 13-53. In addition, construction methods,
developed over the years to facilitate the work and
make for a sound, safe installation, are explained in
this chapter.

WIRES AND CABLES

Electric wire comes in various sizes and forms. The
most common types used in house wiring are BX
and Romex. Romex is a plastic-covered cable having two or three insulated wires and a grounding
wire. BX serves the same purpose and has the same
construction, but the covering—instead of being
plastic covered—has a metal, spirally wrapped
covering. This metal covering is more resistant to
damage than Romex. For this reason, many areas
require BX in all installations.

Other electric wire forms are single wire that
is either solid or stranded. Solid wire is one wire
covered with insulation. Stranded wire is a number
of fine wires twisted together to form one conductor. This type is found in the lamp cords and extension cords. Wire sizes vary from very small to very
large. The sizes used in house wiring range from
No. 14, for branch circuits, to No. 2/0, used for the
wires coming into the building.

Romex

Romex is the most widely used wiring. The following information also applies to BX, with the
exception of the metal covering. Figure 9-12 illustrates how to cut BX. Cable sizes commonly used
are No's. 14, 12, and 10. No's. 14 and 12 are used in
branch circuits such as lighting and appliance circuits. No. 10 is used for circuits supplying clothes
dryers and electric water heaters. No's. 8 and 6 are
used to supply electric ranges. All these wire sizes
are made in copper and aluminum. Do *not* buy or use
wire made of *aluminum*! Aluminum wire used in
homes built during the 1960s caused much damage
to the devices used with it and also caused some
house fires.

Both Romex and BX cables *must* have a

Fig. 13-1. Recessed porch fixture, will have glass cover.

grounding wire included in the cable. This wire is a safeguard for persons and equipment (especially for persons). There might still be Romex on the market without this ground. Do not buy this type of wiring. The correct marking on Romex cable will be: "(UL) Type NM 12-2 with AWG 12 Ground 600 V." This means that the cable has two No. 12 insulated wires and one bare *grounding* wire. The wire has sufficient insulation to be used on 600 volts. The type NM cable may be used in only dry locations. Type UF may be used in damp but not wet locations. Logically UF may be used *also* in dry locations. In this respect it should be stated that if you are doing much wiring or rewiring consider buying one size of Romex, namely No. 12-2. It will be cheaper to buy one large coil of one size than two smaller coils. The standard coil of Romex (or BX) is 250 feet and in this quantity is cheaper by the foot.

Anchoring Cable to Boxes

Connectors are used to anchor cable to boxes. Previously, separate clamp type connectors were used, having locknuts to hold them in knockouts in the boxes. Boxes are now available with clamps inside the back of the box. These line up with knockouts and when the knockout is removed and the cable is brought through the knockout opening it goes under the clamp and is anchored tightly. The top and bottom of the box each have two knockouts available for use with their built in clamps.

Plastic boxes now available have no clamps built in. Therefore, it is necessary to staple the cable to the stud or other support within 8 inches of the box. This is necessary where the wiring is exposed and the finish wall material has not been

applied to the studs. In remodeling work, the cable cannot be anchored this way. Try to get plastic boxes with cable clamps or use metal boxes.

All electrical connections *must* be made *inside* outlet or junction boxes. Cable must also be run so that it is protected from damage. Figures 13-4 and 13-5 illustrate these type of installations. Cable must be run through bored holes in joists or studs. Exposed joists such as in basements may have cable run on the bottom edge if there are wood strips on each side or under the cable for protection. In walls to be finished with drywall or another covering, cable may be run in notches cut in the face of the stud, but the cable must be protected by a metal plate, 1/16 of an inch thick, fastened over the cable lying in the stud notch. See Fig. 13-51.

In attics within 7 feet of the access opening, the cable runs also must be protected by running boards. For anchoring cable, there are available one or two hole straps for use with nails. There are two-point staples with a flat top to prevent cable damage and special staples with a plastic top-part, having one nail through each end, to protect the cable from damage when nailing.

Cable must be anchored every 4½ feet. Cable fished inside walls is exempted from this require-

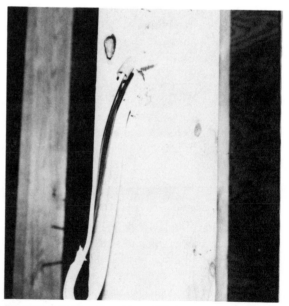

Fig. 13-2. Lead for connection of kitchen exhaust fan.

Fig. 13-3. Hole through plate for cables from basement.

Fig. 13-4. Four-gang switch box. Near front door. Controls inside and outside lights. Rough-in completed. Plastic box.

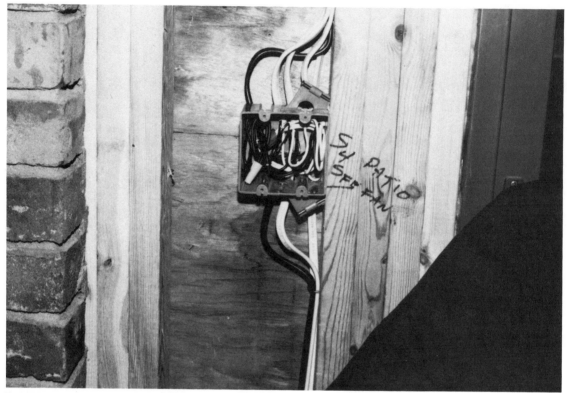

Fig. 13-5. Two-gang switch box with designations. Rough-in completed. Plastic box.

ment. If a new outlet box or ceiling box is installed, any openings between it and the plaster wall must be patched so that any possible sparks have no chance getting inside the wall. This is a code requirement in all cases.

Metal boxes used with cable must be grounded to the equipment ground. Cable designated as "with ground" *must* always be used whether you are using metal or plastic boxes. The bare "grounding" wire in the cable must be attached to the metal box and to the *green* grounding screw on the device mounted in the box. All devices now available have this green *hex head* grounding screw on the device mounting strap, which effectively grounds the metal "non-current-carrying" strap.

Armored Bushed Cable (BX)

This type of cable is commonly known as BX. BX gives better protection than Romex, but it is more expensive. Where the use of BX is mandatory,

Romex may not be used. The grounding method uses a very narrow metal strap that is bent back over the outer metal armor and clamped tightly by the connector either inside or outside the *metal box.* BX must always be used with metal boxes.

To cut BX use a hacksaw. Do not cut the armor at right angles to the length of the cable, but rather at right angles to the armor strip. Mark the length needed plus 8 inches allowed inside the junction box.

Take the marked place in your left hand; step on the cable with your foot allowing enough length to bring the cutting mark waist high. Flex the cable enough to make a hump at the mark plus while also keeping the cable taut. Cut through the armor *almost* fully. Flex the cut point till it breaks loose and then cut the wires with diagonal cutters. To bare the wires, back up the 8 inches (mentioned before) and repeat the sawing.

Be extremely careful this time not to cut into

Fig. 13-6. Three-gang switch box not roughed-in. Cables ready for installation. Plastic.

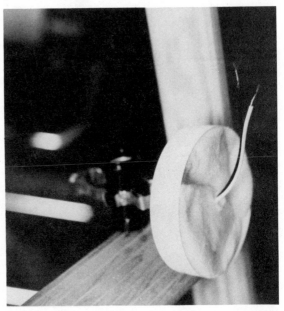

Fig. 13-8. Ceiling box prepared for installation of fixture. Note plaster is patched around edge of box (a code requirement). Otherwise there would be a fire hazard.

the wires. Then remove the armor by bending and twisting. Figures 9-12, 9-13, and 9-14 show the sequence of operations better than words. Prepare the other end of the cable length if you have not already fastened it in place. This method of cutting can also be used in a run of BX already installed in joists or studs. In this case, the cable is already anchored. No foot holding is needed.

Use the same hand method to arch the BX for sawing. Because BX has the steel outer covering that has a sharp cut edge, it is necessary to insert a plastic or fiber bushing between the outer steel

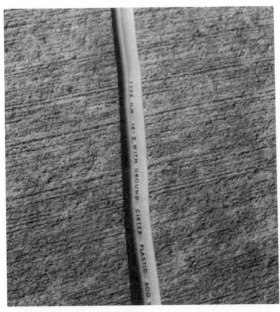

Fig. 13-7. Nonmetallic sheathed cable (Romex). Note the specifications on covering.

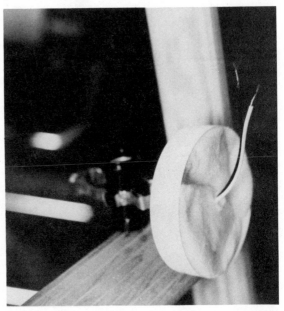

Fig. 13-9. Fixture ready for connection. Note the glass fiber in base to prevent heating of the fixture wires.

Fig. 13-10. Ceiling fixture connected to the wires and ready for bolting to ceiling box. Note this plastic box will not support a fixture heavier than shown.

Fig. 13-12. Ceiling fixture rough-in. Note the cables are run over the joists because this is an inaccessible attic.

casing and the wires inside. This is required by the code and will be checked by the inspector. All BX clamps have slots for the purpose of determining the presence of the fiber bushing without dismantling the connection.

SERVICE-ENTRANCE CABLE (SE)

Service-entrance cable is similar to Romex except that the wire is type XHHW (moisture and heat-resistant insulation) and there are *two* insulated wires, red and black. The neutral wire consists of many fine strands of tinned copper wire wrapped spirally around both insulated wires (see Fig. 4-11 for construction details). This is then covered with a tough outer covering that is very damage resistant. There is no grounding wire as such. The neutral is also the grounding wire.

The cable brings power through the meter and

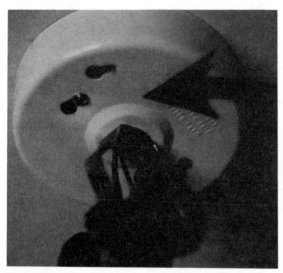

Fig. 13-11. Fixture mounted in place. Note the double set of screw holes to fit either 3½-inch or 4-inch boxes.

Fig. 13-13. Junction box with cover. The code requires covers on all junction boxes.

Fig. 13-14. Two-gang switch box. Wiring roughed-in.

Fig. 13-16. Top row: ceiling box, two-gang switch box, single-gang switch box. Center: duplex receptacle, switch. Bottom: two-gang switch plate.

into the building to the service-entrance equipment. The fine, tinned strands of the neutral are bunched and twisted together and connected to the neutral bar, to the grounding wire in the panel, and in the meter base.

Modern homes usually will need large service-entrance cable wire size such as No. 4, 3, 2, or 1 for 100-amp, 115-amp, or 130-amp capacity respectively. Service-entrance cable also may be used to wire ranges and clothes dryers using No's.

Fig. 13-15. Rough-in for an electric range. Note heavy cable to box.

Fig. 13-17. Replacing a single-pole switch controlling ceiling light with a two-switch combination. Other switch controls wall receptacle as originally wired. There was no ceiling light.

Fig. 13-18. Note that old switch plastic broke when I tried to loosen terminal screw. (Screw is of steel, not brass; try to buy devices having brass screws.) Notice that new devices are connected before old device is completely removed to keep the wiring from getting fouled.

Fig. 13-20. Completed pigtail splice. The wire, not the solder, must be heated enough so that touching the solder to the hot twisted wires causes the solder to melt and flow in and around the complete joint and not lump up just on the surface. The simple "tap" is made the very same way.

6 and 8 respectively. Watertight cable connectors must be used in wet locations such as at the top entrance to the meter base outdoors to prevent moisture entry. A special service head is used at the point where the servicedrop connects to the cable. You can purchase service-entrance cable by the foot at home improvement centers. Measure carefully to be sure you don't run short. This cable

is very expensive. Cable with aluminum wires is also satisfactory for ranges, dryers, and electric furnace uses.

CONDUITS

Conduits take different forms and are made of different materials. The following sections describe them in the order that they were developed.

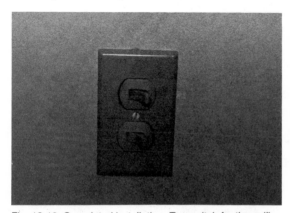

Fig. 13-19. Completed installation. Top switch for the ceiling light. The bottom for the "switched" receptacle. Keep the arrangement logical; top switch, top light, etc.

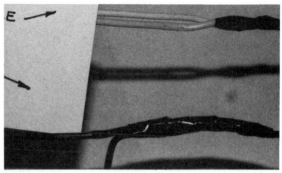

Fig. 13-21. The electrical tape is started at the insulated end and half lapped all the way to and beyond so as to have a half width to fold back on itself (to protect the end). Taping is continued back toward the left end, giving double (really four), layers of tape. Make sure the end has four layers.

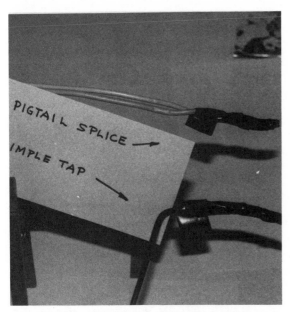

Fig. 13-22. Completed taping. Tape ends up beyond the beginning (slightly). Loose ends show where taping "stops." The "simple tap" has no end to protect, just back and forth.

Fig. 13-24. Leviton ground fault circuit interrupter (GFCI) wired to circuit. Wires capped off go to other receptacles "downstream." They are not used.

ferent forms and are made of different materials. The following sections describe them in the order that they were developed.

Rigid Metal Conduit. Rigid metal conduit has been in use almost as long as wiring has needed

protection from damage. This conduit is similar to water pipe in appearance, but it is specially treated to make the inside smooth and to bend easily. It is threaded similar to water pipe, but it should be cut with a hacksaw rather than a pipe cutter. A cutter

Fig. 13-23. Original duplex receptacle partially disconnected and wires checked out.

Fig. 13-25. GFCI installed and cover put on. Note test and reset buttons in center of device.

145

Fig. 13-26. Handy tester (light bulb with pronged socket) to test circuit for power.

raises a large burr on the inside and the burr must be completely removed with a reamer. Because this conduit requires a bender, vise, and pipe dies, the homeowner might not want to use it. It is readily available at electrical wholesalers. Fittings that eliminate threading are also available.

Electrical Metallic Tubing (EMT). This tubing, commonly known as thinwall, is easy to bend and it can be cut with a hacksaw. It is bent with a *thinwall bender* that can be rented. The bender sells for under $15 and it will pay for itself if you plan to do much work with thinwall. This type of conduit is never threaded and is connected to boxes with thinwall connectors and couplings. These fittings are made in various types:

■ Crimp-on that needs a large crimp-on tool.

■ Compression type using a nut and split ring to tighten onto the thinwall.

■ Setscrew type. The setscrew types are either steel or die cast. These have one or more setscrews depending on the size of the fitting.

■ For use with internally threaded hubs on cast boxes and meter hubs a thinwall "adapter" slips

over the thinwall end and when tightened into the hub grips the thinwall tightly.

Rigid Nonmetallic Tubing. This type of conduit is similar to plastic water pipe except that it is made especially for wiring use and can be used underground. Common sizes are of polyvinyl chloride. While metal thinwall needs supports only every 10 feet, the nonmetallic type needs support every 3 feet in the ½-inch to 1-inch sizes. It is more flexible. Because this conduit needs specialized equipment to bend it, the homeowner might find that it is not practical for home use.

Flexible Metal Conduit (Greenfield.) This conduit appears to be the same as BX. The steel armor is the same but the inside is empty. Greenfield is usually larger than BX. The ½-inch size is larger than ½-inch thinwall in outside diameter. For some areas the ⅜-inch size is approved for lengths under 6 feet for connecting to light fixtures. BX connectors are used for ⅜-inch Greenfield conduit. Larger sizes use Greenfield connectors.

Liquidtight Flexible Conduit. This type of flexible conduit is used commercially for connections to motors, etc., where dampness is present. Special fittings are used to maintain the dampness resistance. The name Sealtite identifies the metallic type. Plastic types also are manufactured.

SURFACE RACEWAYS

As defined in the code, a raceway is designed to hold wires. A *surface raceway* is used for an exposed extension to an existing concealed wiring installation because of building construction or other reasons. Many times it is impossible to conceal needed additional wiring.

The most popular and perhaps the oldest surface raceway system is that manufactured by the Wiremold Company. Their system is complete; it furnishes not only the raceway, but adapters to change from other raceways (thinwall, conduit or Romex) to Wiremold. There are special systems that have been developed by the Wiremold Company. These include receptacle strips, *Plugmold*, and other specialized systems.

Wiremold raceways sizes start at ½ inch wide

by 11/32 inches high to ¾ inches wide by 21/32 inches high. Special shapes are used for over the floor uses such as in offices where the permanent receptacles are not in convenient spots. This style has sloping sides to minimize tripping. While Wiremold raceways are designed to be bent, with the variety of fittings for use with them, you might not have need to bend the raceway. There *are* a variety of tools for use with Wiremold, but you most

likely will not need them for the amount of work you will be doing.

There are many uses for Wiremold in the home even though it was originally designed for commercial use. The raceway is very neat in the smaller sizes. It is enameled in a tan color and is quite attractive when installed neatly. You might like to use it in the basement instead of thinwall as it gives a finished appearance. Switches, receptacles, ceil-

---

While circuit-breakers and fuses protect equipment and structures against high-current overloads and short circuits, they do not protect personnel against electrocution. A person can be killed by as small a current as 200 milliamperes, and sometimes smaller! The most common type of current responsible for electrocutions is the *ground fault,* a leakage of current to ground, often through the body of a person in contact in some way with ground, thus providing the ground path.

A ground fault circuit interrupter (GFCI) will detect such leakage and will open the circuit promptly to avoid further shock or injury to the person.

Such a device can be placed at the distribution center, usually as part of a dual-function circuit-breaker. Underwriters' Laboratories requires that a GFCI trip when it detects 6 or more milliamps of ground fault current. Therefore, a circuit-breaker type GFCI will trip from either this kind of ground fault or from an overcurrent in the circuit greater than its rating, e.g. 15 or 20 amps. Trouble-shooting this trip is not often easy,

since either a ground fault or an overcurrent could have caused the trip, and since the entire branch is shut off by the circuit-breaker.

Today there are receptacles available with built-in GFCI protection. They can be installed to offer GFCI protection only through their own outlets, or they can be used as feed-through devices protecting a part of or the entire branch circuit.

Leviton's SURE-GARD III is such a device, capable of being wired for protection through itself alone or through up to the entire branch. When selective or restricted protection is employed it becomes easy to trouble-shoot the cause of the tripping, since it is localized to areas served by each SURE-GARD III.

To make it still easier to locate the trouble, SURE-GARD III is available with an Indicator Light that tells whether or not it is powered.

See Section D for more information on the GFCI receptacle.

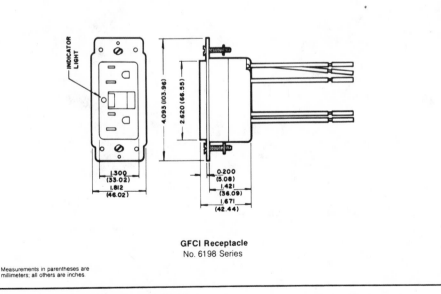

GFCI Receptacle
No. 6198 Series

Measurements in parentheses are millimeters; all others are inches.

Fig. 13-27. Information on GFCI (courtesy Leviton Mfg. Co.).

Fig. 13-28. Built-in timer to suit the needs of the household (courtesy General Electric Co.).

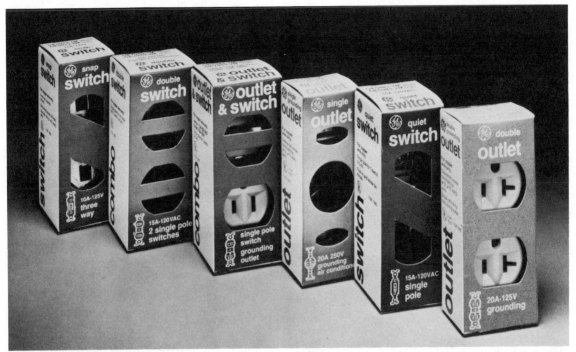

Fig. 13-29. Electrical devices commonly used in houses. Notice the electrical ratings on each device (courtesy General Electric Co.).

ing boxes, and many other special adapters make a very neat installation. The Plugmold 2000 raceway is useful for the workshop over the workbench. For the kitchen, there is a stainless steel style with outlets every 6, 12, or 18 inches.

Wiremold is installed by attaching the supporting clips to the surface, snapping the Wiremold into the clips. The wires are then pulled in to complete the installation. The supporting clips are mounted using the appropriate anchors for the surface. Electrical wholesalers carry Wiremold, but even at retail prices you will save money by doing it yourself.

WIRE TYPES

Wires are technically known as *conductors* and they are bare or insulated, depending on the usage. Wires used in house wiring are either rubber covered with a braid (RHW) or thermoplastic covered (TW or THHN). Sizes commonly used in house wiring range from No. 14 (No. 18 is used only

in wiring ceiling and wall fixtures) to No's. 4, 3, 2, 1, and 0. Lightweight extension cords may have No. 16 wire. The larger the number the smaller the wire. The numbers refer to the American wire gauge (AWG).

Each size wire has an allowable ampacity (or maximum) determined to be safe for its size and type of insulation. If this ampacity is exceeded, overheating and a fire could result. Wires No. 6 and larger *must* be stranded. Solid wire in sizes No. 6 and larger would be impossible to handle to pull through conduit and bend into place in electrical panels.

Romex and BX are used in sizes No. 14, 12, 10 to No. 2. Cables may have two or three wires inside, always with the additional grounding wire included. Do not buy or use cable with *no* ground. It is usually illegal. All cable and wires are marked for use up to 600 volts.

Because Romex and BX are very popular as wiring materials, they are available in any

149

length—even by the foot. I would recommend that you use No. 12 Romex in all your wiring jobs because by so doing you will be buying in full coils and getting the quantity price. In addition, all the branch circuits can then be protected by 20-amp circuit breakers.

Wiring with thinwall is more expensive and it usually is not required. Before proceeding with any wiring project, contact the governing authority to determine the local electrical requirements before purchasing a lot of materials and then finding that you cannot use them. Most home improvement

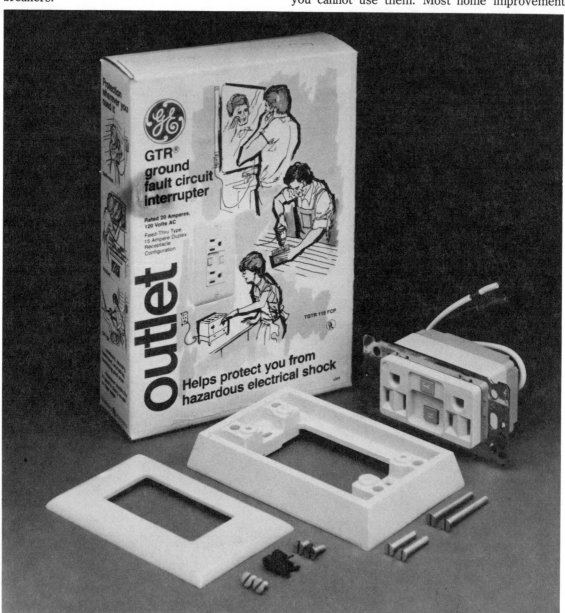

Fig. 13-30. Ground fault circuit interrupter (GFCI) as purchased. Notice the raised adapter to accommodate the GFCI when box is shallow. It is not always necessary to use this (courtesy General Electric Co.).

centers now sell all types of wiring materials by the foot (even single wire used with thinwall). In using thinwall or other conduit, it is necessary to know the number of wires permitted in each size of conduit. Excerpts from code Tables 3-A, 3-B, and 3-C are shown in the Appendix.

DEVICES: CURRENT-CARRYING ITEMS

In electrical wiring, the word *device* means any component part that *carries* current, but does not consume it. Sockets, switches, receptacles, and circuit breakers are devices. Power *consuming* items are called *utilization equipment* and could be motors, toasters, lamps, etc. These items put a load on the circuit and spin the meter disc.

Wiring devices are many and varied, as you can tell by visiting the electrical supplies counter in a hardware store. Each year brings new devices to the market. Some are good and some are not. Be sure to look for the Underwriters' label, UL, on any device you purchase. This listing label gives assurance of a quality product that will serve the purpose for which it was designed. Voltage and amperage ratings are stamped or printed on the device and its container. In using any device, keep within these limits or buy a higher-rated device.

OVERCURRENT DEVICES

If a wire is carrying too much current (amperes), it will overheat and damage the insulation. If insulation overheats, it could melt, become brittle, and break off or drip off. This will leave a bare wire to cause more trouble. To overcome this dangerous condition, overcurrent devices were developed to limit the current allowed to flow in the wire. This maximum depends not only on the wire *size*, but the insulation material and whether the wire is enclosed with other cable or in free air.

I can remember as a youngster holding a candle while my father replaced a fuse in the fuse holder in an upstairs bedroom. The actual *fuse* was a strip of low-melting point material (similar to wire solder) connected between two terminal screws. The wiring was exposed along with the meter on the bedroom wall. The service drop entered the house at a point outside, came through the wall, through an open knife switch, into the meter, and then through the "fuses." Even this simple method provided protection for the house wiring.

Fuses

With the exception of the wire solder fuse, plug fuses are the oldest type of fuse. The plug fuse requires no tools to change and it is safe if only the outer rim is touched when installing or removing the fuse. When a new fuse is installed, be sure to tighten it in place because a loose fuse can blow or overheat the holder and damage it.

If you look in the fuse window, you will see the actual *fusible* link. This link has a narrow center part which is the part which blows or melts. An overload will melt the narrow part and it will just disappear. A short circuit will actually blow (explode) and the window will be blackened. These indications will give some hint as to the trouble on this circuit. Plug fuses 15 amp and smaller have a hexagon window. Larger fuses up to 30 amp have a round window. *Always* replace a defective fuse with one of the *same* size. Plug fuses may be only used on circuits of 150 volts to ground.

Time-Delay Plug Fuses

Time-delay plug fuses, known by the trade name of Fusetron (now called Tron), are designed to carry a greater current for a short period (about one minute) such as is developed when a motor starts. Examples are washing machines, furnace blower motors, and air conditioners. This current draw may be three to five times the normal running current, although it lasts only a few seconds. This current in rush would blow a standard fuse. Therefore, the time-delay fuse was developed.

The delay fuse consists of two parts: a *fusible strip* just like the standard fuse and a *solder pot* at the bottom of the fuse body. The solder pot has a wire inserted into the solder in the pot. The other end of the wire is attached to a spring.

In addition, the wire is connected to the standard fusible link that is part of the standard fuse type. The spring puts tension on the wire in the solder. When an overload occurs, the solder starts heating. If the overload is of short duration (say the

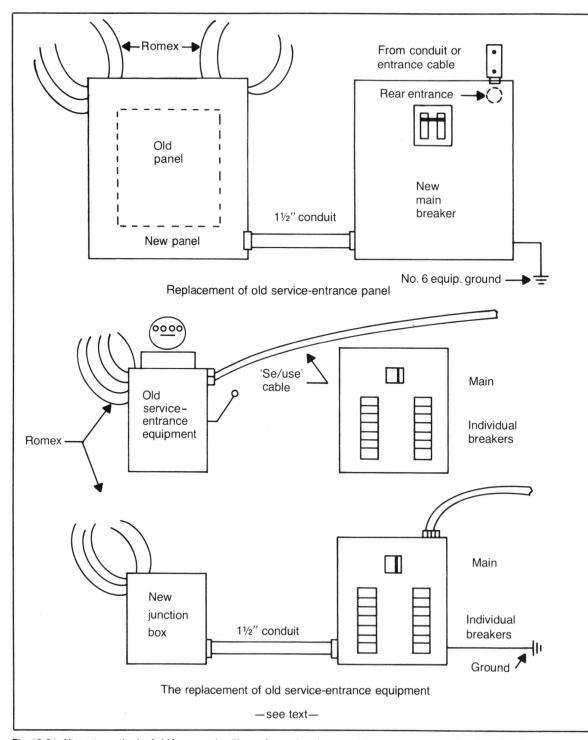

Fig. 13-31. Alternate methods of old fuse panels with new fuse or breaker panel. In both cases the old fuse panel is discarded.

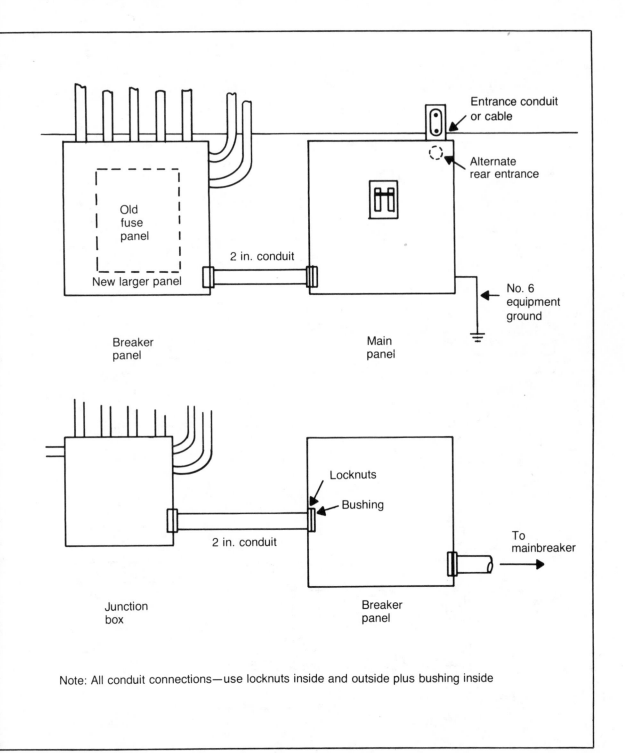

Old
fuse
panel

New larger panel

Breaker
panel

2 in. conduit

Entrance conduit
or cable

Alternate
rear entrance

No. 6
equipment
ground

Main
panel

Locknuts

Bushing

To
mainbreaker

2 in. conduit

Junction
box

Breaker
panel

Note: All conduit connections—use locknuts inside and outside plus bushing inside

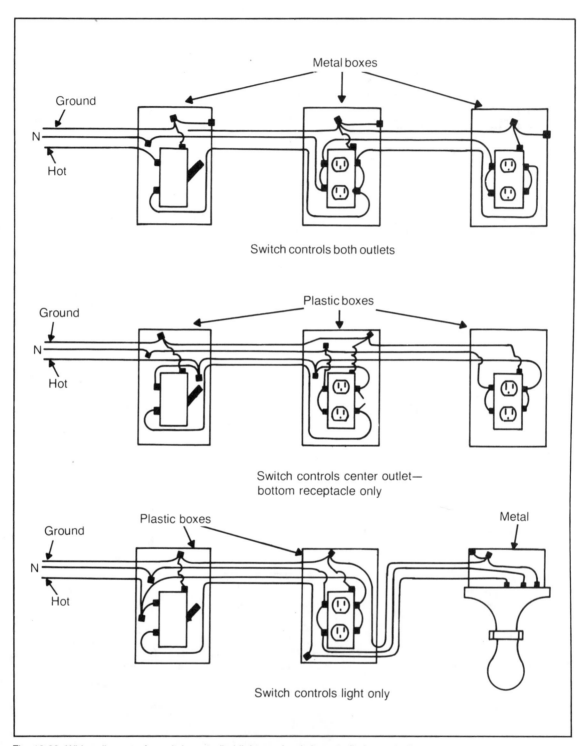

Fig. 13-32. Wiring diagrams for switch-controlled lights and switch-controlled receptacles.

motor starts promptly), the solder does not melt and nothing happens.

If the motor has tight bearings and cannot start within a reasonable time or is unable to turn, the solder melts and releases the wire because the spring pulls it out. If a short circuit occurs, the fusible link blows. Both methods serve the same purpose: to protect the circuit and equipment.

TYPE S NONTAMPERABLE FUSE

The type S fuse has the same characteristics as the Edison-base, time-delay fuse (Fusetron of Tron). The Type S fuse has a smaller threaded part so that a coin cannot be inserted nor can foil be used (threads will chew up the foil). These fuses are called Fustats when made by Bussman Company. They are used in Edison-base fuse receptacles by inserting an adapter. The adapter has a prong on the side that effectively prevents the adapter from being removed from the fuse receptacle.

Fusestats and their adapters are sized to-gether so as to prevent overfusing the circuit. This means: a 0-to-15 amp adapter will only accept a 0-to-15 amp Fustat. All types of plug fuses may be used on circuits of over 150 volts to ground. This allows them to be used on residential circuits because, with 240-volt service, either side of the 240 volts is only 120 volts to ground. The 240 volts is *between* the two hot wires.

Cartridge Fuses

Cartridge fuses are different in shape from plug fuses. They are cylindrical in shape. Up through 30 amp they are 9/16 inches in diameter by 2 inches long. The next larger size, 35 through 60 amps, are 13/16 inches diameter by 3 inches long. The ends are made of brass while the center is made of fiber.

The actual fuse link is inside the fiber center and is surrounded by an inert powder to smother the arc when the fuse blows. Larger than 60-amp fuses are of the knife blade type. The appearance is similar to the smaller-capacity fuse, but on each end are

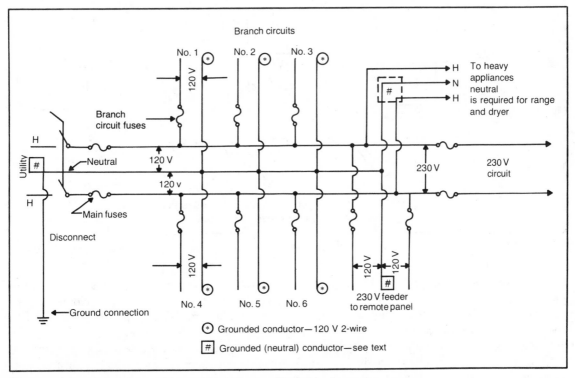

Fig. 13-33. Wiring layout for a residence. This is the usual layout for the modern house.

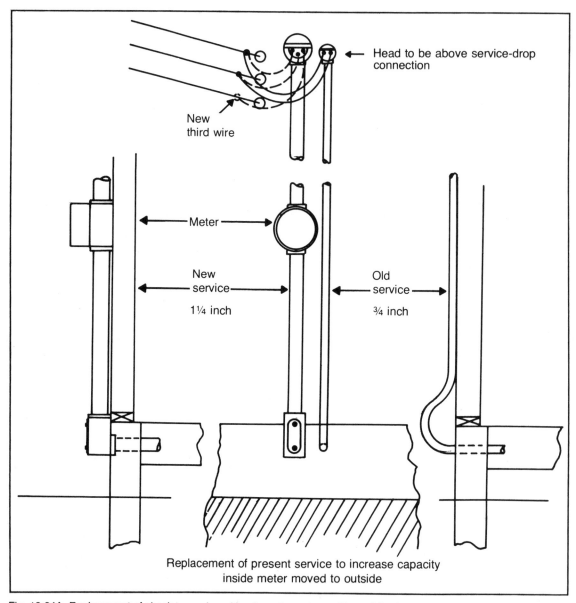

Fig. 13-34A. Replacement of obsolete service with adequate modern wiring, while also moving the meter to the outside.

flat copper blades—hence the knife blade designation.

These blades slide into parallel jaws to make contact with the fused disconnect wiring. Use of the term cartridge comes from the similarity to a rifle cartridge. The 70-amp size is 1-inch diameter by 5 ⅞ inches long. Larger capacities are larger in physical size. The cartridge fuses from 30 to 60 amps are used to protect ranges, clothes dryers, and water heaters. Modern installations are usually the pull-out-type fuse block.

In a situation where they are exposed, the fuse must be able to be de-energized by a disconnect to be safe to remove. Even then, use a fiber fuse puller to remove and replace the fuse. This will put your hand further from any live (hot) wires or terminals.

The above types are made for circuits up to 250 volts. Other types are for up to 600 volts. These high-voltage types are not used in the home. *Renewable* fuses are made in both the cartridge and knife blade type. Both ends are removable and the fusible link can be replaced. These are usually found in factories and office buildings. The first cost is higher but replacement links are very reasonable.

Circuit Breakers

Circuit breakers, commonly called breakers, are the latest development in overcurrent devices. They can be opened or closed manually and they will open automatically on a short circuit or overload. The amount and duration of the overload is determined by the setting of the breaker. Circuit breakers incorporate the *time lag* feature and will carry overloads for a very short time, but they will trip immediately on a short circuit.

SOCKETS

Various types and sizes of sockets are available for general lighting and decorative effects. Sizes vary from the candelabra at 0.465 inches diameter, intermediate at 0.65 inches, medium (Edison base) at 1.037 inches, to mogul at 1.555 inches. There are other specialized sockets for industrial and commercial use. Three-way table and floor-lamp sock-

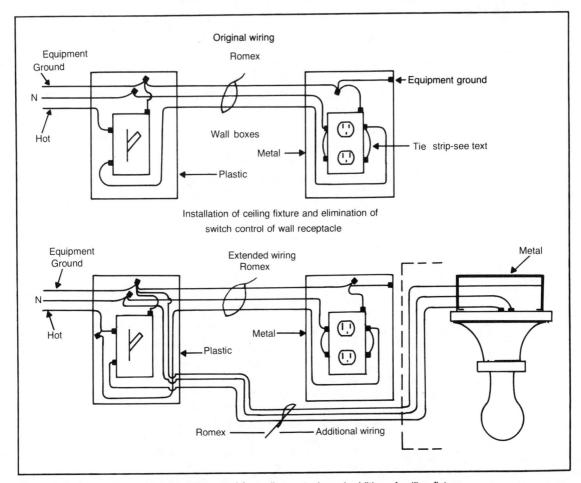

Fig. 13-34B. Shows elimination of switch control for wall receptacle and addition of ceiling fixture.

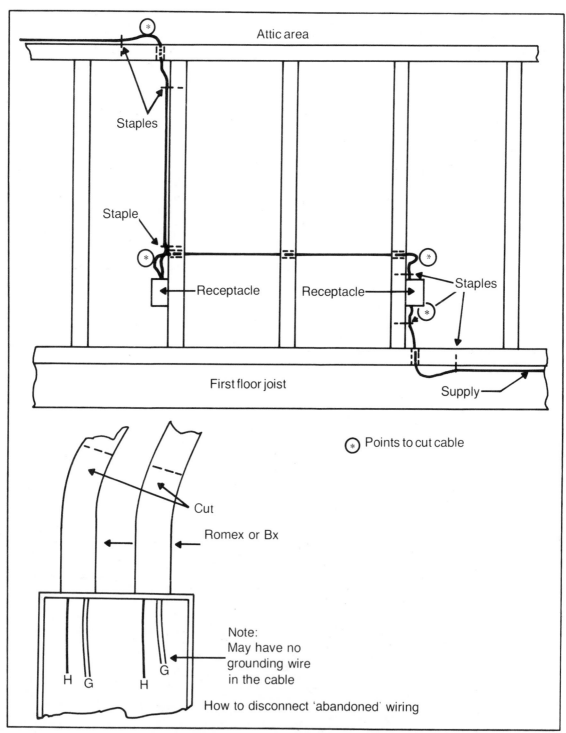

Attic area

Staples

Staple

Receptacle   Receptacle   Staples

First floor joist   Supply

⊛ Points to cut cable

Cut

Romex or Bx

Note:
May have no
grounding wire
in the cable

H G   H G

How to disconnect 'abandoned' wiring

Fig. 13-35. How to disconnect abandoned wiring. Cut back far enough to prevent any possible contact with new wiring.

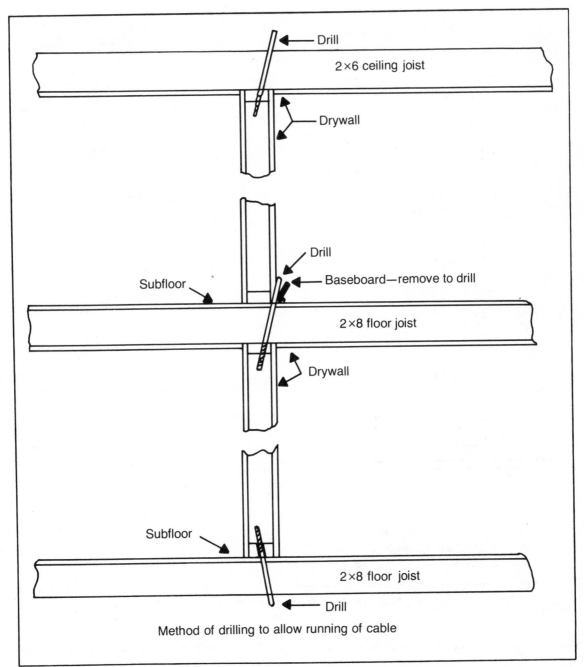

Fig. 13-36. Method of drilling to allow concealed cable to be run from basement panel to attic.

ets contain an extra contact for the special three-way light bulbs so that three levels of light are supplied.

INTERCHANGEABLE DEVICES

Interchangeable devices were developed to accommodate more than one device in a single gang

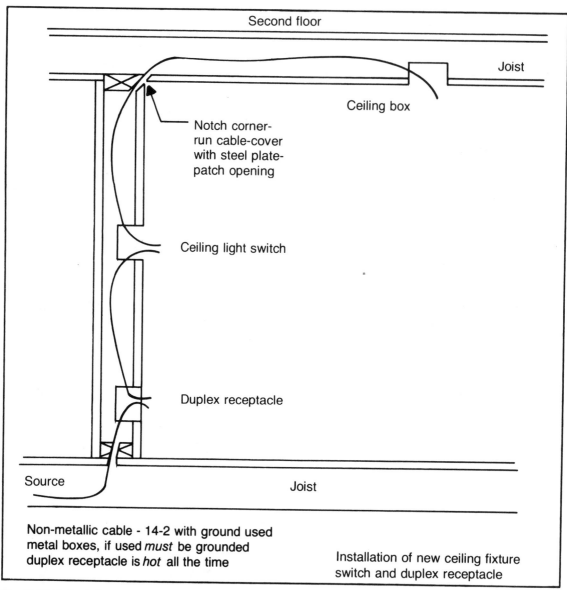

Second floor

Joist

Ceiling box

Notch corner-
run cable-cover
with steel plate-
patch opening

Ceiling light switch

Duplex receptacle

Source

Joist

Non-metallic cable - 14-2 with ground used
metal boxes, if used *must* be grounded
duplex receptacle is *hot* all the time

Installation of new ceiling fixture
switch and duplex receptacle

Fig. 13-37. Method of running cable to supply a switch, ceiling fixture and receptacle. Note the methods of access to various wall cavities.

wall or handy box. These separate, smaller devices are:

■ Single outlet grounding receptacle.
■ Toggle switch, single pole or three way.
■ Pilot light.
■ Push button.
■ Blank insert.

The devices can be combined in any arrangement of the five types listed. A steel mounting strap holds them in correct position to accommodate a cover plate (as would be a single device in the same space). This strap is furnished with one or three openings. When used for only two devices, the center opening is not used. Devices are inserted from the back of the strap and locked in place by prying a thin portion of the bar over into the plastic part of the device to anchor it. Cover plates come with one, two or three openings. The one opening strap and cover position or the device vertically. The two and three device positions are horizontal.

Although these devices are approved for all the uses that standard devices are approved for, I prefer not to use them. They take up more box space and especially when three devices are used in a single gang box. Many more wires are introduced into a small wall box and this might exceed the rated capacity of the box. In any event, wiring connections must be made very carefully and the wires must be folded neatly back in when fastening the

assembly to the box ears. Where wall space is at a premium, these devices are useful. If you are able to use standard devices, do so because they are easier to work with.

I have found lightning is apt to burn across these devices because of the closeness of the terminals. I found after replacing one switch assembly that the second one also shorted out. I then replaced the assembly with standard switches in separate boxes and had no more trouble.

COMBINATION DEVICES

Combination devices are similar to interchangeable devices. They differ because they are furnished in selected combinations such as: switch/outlet;

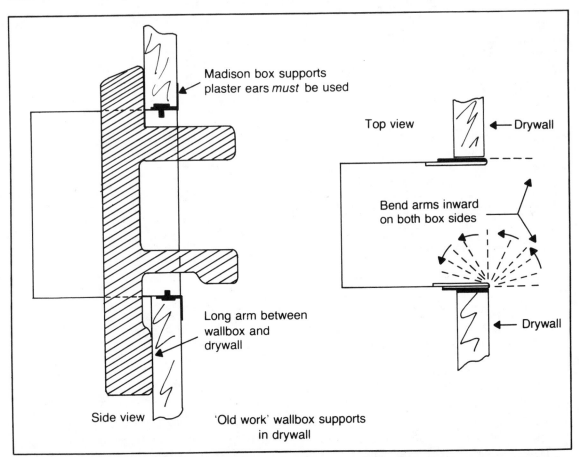

Fig. 13-38. Madison patented "old work" metal or plastic wall box support. Wall box and two supports are inserted into opening, positioned as shown. Box is pushed in and supports are pulled tight. Short arms are bent tight against each side wall of the box. Use pliers to pinch them tightly.

switch/switch, and switch/pilot light. These combinations are cast in one plastic housing and must be purchased in the arrangement desired. Only *two* devices are combined in one housing. Standard duplex receptacle plates are used. This type is preferred over the interchangeable style.

WALL RECEPTACLES

Wall receptacles are as varied as switches. The old types had a screw socket (same as a light socket) with a brass plate and a hinged cover. Lamps and extension cords had a plug with a freely rotating brass threaded shell. When this shell was screwed into *any* socket, including this wall socket, the cord would not twist. Later, the threaded part of this plug was made separately from the other half which had the two blades. This then became the standard attachment plug we know now. These plug bases are still available.

The first wall receptacle I remember was mounted 7 feet high on my parents' bedroom wall. It was recessed porcelain and had a brass plate with small hinged doors that opened outward like cupboard doors. Inside was the recess about 1½ inches high and 1 inch wide. It was about 1½ inches deep. On each side was a brass plate (the two contact bars). The plug consisted of a porcelain *block* having on each side a contact bar that when inserted into the recess, made contact with the mating bars in the receptacle recess. The two brass doors of the cover plate closed around an extension cord consisting of two twisted wires (green cloth covered) that were attached to a plug. At the other end of the cord, was an open socket. This was my first "contact" with electricity. I found out what was in the socket.

Receptacles have different configurations of openings in their faces. One reference shows 18 different receptacles for as many applications. You may be familiar with the difference between electric range and electric dryer receptacles. The range receptacle accepts three straight blades while the dryer receptacle will only accept two straight and one L-shaped blade. This prevents a dryer cord from being plugged into a higher-amperage range receptacle.

Receptacles for lamps, radios, televisions,

vacuums, etc., are fused at 15 amps and they are the common type found in homes. Inspect one and note the longer slot on one side. This slot is connected to the neutral (white) wire. The newer radios and other appliances now have one blade of the attachment plug wider than the other. This prevents the plug from being inserted the wrong way. This helps to ground the equipment better.

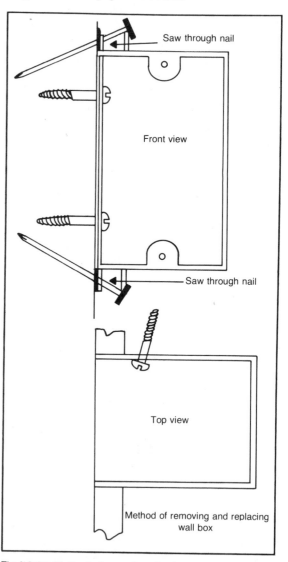

Fig. 13-39. Method of removing plastic or metal box to add additional wiring, then replacing box. You should put electrical tape over metal screw heads just in case a bare wire touches them.

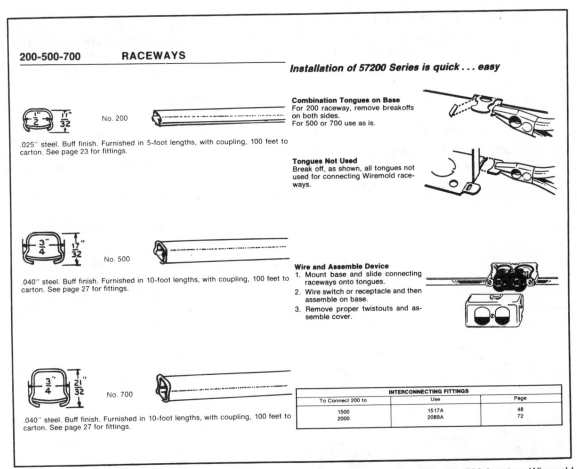

Installation of 57200 Series is quick . . . easy

No. 200

.025″ steel. Buff finish. Furnished in 5-foot lengths, with coupling, 100 feet to carton. See page 23 for fittings.

Combination Tongues on Base
For 200 raceway, remove breakoffs on both sides.
For 500 or 700 use as is.

Tongues Not Used
Break off, as shown, all tongues not used for connecting Wiremold raceways.

No. 500

.040″ steel. Buff finish. Furnished in 10-foot lengths, with coupling, 100 feet to carton. See page 27 for fittings.

Wire and Assemble Device
1. Mount base and slide connecting raceways onto tongues.
2. Wire switch or receptacle and then assemble on base.
3. Remove proper twistouts and assemble cover.

No. 700

.040″ steel. Buff finish. Furnished in 10-foot lengths, with coupling, 100 feet to carton. See page 27 for fittings.

INTERCONNECTING FITTINGS		
To Connect 200 to	Use	Page
1500	1517A	48
2000	2089A	72

Fig. 13-40. Illustration of Wiremold surface raceway giving dimensions of various series: 200, 500, 700 (courtesy Wiremold Co.).

Some equipment has one wire grounded to the frame and it needs this polarized plug. Receptacles for many years have had one slot wider than the other. This was the design even before the grounding receptacles were developed. The wide slot is connected to the grounded wire (the white wire). When used with a polarized plug, this effectively grounds the frame of the appliance thus connected.

Receptacles in the kitchen and dining room are on 20 A circuits. Generally, only 15 A receptacles are installed on these circuits because standard attachment plugs are furnished with appliances used in these areas. This is a code-approved method.

TIMERS, PHOTOCELLS, AND CONTACTORS

Timers control many current-using items such as lights, thermostats, water heaters, pumps, and so on. They are in series with current-using items and are actually automatically operated switches. Photocells are also switches, but they are dependent on light levels in their area. They are completely automatic and need no adjustment. Timers do need to be adjusted for changing sunset and sunrise hours while photocells do not. They react to sunlight. Buy a good brand at a cost of about $10. I installed one and later the neighbor complained that it blinked on and off all the time. I purchased a better one and had no more trouble.

Contactors are switches with the capacity to

carry larger-size loads. They are operated by a magnetic coil energized by either a photocell or timer or other controller. Parking lot, stadium, or other heavy lighting loads are operated by contactors. Your home central air conditioner has such a contactor built into the control system.

Ground Clamp

This device clamps tightly to a water pipe or ground rod by means of two screws clamping the two parts. The grounding wire is held by a setscrew, making a tight connection mechanically *and* electrically.

Electric Utility Meter

Even though this is utility property it is still a device because it carries current. It is also current

using as it uses a small amount to "spin its wheels" so you can be billed. If you must remove the meter from its base or open the meter cabinet, notify the utility. If you remove the meter to work on the service-entrance panel or other "hot" wires, be sure to put a circle of corrugated cardboard in place of the meter. Children are very curious and this would legally be an attractive nuisance and you would be liable for damages. Be *cautious!* Notifying the utility beforehand and afterward puts you in good standing with the utility and shows that you are not trying to cheat the utility.

WIRE HOLDING ITEMS

Wire holding (containing) items are numerous. Conduits have been covered. Other items are, cabinets, pull boxes, and wall and ceiling boxes.

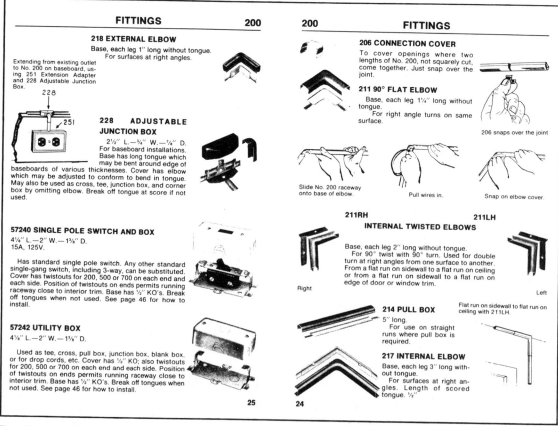

Fig. 13-41. Representative selection of Wiremold fittings (courtesy Wiremold Co.).

HOW TO INSTALL WIREMOLD
200, 500 and 700 RACEWAYS

Each length of raceway is furnished with a coupling.

1st. Push out coupling.

2nd. Fasten to surface, using No. 6 flat-head wood screws with No. 200, and No. 8 flat-head wood screws with Nos. 500 and 700.

3rd. Couple lengths together.

4th. Pull wires in.

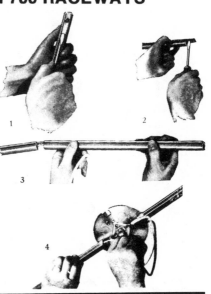

HOW TO INSTALL
WIREMOLD 200, 500 AND 700 FITTINGS

1st. Line up run and fasten base of fitting to surface, using a No. 6 flat-head wood screw for No. 200 and No. 8 flat-head wood screw for Nos. 500 and 700, or the equivalent size expansion shield, toggle bolts, etc.

2nd. Couple base of fitting to raceway by slipping tongue of fitting under the base of the raceway (between the curled edges). When 57200 series fittings are used with 200, break-offs in combination tongues for 200, 500, and 700 should be removed.

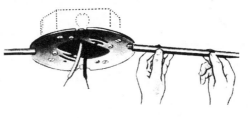

Fig. 13-42. How to install Wiremold raceways and fittings (courtesy Wiremold Co.).

Long ago boxes were not used. Wires were run inside walls using *loom*, a formed fiber covering shaped like tubing. The wire was run through this loom from the last porcelain knob in the attic or cellar to the "turn" switch on the wall. There were no wall receptacles. It then was decided that be-cause of fire and safety hazards metal boxes should be used wherever splices or connections to terminals were located. This has now become mandatory.

Boxes must be supported in walls and ceilings so that they will be mechanically solid and secure.

RACEWAYS 200-500-700

200 WIRE CAPACITY	Single Conductor						
TYPE	No. 6	No. 8	No. 10	No. 12	No. 14	No. 16	No. 18
THHN, THWN	—	—	—	3	5	6	7
TW	—	—	—	3	3	4	5
THW	—	—	—	2	2	4	5
RHH, RHW	—	—	—	—	—	4	5

500 WIRE CAPACITY	Single Conductor						
TYPE	No.6	No. 8	No. 10	No. 12	No. 14	No. 16	No. 18
THHN, THWN	—	2	4	7	9	10	12
TW	—	2	3	4	6	7	9
THW	—	—	2	3	4	7	9
RHH, RHW	—	—	2	2	2	7	9

700 WIRE CAPACITY	Single Conductor						
TYPE	No. 6	No. 8	No. 10	No. 12	No. 14	No. 16	No. 18
THHN, THWN	2	3	5	8	11	12	15
TW	—	2	4	6	7	9	11
THW	—	2	3	4	5	9	11
RHH, RHW	—	—	2	2	3	9	11

Note: No. 16 and No. 18 not covered by U.L. Guide Cards.
Capacities are given as a guide to installers of low-potential wiring.

Fig. 13-43. Special fittings for Wiremold also wire capacities for the 200, 500, and 700 series (courtesy Wiremold Co.).

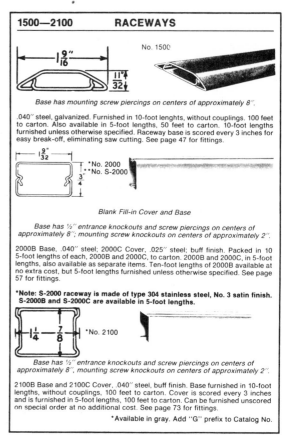

1500—2100   RACEWAYS

No. 1500

Base has mounting screw piercings on centers of approximately 8".

.040" steel, galvanized. Furnished in 10-foot lenghts, without couplings. 100 feet to carton. Also available in 5-foot lengths, 50 feet to carton. 10-foot lengths furnished unless otherwise specified. Raceway base is scored every 3 inches for easy break-off, eliminating saw cutting. See page 47 for fittings.

*No. 2000
**No. S-2000

Blank Fill-in Cover and Base

Base has ½" entrance knockouts and screw piercings on centers of approximately 8"; mounting screw knockouts on centers of approximately 2".

2000B Base, .040" steel; 2000C Cover, .025" steel; buff finish. Packed in 10 5-foot lengths of each, 2000B and 2000C, to carton. 2000B and 2000C, in 5-foot lengths, also available as separate items. Ten-foot lengths of 2000B available at no extra cost, but 5-foot lengths furnished unless otherwise specified. See page 57 for fittings.

Note: S-2000 raceway is made of type 304 stainless steel, No. 3 satin finish. S-2000B and S-2000C are available in 5-foot lengths.

*No. 2100

Base has ½" entrance knockouts and screw piercings on centers of approximately 8"; mounting screw knockouts on centers of approximately 2".

2100B Base and 2100C Cover, .040" steel, buff finish. Base furnished in 10-foot lengths, without couplings, 100 feet to carton. Cover is scored every 3 inches and is furnished in 5-foot lengths, 100 feet to carton. Can be furnished unscored on special order at no additional cost. See page 73 for fittings.

*Available in gray. Add "G" prefix to Catalog No.

Fig. 13-44. Special Wiremold raceway for overfloor use. Also shows larger square 2000 and 2100 series (courtesy Wiremold Co.).

Ceiling boxes must be so anchored that they will be able to support heavy chandeliers that sometimes weigh 20 pounds or more. Wall boxes are supported in new work by nailing to the side of the stud. Plastic wall boxes have nails in place through ears on the top and bottom of the box.

Ceiling boxes and wall boxes for fixtures are mounted on adjustable bars that are nailed between studs for wall boxes and between joists for ceiling boxes. These adjustable bars have bent over ends to be nailed to the framing. The box is mounted in the center, but by loosening the setscrew the box can be moved so as to center it on the ceiling or to center a wall box on a wall space. Certain wall boxes have removable sides and can be attached together (ganged) to make long horizontal switch boxes for uses such as stores and office buildings. The most a homeowner would need might be a four gang for four switches.

Octagonal boxes resemble a 4-inch square box, but with the corners cut off. The *square*, 4-inch box can be used for ceiling fixtures with the addition of a plaster ring. This is a raised cover with a round center ring with ears having tapped holes to accept a fixture bar. This bar comes with every fixture and is part of the mounting kit. Most boxes come with BX or Romex clamps (except the 4-inch square and the larger 4 11/16-inch box; these are more for commercial work). Very shallow ceiling boxes are made with one-half inch depth for mounting where a joist is in the way of centering a ceiling box. I just had to use one myself.

PLUGMOLD WIRED SECTIONS for special applications

STAINLESS STEEL

Plugmold S-2000 Wired Sections are made from heavy gauge, type 304 stainless steel, a material with high resistance to corrosion and heat. It is ideal for any application where multiple electrical outlets are needed and a clean, sterile environment must be maintained, such as in cafeterias, restaurants, hospitals, clean rooms and laboratories.

The multioutlet strip is easily kept clean with a damp cloth or sponge, wiping carefully around the outlet, not over it.

NOTE: The following fittings are available also in stainless steel: S-2010A, S-2010B, S-2018C, S-2051H. When ordering be sure to add "S" prefix to the catalog number. S-2000B base and S-2000C cover are available in 5-foot lengths.

IG SERIES

Plugmold 2000 IG Wired Sections feature an insulated-isolated "pure ground", reducing electromagnetic interference in sensitive electronic equipment. Receptacle faces are orange.
To preserve the integrity of an IG isolated grounding circuit, all receptacles on that circuit must be restricted for use by equipment requiring interference-free operation. All other equipment should use standard circuits with non-isolated grounding receptacles.

GROUNDING METHODS...

RECEPTACLE

GROUNDING
CONTACT TO
RACEWAY

20G, 20GA, 20GB, 20DG,
20GBA, 20DGB SERIES

RECEPTACLE

WITHOUT
GROUNDING
CONTACT TO
RACEWAY

20IG SERIES

PLUGMOLD® 2000

FITTINGS FOR USE WITH PLUGMOLD 2000 SURFACE METAL RACEWAY, MULTIOUTLET SYSTEM, WIRED SECTIONS, PLUGMOLD WITH SNAPICOIL°

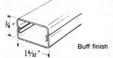

Buff finish

Description — page 10.
Wire Capacity table — page 11.
Installation Instructions — page 64.

15 Amp. Specification Grade receptacles (conforming to NEMA specification WD1-3.02 to 1-3.10, "Heavy Duty, General Use, 15A, 125V Grounding Receptacles") are furnished in all Plugmold 2000 multioutlet products. These receptacles are designed for use on 20 Amp branch circuits: See NEC Article 210-21(b)(3). All conductors are No. 12 A.W.G.

Plugmold 2000 is furnished prewired as: (a) Plugmold wired sections (6' maximum), and (b) Plugmold with Snapicoil (500' maximum, 48' minimum), which eliminates multiple splicing that would result from using a number of short wired sections in long run installations.

Prewired sections are furnished in 1', 3', 5', and 6' wired sections, with prewired receptacles factory installed in the cover. A wired section is used where a short length will suffice — along the back of a workbench, for example. Whenever plenty of outlets are required use Snapicoil packages to eliminate need for tedious, repetitive outlet wiring in the field.

Plugmold with Snapicoil is the most economical way to install long, continuous runs, since multiple splices are eliminated. It consists of a harness of receptacles factory-wired at regular intervals, matching holecut cover, base, and the required number of wire clips and couplings.

Fig. 13-45. Wiremold Plugmold wired sections with receptacles prewired; Series 2000 (courtesy Wiremold Co.).

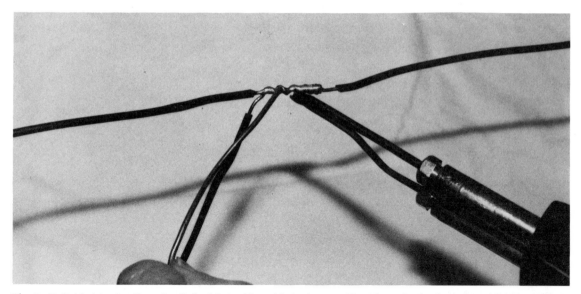

Fig. 13-46. Soldering a "tap" on a "run" of solid wire. The soldering iron must heat the splice itself, not the solder. The solder is melted and runs and blends with the splice solely from the heat in the splice. This way you will have a perfectly soldered joint. Notice the shiny, smooth, evenly blended turns.

The code limits the number of wires allowed in any wall, ceiling, handy box or junction box. This eliminates crowding and the sharp bending of wires. Any box packed full of wires and devices is sure to generate heat. The heat could build up and damage the insulation or the device. Plastic boxes have the limit of the number of wires embossed inside along with the cubic inch figure. A typical single-gang plastic wall box might have the following designation: "18 cu. inch. - 9/14, 8/12, 7/10." The maximum number of conductors that may be installed in a designated-size box is given in code Table 370-6(a).

The extensive use of cabinets in home wiring is unlikely except if they are used as fuse or breaker cabinets or disconnect cabinets. When installing new service-entrance equipment, a junction box/ cabinet will need to be installed if the new equipment has to be moved (thus leaving the old wires too short to reach). In all boxes of any kind, *unused* and open knockouts must be closed with knockout plugs. These are snap-in metal plates that seal the opening. Metal plugs in plastic boxes *must* be recessed ¼ of an inch from the *outer* surface, as stated in code Section 370-8. Try to avoid making extra openings in plastic boxes. It will be hard to close those not used.

Metal raceways are not used in home wiring, but they are common in large installations such as office buildings.

NEW WORK

New work is electrical wiring installed *before* any of the finish materials such as drywall or paneling are applied to the studs or joists. It also means any place where the framing members are exposed such as basement and attic areas. The term new work refers to the *method* used to install such wiring, not the age of the building. In fact old work can and is installed in *new* buildings in cases where changes and additions to the original construction plans have to be made after the building is completed.

Romex and BX in new work is run through holes bored in joists and studs. Cables must be anchored within 12 inches of the box and every 4½ feet when run parallel to framing members. Nonmetallic boxes require stapling within 8 inches of the box.

Nailing supports are an integral part of the box construction. On nonmetallic boxes tight hooks hold nails on the top and bottom. Some metal boxes have nails going through near the top and bottom inside the box. These come out on the other side to go into the wood stud. Code Section 370-13 describes this in detail. Other boxes have an angle bracket on one side for nails or self-formed nailing prongs. Supports will position the box so that it will be flush with the finished surface.

THE WIRING LAYOUT

It will be necessary to have a blue print or drawing of a new wiring layout for a new dwelling or an addition. This might be required when you apply for a permit. Contact the utility to find out their preferred location for the service-entrance mast and meter. They will advise the best location after conferring with you. Certain locations are preferred; others may be acceptable to the utility. Underground service is not so flexible as to location. Again, the utility has the final say.

If the service is completely underground you will have to furnish conduit from the bottom of the meter housing down into the ground. Some utilities require a 90-degree elbow turned to the supply source. The service may only be underground to the utility pole. In this case, conduit will be required also from underground at the pole up the pole to a minimum height of 8 feet (or as the utility requires). When talking to the utility representative, mention the proposed location of the interior service-entrance panel. They might suggest an alternate meter location. The overhead servicedrop restricts the meter location because of clearance requirements. Roof clearance is 8 feet minimum; ground clearance is 12 feet for 240-volt service (less than 300 volts to ground). Connection at the building requires a minimum clearance of 10 feet (more if possible). The higher the better.

SERVICE EQUIPMENT AND DISTRIBUTION PANEL

Service-entrance/distribution panel equipment must be adjacent to the meter location. Warm climate areas have these items outside. More often, the equipment is inside directly opposite the meter outside. The service equipment and distribution panel come in one enclosure for the average dwel-

ling. The capacity will be 100 amp minimum, often 150 amp.

With the equipment location decided, the branch circuit wiring can now be run. Take your print and go around and mark locations for receptacles, switches, ceiling fixtures, and any other junction box locations. Mount these items to studs or joists. Next, bore holes for the Romex or BX cables. Route these cables by the most direct path, but do not skimp on length. A little extra on each end of the run is better than a length 6 inches too short. True, a short length *can* be pulled out and used elsewhere, but that takes time and labor.

The code requires that no wall space be more than 6 feet from a receptacle. Also, any wall space 2 feet or wider must have a receptacle. Counter tops wider than 12 inches must have a receptacle. Bathrooms, outdoors, and laundries must have one receptacle each. Boxes for switches are 46 inches high. Boxes for receptacles are 15 inches high. This required spacing of outlets is illustrated by Figs. 6-1 and 6-2. Note the arrangement of outlets. This or any arrangement seems never to be where the

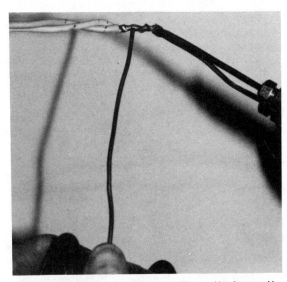

Fig. 13-47. Soldering of a pigtail joint. The end is obscured by the solder gun tip. This is also a perfectly blended joint. A small propane torch could also be used. Very little heat is needed, Caution: Never use any open flame on any construction work and then immediately leave the premises. Stay at least another half hour to allow any fire that might have started to show itself.

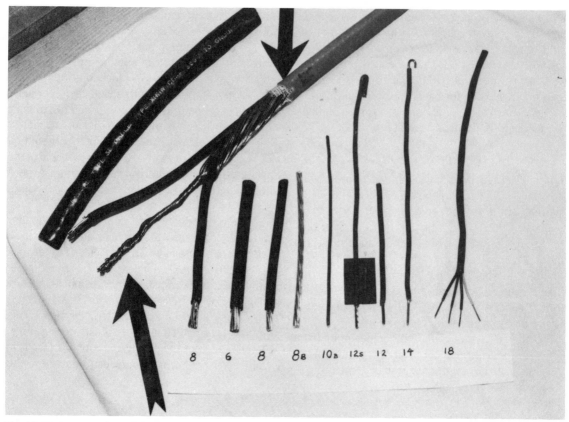

Fig. 13-48. Assortment of different size wires. From the left, empty cable casing, contained three insulated No. 6 wires (two black, one gray, for neutral) and one bare for equipment ground. Service-entrance cable, two insulated black wires with a bare neutral wrapped around the other two wires, all No. 8. The No. 8 B and No. 10 B are bare (used for grounds). No. 12 S means stranded. No. 18 is thermostat cable. The black rectangle has the clear plastic covering removed from the blue insulation stranded wire. This is oil-proof insulation. Small stranded wire is easier to pull through conduit or thinwall.

homeowner would like to have them. Perhaps you can do better for your own home.

Centering Ceiling Outlets in a Room

Ceiling outlets are installed in the center of most rooms. Some living rooms have at one end an alcove for use as a dining area. Because most living rooms do not use ceiling fixtures, only the dining area would require a ceiling box. To center a ceiling box, use a long 1×2 or similar piece of wood about half as long as the longest room dimension. Put one end of the stick against a wall that will allow it to be laid against the bottom of a joist. Mark the end of the stick. Now shove the stick along the same joist to the other end of the room (opposite the first wall)

and again mark the stick. You will be doing this first marking on a joist near the center of the room's cross dimension.

You now have two marks on this joist a short distance apart. Divide this distance in two with a steel tape or wood rule. You now have the center in one direction. Gauge by eye to determine between which two joists to mount the box carrying bar and box. Mount the bar and box where you marked the room lengthwise first. Leave the box loose on the bar. Again use the stick. If the room crosswise dimension is less than the lengthwise dimension by quite a bit, make a pencil mark on the stick somewhere near where the box sits on the bar. Also mark, on the bar at the same time, so that both marks coincide. Change ends with the stick and mark the bar again from the mark you made on the stick.

Actually this whole marking, centering, mounting the bar and box, and locking the box on center takes very little time. Figures 9-20 and 9-21 illustrate how to do this.

On an already plastered ceiling, centering is accomplished much faster. Positioning the stick lengthwise and then crosswise is all that is needed. In case the box location falls on a joist, try to "fudge" a small amount either way from the joist location. But to fudge very much will look bad. Instead buy a 4-inch by ½-inch deep box. To mount this box flush with the ceiling surface, you will need to chisel out some from the bottom of the joist. Then mount the box with wood screws. Never use nails because removal would be very difficult. Always look ahead to what you might have to do next or might have to change. Be sure to arrange the box so that a knockout is clear so the cable can be brought into the box alongside the joist.

Measuring

Measuring accurately is very important. The old saying, "Measure twice and cut once," is very appropriate. When holding your rule upside down, be careful not to misread the figure on the rule. Cabinetworkers doing fine furniture use a knife blade to mark wood because it is as more accurate than a blunt pencil. Rough electrical work allows some leeway, but still be as accurate as possible and measure twice.

BRANCH CIRCUITS

With the location of devices established, plan the layout of the branch circuits. For residential occupancies, the code requires 3 watts per square foot of floor area (measuring the *outside* dimensions of the building). Include a basement for a possible recreation room and workshop. Not less than one circuit should be installed for each 500 square feet of an area. Plan to have most areas served by *two* separate circuits; if one goes out, the other will still be usable. These circuits can be 14-2 Romex with ground and be protected by a 15-amp fuse or

breaker. These circuits could also be 12-2 with ground protected by 20-amp breaker or fuse.

Small Appliance Branch Circuits

Outlets in the kitchen, pantry, family room, dining room and breakfast room *must* be supplied by *two or more* 20-amp appliance circuits wired with 12-2 with ground Romex. No other outlets shall be on these circuits. The kitchen area must have outlets supplied by two circuits. This way more than one high wattage appliance can be used at one time without blowing a fuse. These could be a toaster and

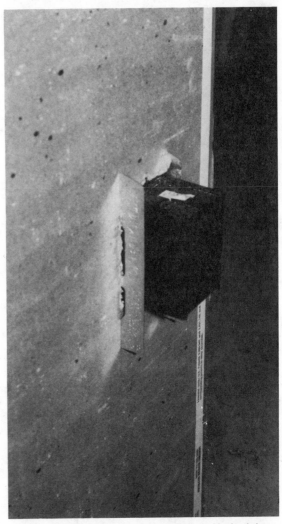

Fig. 13-49. Madison drywall anchor installed with plastic box.

171

Fig. 13-50. Face side showing Madison anchor in place. One side has ears bent in, but the other ears are not bent.

a counter-top oven. Laundry outlets must be on a separate 20 amp circuit.

Electric Ranges

The feeder loads for electric ranges or other cooking appliances are calculated from code Table 220-19. Range circuits are sized according to a demand factor rather than the actual name plate rating (connected load). This is because all heating elements of a range will seldom be on at one time. If the cooking units consist of one cook top and not more than *two* wall-mounted ovens, it is permitted to add the nameplate ratings together and treat this as *one* range. This provided all components are in the same room. Note 1 to Code Table 220-19 explains how to arrive at the demand rating if there is more than 12 kW for one range. Be sure to read all notes to tables as you use them.

Electric Clothes Dryer

The electric clothes dryer demand factor is 100 percent of the nameplate rating. It is recommended that No. 8 wire be used for this circuit and be protected with a 40-amp breaker. No. 10 wire can be used, protected by a 30 amp breaker, but the heating elements in clothes dryers are being made in heavier wattages. When a dryer replacement is needed, the circuit might not handle it and will need to be rewired.

Heating and Cooling Loads

Because heating and cooling equipment is never used simultaneously, the effective load is taken as the cooling load. This load is the greater of the two loads. This load is taken at 100 percent of the nameplate rating. As an example, my own air conditioner load is 19.00 amps while the heating load is 2.4 amps. Therefore the effective heating cooling load is included as 10.00 amps × 230 volts = 4370 W.

OLD WORK

Old work refers to additional wiring installed in those buildings already finished. It also refers to repairs or the replacement of obsolete wiring. This work is much more difficult than new work because of the problems encountered in "fishing" cables

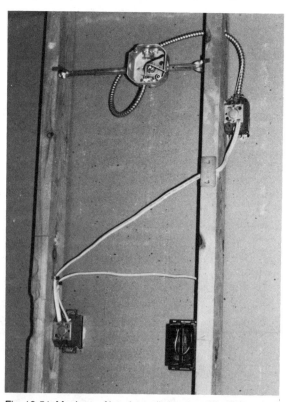

Fig. 13-51. Mock-up of interior wall showing different types of wall box installations, including plastic and metal wall boxes. Also a ceiling type octagon box with BX running to it from a wall box. Because this is a mock-up, distances are not to scale.

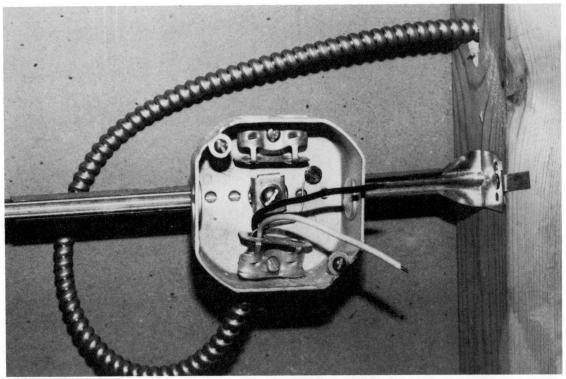

Fig. 13-52. Close-up of the ceiling box installation. Notice the adjustable mounting bracket. Nails and clips to keep bracket from going too far back in the wall overlap the studs. Clips can be removed when not needed. Notice the grounding wire under the green hex head screw in the bottom of the box.

through walls and ceilings. All wiring is concealed for appearance and protection.

A one-story dwelling is fairly easy to rewire because the attic and basement or crawl space should be accessible for work. The rewiring work can be done one section at a time or one circuit at a time. Not only should an old dwelling be rewired, but it should be updated and wired for today's needs. Be sure to allow for additional circuits not included in the old wiring system. Add three-way switches so that you can walk through the house without retracing your steps to turn lights on and off. In new dwellings, the outlets in the various rooms—even though they are located according to code requirements—are sometimes located at inconvenient spots. When doing rewiring, you now are able to locate the outlets where they are most convenient. Just remember to maintain minimum code requirements.

REPLACING THE OLD WIRING

Removing and rewiring work will tax your ingenuity a great deal. Some old wiring will have to be cut off as far as possible *inside* walls and pushed out of the way. There must be no possibility of the abandoned wiring contacting any of the new wiring. Reach in through where the old wires came out of the wall and cut them *inside* the wall itself. If Romex is used it will be stapled close to the old outlet location so that it cannot be pulled out. Cut it off.

Other routes may be horizontally through the studs and this also will be stapled. New cable will have to be run either up and over the attic or down and under the first floor if you are lucky enough to be working on a one-story dwelling. Refer to Fig. 9-16.

A two-story dwelling will give you other problems. Sometimes a pipe chase (opening through the top and bottom of a wall for drain pipes)

Fig. 13-53. Drywall in place on a mock-up ceiling. The person who cut the opening for the box did a poor job. Plaster will have to be used to patch this opening. The code requires that this be done.

Use a piece about 12 inches long. One end is bent with a hook in an L shape, but pointing a little back to the long end. The other end is formed into a handle for ease in holding. Make a hand-size loop. The center is formed as needed to reach inside a wall opening and retrieve the "mouse" hanging from the chalk line inside the wall.

Figure 3-8 shows how to make and use these items. The lead mouse is best because it is heavy for its size. A large nut could be used, but it might not go through holes bored in the framing or wall. To find studs in a finished wall, use a commercial stud finder or tap with a screwdriver or your knuckles. A long, slim nail pushed through drywall or plaster will locate studs if they are hard to locate otherwise.

Make a stud finder from a coat hanger wire. Form a loop handle and bend an angle on the other end. Push this through a nail hole in the drywall and rotate the bent end. This will hit a stud that is close and therefore locate it. Be sure to align the loop handle with the bent end so as to know which way the bent end is pointing. These small nail holes are easy to patch. Taking off the baseboard will sometimes help you locate studs. Make sure of your results before cutting a large opening for a wall box. Such holes are hard to patch.

When working alone, you will be running back and forth, dropping the mouse inside the wall and fishing for it below. Be sure to have enough length of cord for the mouse to hit the bottom of the wall inside the partition. When the mouse hits the bottom, raise it slightly so that the cord hangs free and does not lie against either inside surface of the hollow partition. Hold the mouse just free of the bottom by laying a weight on the cord at the upper end. Do not tie it. If you hook the mouse, you will be able to pull the mouse out from inside the wall without any trouble. If you tied the top end of the cord, you would not be able to pull out the mouse from the inside. At a greater distance back on the cord, tie it to something so the cord does not fall completely inside the wall. These things seem complicated in the telling of them but are very simple in actual practice.

Figures 9-17 and 9-19 show how to do these

can be used for cable. If you use a pipe chase, be sure that there are no heating pipes or ducts or even hot water pipes. This would increase the wire temperature and affect the insulation. Many times, access can be gained in closets and other hidden areas and cutting floor and ceiling openings will not affect the appearance of a regular room or need extensive redecorating.

When running concealed wiring, a person has to be resourceful and plan ahead. You might need to run three or more cables up from the basement to supply the second floor circuits. If you have to remove flooring, refer to Fig. 9-21. To "fish" cable up or down finished walls, you will need a chalk line at least 20 feet long or longer. You will also need a handmade "mouse" and a handmade "fish hook".

A mouse is made from 3 inches of ⅛-inch wire solder. The solder is bent back upon itself about 1 inch from one end and then a loop is formed and the rest is wound tightly around the 1-inch end so as to form a compact weight about 1¼ inch long and ½ inch in diameter.

The fish hook is made from coat hanger wire.

simple maneuvers. The fish hook might need to be bent in various shapes. Sometimes the hook itself is bent at various angles. Make very sure that your measurements are correct, because a 4-inch error can bring the hole in the ceiling of the room rather than inside the wall. When finishes such as paneling or wallpaper are to be installed, small error will be covered. It is best to work carefully and not make mistakes.

When you want only to modernize or extend your present wiring, this will still be "old work." Such a situation would be where a wall switch controls a wall outlet only. You might want to control a newly installed ceiling fixture from the present wall switch and leave the outlet hot all the time. Another way would be to make half of the outlet hot and the other half switch controlled. Many outlets are wired this way where there is no ceiling fixture in the room.

To remove a plastic switch box from the wall, remove the device from the box. The box will usually be nailed to the stud next to it. With a screwdriver, gently pry the box—side, top and bottom—from the stud enough to insert a hacksaw blade, less frame, between the box and stud. Saw both nails completely through and the box will now be loose from the stud. When you use a hacksaw be sure to put tape on the end you hold. Pull the box from the wall and remove the cables. You can now add additional cables or reroute those already there, depending on what you want to control.

When you are ready to replace the box, drill two holes in the side of the box to pass a No. 10 roundhead wood screw. Drill one hole ½ inch down from the box top and 1 inch in from the front edge. Drill another hole ½ inch from the box bottom and 1 inch in from the front edge. Now replace the box in the opening with the cables in place. Hold the box flush with the finished wall and drive two screws in the holes you just made in the box directly into the side of the stud. It is advisable to ground these screws just as if they were part of a metal box.

You can now connect the new wiring as you planned. Any openings in the boxes not used must be closed so don't open any more than you will be using. Openings in plastic boxes are hard to close.

This original plastic box may be replaced by a metal box and the screws holding the box to the stud would not have to be grounded. Be sure to patch the wall surrounding the box after replacing it in the opening. The metal box, if used will probably be smaller than the plastic box and will need patching. The code requires this.

COPPER SOLDERING TECHNIQUES

The soldering of copper splices has almost become a lost art because of the many devices for connecting wires to each other and terminals. Sometimes wires do have to be soldered. As in every soldering job, the material has to be heated and the solder then applied to the hot area (now referring to temperature and not being energized with electricity). If the material, wire, or whatever is heated high enough, the solder will melt and blend in with the material (copper in this case). To prepare the joint, make sure the wires are absolutely clean. Sometimes sandpaper works; usually a pocketknife is enough. Twist the wires together *tightly* because the code requires that the joint be mechanically *and* electrically secure without solder and then soldered. All splices and any other exposed current-carrying parts must be covered with an insulation equivalent to that used on the conductors themselves. Modern insulation, when removed from the wire, leaves a very clean surface.

I remember scraping and scraping the old fabric and rubber insulation from the wires before soldering them (there were no wirenuts then). Every joint had to be soldered. After soldering, the joint had to be taped with "rubber" tape, then the warm hand tightly gripped the tape to somewhat "vulcanize" it (weld it together, so to speak). Friction tape was added to hold the rubber tape in place.

Tape application methods were as they are now. Start at one end a half inch or so onto the insulated wire. Wrap round and round lapping the tape half onto the last turn. For a "pigtail" splice, continue past the soldered end, and then continue back toward the starting point. This method actually gives four layers of tape.

The new "plastic" electrical tape is a great improvement over the old two-tape method. It is faster and it sticks better. The disadvantage, discovered shortly after the plastic tape was introduced, was its extreme thinness, 8.5 mills (trash bags are 2 mills). Electricians not familiar with this property often did not tape the soldered joints with enough layers on the *end* of the pigtail joint. Often the tape would be scraped off this end, causing a short circuit. This condition is easily overcome by using care when taping. The old rubber tape was much thicker and did not cause this problem. When pushing a plastic taped joint back into a box, keep the end of the joint away from the box wall.

This discussion about soldering and taping should be reviewed again when you need to solder electrical wires; just tape your soldered connection with care. Generally you will use wirenuts.

Chapter 14
Special Projects

THERE ARE MANY IMPROVEMENTS AND ADDI-tions that will increase the value of a home. A homeowner will save on installation costs by doing the work himself and can save on heating and air conditioning operating costs. Figures 14-1 through 14-2 illustrate numerous products and projects.

REPLACEMENT OF THE PRESENT THERMOSTAT

The standard heating thermostat (*stat* in industry terminology) selling for about $20, can replace your present stat. It has the potential to save you money *two ways*. You can install it yourself and you can buy it at a discount. In addition, a new stat will operate the furnace more efficiently—saving fuel.

To get the most efficient operation from your equipment, the stat must be properly located. Evaluate the location of the old stat. Living room or family room locations are best. Hallways with good air circulation are the next best locations. If the stat is in a poor location, furnace operation will be af-fected and may cause longer or erratic furnace op-eration. This will cause needlessly higher fuel bills.

Cold drafts cause the same type of problem. This is why a stat must never be installed on an outside wall. For even more fuel economy you might want to buy and install a night set-back type stat.

The best stat on the market is the Honeywell Model T87-F. This three-wire stat can be used for heating only, cooling only, or both heating and cooling, depending on which *two* wires are used for one function. For both functions, three wires are used. So as not to confuse you, some old stats also had three wires (red, white and blue). Thermostat cable *is* color coded because this control work, as it is called, is very dependent on correct wiring, as is line voltage house wiring.

The old three-wire stat was for heating only and it is now obsolete; but it is still in use in many older homes. This stat is Series 10 (the T87-F is Series 80). If the Series 10 stat is controlling a relay that is operating a gas valve, oil burner, or hot water circulating pump, the relay will have three terminal screws: red (R), blue (B), and white (W).

To use the new T87-F, the R and B terminals

Fig. 14-1. Shows Honeywell T-8082A stat with cover in place.

must have a jumper wire connected between them. This can be a short *bare* piece of No. 18 stat wire. The old stats were the vertical *open contact* type Series 10. These stats are 4 inches high. The new T87-F, which is round, will not cover the area left by the old stat. Solutions vary from painting the bare spot or papering the bare area. If you are lucky, you will have a remnant of the identical paper. A very unattractive cover plate is available from Honeywell. It is about 5 inches round.

Fig. 14-2. Honeywell T-8082A stat cover removed to time setting pins and control mechanism.

Fig. 14-3. Close-up of heat anticipator scale and pointer for setting.

To proceed with the installation, first buy the stat. Try to find one in a sealed carton rather than one that has been opened and examined. Some small parts might have dropped out. Mounting screws and instructions are the loose parts. At home, shut off the furnace switch; this is usually on the side of the furnace cabinet. This switch should be plainly marked, "main furnace shut-off switch" so that it can be turned off in an emergency.

After you have turned the switch off, you can remove the old stat. The vertical model has one cover screw (top or bottom). Loosen this screw and take off the cover. The three terminal screws will be visible. Loosen them, straighten the wires off from the screws, and arrange them so that the stat can be pulled away from the wires and off the wall

(after removing the mounting screws). If the hole in the wall is open, stuff glass fiber insulation in it to prevent drafts from affecting the operation of the stat.

The new stat is round and there are level lines on the backplate that is to be mounted to the walls with the screws furnished. This backplate must be level because the stat has a small mercury-filled bulb that acts as the contact points instead of open contacts. If the stat is not level, the *set point* (degree mark, 68° F or 70° F, at which the stat pointer is set) will not reflect the actual *operating point* because of the stat being off level.

Use a small pocket level to give you the horizontal line. Level the base. While holding the base steady, mark the three mounting screw holes with a pencil. These holes are elongated on a curve to allow some adjustment. While still holding the base in place, recheck with the level. Measure twice; cut once. Remember? As an example, an opening cut in either drywall or plywood in the wrong place might cause you to have to use another new sheet of either material.

If you use a very small drill to drill into the drywall, you will not need screw anchors. Just use the screws furnished. For this type of drilling (small-size drill bits) in plaster and the like, I use the Yankee nickle plated push drill. This drill seems to always be part of telephone installers' tool kits without fail. It is very handy; mine is 40 years old, but it still works.

Mount the stat base on the wall and tighten the screws. You will have fed the three wires through the hole in the stat base. The red wire can be taped up and pushed back through the wall to get it out of the way. White and blue are the only ones used. Either wire goes on either terminal screw. It makes no difference. On other than two-wire stats, a color code is very, very important. After you have the base wired, mount the stat body on the base with its three captive screws.

The stat heat anticipator must be set according to the rating of the primary control. This control is usually a gas valve, relay or an oil burner control. The stat wires are connected to this control. The current rating of the control will be printed or

thermostats—single-stage

━━━━━━ T87F THERMOSTAT—THE ROUND ━━━━━━

PROVIDES TEMPERATURE CONTROL FOR 24 TO 30 VOLT RESIDENTIAL HEATING, COOLING, OR HEATING-COOLING SYSTEMS.

Features dustproof, spdt mercury switch, adjustable heat anticipator, and a 2- or 3-wire wallplate for heating only, cooling only, or heating-cooling systems with remote switching. Add a Q539 subbase in systems requiring system and fan switching at the thermostat location. Q539 also provides cooling anticipator. For T87F models designed to meet Department of Defense specifications, see page 111. Also see Thermostat Guards section, page 96, for THE ROUND WITH KEY LOCK COVER.

APPROXIMATE DIMENSIONS:

	Diameter		Depth	
	in.	mm	in.	mm
T87F	3- 1/4	82.6	1-1/2	38.1
T87F with 137421 Wallplate or Q539 Subbase	3-11/16	93.7	1-3/4	44.5

ELECTRICAL RATINGS:
Mercury Switch: Full Load—1.5 A; Locked Rotor—3.5 A at 30 Vac.
Adjustable Heat Anticipator: 0.1 A to 1.2 A.
Cooling Anticipator: 0 A to 1.5 A, 24 to 30 Vac.

REPLACEMENT PARTS:
104456B Wallplate Assembly, 2 terminals (heating only models). Includes terminal screws.

114854 Crystal, 1.9 in. [48.4 mm] dia.

114855-01370 Thermostat Cover Ring.

ACCESSORIES:
104994A Calibration Wrench.

129044A Adapter Plate Assembly. Includes 6 in. [152.4 mm] cover ring and adapter plate. For mounting T87F thermostat on outlet box and for covering old thermostat mounting marks.

137421A Wallplate for heating and cooling systems. For T87F without positive OFF. Includes spdt heating only (series 20) alternate terminal markings and cooling (also series 20) anticipator.

137421B Wallplate for heating and cooling systems. For T87F with positive OFF.

TG503A1000 Metal Thermostat Guard. Includes locking cover, backplate, and bracket for mounting on a standard size outlet box. Also includes 104456B 2-terminal Wallplate. Not for use with T87F mounted on 137421 Wallplate or Q539 Thermostat Subbase.

TRADELINE models. • *SUPER TRADELINE model.*

Order Number	Range[b]		Features	Includes
	F	C		
•T87F1859[a]	40 to 90	4 to 32	Replaces heating, cooling, and heating-cooling models (use Q539 for heating-cooling). Alternate series 20 terminal markings on 137421A Wallplate.	6 in. [152.4 mm] cover ring, 137421A 3-terminal Wallplate.
T87F1867	50 to 90	10 to 32	With positive OFF.	6 in. [152.4 mm] cover ring, 137421B 3-terminal Wallplate.
T87F2360	45 to 75	7 to 24	Limited set point range.	104456B Wallplate.
T87F2782	35 to 65	2 to 18	Heating only; limited set point range.	Locking cover and locking dial. Allen-head screws and wrench included for locking cover. 137421A 3-terminal Wallplate.
T87F2873	40 to 90	4 to 32	Concealed 2-terminal heating only wallplate.	104456B Wallplate.

[a]Use T87F1859 as a replacement for former TRADELINE model T26A1433 and T87C1252.

[b]Temperature scale in Fahrenheit on thermostat.

TRADELINE ━━━━━━

Fig. 14-4. The T87F round stat for heating only, cooling only, or heating-cooling systems (courtesy Honeywell Inc.).

180

Q539 THERMOSTAT SUBBASES

PROVIDES SYSTEM AND FAN MOUNTING AND SWITCHING FOR T87F THERMOSTATS.

Includes cooling anticipator and letter-coded screw terminals for electrical connections. Wide range of switching functions fits most cooling or heating-cooling applications. Electrical Ratings: 2 A at 24 Vac. Optional Indicator Lamp: 28 Vac. All Q539 subbases mount directly on wall. To mount on an outlet box, use 6 in. [152.4 mm] cover ring (included with some T87F models) or order 129044A Adapter Plate Assembly. Approximate Dimensions (with T87F): 3-11/16 in. [93.7 mm] dia., 1-3/4 in. [44.5 mm] deep.

REPLACEMENT PART:
129571 Filter Light.

TERMINAL DESIGNATIONS:a

Terminal	Connection
R	Transformer.
R_H	Heating transformer with isolated heat-cool circuits.
W	Heating relay or valve coil.
Y	Cooling contactor coil.
B,4	Heating damper (if used). Circuit only completed between R and B with system switch in heat position; "4" terminal is the same as Honeywell "B" terminal.
O	Cooling damper (if used). Circuit only completed between R and O with system switch in cool position.
G	Fan relay coil.
X	Clogged filter switch. Only available on subbase with malfunction light.
P	Heat pump contactor coil.
Z	Q539D,H—low voltage fan switch for control of fan relay in AUTO position for both heating and cooling control.

[a] R_1, W_1 and Y_1 are not marked on thermostat subbase. They are mounting posts and electrical connections for the thermostat.

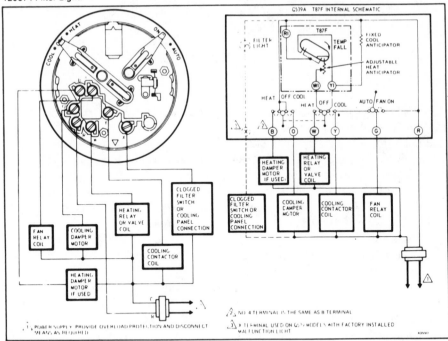

Typical hookup and internal schematic for Q539-T87F heat, cool, and heat-cool applications using common power supply.

continued next page

TRADELINE

Fig. 14-5A. Shows Q539 stat subbase for use with T87F stat. Includes wiring diagram (courtesy Honeywell Inc.).

Fig. 14-5B. Shows Q539 stat subbase for use with T87F stat.

stamped on the body and will be a number such as 0.2, 0.4, or 0.45. The heat anticipator is the scale with the small pointer directly under the mercury tube of the stat. The scale has markings corresponding to the primary control markings. Set the pointer at the control rating. Install the cover and set the stat at 68 degrees. Go downstairs and turn on the furnace switch. If the furnace does not start, the stat set point was lower than the room temperature and the furnace will not start. Gradually raise the set point until the furnace starts. Now leave the stat alone unless the setting is too high for your needs. Adjust the set point as you prefer. Monitor the new stat. Calibration is seldom needed. If it is needed, detailed instructions are furnished with the stat.

RELOCATION OF THE PRESENT STAT

The installation of a stat in a different location is the same as installing any new electrical device in a hollow wall. Select the new location bearing in mind the most suitable place. Drill a pilot hole down through *behind* the base shoe molding. Or drive a long, thin nail or spike. This will give the location for drilling up from the basement or crawl space. It is also necessary to either measure very carefully where to drill down from the attic if that is the way to go. What a way to go! Be careful not to step through the ceiling. The other way would be to also drill a very small hole at the point where the wall meets the ceiling. Drill upward at an angle similar to locating for the basement drilling. This hole is easily patched with spackling compound and will not be visible.

Stats are mounted five feet above the floor. Drill or pound a ½-inch hole in the drywall. It is easy to use a ⅛-inch wide screwdriver and your electrician's side cutters (pliers). Hammer the screwdriver handle with the pliers. This operation will hurt neither tool because the drywall is very soft.

If you have already drilled up or down to get inside the wall, drop a mouse (solder formed into a weight, tied to a cord) down from the stat hole or down from the attic. Fish out the mouse with the "fish hook" described in Chapter 13.

If the new location is farther from the furnace than the old location you might need more *thermostat* cable. This cable consists of three or more No. 18 copper wire in a covering similar to Romex cable. This added-on length may be spliced in the open. A junction box is not required for *low-voltage* wiring. You can also run all new cable if you prefer. If the cable is spliced use wire nuts. Always splice color to color if the individual wires have colored insulation. Very old cable might have all-black wires. Be sure to staple the cable so that it will not be damaged. Keep it close to the framing members.

Sometimes you will want to drill holes to run it through framing members. Keep it neat. Insulated staples are available at hardware stores.

NIGHT SETBACK WITH TWO STATS AND A TIMER

Using two stats and a time clock (timer) saves you money over the standard night setback stat sold in hardware stores and home centers. Stats cost about $15 to $20 and a timer costs about $25. The store price of the fancy model is usually $80.00 to $90. You will save on installation labor.

Your original stat can be used as the night stat and put in a hallway. The new stat is installed in place of your old one. Stat cable from each stat is brought to a common spot in the basement where the timer will be located. A hallway location for the night stat is desirable because two stats side by side

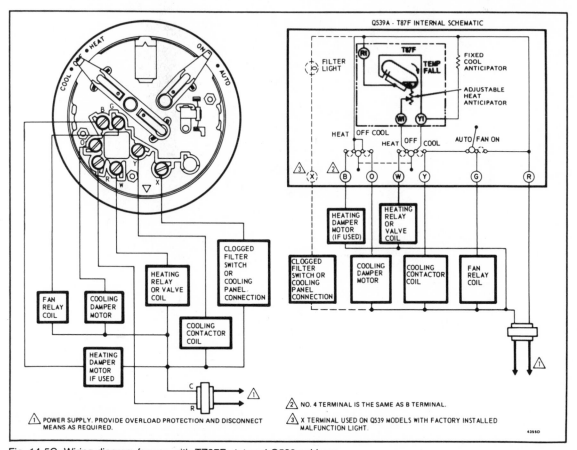

Fig. 14-5C. Wiring diagram for use with TZ87F stat and Q539 subbase.

Fig. 14-6. Timer for day/night changeover installed in home. Switches from day to night settings and back to day according to times selected (courtesy Intermatic, Inc.).

in the living room would look strange. This is up to you if you want them side by side; wires from both still must go to the timer. The installation of stats is described in Chapter 13.

You will need to modify the timer switching mechanism to isolate the *low* voltage (24 V) from the *line* voltage which is to operate the clock of the timer only. One wire between the two stats is broken by the timer contacts. The two stats are wired in parallel. The wire that is broken (disconnected) actually *disconnects* the day stat so that it cannot control the furnace. This action usually takes place at night.

The night stat is usually set at 6 degrees to 8 degrees below the set point of the day stat that is set at perhaps 68° F. This higher day set point keeps the night stat satisfied so that it never calls for heat. At a set time, the night stat is on its own

Fig. 14-7. Timer also used for night stat setback (courtesy Intermatic, Inc.).

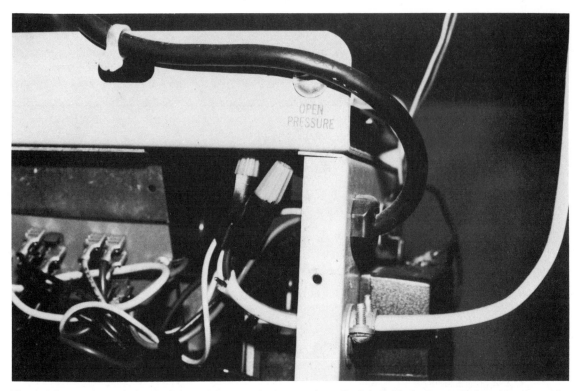

Fig. 14-8 Connection replacing the light on the garage door opener by a pilot light inside the house. Notice wire nuts and the Romex leaving the housing.

and does its job. It will keep the house at 60° F or whatever its set point is. At perhaps 6:00 AM, the *day* stat is reconnected in the circuit and then maintains the daytime 68° F temperature.

The timer you will have to use may or may not have to be modified. Intermatic Incorporated manufactures a timer that has the timer motor terminals isolated from the switching terminals. The timer is their Model T-101B(a). This would be ideal because no modification is necessary. This arrangement seems quite difficult, but in reality it is very simple. Usually a home improvement store will be able to order the Intermatic timer for you or an electrical wholesaler might sell you one.

One disadvantage with this type of system is that there is no visible clock on either stat. This might or might not be something that is desirable to you. Generally, timepieces are selected for their appearance and there is really no need for another one. The timer will have to be wired to a source of power that will not be interrupted at any time. This is a standard type of installation and is no different from the wiring of a receptacle. Just make sure that the power supply is uninterrupted.

Should a power interruption occur, you will have to reset the dial on the timer. Open the cover and turn the dial manually to the time of day. Check all timers for correct time of day occasionally as power outages at night may not show up unless you have an electric clock that has no battery carryover.

The day-night thermostat described in the following section does have the battery carryover feature. Other night setback stats are on the market. Some have expensive, exotic features that are not needed. Be a prudent buyer and buy the best you can afford, but always buy when on sale.

THE STANDARD NIGHT SETBACK STAT

Many manufacturers of controls offer night setback stats. I recommend the Honeywell T-8082A Fuel

Fig. 14-9. Toggle switch to disconnect door radio receiver on door operator when leaving for an extended time (vacation). Thus no other car transmitter will be able to open the door. A key switch must be installed to operate the door when this switch is turned off. This is low voltage (24 V). No box is needed.

Saver Thermostat. This stat comes complete with instructions. Be sure to wire all terminals correctly, color to color, or according to instructions.

The T-8082A stat has a carryover feature so that the clock continues to run in the event of a power outage. Figures 14-1, 14-2, and 14-3 show the complete stat with the cover removed. The anticipator scale pointer must be set as described in the previous section to match the amp rating of the primary control that it will operate. The instruction booklet provided is complete and it shows wiring diagrams for almost any stat to be replaced.

I recommend that any device purchased be thoroughly inspected before leaving the store. A defective device means a trip back to the store.

Save money by saving needless trips. Sometimes parts are broken or missing. If you find the stat OK, remove the shipping tabs. The stat will not operate with these in place.

Take your time, work carefully and accurately, and check your finished work. I once checked out from the company stock a new brass cock for a gas line shut-off use. After screwing it on the gas line, I tried to screw a nipple into the opposite end. That end had never been threaded at the factory. This forced me to drive to a wholesale supply house to obtain a new valve. You can be sure I inspected *both* ends of this second valve. This not only caused loss of time, but it made necessary the relighting of numerous pilot burners on other gas unit heaters. I probably lost over an hour by not inspecting the cock.

PILOT LIGHT TO INDICATE OPEN GARAGE DOOR

Garage doors on attached garages that are operated by remote control sending units in the car and from a push button inside the garage are sometimes open. An indicating pilot light will alert you to this condition. An open garage door after dark is an invitation to thieves to help themselves to items stored there. See Fig. 14-8.

Garage door operators usually light an integral light when the door is opened. This allows persons to get out of the car and remove packages in a lighted garage. Other door operators, after a short

Fig. 14-10. Double pilot lights. Left: garage ceiling light. Right: garage door open position indicator light.

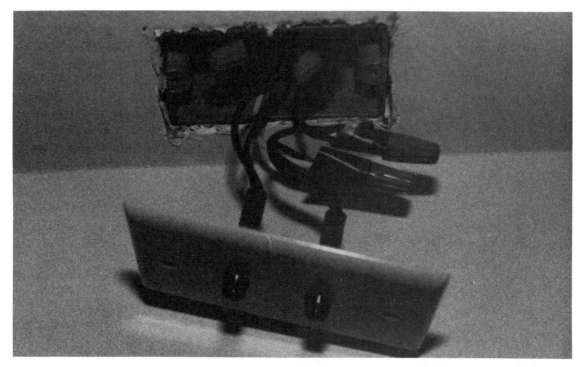

Fig. 14-11. Double pilot lights. These lights are each from different circuits. Therefore, each light has its own *two* wire circuits coming to it. Notice the four wirenuts protected by electrical tape.

time, turn off the light. Either the continuous light or the delayed turn-off light can be adapted to the pilot light installation.

To proceed with the installation, determine where you want to locate the pilot light. I have mine installed in the ceiling over the door to the garage. A convenient wall is also suitable. The logical place is where the light will be easily noticed. For the installation, you will need enough Romex to reach from the operator power unit to the pilot light location. Run this cable as you would any electrical circuit.

The cable should be run up to a ceiling joist or above the finished ceiling over to the light location. Leave enough at each end for proper connections. Also needed is a wall box and a cover. The cover plate will depend on the type of pilot you use. There are many types of pilot lights on the market:

■ The oldest type has a small (7½-watt) bulb and socket. These take up a whole wall box alone.

■ The interchangeable line (Despard brand)

Fig. 14-12. Garage door operator. This is a replacement, so the electrical outlet has been left hanging. As the owner, you would anchor the outlet or move it. The door operator mechanics were not electricians.

uses a 7½-watt, the same bulb that extends through the cover plate with a metal guard over it. A newer model of the same style uses a neon bulb and is flush with the cover plate.

■ A third type is sold by Radio Shack and is used in electronic equipment. It is rated at 120 V. I used this type for my lights. A blank plastic cover plate has to be drilled for this light. The light is pushed through a snug fitting hole in the plate and held by a metal friction ring on the back. The two leads are connected to the Romex wires in the box.

■ Another type uses a *duplex* receptacle and plate and a plug-in night light socket and bulb. One on the market is very small. It is about the size of a small attachment plug. The neon bulb is inside a clear plastic cover. This type is very convenient because the light is easy to change. Unplug and insert a new one.

Unplug the door operator from the ceiling receptacle, and then remove the cover from the power unit. Trace the leads (wires) from the light socket in the power unit to their connections at terminal screws or push-on connectors. If you want this light to continue to operate as before, you will have to splice into the leads *between* the socket and the terminals. Cut one wire at a time and splice in the Romex wires, white to white, black to black. Each color will have *three* wire ends to splice together with a wire nut.

Install the wall box and run the Romex to the operator power unit. There might be an unused knockout in the cabinet that you can use. If not, you will have to make one. Use a hole saw that is ⅞ of an inch in diameter. Be sure that there is nothing inside where you will be drilling. Use a Romex clamp in the knockout. Connect the Romex wires to the light leads or directly to the terminals if you don't use the light. Mount the pilot light wall box where you prefer and run the Romex into the box. Connect the pilot light you have selected and install the cover plate. Recheck all of your work carefully and make sure nothing is left undone.

Plug the door operator cord back in the receptacle. If the door is open, the light *should* come on. If not run the door closed. If nothing operates check the circuit. Use a bulb adapter to test the recepta-

cle. You should now know how to test fuses and circuit breakers. There really should be no problem.

If the door operator turns its light after a short period, you will be able to bypass this delay mechanism. If you cannot do this easily, it will be necessary to devise another means of energizing the pilot light. A limit switch can be installed on the door track at the far inside end where the *top* of the door stops. Mount the limit switch so that its lever is moved and closes its switch. Instructions with the switch explain how to make this adjustment. You can get power from the receptacle where the door operator is plugged in. The expensive item is the limit switch; the list price is about $18. You might be able to get a discount at the wholesaler or perhaps find one at a surplus store. Make sure the surplus store unit operates properly. The limit switch must have the terminals enclosed; the code requires this. Also check to see if the actuating arm *makes* contact when pushed and returns by spring action when released.

Wiring consists of a two-wire cable from the limit switch to the power source (junction box), and then to the pilot light. While most operators are

Fig. 14-13. Photocell mounted under eaves to control outdoor lighting.

Fig. 14-14. Water heater timer (supposed to save 33 percent on your electric bill). Courtesy Intermatic, Inc.

The "LITTLE GRAY BOX" ®

OFF ⟵ ⟶ ON

(UL) (CL)

MODEL NUMBER	SWITCH	VOLTS 60 Hz	AMPS. PER POLE INDUCTIVE
T103-20	DPST	125	40
T104-20	DPST	208-250*	40

For additional trippers, order No. 156T1978A.

ELECTRIC WATER HEATER TIME SWITCH
SERIES T104-20
- Can be set to shut electric water heater off during periods of your utility's peak power usage.
- Time switch can be automatically programmed to meet the needs of individual family.
- Save up to 33% of your water heating dollars by reducing hot water temperature and quantity.

Electric water heaters consume more energy than any other appliance. The average homeowner spends $216.00 per year on electric water heating costs (based on 4500 kilowatts per year, a utility rate of 4.8¢ per kilowatt hour). With energy costs on the rise, there is now a way to help you reduce water heating costs. The water heater, unless timer controlled, automatically maintains the hot water temperature set by the homeowner, night and day, whether needed or not. By automatically limiting water heater energy usage to those hours needed, the homeowner can reduce energy consumption and save money.

For maximum savings, set timer to turn on one hour in the morning and two hours in the evening. Set trippers to turn water heater on one hour ahead of expected morning and evening periods of major hot water usage. This will normally provide sufficient hot water for the average family and will cut the electric water heating bill by an average of 33%.

SPECIFICATIONS
CASE — Drawn steel 7¾" (19.7cm) high, 5" (12.7cm) wide, 3" (7.6cm) deep in gray finish. Spring hasp, with hole for lock, holds permanently attached side hinged door closed. Three mounting holes on back.

KNOCKOUTS — Combination ½" — ¾" nominal knockouts, one on back and each side of case, and two on bottom.

SPECIAL VOLTAGES AND CYCLES — All models 125v, 50 Hz; 250v, 50 Hz.

SWITCH RATING — 40 max. load amps. per pole, 35 amps. tungsten; 2 H.P., 125V. A.C. and 3 H.P., 250V. A.C.

Fig. 14-15. Water heater time specifications and time mechanism (courtesy Intermatic, Inc.)

plugged into a receptacle, some can be wired directly to the circuit. This is no problem when there is a junction box near the operator. You will find an unswitched circuit there from which to get power.

In addition to operating the door operator with the radio sender kept in the car, there might be times when you would like to close or open the door from outside the garage. When all family members are away, a neighbor might need to have access to the garage. In such a case, it is necessary to provide a key operated switch on the outside of the garage, usually on the door frame. Door operator manufacturers will furnish these key switches. To install a key switch, locate the wires from the inside push button (this closes or opens the door from inside the garage and out of the car). These wires will be in the garage attic or above the door track area. These will be *two* wires, singly or twisted together. Usually, a ¾-inch hole needs to be drilled for the key switch.

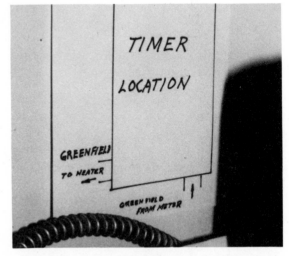

Fig. 14-16. Tentative location for heater timer. Insulated top in foreground. You might be able to have the Greenfield enter timer case from the rear, then leave the side of the case for the heater. Shown by lettering in photo.

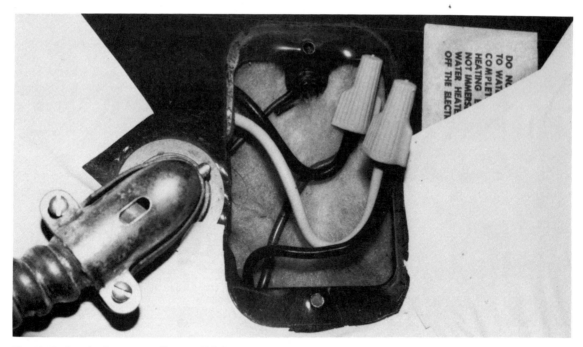

Fig. 14-17. Junction box on top of heater. This has no terminals (just pigtail joints). Be sure power is off before removing the cover plate. Ground wire is wrapped around screw, top center.

Because the voltage is low, the wires can be concealed in slots on the inside of the door jamb and led up to where the push-button wires are located. Pull the plug of the operator before working on the control wiring. This is to prevent the door from going up and down while you are working on the wires.

Drill the hole for the switch. Route the wires from the area of the push-button wires down to the push-button hole that you have drilled. You can use bell wire or thermostat cable. Cable is better because it has a heavy covering over both wires for protection. When concealing the cable (or wires), be sure they will be out of the way of any construction work done later in the garage. You might drive a nail and have the garage door operate.

Connect the wires to the two terminals of the switch. Push the switch back into the hole you drilled as you pull on the wires to take up the slack. No slack is needed here. Continue taking up the slack and keep the wires snug and hidden in their groove or whatever route you take. Staple where necessary.

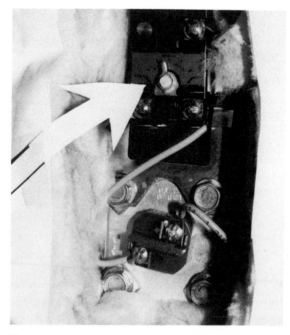

Fig. 14-18. Heater thermostat dial (under a cover plate). Cut off power before removing cover plate. Be careful. For cooler water move pointer away from "hot" to "warm."

Fig. 14-19. Built-in timer for such uses as attic fan, sun lamp, garage, or basement lights (courtesy Intermatic, Inc.).

When you have the new wires adjacent to the push-button wires, cut one push-button wire if you have slack enough to provide for a pigtail splice. Bare both cut ends, plus one end from the new key switch pair and make a pigtail splice of all three (making it tight with a wirenut). If you have no slack, then bare a 1½-inch section and make a tap splice. Solder it if you like (that's the best way) and tape the joint. Don't forget to do the other wire, it won't work with one wire.

GARAGE CEILING PILOT LIGHT

A pilot light can be housed in the same single-gang wall (ceiling) box as the door operator pilot. Consider doing this work when you are installing the door operator pilot light. All that is needed is one length of 14-2 with ground cable from the ceiling light junction box to the pilot light wallbox. Two original *large size* pilot lights will not fit in a single-gang box. Use a two-gang box or use one of the small pilot light devices. Keeping this light off will save money.

PILOT LIGHT ADDED TO EXISTING SWITCH

A room or area that has the light switch remote from that room, such as outside a closed door, should have a pilot light to indicate when that light is on. This will save money. Likely areas would be the basement or attic. Both these areas often have the switch located in the hallway outside adjacent a closed door to that area. Two arrangements are possible. If the present switch is visible and is *outside* the area, it can be combined with the pilot in the existing single-gang box. This is a combination device and it costs about $5. The price is not too bad considering you will gain a toggle switch. This combination uses the standard duplex receptacle cover.

The second arrangement is where the switch is not visible or is inside the area. This condition will call for another wall box to be installed outside the area in a visible location. In this case, you will have to run a length of two-wire grounded cable from the light fixture in the room out to the pilot light location. Save money, basement and attic lights are notorious for being left on—all night.

Another area where lights are left on is the front and rear outdoor entrance lights. This is most often very easy to do because the switch is at the door and is ready-made for this change (both the "feed" and the "load" to the outdoor light). There can be a second switch for an inside hall light. These two switches may be in a single-gang box or a two-gang box. A single-gang box poses the problem of assembling a *three* device interchangeable assembly. While this will crowd the box some, it should not exceed the limit of wires. Two switches in a *two*-gang box is the perfect condition as the inside switch is left and the outdoor switch is exchanged for the switch pilot light combination. You will use a switch-duplex receptacle plate.

CONTROL OF OUTDOOR LIGHTING

Control of outdoor lighting can be accomplished by turning it off by hand, a clock timer switch, and by a photocell. In each case, the wiring is the same, but the operation of each control differs. The photocell turns the lights on at dusk and off at dawn. The timer turns the lights on and off at the times you select. Because dusk and dawn vary during the year, it is necessary to move the settings to correspond to these changes. One special time control called the "astronomical" timer does this for you, but it will

Fig. 14-20. Portable timer with cord and attachment plug and built-in receptacle. Has many uses on the farm and home. Controls protable heaters and other portable appliances. Courtesy Intermatic, Inc.

Fig. 14-21. Eight-day timer to control heating or air conditioning, usually commercial. Can be programmed to skip selected days, plus different on and off settings each day. Courtesy Intermatic, Inc.

also cost you, $45 and up. The standard timer is $18. The photocell is about $15. So the astronomical timer is at a serious disadvantage—the "astronomical" price! Timers have a more positive action, but the photocell is entirely satisfactory for the homeowner. Just buy the best you can afford. Many inexpensive photocells are erratic in operation and flash on and off, disturbing neighbors if not the owner.

You might not now have any outdoor lighting except for the decorative lights at the front entrance and side or rear doors. This lighting can be left as is or expanded to include side floodlights or other all-around lighting for security reasons. If you plan on installing extensive security lighting or just mainly decorative lights, decide on a layout and locate the positions for the fixtures. Spot lights on the front corners that shine along the four outside

PRODUCTS TO CONTROL ENERGY

INTERMATIC®
photo controls

MODEL K1731

| MODEL | WATTS | | AMP. BALLAST | VOLTS |
	Tungsten	Ballast*		
K1731	1800	1000	8.3	120

*Ballast wattage rating shown is based upon 50% power factor.

MODELS
K4021
K4024
K4022
K4033
K4035

5 YEAR WARRANTY

MODEL K4321

| MODEL | WATTS | | AMP. BALLAST | VOLTS | FORMERLY |
	Tungsten	Ballast*			
K4021	1800	1000	8.3	120	K7341
K4024	2000	1700	8.3	208	—
K4022	2000	2000	8.3	240	—
K4033	3000	2300	8.3	277	—
K4035	3000	4000	8.3	480	—
K4321†	1800	1000	8.3	120	K7351

†Wall plate included.
*Ballast wattage rating shown is based upon 50% power factor.

MODELS
K4121
K4124
K4122
K4133

5 YEAR WARRANTY

| MODEL | WATTS | | VOLTS | FORMERLY |
	Tungsten	Ballast*		
K4121	1800	1000	120	K2011-9
K4124	2000	1700	208	—
K4122	2000	2000	240	K2013-10
K4133	3000	2300	277	K2313-10

*Ballast wattage rating shown is based upon 50% power factor.

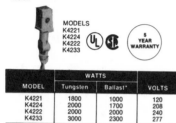

MODELS
K4221
K4224
K4222
K4233

5 YEAR WARRANTY

| MODEL | WATTS | | VOLTS |
	Tungsten	Ballast*	
K4221	1800	1000	120
K4224	2000	1700	208
K4222	2000	2000	240
K4233	3000	2300	277

*Ballast wattage rating shown is based upon 50% power factor.

MODELS
K4521
K4524
K4522
K4533

5 YEAR WARRANTY

| MODEL | WATTS | | VOLTS | FORMERLY |
	Tungsten	Ballast*		
K4521	1800	1000	120	K1231
K4524	2000	1700	208	K1231B
K4522	2000	2000	240	K1231C
K4533	3000	2300	277	K1231D

*Ballast wattage rating shown is based upon 50% power factor.

MODELS
K1121
K1122

| MODEL | WATTS | | VOLTS |
	Tungsten	Ballast*	
K1121	1500	1500	105-130
K1122	1500	1500	210-240

*Ballast wattage rating shown is based upon 50% power factor.

MODELS
K1221
K1222

| MODEL | WATTS | | VOLTS |
	Tungsten	Ballast*	
K1221	1000	1800	105-130
K1222	1000	1800	210-240

MODEL K122 POLE BRACKET ADAPTER —
For use with K1200 Series twist lock, plug, type controls.
*Ballast wattage rating shown is based upon 50% power factor.

MODEL
K1611

| MODEL | WATTS | | VOLTS |
	Tungsten	Ballast*	
K1611	1000	1000	105-130

*Ballast wattage rating shown is based upon 50% power factor.

Fig. 14-22. Different types of photo controls (courtesy Intermatic).

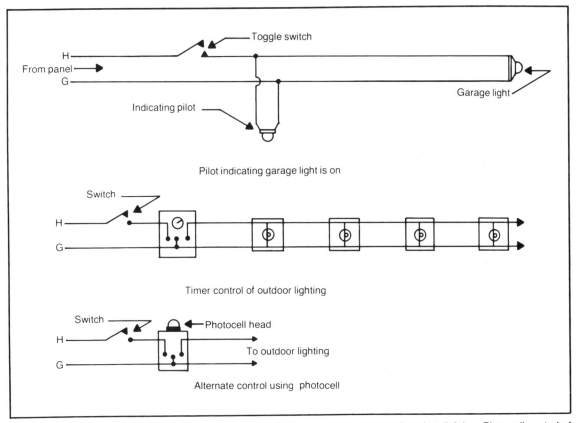

Fig. 14-23. Installation of pilot light to indicate the garage light is on. Timer control of outdoor lighting. Photocell control of outdoor lighting.

walls can be either fed from the attic at each corner or light colored non-metallic cable (Romex) can be run under the eaves to the various fixtures. Use type NMC cable (waterproof) and keep the fixtures *under* the eaves. Use the special waterproof boxes and covers to mount the outdoor sockets. You can also use thinwall tubing (EMT), but that is expensive and not necessary.

The installation of the photocell or timer is very easy. In effect, both devices are switches, as is a stat. The timer should be mounted inside to prevent vandalism or damage. There are timers in weatherproof cases, but do not use them. They are not necessary and they are more expensive. If your outdoor lighting was installed sometime ago, it will have a manual switch to turn it on and off. The timer must go between this switch and the outdoor lighting. This also applies to the photocell location. This

is the sequence: power supply, switch, timer (or photocell), lighting.

By its nature, the photocell must be installed outdoors. The north side is preferable but not necessary. As it senses light, it *must not* be facing any lights such as other controlled outdoor lighting, traffic signals or street lights. Any light "seen" by the cell will cause erratic action.

Figure 14-13 shows a cell mounted facing south; it has always operated satisfactorily even though it is close to the adjoining house. This installation could have been improved by mounting the handy box tight to the wall or by using a wall box and recessing it flush to the wall. The cell is mounted by means of an adjustable swivel to aim the cell away from lights. The swivel mount is attached to a "blank" handy box cover that has had a knockout opening punched in it by a Greenlee brand knockout punch. These punches come in all sizes. You might like to buy the ½-inch and ¾-inch sizes for your own use. They are much handier than a hole saw and not much more expensive. The hole saw has more uses. Once you buy the mandrel, all size blades (up to a limit) will fit on it. The knockout punch will only punch thin metal such as junction boxes and panels.

ELECTRIC WATER HEATER TIMER

Installing this timer will save you money. Water heaters can be cycled so that water necessary for household use is heated, but the rest of the time is not kept hot. As much as a 33 percent saving on energy costs can be realized.

Some utilities such as where I live have the water heater on its own meter and the rate is different from the power rate. Power to the heater can be interrupted by a radio signal from the utility. A special device is next to heater electric meter. If your heater has such a device, you should question the utility about times when power is cut off by radio. Other utilities have their own timers (outside).

If you have made the decision to install the timer on your water heater, first buy the timer. They cost about $30. You will also need two more Greenfield connectors because you will cut the present Greenfield to allow it to go into the timer case. From there, it will go to the heater junction box. If you can visualize the layout, you will be able to tell if the connectors should be straight or angle. You could get two of each. The timer must have a 40 A rating; most do if they are sold for heaters. Locate a spot near the heater so that the Greenfield will attach to the case easily.

Turn off the power to the heater. Next, test to see if the power really is *off*. Lock the breaker or remove the fuses and take them with you. Be safe.

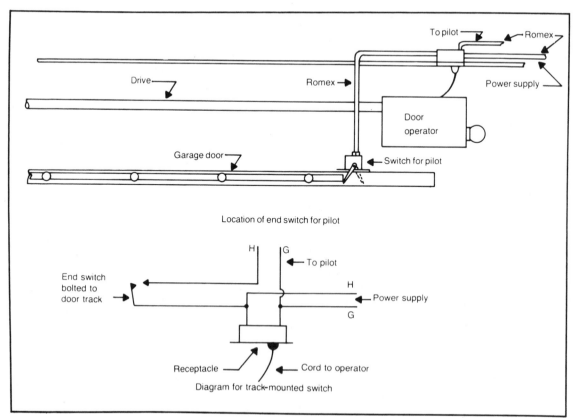

Fig. 14-24. Location of end switch for "door open" pilot light. Wiring diagram for track-mounted switch.

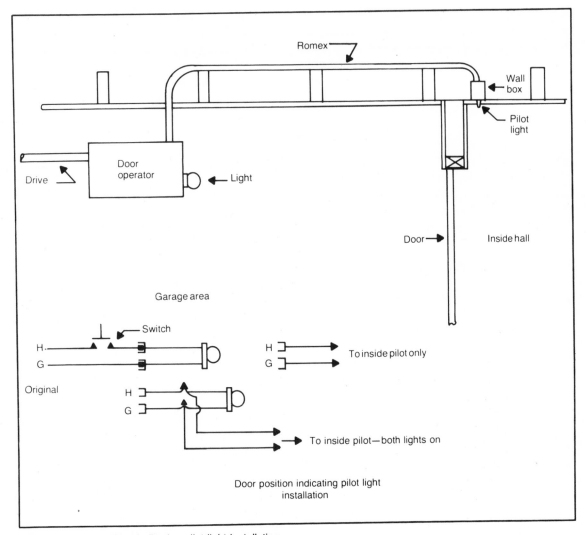

Fig. 14-25. Door position indicating pilot light installation.

To disconnect the wires from the heater, remove the cover plate. This is either on the actual top or near the top on the rear side. The wires from the distribution panel will end at screw or nut terminals in the small area under the access plate. Some heaters have an external octagon box as a terminal cover. Other heaters just have wire nuts.

Be careful when loosening the terminals because they might be corroded and you might break some plastic part. Measure and cut the Greenfield. Make sure you saw at right angles to the spiral and not straight across the length. You should attach the box connector before cutting for a more accurate measurement. If you have enough length left, you can use this piece to go from the timer case to the heater. Sometimes the wires in the Greenfield will be long enough; other times they will be too short. It is better to buy 10 or 15 feet of No. 10 copper and have enough slack to make proper connections. Allow for neat loops rather than tight, short connections.

Basement heaters will have the wiring coming from the ceiling. In this case, you should be able to install the timer by the distribution panel and connect it by means of an offset nipple. You will not have to touch the heater connections. First-floor heaters usually have the Greenfield coming out of the wall. In this case see the preceding paragraph. If you need extra wire, use black for the hot and grounded wires.

Paint the grounded wire white at both ends or put on tape. Strip the insulation for the equipment ground wire. Use white wire if you can buy it. When you install the box connectors, be sure to tighten the locknuts securely to complete the equipment

ground continuity of the metal housing and Greenfield.

Remember, if you have a 230-V water heater you will *not* have a white wire; you will have two black wires and one bare wire for grounding the noncurrent carrying parts such as the timer case, Greenfield, etc. A 115-V heater will have one black wire, one white wire, and one bare wire.

When you have rerouted the Greenfield, you can now pull the wires in. In the timer, the terminals will be marked "line 1, load 1; line 2, load 2." Line is

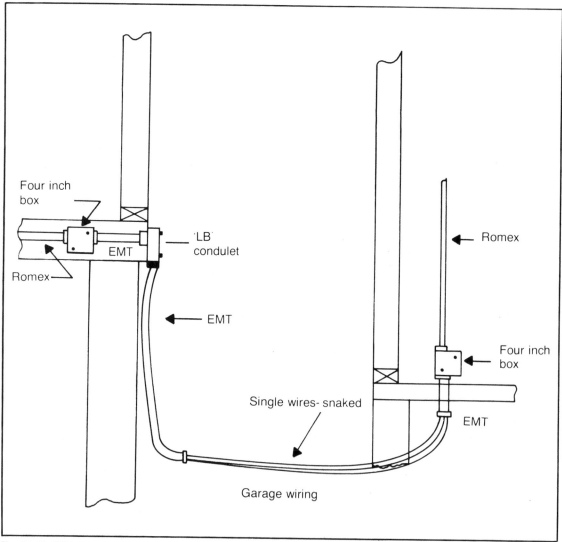

Fig. 14-26. Wiring a garage by running the feed wires underground.

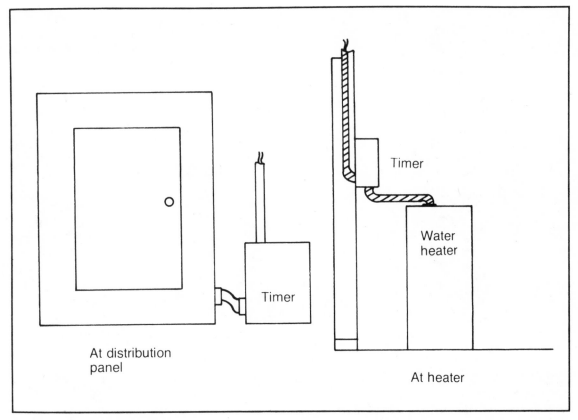

Fig. 14-27. Locating a water heater timer.

from the power supply and load is to the current using device (in this case the heater). Do not try to skimp on either the Greenfield or the wires. Buy more rather than try to make do. Route the wires neatly in the timer case with a nice "S" loop.

If everything is OK, restore the power (put the fuses back or turn ON the breaker). Check for power at the heater and timer. There is an off-on lever for manually operating the timer. Do *not* use this lever to disconnect power from the circuit. Use the fuses or breaker to disconnect power, *always!*

The on-off lever may be in the OFF position. While this lever is OFF, set the time of day and the on and off trippers to the times you want the heater to be ON and OFF. Usually two ON periods, morning and evening, are sufficient for the average family. Figures 14-14 and 14-15 show a representative timer. The mechanism is removable for installation purposes or for replacement. Now you will be sav-

ing money on your electric water heater operating expense. One additional money saver tip is to install a water heater insulating blanket on the outside of your heater. You can feel the difference just by touching.

WIRING A DETACHED GARAGE OR OUTBUILDING

Even though many garages are now attached to the house (a great convenience), there are thousands set back in the rear of lots, separate from the house. They sit in the dark, unlighted. Save money; wire your own garage. An outbuilding should be wired underground. This eliminates low overhead wires with their dangers and maintenance Use underground cable type UF (underground feeder).

I recommend 3 No. 10 UF cable to your garage or outbuilding. Try home improvement centers and hardware stores for the cable. Near where I live there is a "pipe and supply" company (actually a

Fig. 14-28. Key operated switch for garage door operator. This is a must when radio control is turned off. See Fig. 14-9.

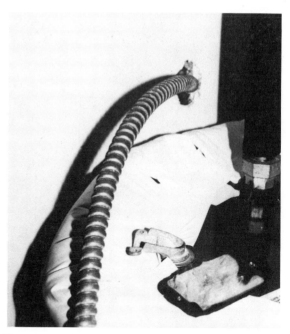

Fig. 14-30. Greenfield has been pulled from connector.

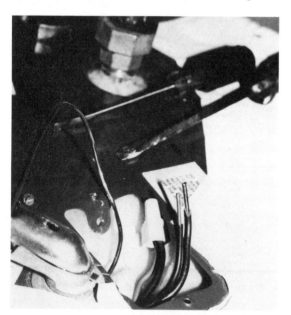

Fig. 14-29. Installing timer on electric water heater. Start of job; leads have been disconnected from water heater wires in junction box.

Fig. 14-31. After pulling Greenfield from wall, wires are found to consist of No. 10 Romex with ground (bare) the white wire is from the Romex. Wires leaving box are all black. Black bracket in upper part of box is the spring door latch of the cover. Mechanism of timer has been removed to allow wiring to be installed.

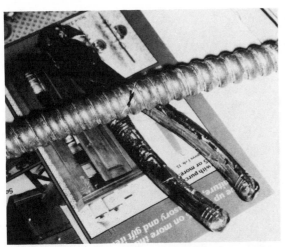

Fig. 14-32. Hacksaw cut in Greenfield. Two parts will be twisted to separate them. Shorter length is now needed.

Fig. 14-34. The installation is complete; the fiber cover is over the live terminals and the tripper fingers are set for on at 3:45 P.M. and off at 7:00 P.M. This is an experimental setting and is in my residence to see the shortest on time to provide enough hot water supply.

Fig. 14-33. Mechanism has been installed and wiring is connected to the correct terminals. Note the white wire on the far right terminal post; This wire is "hot" and it is so identified by black electrical tape. This is the Romex white (grounded) wire. The supply from the meter comes to the far left and far right terminals. The load to the water heater is taken off from the two center terminals. The time of day is 2:00 P.M. Note the pointer. The ground wires are connected to the box screw in the center.

Fig. 14-35. The installation of wall fixtures where the attic is inaccessible due to low eaves at this point. Power for the fixtures is from the double switch box having one switch for the outside light and the dimmer knob for the wall fixtures. Arrows show routing of Romex cable.

Fig. 14-36. Arrow shows route of cable from outlet box towards double switch box.

Fig. 14-38. Cable has been fished through wall spaces and around bottom of stud.

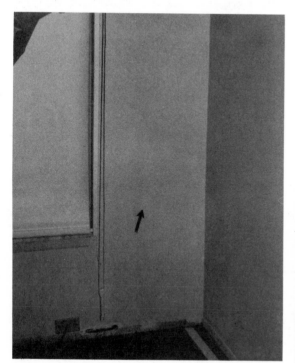

Fig. 14-37. Cable route to right fixture. Note below the cable notch in the plaster of drywall with cable showing.

Fig. 14-39. Metal plate has been applied to cover cable. Plate must be 1/16-inch thick.

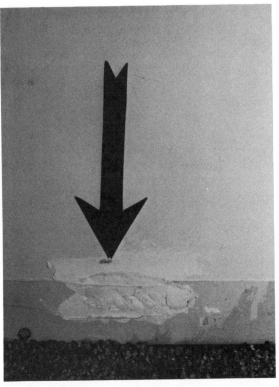

Fig. 14-40. Plate and hole have been covered with patching plaster. Note line where baseboard has been. Plaster will have to be painted above baseboard.

Fig. 14-42. Cable is covered with 1/16-inch plate of steel.

Fig. 14-41. Second place where cable goes around bottom of stud. To the left is the cable TV connection plate. Object above cable is traverse drapery cord holder.

Fig. 14-43. Plastering is completely ready for baseboard.

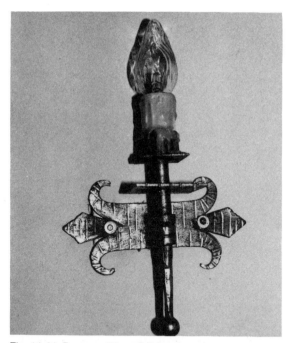

Fig. 14-44. Because this wall fixture base is very narrow, a partition box is used. The box is 1 5/16 inches wide by 1 ⅝ inches deep by 3 ¾ inches long. The cubic capacity is 6.5 inches. A special handy box, 1½-inches wide by 1½ inches deep by 3 ¾ inches long, could also be used. Raco makes these.

large hardware store) that has everything the homeowner could want in electrical supplies. In such a place you will be able to buy the length you need. Be sure to buy enough. Splices are prohibited underground.

The No. 10 three-wire cable allows you to have 230-V power in the building. This allows you to operate power tools with little voltage loss. This cable *must* have overcurrent protection (fuses or breakers) at the *starting point*. This means at the distribution panel in the basement or other location. Use 30-A overcurrent protection in the *house* panel. If you use 30-A protection there, you will need to install a fuse/breaker panel in the outbuilding to protect the smaller wires used there.

If you do not want to have a fuse/breaker panel in the building and are using No. 12 or 14 Romex, protect this circuit at the house. It must be protected by 20-A or 15-A overcurrent devices respectively. You can also use No. 12 three-wire UF cable

and fuse it in the house panel at 20 A. Then the whole length of the circuit will be protected by one fuse/breaker.

If you use No. 10 UF cable underground and provided protection for 30 A, you must also use No. 10 Romex or BX between the distribution panel in the basement and the junction box at the outside wall where the UF cable starts. If you protect the UF cable with only 20 A, then use No. 12 Romex or BX in the basement. Never over fuse *any* part of a complete circuit. As the smallest wire is the weakest link, the overcurrent protection must protect the weakest part. The weakest link in any circuit *must* be the fuse or breaker. This is the fail-safe link; its duty is to fail when needed.

The code requires that where underground cable rises out of the ground it be protected with conduit or thinwall (EMT). The method used is to run conduit through the house wall from a junction box mounted on the side of a joist (this is to make the change from other types of cable to the underground UF cable).

On the outside is a special fitting called a Condulet. The position of the openings in this Condulet is designated by letters, in this case LB, meaning L=left; B=back (angle fitting, back outlet, and bottom outlet). See Fig. 14-26. This LB is connected to the conduit with the compression connector (part of the Condulet).

Another piece of conduit is attached to the downward pointing opening in the Condulet and arranged to go down into the ground at least 12 inches. This piece can be straight or have a sweep 90 degree bend pointing toward the outbuilding. A bushing must be on the end that is in the ground. The trench must be at least 12 inches deep. Snake the cable in the trench. Do not pull it taut. This might look sloppy, but it prevents tension on the cable that could damage it.

All wiring must be neat and must not be stretched out taut. Many persons when wiring receptacles or switches leave *no* slack even for pulling the device out of the box (they must have wired the device, then gone around to the back of the box and pulled the device into the box by pulling on the Romex cable. I have seen devices that looked

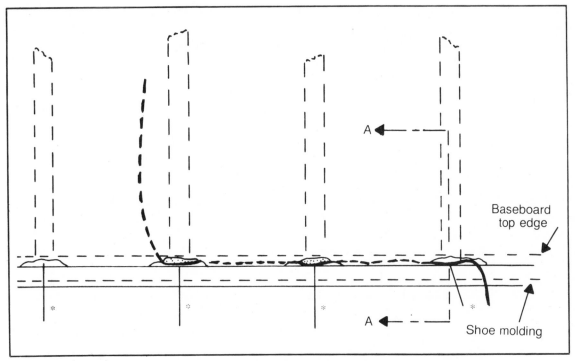

Fig. 14-45. Cable routing for two wall fixtures. This type of "old work" is customary in finished buildings.

exactly like this. It would take a feat of magic to disconnect such a device!

Wiring the garage is just like wiring any building that does not have the inside finish on the studs (some garages do have drywall on the studs). You will want two or more ceiling lights, depending on the positioning of vehicles, and perhaps a workbench to the side or rear. If you intend to build a shop in the garage or other building, do run No. 10 copper wire (cable) all the way from the distribution panel in the basement to a fuse panel in the garage. Use No. 10 three-wire interior Romex and No. 10 three-wire UF cable in the ground.

Two or more receptacles over the workbench should be installed. A neat way to do this is to use handy boxes with short (2-foot) lengths of ¾-inch thinwall with appropriate box connectors separating the boxes. This will give you six receptacles over the workbench.

You can even have two separate circuits in this arrangement. To do this install four boxes and three conduit lengths. Put alternate receptacles on dif-

ferent circuits. Separating the individual outlets on the duplex receptacle is unnecessary and I recommend boxes 1 and 3 on one circuit and boxes 2 and 4 be on another circuit. If you have a 230-V appliance or welder, provide a special 230-V receptacle for this. An electric dryer 230-V receptacle will be ideal for this application. Be sure to buy a receptacle with the correct configuration such that no attachment plug for an appliance intended for 115 V only is able to be plugged into this receptacle.

Fuse panels are sold with the fuseholders already installed. Breaker panels are bare (service-entrance panels usually have the main breaker). Buy either type panel so that you will have space for four circuits: two for the 230-V circuit and the other two for two 115-V circuits.

Save money. I had been looking for a two-position breaker cabinet. Prices ran from $12 to $14. I did not buy because I was in no hurry. Later, in a local retail hardware store, I found exactly what I wanted—Sylvania brand at $8.39 (brand new).

Be sure what you buy has the UL label and is in

new or in perfect condition. Find out if you can return the item if necessary. Circuit breakers should always be purchased brand new in order to eliminate trouble. It would be better if for the 230-V circuit the breaker would be "two-pole" with both handles bar-tied together (both poles of the 230-V circuit trip at once). This type will take two spaces in the cabinet. One pole breaker comes in ½-inch thick and 1-inch thick sizes. My preference is the 1-inch breaker. It even *looks* stronger!

Garage builders sometimes provide a piece of curved ¾-inch conduit coming up through the concrete floor, through the plate, and up into the stud space of the wall. This allows underground wiring to the garage without the need for an arrangement such as at the house end. Install a bushing at the below-grade end of the thinwall and mount a 4-inch junction box on the end inside using a box connector. I had this arrangement in a garage of mine. From this box, I ran thinwall up to a 4-circuit fuse panel.

AUXILIARY POWER SUPPLY

The use of auxiliary power has become more prevalent as certain electrically operated equipment necessary for life support and back-up facilities is being used. This equipment is not only used in hospitals and nursing homes, but also in private homes. For such equipment to be dependable, it must have a constant power supply. Such a power supply can be provided by an auxiliary power source.

Auxiliary power, or as it is sometimes called, standby power is generally available as a portable generator. Such a system consisting of the generator, a transfer switch, and the related wiring can be installed, by you, for about $1500 to $2000. Units range in capacity from 1350 W to 5000 W for this price. Because the setup is basic, greater wattage does not increase the cost in proportion. Therefore, you might want to buy a greater-capacity system. Wiring is simple. The running of the conduit or thinwall is the hardest part of the job. The standby

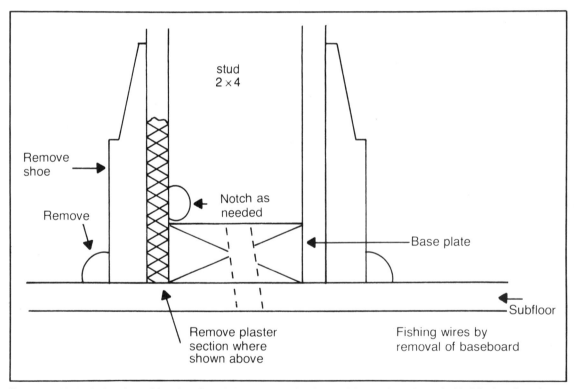

Fig. 14-46. Method of routing cable, when the attic is not accessible, by notching studs or plaster behind the baseboard area.

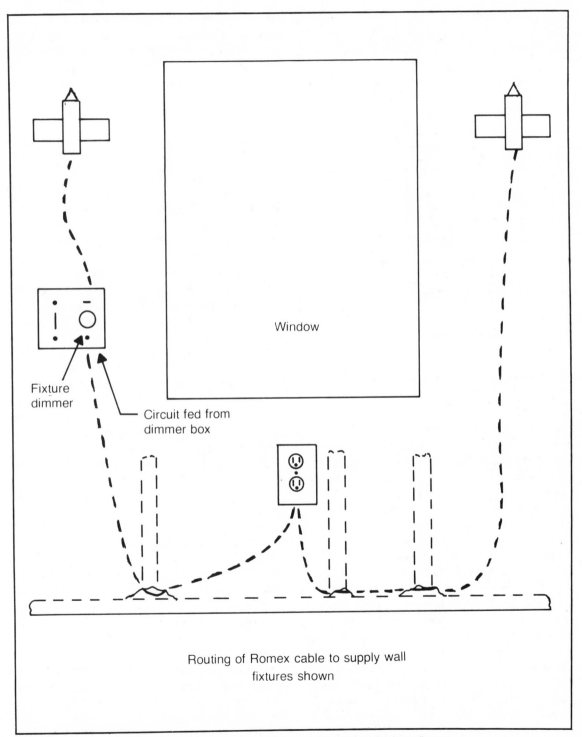

Window

Fixture
dimmer

Circuit fed from
dimmer box

Routing of Romex cable to supply wall
fixtures shown

Fig. 14-47. Layout of cable run to supply power to wall fixtures and control them by a dimmer.

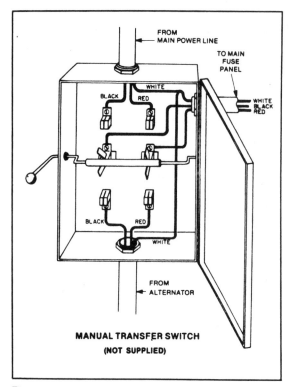

FROM
← MAIN POWER LINE

TO MAIN
FUSE
PANEL

WHITE

BLACK   RED

WHITE
BLACK
RED

BLACK   RED

WHITE

FROM
← ALTERNATOR

MANUAL TRANSFER SWITCH

(NOT SUPPLIED)

Fig. 14-48. Manual transfer switch to transfer house wiring from utility to standby generator.

connection box and cord are on the outside near the meter (as is the standby generator location).

The wires and conduit from the connection box lead inside to *near* the service-entrance equipment (as do the wires and conduit from the utility meter). Both supplies, the standby power and the utility power, terminate at a *transfer switch* in a cabinet. This transfer switch can connect *either* the standby or the utility power to the service-entrance equipment, but not both at the same time.

Even though the generator is not operating, it is illegal to connect both power sources to supply power to the service-entrance equipment *without* providing a transfer switch. If the standby generator is operating *without* a transfer switch to separate the two power sources, power will be fed to the utility's lines with the possibility of electrocution of a lineman who might be working on the lines of the utility. See Figs. 14-48 and 14-49.

The auxiliary generator can be portable, to be

wheeled outdoors when needed, and the system can be plugged into the generator receptacle by means of a flexible cord. If the generator is to be used inside a building, the exhaust *must* be piped to the outside to eliminate any chance of carbon monoxide seepage into the building during operation.

If the generator is to be permanently connected it can be either inside or outside. An outside generator needs protection from vandalism and theft. This should take the form of a cage and perhaps lighting.

If a small-capacity system is installed, only certain loads may be connected to the system. The connected load might be the heating plant, refrigerator/freezer, a few lights, and a sump pump or well pump. These few circuits should be fed from a *separate* distribution panel to make it easy to connect as a separate entity directly (through the transfer switch, of course) to the standby generator. *Caution:* In any event, no auxiliary power may be connected to wiring supplied with power from a utility *unless* connected through a transfer switch. See Figs. 14-48, 14-49, and 14-50.

If the generator set is to be permanently installed, a concrete pad should be made. This pad should be 4 inches larger all around than the generator base. This allows an area for the concrete anchors to be installed with no cracking of the concrete near its edges. Securely fastening down the generator in this manner will help prevent theft.

The connection box will be of weatherproof construction because it is to be mounted outside. The connection plug should be four-wire 240 Vac if your generator is to supply 240 V. If the generator supplies 120 Vac, the plug will be three-wire 120 Vac. Be sure the assembly is of weatherproof construction. All wiring including conduit or thinwall requires standard construction methods. You may need to rent a bender to bend the thinwall. Rigid conduit, long-sweep elbows can be purchased. Three, at the most, might be needed. These elbows are connected to conduit lengths by means of conduit couplings. You will also need LB condulets, offset nipples, straight nipples, and other common fittings.

Small-capacity generating systems are arranged for pull starting similar to a lawn mower or garden tractor. These small systems are strictly manual and cannot be retrofitted to operate automatically. Because these systems are not designed for heavy loads, a simple manual changeover arrangement can be installed. This method requires two 50 A three-pole, four-wire electric range cord sets. Each set consists of a cord with two No. 6 and two No. 8 conductors. These cord sets come in 3-, 4-, and 6-foot lengths.

In addition you will need two 50 A three-pole, four-wire range receptacles (outlets). This small, simple system will handle *only* essential needs. You will have to decide what loads are absolutely necessary. These loads are:

■ The heating system.

■ In rural areas, the well pump and related accessories.

■ The refrigerator/freezer.

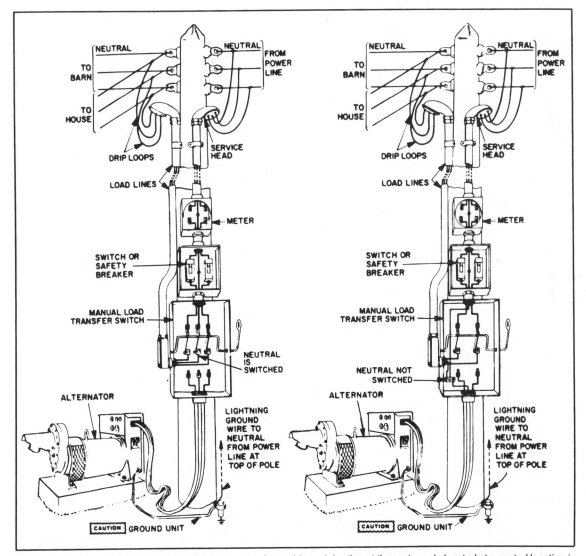

Fig. 14-49. Wiring diagram for connecting generator to farm wiring originating at the meter pole located at a central location in the farm yard.

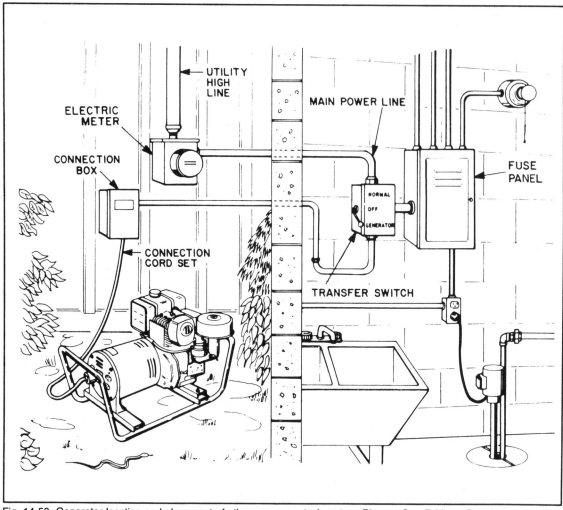

Fig. 14-50. Generator location and placement of other components (courtesy Pioneer Gen-E-Motor Corp.)

If a "life support" system is to be operated from this standby generator system, then its connected load must also be considered when calculating the total connected load to the generator. A 25 percent excess capacity should be added for safety.

Assemble the installation in this manner. Mount a four-circuit breaker/fuse panel adjacent the main distribution panel. Do not connect this four-circuit panel to the main panel. Install next to the main panel one of the 50-A range receptacles in an appropriate metal box. Connect this box to the main panel by a 1¼-inch nipple, locknuts, and

bushings. You might be able to get an offset nipple to make an easier connection.

Using No. 6 stranded copper wire, connect the appropriate terminals on the receptacle to the bottom ends of the main panel bus bars. These will have terminals for this purpose. A 3-foot piece of wire should be long enough for the connection.

Attach the terminal end of the range cord to the *line* terminals of the new auxiliary panel (this is the *standby* panel). You will connect all the essential equipment to this panel. Watch the total connected load. Because where there are four circuits there should be enough to have each essential item on its

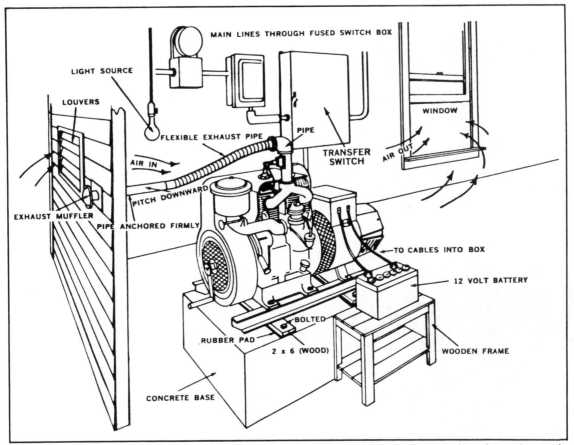

Fig. 14-51. Alternate layout where generator (including engine) is housed inside a dwelling area. Note the requirement for adequate ventilation. Engine exhaust must be piped outside. Courtesy Pioneer Gen-E-Motor Corp.)

own circuit. Be sure to provide for a few lights on one of the circuits.

In all instances the fourth terminal will be the ground. This range cord plug will now plug into the range receptacle you have installed and connected to the main panel bus bars. If it is more convenient and easier, you can turn the four-circuit panel upside down or sideways to accommodate the range cord so that it can plug into the receptacle without kinking.

The second range receptacle should now be installed near the first receptacle. Make sure the range cord plug can be plugged into either receptacle easily. This second receptacle is to be wired to the generator junction box with conduit. You *can* use four-wire Romex, size No. 6, between the re-

Fig. 14-52. Typical portable generator/engine assembly (courtesy Pioneer Gen-E-Motor Corp.)

213

Russelectric Inc.
"emergency power control systems"

enclosed automatic transfer switches
100 through 4000 amperes

Bulletin 74B

RMT 4003CE

400 Amperes, 480 Volts
Nema I, Wall Mounted
Fully Front Accessible
Rear Wiring Gutter behind Relay Plate

RMT 20003CEF

2000 Amperes, 480 Volts
Nema I, Free Standing
Rear Access Only
Bus Duct or Cable Connections Optional

Russelectric Inc. 99 Industrial Park Road, Hingham, Massachusetts 02043   (617) 749-6000   TELEX 94-0328

Fig. 14-53. Large automatic transfer switch (manual or automatic). Courtesy Russelectric, Inc.).

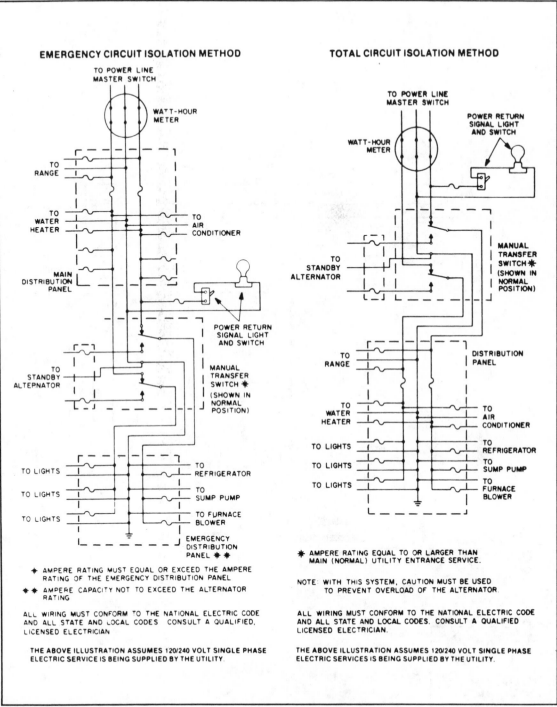

EMERGENCY CIRCUIT ISOLATION METHOD

TO POWER LINE
MASTER SWITCH

WATT-HOUR
METER

TO RANGE

TO WATER HEATER

TO AIR CONDITIONER

MAIN DISTRIBUTION PANEL

POWER RETURN SIGNAL LIGHT AND SWITCH

TO STANDBY ALTEPNATOR

MANUAL TRANSFER SWITCH ✱ (SHOWN IN NORMAL POSITION)

TO LIGHTS

TO LIGHTS

TO LIGHTS

TO REFRIGERATOR

TO SUMP PUMP

TO FURNACE BLOWER

EMERGENCY DISTRIBUTION PANEL ✱✱

✱ AMPERE RATING MUST EQUAL OR EXCEED THE AMPERE RATING OF THE EMERGENCY DISTRIBUTION PANEL

✱✱ AMPERE CAPACITY NOT TO EXCEED THE ALTERNATOR RATING

ALL WIRING MUST CONFORM TO THE NATIONAL ELECTRIC CODE AND ALL STATE AND LOCAL CODES. CONSULT A QUALIFIED, LICENSED ELECTRICIAN

THE ABOVE ILLUSTRATION ASSUMES 120/240 VOLT SINGLE PHASE ELECTRIC SERVICE IS BEING SUPPLIED BY THE UTILITY.

TOTAL CIRCUIT ISOLATION METHOD

TO POWER LINE MASTER SWITCH

POWER RETURN SIGNAL LIGHT AND SWITCH

WATT-HOUR METER

TO STANDBY ALTERNATOR

MANUAL TRANSFER SWITCH ✱ (SHOWN IN NORMAL POSITION)

TO RANGE

DISTRIBUTION PANEL

TO WATER HEATER

TO AIR CONDITIONER

TO LIGHTS

TO REFRIGERATOR

TO LIGHTS

TO SUMP PUMP

TO LIGHTS

TO FURNACE BLOWER

✱ AMPERE RATING EQUAL TO OR LARGER THAN MAIN (NORMAL) UTILITY ENTRANCE SERVICE.

NOTE: WITH THIS SYSTEM, CAUTION MUST BE USED TO PREVENT OVERLOAD OF THE ALTERNATOR.

ALL WIRING MUST CONFORM TO THE NATIONAL ELECTRIC CODE AND ALL STATE AND LOCAL CODES. CONSULT A QUALIFIED LICENSED ELECTRICIAN

THE ABOVE ILLUSTRATION ASSUMES 120/240 VOLT SINGLE PHASE ELECTRIC SERVICES IS BEING SUPPLIED BY THE UTILITY.

Fig. 14-54. Left diagram is for generator to supply only certain circuits during an emergency. Right diagram is for generator supply all circuits in the system during an emergency. Courtesy Russelectric, Inc.

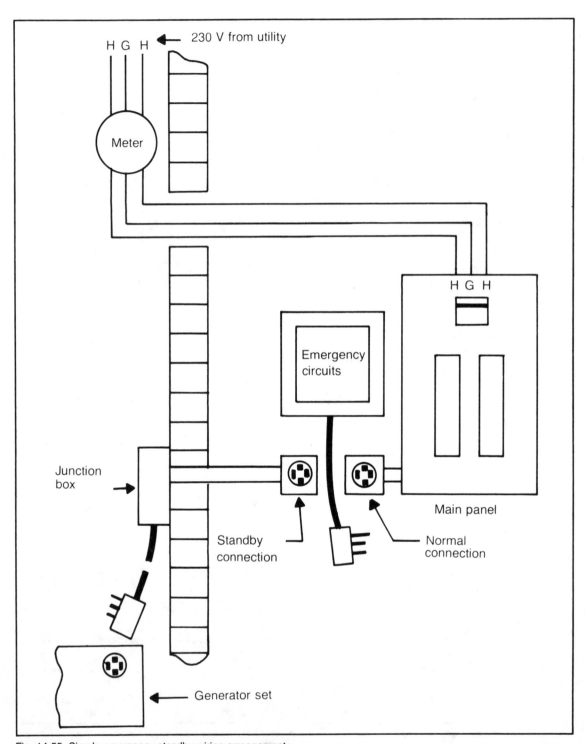

Fig. 14-55. Simple emergency standby wiring arrangement.

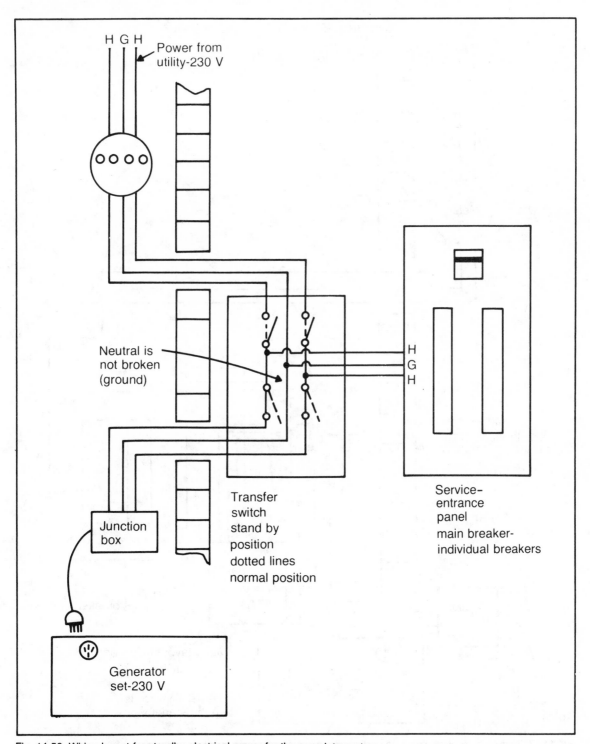

H G H

Power from
utility-230 V

Neutral is
not broken
(ground)

H
G
H

Transfer
switch
stand by
position
dotted lines
normal position

Service-
entrance
panel
main breaker-
individual breakers

Junction
box

Generator
set-230 V

Fig. 14-56. Wiring layout for standby electrical power for the complete system.

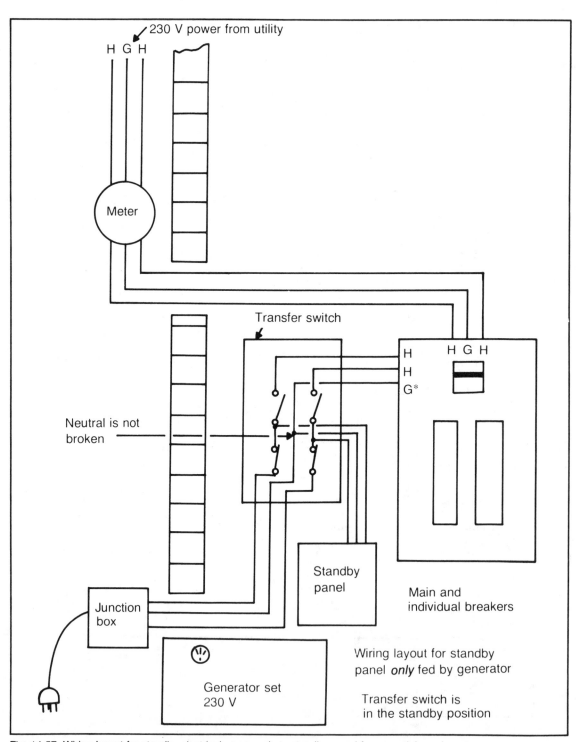

230 V power from utility

H G H

Meter

Transfer switch

H
H
G*

H G H

Neutral is not broken

Standby panel

Main and individual breakers

Junction box

Wiring layout for standby panel *only* fed by generator

Transfer switch is in the standby position

Generator set 230 V

Fig. 14-57. Wiring layout for standby electrical power only to standby panel for essential needs.

PS5
AIR-COOLED

WINCO 3600 RPM Package Standby Units are the low cost answer to automatic standby power. When the utility power is interrupted, the WINCO Package Standby Unit automatically starts. When the utility power comes back on, the WINCO Package system automatically shuts itself off. This system is completely prewired and pretested at the factory to insure proper operation and minimize the installation costs. Gasoline storage is not a problem, since the WINCO Package Standby runs on LPG or Natural Gas. A built-in battery charger keeps the starting battery at a full charge. All components for a completely automatic system are standard equipment (except the battery). All WINCO Package Standby systems carry a one-year limited warranty and are backed up by a worldwide service organization.

SELECTION GUIDE

MODEL	LP KW	NG KW	VOLTAGE	PHASE	TRANSFER SWITCH RATING	ENGINE	TYPE OF COOLING	DIMENSIONS			WEIGHT	
								L	W	H	NET	SHIP
PS5BH-3R	5	4	120/240	1	30 amp	Briggs-Stratton	Air	27	24¾	30	214	254
PS7BH-3R	7	6	120/240	1	30 amp	Briggs-Stratton	Air	26	24¾	30	311	351
PS10WH	10	8	See Chart	1 or 3	60 amp	Wisconsin	Air	40¼	25⅛	48	600	640
PS20WH	20	19	See Chart	1 or 3	200 amp	Wisconsin	Air	45	35	35	907	960
PS75CH	75	70	See Chart	1 or 3	400 amp	Chrysler LH318	Water	80	47	51	1900	2200

STANDARD EQUIPMENT
- 3600 RPM power plant
- Automatic transfer control
- LPG or natural gas carburetor (Air-cooled units standard natural gas, field adjustable for LPG)
- Low pressure solenoid valve
- Built-in battery trickle charger
- Battery rack and cables
- Muffler
- Flexible exhaust connection
- Vibration dampeners

ADDITIONAL STANDARD EQUIPMENT FOR PS75
- A.C. voltmeter
- A.C. ammeter
- Phase selector switch
- Combination frequency/running time meter
- Water temperature gauge
- Battery charging ammeter
- Oil pressure gauge
- High water temperature shutdown
- Low oil pressure shutdown
- Overspeed shutdown
- Overcrank shutdown
- 4 fault light indicators
- Voltage adjusting rheostat
- Residential grade silencer

- Stainless steel flexible exhaust connection
- Electronic governor
- Start delay relay
- Cool down relay

PS75 ENGINE CONTROL
1. Start Delay: Adjustable from 0 to 30 seconds in 3-second increments.
2. Engine Warm Up: Engine idles for 12 seconds after start. Non-adjustable.
3. Cool Down Delay: Adjustable from 0 to 8 minutes in 48-second increments.
4. Lamp Test: Pushbutton for testing all alarm lights.
5. Alarm Silence: Pushbutton to silence the alarm if shutdown occurs.

VOLTAGE SELECTION GUIDE

VOLTAGE CODE	VOLTAGE	PHASE
—3R	120/240	1∅
—4R	120/208	3∅
—17R	120/240	3∅
—18R*	277/480	3∅

Other voltages available on request
*PS75CH only

Fig. 14-58. LPG/natural gas package standby system (courtesy Winco Co.)

Fig. 14-59. Small portable generator. Model KP3000R2 KOOL-POWER generator (courtesy Over-Lowe Co.).

ceptacle and the junction box. This junction box will then have the second range cord connected to the ends of the wires from the "standby" receptacle at the standby panel location. The plug of this cord will then plug into the generator receptacle that will be on the generator panel.

If the generator is to operate inside the dwelling (as in the garage). The exhaust pipe *must* lead the fumes outside and away from the building. This is *very* important! Also, if the generator set is to be housed indoors, two louvered openings *must* be provided for engine ventilation; one for air intake mounted near the ceiling and one for exhaust near the floor line.

In normal use, the range cord and plug dangling from the standby circuit panel will plug into the main panel receptacle. In an emergency (standby) use, this plug will plug into the emergency receptacle. Be sure to mark these two receptacles correctly so that they can be easily seen and properly used. Depending on the nearness of the two receptacles to the cord plug, you may only need a 3-foot range cord. Refer to Fig. 14-55.

Figure 14-58 illustrates a standby generator complete with transfer switch. This generator operates on natural gas or LPG and is fully automatic. The battery is not included, but the battery bracket and battery cables are included. A manually operated generator varies in sizes from 2250 watts to 7500 watts. The manual transfer switch (or two receptacle switching method) must be changed to the standby position *after* the generator has come up to speed.

If the generator is to run on natural gas, note that the natural gas supply *might* be cut off in event of an emergency. If the generator is to supply power for life support systems, it would be wise to use LPG for engine power. The use of gasoline is not recommended because of the high flammability of the storage facility and leaks dripping on the floor. Both natural gas and LPG have odor detectors added to the supply for leak detection. When you decide to install such a system, contact various manufacturers to help you decide on the best system for your needs.

Chapter 15
Rewiring a Dwelling During Renovation

WITH THE BLOSSOMING OF MANY URBAN renewal projects, particularly in the inner-city areas, there is a great need for the know-how to do these jobs correctly and in a workmanlike manner. This is an important part of the "do it yourself and save money" theme of this book. Most of the inner-city urban renewal projects involve very old and run-down buildings. See Figs. 15-1 through 15-10.

It is easier to work on this type of building if the interior plastered walls are stripped down to the studs. This serves a dual purpose. It allows blanket insulation to be installed in the exterior walls in addition to making it easier to install wiring, plumbing, and heating work.

At the same time the other trades could install their work with less expense and time involved on their part. In other words, this would be new work and it would be installed exactly as in a new building under construction. Generally in buildings this old, the plaster would be in very poor condition. New drywall would be installed and then taped after all concealed work had been done. The old plaster on the ceiling would also be removed to allow for wiring in that area. Friends of my parents did this very thing. They bought an old house and gutted the inside and started over as if it were a new building. Note that after the plaster has been removed, the studs and joists can be inspected for defects or broken framing.

In addition, plumbing, heating, air conditioning and, of course, the wiring will go much faster. Don't forget to have installed or to install yourself, telephone and television wiring. In many areas, homeowners are now permitted to install wiring for their own phone system. If the original plaster is to be left, there will be much additional labor needed. See Figs. 15-2, 15-3.

The removal of wiring can be started at any point. Consider salvaging attractive and antique lighting fixtures. These old fixtures can be refurbished and rewired to become very attractive additions to the renovated dwelling. Also usable and attractive are old metal (brass) switch and receptacle plates. I remember some that were called *oxidized copper*, a mottled antique copper finish.

Accessories

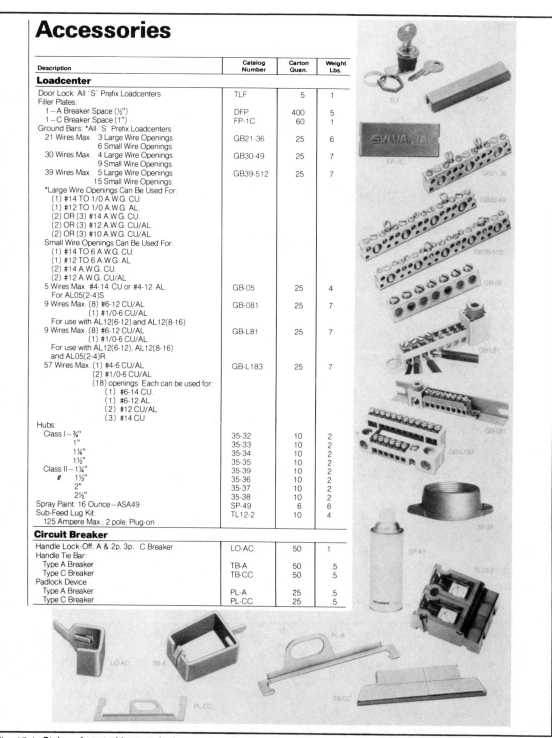

Description	Catalog Number	Carton Quan.	Weight Lbs.
Loadcenter			
Door Lock: All "S" Prefix Loadcenters	TLF	5	1
Filler Plates:			
1 – A Breaker Space (½")	DFP	400	5
1 – C Breaker Space (1")	FP-1C	60	1
Ground Bars: *All "S" Prefix Loadcenters			
21 Wires Max. 3 Large Wire Openings	GB21-36	25	6
6 Small Wire Openings			
30 Wires Max. 4 Large Wire Openings	GB30-49	25	7
9 Small Wire Openings			
39 Wires Max. 5 Large Wire Openings	GB39-512	25	7
15 Small Wire Openings			
*Large Wire Openings Can Be Used For:			
(1) #14 TO 1/0 A.W.G. CU.			
(1) #12 TO 1/0 A.W.G. AL.			
(2) OR (3) #14 A.W.G. CU.			
(2) OR (3) #12 A.W.G. CU/AL.			
(2) OR (3) #10 A.W.G. CU/AL.			
Small Wire Openings Can Be Used For:			
(1) #14 TO 6 A.W.G. CU.			
(1) #12 TO 6 A.W.G. AL.			
(2) #14 A.W.G. CU.			
(2) #12 A.W.G. CU/AL.			
5 Wires Max. #4-14 CU or #4-12 AL.	GB-05	25	4
For AL05(2-4)S			
9 Wires Max. (8) #6-12 CU/AL	GB-081	25	7
(1) #1/0-6 CU/AL			
For use with AL12(6-12) and AL12(8-16)			
9 Wires Max. (8) #6-12 CU/AL	GB-L81	25	7
(1) #1/0-6 CU/AL			
For use with AL12(6-12), AL12(8-16)			
and AL05(2-4)R.			
57 Wires Max. (1) #4-6 CU/AL	GB-L183	25	7
(2) #1/0-6 CU/AL			
(18) openings Each can be used for:			
(1) #6-14 CU.			
(1) #6-12 AL.			
(2) #12 CU/AL			
(3) #14 CU			
Hubs:			
Class I – ¾"	35-32	10	2
1"	35-33	10	2
1¼"	35-34	10	2
1½"	35-35	10	2
Class II – 1¼"	35-39	10	2
1½"	35-36	10	2
2"	35-37	10	2
2½"	35-38	10	2
Spray Paint: 16 Ounce – ASA49	SP-49	6	6
Sub-Feed Lug Kit:			
125 Ampere Max.; 2 pole; Plug-on	TL12-2	10	4
Circuit Breaker			
Handle Lock-Off, A & 2p, 3p. C Breaker	LO-AC	50	1
Handle Tie Bar:			
Type A Breaker	TB-A	50	.5
Type C Breaker	TB-CC	50	.5
Padlock Device			
Type A Breaker	PL-A	25	.5
Type C Breaker	PL-CC	25	.5

Fig. 15-1. Styles of neutral bars and other accessories for entrance panels (courtesy Sylvania, Inc.).

Fig. 15-2. Renovation project underway. Lath and plaster has been removed. Framing members are now ready for installation of wiring and other installation work.

Push-button switches can be salvaged, but they must be in top condition; make sure that the contacts are not burned or pitted. Look closely, using a flashlight, to inspect the moveable contacts. Slight pitting does not matter. The porcelain body must not be cracked. Porcelain can stand high heat.

With all of the materials worth salvaging removed, you can now proceed with the removal or abandonment of the rest of the wiring.

REMOVAL OF ALL OLD WIRING

If the original plaster is to stay, as much of the wiring as possible must be pulled from the interior of the walls. Try to reach inside the wall cavity and cut loose as much of wiring as possible. The main purpose is to eliminate any contact or even closeness of the new wiring to the old wires. Take no chances that *any* of the old wiring is ever able to be connected to the new wiring.

After all of the old wiring is removed, the building is now ready for rewiring. If the plaster is in place, you will use old work installation methods. You will have to cut holes in order to run the cable properly.

On outside walls where there are eaves, notches will have to be cut at the ceiling-to-wall junction to bring cable from the attic down this wall. Use this method on one-story buildings and for the second story on two-story buildings, gable ends will not need this treatment as there is available room for working. You will have to be very resourceful and find methods of running the cable so as to minimize cutting and patching. This might mean using more cable to take a roundabout route to achieve the result.

Spend some time laying out the route so make sure you *can* go this way. Think before you cut and measure before you cut. Measure *twice* and cut *once*.

Fig. 15-3. Showing lath and plaster removed from front side of wall. Back side of wall still has to have lath and plaster removed. Room to right still has to be done.

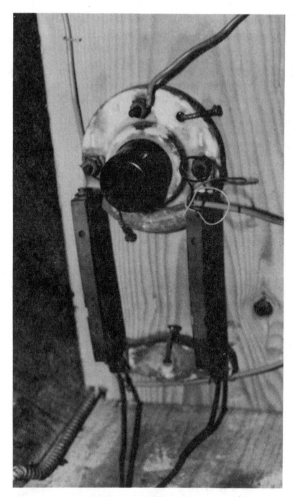

Fig. 15-4. The electrical protector provided by the phone company. This installation is not neatly done. Unit has been *nailed* in place.

Usually, first floor receptacles and switches can be fed from the basement or crawl space. First-floor ceiling outlets as for a fixture might need to have the flooring cut in second-story rooms to run cable from the attic or basement. Try to cut flooring in halls or closets if possible. See Figs. 9-21 and 15-10.

If the old plaster is completely removed then the wiring method will be new work. This type of wiring work will be straightforward and go much faster. I would be in favor of removing the plaster. Very old plaster tends to crumble and does not take

wall paper or paint well. The speed and economy of new work over old work might pay for most of the drywall installation. You can remove the plaster and wiring, plumbing, and heating yourself. This work is very hard and dirty so wear a dust mask and goggles.

REMOVAL OF OLD SERVICE EQUIPMENT

Sometimes the meter and service equipment is so old and primitive it can hardly be called that. It might be only an open knife switch with two fuses instead of one for 115 V. If you are doing a complete renovation, there will be no power in the building. You might need to arrange to have temporary power furnished or buy it from a neighbor. Always buy from neighbors; never borrow. If you hire other workman, they will need power and you will have to make some arrangements.

With no power, the service equipment can be removed. Tear it all out. If you want to save anything for nostalgic reasons, do so. Do *not* reuse these items.

Before installing any *new* service entrance equipment, talk with the utility and get their recommendation for the meter location. The utility might not connect their lines to a location on the building if it has not been approved by them. The utility needs a direct route for their overhead lines. Usually the original connection point to the building will be satisfactory to both you and the utility.

The service-entrance panel in the basement or first floor *must* be immediately inside of where the entrance cable or conduit enters through the wall. Because this cable or wire is not fused or protected from overcurrents until it is connected to the main breaker or fuses, it must be as short as possible. You must make arrangements for space to mount the main disconnect and distribution panel or the combination main/breaker panel. This location must be adjacent the entrance of the cable or conduit from the meter. Be sure you have room for the equipment that you choose. Measure carefully.

Combination main/branch circuit panelboards will usually need less space. Even though they are more expensive, they will fit in a small area. If the original panel was some distance from the cable entrance point, you will want to install a main breaker *only* panel there and continue on to the distribution panel location with cable or conduit.

In my parents' home, the meter was in an upstairs bedroom and included fuses. These "fuses" were wire made of lead and secured under screw terminals. Many meters were located in an upstairs bedroom. This was because the wires from the utility pole entered the house at a high point. Again, fuse the service as soon as it enters the building. Refer to Figs. 15-7, 15-8, and 15-9.

Remove or abandon *all* wiring such as obsolete service-entrance wiring. This wiring might have been only size No. 10 because the usual service switch was only 30 A. There were only *two* wires from the pole to the building and therefore only 115 V was available. Later buildings had ¾-inch conduit on the outside of the building from the point of attachment from the pole down and into the basement by means of a gooseneck bend to make the 90-degree turn through the wall.

Present conduit size is 1¼-inch conduit or thinwall. This will accommodate No. 3 wire to carry 150 A ampacity. The ¾-inch conduit *must* be replaced by the 1¼-inch conduit/thinwall or cable. Conduit looks nice especially when used with a mast and service head at its top.

Below the meter where the conduit enters the wall use an angle fitting (known as an LB for *angle* fitting with *back* opening). This has a waterproof cover with gasket and makes a neat job. Most fittings made for this purpose are offset back against the house wall to allow the conduit to lie flat against this wall. As my son says, this makes it "more neater."

Condulet bodies are designated by location of openings. Example: type LB is an elbow body having a "back" opening and an "end" opening. Therefore it is an elbow (L) with a back (B) opening. The cover is on the front with a rubber gasket to make it weatherproof. LL has the opening on the left: LR has the opening on the right.

Fig. 15-5. Four "entrance bridges" for connecting various phone jacks in the dwelling.

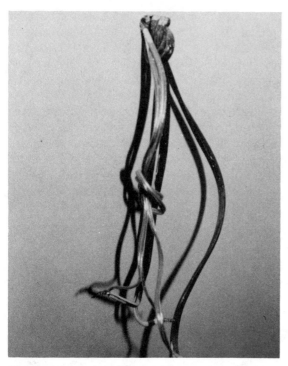

Fig. 15-6. Wiring for stereo system to allow music in many of the rooms in the dwelling.

Remove any service-entrance conduit. Cut it with a hacksaw at the gooseneck. It is best to get help when taking down conduit. Many things appear lighter than they actually are and thus cause accidents. Long pipes or planks, when cut free, can be overbalanced when you grasp them and get away from you.

Work carefully after removing the vertical conduit. Go inside and disconnect the conduit connection at the service-entrance equipment. After you have done this, the rest of the gooseneck and straight part will pull through the wall easily. Plan the layout for the new service. Thinwall (conduit) looks best for the part from the service head down to the meter base. You can use cable from the meter base all the way inside to the service equipment.

Cable is easier to work around bends and through holes in the outer wall. Where the cable enters the building wall will leave a space that will need to be caulked. Fill this area well and then cover it with a *sill plate*. This plate is formed to cover the cable as it turns into the wall and be held against the wall by wood screws. Push the plate into the caulking compound and fasten it with screws. The caulking under the plate should be sufficient; if not fill it in with more.

Be sure that the cable is not bent at too sharp an angle. Cut away the top edge of the hole through the wall to allow the cable to make a long sweep curve. The minimum radius allowed is five times the diameter. Therefore, a 1-inch cable should not be bent in a radius less than 5 inches. Trim the hole edge accordingly. Sharper bends damage the covering.

Apply at the utility for the meter base. If you use conduit above the meter only, assemble the meter base, conduit and service head as one piece. Some bungalow houses, with low hanging eaves, need to have the conduit go up through the roof at the point where the roof boards meet the wall. The mast (the extension of the conduit above the roof surface) must conform to certain code requirements as follows:

■ The service drop connection at the service mast *must* have a minimum of 3 feet clearance from the roof surface, provided the roof has a pitch (slope) of 4 inches in 12 inches. The connection of the service drop to the mast *must* be *below* the service head to prevent moisture from entering the service head.

■ The servicedrop connection *may* be a minimum of 18 inches if the conductor cable passes over no more than 48 inches of roof surface. This refers to a 48-inch roof overhang (eaves).

■ The servicedrop cable must maintain a minimum of 10 feet above the ground at any point between the building and the connection at the utility pole.

All of these conditions refer to *cabled* service-drops having two insulated wires and the grounded messenger (support) cable, used as a neutral, and limited to 150 V to ground. All this applies to residential service only. If the service mast must extend some distance above the roof, the mast should be the 2-inch pipe and it might need guying to take the strain of a long service drop span.

In winter snow and ice conditions combined

with strong winds put a severe strain on the servicedrop and in turn on the mast. Guying the mast is important for these reasons. The 2-inch pipe conduit used as the mast will need to be bushed down at the meter base. The hub is usually 1¼-inch female thread.

Many old two-story buildings have a servicedrop consisting of three separate (or two separate) wires supported by a metal rack holding three porcelain insulators separated from each other by about 6 inches. Sometimes the wires are attached to individual insulators screwed directly into the building framing by means of lag screws cemented into the insulator base. Be sure to check with the utility to find out if they want to run a new cable servicedrop rather than reuse the separate wires. The cable drop is stronger and causes fewer problems.

Beginning in the attic, above the first or second floor, cut and remove *all* the old wiring you can see. Where wires go down through the walls, try to pull them out. Wear gloves so that you do not cut your hands. The old insulation can break off and leave bare No. 14 wire that, when pulled through your bare hands, can give a nasty cut. Such a cut might become easily infected. You will need your hands in good shape to finish the job; be careful.

On the floor below the attic, remove all electrical devices in walls and ceilings. After removing these devices, pull all the wires from inside the walls. Again, watch your hands for the same reasons. Any wires that cannot be pulled loose and removed must be cut off well inside the walls. Remove all the old wiring and then go to the basement and do the same there.

With all the old wiring removed, lay out the new wiring plan. You will have a tentative wiring plan on paper as required by the inspector. Remember, no spot along any wall may be farther than 6 feet from a receptacle. Provide for three-way switching where needed. Three-way control is necessary in hallways, stairways, and for large rooms such as family rooms and living rooms having more than one entrance to the room. Rooms such as bedrooms, living rooms, and dens usually have no ceiling fixture.

Consider installing ceiling fixtures. You can provide for this by wiring for the ceiling fixture and covering the ceiling box with an attractive ceiling canopy cover made for this purpose. This is a decorative cover held by a knurled brass cap nut. This forethought will eliminate running wiring later after the ceiling has been decorated.

I installed fixtures in both of my bedrooms (I bought the house after completion) and find it very convenient. I removed the switch control from the wall receptacle and now control the ceiling fixture from this switch. This is approved by the code.

Living areas need switch control of receptacles so that lamps which are plugged into them can

Fig. 15-7. How not to do wiring. No inspector would approve of this.

Fig. 15-8. A fairly neat installation of BX cable.

be controlled from a wall switch when entering or leaving the room. Many contractors "split-wire" these receptacles so that the upper outlet is hot (live) at all times and the lower one is controlled by the wall switch. The reason the upper outlet is left hot is for appliances such as a vacuum cleaner or electronic equipment. A clock radio must be energized continuously even though it has a means of "carryover" for the clock portion.

Wiring for stereo, TV antennas, and telephone service is low voltage or no voltage work, but you must be careful to make proper connections just as with line-voltage wiring. While there is absolutely no fire hazard, work accurately so that you will not have to tear a wall apart to repair defects. Check all circuits and route all wires to prevent damage to these wires. Use the same construction procedures as when working with line voltage wiring.

Wall boxes may not be necessary (only for protection perhaps (because the code does not apply to this class of wiring). The code does prohibit this class of wiring being in the same cabinet or wall box as line voltage wiring because this wire does not have enough insulation for line voltage. The only allowable situation is where there is a so-called metal partition (barrier) in the box separating these two classes of wiring systems. See Figs. 15-4, 15-5, and 15-6.

OLD WORK WIRING METHODS

Old work wiring is different from new work because in old work cables must be drawn through inside the walls without doing extensive damage. In addition, the walls must be patched where access openings have been made. To do work that is acceptable, the patching must be practically invisible. By careful cutting, the patching is made easier and less noticeable.

Cable can be run behind baseboard for a horizontal run between two receptacles where no other route is possible. To do this carefully, remove the baseboard by prying slowly with a wide wood chisel driven behind the baseboard. Pry outward gently along the full length, a little at a time. The modern thin baseboard tends to split or crack so be extra careful.

Do *not* drive the nails back through the face of the board. Use your electrician's side cutters to grasp the shank of the nail close up to the back of the board. The point of the nail is facing you. Now pry up using the jaws of the pliers as a fulcrum. If the nail is a finishing nail, it will pull right through the wood. If the nail has a flat head, you should drive this type *back* through the front of the baseboard. One pry should pull the finishing nail through; if not, grasp and pry again. See Figs. 14-46 and 14-47.

Caution: In any type of remodeling work, always remove *all* protruding nails. It is extremely dangerous to step on a nail. On lumber to be discarded, the nails *should* be bent over and the lumber discarded. Just be sure the nails do not stick up. After removing the baseboard, you will find the bottom 2×4 (plate) and the bottom ends of the studs nailed to the plate.

If the baseboard is high (width), say 4 or 5 inches, you should be able to cut away the plaster to within 1 inch of the top edge of where the baseboard top edge covers when it is replaced. This method will allow you to drill holes through the part of the studs showing behind where the baseboard will cover. You might need to use a drill extension (available in hardware stores) to use an electric drill motor. Be sure to drill in the exact center of these studs. This is a code requirement.

If the baseboard is narrow, you will have to notch the stud or the base plate. The very bottom of the studs should be behind the baseboard. You will have to cover the cable with a 1/16-inch metal plate to protect the cable from nails. Do this to protect yourself and prevent the house from burning down. It might be necessary to recess these plates to allow the baseboard to fit back in place. Do not replace the baseboard until inspection has been made.

When you bring cable down from the attic on an outside wall, there will be places where low roof lines do not allow access to the top plate. In this case, you will have to cut a notch in the interior wall and ceiling corner. To do this, cut a notch half in the ceiling and half in the wall to make an area exposing the top plate. The notch should be about 1½ inches wide by 1½ inches deep, both on the wall and on the ceiling. You also will have to notch the plate and then cover it with 1/16-inch metal.

Installing Wall Boxes in Lath and Plaster

When cutting lath and plaster for wall boxes, center the box vertically on one lath even if it means raising or lowering the box location slightly. If you do not do this, it will be more difficult to install the box. To locate the center lath, probe with a nail or screwdriver to locate the top and bottom edges of the lath. Mark the box outline on the wall.

Carefully remove the plaster for the full *width*

of the box *horizontally* from the lath and by the full width of the lath *vertically* plus the space between this center lath and the edges of the laths on either side of the center lath. This will give a plaster-free space about 2×2 inches.

Now carefully remove the plaster from the box outline top and bottom of the plaster-free opening. Note that the center lath part showing will be removed. Allow a slight amount of slop (short for sloppy fit) when removing the plaster. Try the open front of box into the plaster-free area to see if it fits. This opening should be ⅛ of an inch larger, in both dimensions, than the box dimensions.

Fig. 15-9. An old installation of BX cable and thinwall conduit. The "pigtail" splices have been wrapped with rubber tape and then covered with friction tape. The actual wires might or might not have been soldered. The code requires soldering. Wire connectors (nuts) are now used here.

Fig. 15-10. Porcelain insulators. These are seldom used in homes.

Starting with the center lath, saw down one side of the lath, next to the plaster edge, with a coarse tooth hacksaw blade (tape one end of the blade to make a handle) or a keyhole saw. *Caution:* Do not saw either side of the lath all the way through; saw about half way on each side. Insert a wide blade screwdriver in either side and twist the blade. The sawed portion will split off (usually). If you have no luck, try the other side. If the grain is slanting, you may have to saw more on one side for the piece to split off. Also saw up from the bottom edge and split off this piece.

Now hook one finger behind the remaining center piece to support it while you saw through both ends. This is to prevent the sawing from loosening the lath from the plaster "keys" (the plaster that squeezes through between the laths and locks the plaster to the laths). Saw gently.

Now do the same with the *part* laths for about half the width. This will provide the full opening for wall box. Be sure to hold these laths to prevent breaking the plaster key. You will have to provide a notch in these half laths to allow the device mounting screw to clear them. Just make a small notch in the lath edge with the hacksaw blade. If the wall box will not fit, you might have to pare the edge of the lath with a pocketknife.

There are two methods of using the mounting ears furnished with the box (plastic boxes usually have permanently mounted ears). Metal boxes are built so that the ears are reversible. With the ears *flush* to the box front edge, the ears will be on the surface of the plaster. With the ears *reversed,* the plaster will have to be removed and the ears screwed directly to the wood lath. This is the better method because it is easy to crack the plaster and you have to remove it anyway.

In either case, use No. 6 or 8 flathead screws.

Do not remove too much plaster or the cover plate will not cover the space. You will have to plaster around the box to comply with the code requirement. Any trouble encountered with the wood laths can be overcome by using the patented Madison Supports or a box with a clamp arrangement built in. When surface mounting box ears, you should remove some plaster to allow the ears to lie flush with the wall surface.

Where ceiling boxes are to be installed in rooms, find the room center. Figure 9-20 shows the method for doing this. If you run into a joist at the exact center, move the box slightly to one side. More than 1 inch will be noticeable. You can use a shallow, ½-inch box and notch the joist a small amount if necessary. Secure the box to the joist with No. 10 ¾-inch wood screws or sheet-metal screws. Do not use nails because you might have to remove the box for some reason. When the room center falls between joists, use the standard adjustable bar hanger, made from 11½-inch to 26½-inch adjustment (two sizes). Separate the two halves and reverse the stud that holds the box in place on the bar.

If you can gain access to the attic or have cut access openings in the second story flooring, this hanger can be nailed to the joists on each side of the box location. If this is the case, use a standard 1½-inch deep box to allow more wiring space.

If the top side of the ceiling is not accessible, use the ½-inch deep box and let the bar hanger lie on the top (back) side of the ceiling finish (drywall or lath and plaster). The other alternative is to use the spring out clamp shown in Figs. 9-1 and 9-2. This type will work with a ceiling box to support a lightweight fixture *only*. Don't forget to plaster around the box after installation.

All concealed wiring, such as rewiring an old house, must have the *new* wiring in place before the boxes are installed. This is just the opposite of new work where all the boxes are mounted before the wiring is run. All cutting of openings and drilling of framing members should precede any pulling of cable.

You should now have replaced the old service-entrance equipment with new and be ready to have the utility connect the house to their lines. This way you can use power tools and save time. After you have finished the entrance equipment and have had it inspected, call the utility for the connection. You should already have done any outside remodeling of the building (aluminum siding or face brick) before mounting the service mast and meter base. Be sure to check with both the inspector *and* the utility before proceeding too far with the service-entrance equipment installation. Remember to do the work yourself (family help is OK). The hiring of outside contractors will get you in trouble with the inspector.

Review Chapter 4 and Chapter 5. These chapters give detailed instructions and advice for working with these parts of the system. Also refer to Chapter 13. Figure 13-31 shows methods of reconnecting the separate circuits using service-entrance cable, a new combination main, and a distribution panel. A junction box takes the place of the old service-entrance equipment. Figure 13-34 details the replacement of old ¾-inch service-entrance conduit with a new service mast and outside meter. A third wire will need to be added, if it is not already in place, to provide 230-V service for a range, air conditioning, and water heater. Figure 13-35 shows procedures to remove or abandon old wiring in a building being remodeled.

Details of drilling for cable from the basement to the attic are shown in Figure 13-36. Figure 13-37 shows the arrangement of a receptacle (hot all the time) and a switch and ceiling outlet controlled by the switch. The source is from the basement.

Chapter 9 shows other old work methods. Figure 9-19 shows the use of a mouse (weight) and the method of hooking the cord holding the mouse from inside the hollow wall. Figure 9-20 details finding the center of a room to install a ceiling fixture. Also shown are box supports. These supports can also be used for mounting *wall* fixture boxes. Figure 9-21 shows a method of removing and replacing finished flooring to gain access to a ceiling fixture location on the floor below.

Figure 13-31 details how to install a new service-entrance panel and new fuse/breaker panel. If the new panel is some distance from the old fuse panel, replace the old fuse panel with a junction box.

Some of the circuits leaving the panel might be too short (the cables might be too short to connect to the new terminals). Note that the new equipment can be a combination main/distribution panel or each part can be separate.

In certain areas, Hawaii for example, the meter and main breaker are mounted outside in a weatherproof enclosure. Condominiums are usually arranged with the meters and main breakers outside in a weatherproof enclosure. In both cases, the wiring between the main breaker and the distribution panel is four-wire service-entrance cable using an insulated neutral wire rather than the common bare neutral in standard service-entrance cable.

In this situation, the code requires this type of cable. If the new junction box is within 2 or 3 feet of the new distribution panel, you can use conduit or thinwall between the two enclosures. Usually, though, four wire entrance cable is better and more convenient to work with. It might be difficult to purchase short lengths of insulated wire in large sizes of No. 6 or No. 4.

When using thinwall or conduit, buy all black wire and tape the neutral with white adhesive or plastic tape to designate the neutral. Tape each end of the neutral. You should identify the two hot wires from the main breaker. Put *one* band of *black* tape on the *left* hot wire. Put *two* bands of *black* tape on the *right* hot wire. The left and right is looking at the main breaker terminals. The four-wire service-entrance cable will come color coded: red, black, white, and bare. The bare wire is the same as that in Romex or BX and is used to ground the cabinets and other noncurrent-carrying metal parts of the system.

Be sure when using conduit or thinwall to tighten all locknuts and bushings tightly so as to provide a continuous ground path for fault current anywhere in the system.

The grounding of any electrical system is extremely important for personal safety as well as providing for prompt blowing of fuses and breaker operation when necessary. In case of a poor grounding system or no system at all, the overcurrent protection might not operate and could cause untold damage to personnel and property. The best ground is that provided by a cold-water pipe connected to the city water supply. This is the common grounding connection in urban dwellings.

This ground connection is attached to the neutral bar in the service-entrance panel. The neutral bar is the *white* multiple terminal connector bar where the *white* wires from Romex and BX cables terminate (connect). Figure 4-18 shows this bar on the left side of the panel. The neutral from the service-entrance cable connects to the bar usually at the top end close to where the cable enters the cabinet. This terminal is larger than the branch circuit connections. Refer to Fig. 15-1 that shows a view of the neutral bar. Figure 4-17 shows a combination main service-entrance panel (including the main breaker and individual branch breakers). Figure 4-23 shows the method of grounding the neutral in a dwelling. As noted in Fig. 4-23, the water meter *must* have what is called a jumper wire to bypass the meter space in case the meter is removed for any reason. Some meters are connected to the water pipes by unions that have rubber gaskets. This will provide a very poor ground connection. Therefore the jumper is needed.

Review Chapter 8 for a better understanding of the ground principles. This chapter stresses many important points. Important is the continuity of the ground path from the furthest receptacle or switch all the way to the actual connection to ground (meaning the earth). The ground wire from the service-entrance equipment *must* be continuous all the way to its connection onto the cold water pipe.

Buy the best-quality wiring materials and devices that you can afford. Use only copper wire. Do not use aluminum wire. Follow approved wiring methods and practices. Make all electrical connections tight. When running Romex or BX, leave 8 inches sticking out from the wall and ceiling boxes for making connections. The code requires only 6 inches, but sometimes a little longer is better.

Notice that each box has the cubic inch volume stamped or embossed on the inside. Section 370-6 of the National Electrical Code specifies the number of conductors of a specified size allowed in each size box. Tables 370-6(a) and 370-6(b) list these requirements. I advise that you obtain a copy of the code in complete form for about $10.50 or the abbreviated edition for about $8.50. Calculation examples for determining the connection load for a single dwelling appear at the end of both editions.

Caution: Some areas will not issue a homeowner's electrical permit to wire a two-family dwelling. Check this requirement before doing any work. You might be prevented from doing wiring for the unit you do not occupy. For calculating the connected load use the code Example No. 1(c). Chapter 5 gives an example that is already worked out. Also review Chapter 7.

Never forget to ask the inspector about anything you don't understand. Most inspectors are interested in having you take out a permit because they want to see that you are doing the work properly and making an electrically safe installation.

Additional Items to Consider Installing

Consider installing outdoor perimeter lighting to be controlled by a photocell. The photocell method is the best method because it requires no adjustment for length of day or night. The only requirement is that the photocell *must* be installed where it can sense darkness, but is not affected by lights such as car headlights, street lights or lights on the building next door.

Photocells are usually mounted at least 8 feet above ground level to prevent vandalism. Use an approved installation method. Figure 14-13 illustrates a photocell to control external lights on an attached garage and front entry. In this case, the handy box should have been replaced with a flush wall box for a better appearance. In any case, a metal box cover must be used to support the weight of the photocell.

If you expect to heat domestic hot water with electricity, you should consider installing a water heater timer. This can save 20 percent or more of the electrical consumption needed to heat water. Certain models of timers have additional trip levers to allow more than one operation (on and off cycle) in 24 hours. If no one is home during the day, the heater can be turned off for a daytime period and also during the night to achieve greater savings. Install it yourself and save money *and* electricity.

If you have an attached garage or expect to add one to the dwelling, you should install a garage door operator. The operator will require a separate fused/breaker circuit with no other load connected to it except the operator. For the connection, install a receptacle in the garage ceiling about 24 inches beyond the *top* edge of the door (when it is in the open position and centered between the door tracks). This location should be within reach of the attachment cord of the opener motor. Chapter 14 suggests other projects that you can incorporate into your wiring plans. Reading about these projects will give you ideas for your own pet projects. The instructions given will usually apply to any additional work you will do.

As a suggestion not strictly electrical, be sure to make arrangements to have all meters (gas, water, and electrical) located outside so the meter readers will not have to enter the premises. You can move the electric meter outside yourself. The gas meter usually has to be moved by the gas utility (for a fee). The water meter can be retrofitted with a remote reading indicator (a small plastic case mounted outside on the building) to be read from outside.

Make complete detailed plans so as to include all special wiring you feel you want now or will need at a future time. Electric clothes dryer, air conditioning, and electric water heating circuits should either be installed (roughed in) or provision made in calculating the load requirements so that the service-entrance equipment can be sized properly for later installation of these fixed appliances.

Unless there is *no* alternative, electric resistance space heating is very costly to *operate*. Even though the installation cost is the lowest of all types of space heating, the operating cost is prohibitive. The low installation cost lulls people into having this type of heating installed. When the monthly bills start coming, the homeowner is usually extremely disappointed.

HOME CONTROL SYSTEMS

Because of break-ins, burglaries, and vandalism, there is much concern about protection of property. Homeowners are pursuing methods of discouraging such actions by means of outside lighting and varying lighting patterns inside the house to give the impression of occupancy when the premises are not occupied due to vacation or other reasons. Such systems can be programmed to operate various appliances as well as control heating and air conditioning.

Typical home control system applications can be separated into four categories

- Convenience.
- Security.
- Energy savings.
- Cost effectiveness.

A representative system has been developed by Leviton Manufacturing Co., Inc., Little Neck, New York. This system operates in all four areas. Because special wiring is not needed, costs are reduced over other systems on the market. Modules consist of devices that replace receptacles and switches. In addition, a wall-mounted controller can be used to turn on or off all outside lighting or operate other functions of the system.

The brain of the system is a wall-mounted programmer. One excellent feature is that the program signals are sent over the present electrical wiring by a special signal imposed on the wiring. All modules respond to their signal only and perform their functions. A wall-mounted controller can be installed in the master bedroom or in other rooms as well.

The wall-mounted programmer functions range from turning on the coffee maker (or the Christmas lights) to turning off the lights in a detached garage (no extra wires to run to the garage either), to night setback of heating equipment or night operations of air conditioning.

MINIMUM REQUIREMENTS
FOR EXISTING DWELLING UNITS

Minimum standards for existing dwelling units regarding service-entrance equipment require 100 A service equipment having three-wire capacity, dead front (no live parts exposed) and type S fuses (time delay, nontamperable).

There is an exception to this rule that provides for the continued use of 55-A service equipment

having three-wire capacity and feeders of 30 A or larger. Two- or three-wire capacity shall be accepted if adequate for the load served. The existing wiring shall be in good repair. Evidence of inadequacy shall be any of the following:

(a) Use of cords in lieu of permanent wiring.
(b) Oversizing of overcurrent protection for circuits, feeders or service.
(c) Unapproved extensions to the wiring system in order to provide light, heat or power.
(d) Electrical overload.
(e) Misuse of electrical equipment
(f) Lack of lighting fixtures in bathroom, laundry room, furnace room, stairway or basement.

These rules are excerpted from the *Reciprocal Electrical Council, Inc. Handbook*. Their address is 151 Martin Street, Birmingham, MI 48012. The amendments are adopted by the Department of Housing and Urban Development (HUD) Washington, D.C. available as: *HUD-PDR-631-6* P.4 of cover v. 6. The handbook is available from the Council for $1.50 plus postage and handling.

As the above rules specify, some of the present wiring *may* be reused. In very old buildings, however, the wiring is suspect and it should be carefully inspected. Any parts that do not appear in excellent condition should not be reused. Be cautious in this respect and make sure everything is safe.

TELEPHONE WIRING

Telephone companies will install directly inside a dwelling an "electrical protector" to protect against lightning and electrical accidents to its wires *external* to the dwelling such as overhead wires on poles or from the pole to the dwelling. This protector is familiar as the porcelain-base device near the basement ceiling where the phone cable comes in to the basement or other area. It consists of the porcelain base, two rods (one on each side), and a central round "gizmo." The whole device acts as a fuse and blows when excessive current flows in the outdoor phone lines.

Various phone jacks can be found in electronic stores (Radio Shack is one) and hardware stores.

Hookup wire or line wire is about 3/16 of an inch in diameter and it is usually gray or light brown. The wire size must be at least No. 24 AWG and copper (do not use aluminum). Be careful when stapling not to injure the insulation. Use insulated staples (the same as for doorbell wiring) and don't pound the staple in too tightly.

As with any wiring, be careful to make good, tight connections. Run the cable along the run of the building framing not across open joist spaces. Especially in basement areas do not run across the undersides of floor joists. People will hang clothes hangers on the cable.

In the condominium complex where I live, the phone wiring was done before the wall surfaces (drywall) where installed as new work. This cable was run from phone outlet to phone outlet and to the Network Interface (NI) at the building entrance. At each jack location, enough cable was coiled up to allow a connection to be made. No wires were cut at any point except to connect to the NI. After the building was finished, blank plates were installed. When phone service is wanted, any blank cover is removed, the wires are stripped and a phone jack is installed. Any number of jacks can be installed as preferred. Thus all wiring was concealed.

As an installer, you can run cable concealed using old work methods inside the building walls. The code requires that any splices or connections be accessible as in line voltage wiring. This can be done by making splices behind a blank wallplate (no boxes are used with phone wiring).

The cable must have four No. 24 AWG wires, red, green, black, and yellow. The wire insulation and outer sheath are similar to Romex construction except that they are a smaller size. The wire size must be at least No. 24 AWG, copper. The phone company suggests that bridges (junction blocks) be used. This eliminates using wire nuts or soldering connections.

Appendix

Procedures and Products

SOMETIMES IT IS EASIER TO SHOW SOMEONE how to do a job or procedure than describe it. The information in this appendix shows how to install and wire a receptacle using a "gangable" metal wall box. The gangable wall box is so made that both sides are removable. In this manner, individual boxes can be combined to provide room for more devices.

MOUNTING A RECEPTACLE
IN A GANGABLE WALL BOX

The gangable box gives a chance for the wiring of a duplex receptacle to be seen as if the box had a transparent side. These boxes have a screw on one of the side plates that is removable by loosening this screw. The side plate is then swung free of the screw and is off. If you do this with another box, the two boxes can be locked together by tightening one screw on each box center section. Three or more boxes can all be ganged together as you need.

Figure A-1 shows a receptacle that has just been wired to the Romex, supposedly coming into the box. The bare wire is the *grounding* wire. There are three of these wires showing, 1) from the Romex, 2) to the receptacle green *grounding* screw and 3) to the box *grounding* clamp. This clamp is on the front edge of the removed side (in the lower left).

Figure A-2 shows the receptacle about to be pressed back into the box. All wires are attached (black to brass screw, white to white screw, and bare to green hex grounding screw on the receptacle). The grounding clip is on the box side up near the top of that side.

Figure A-3 shows why the screw holding the receptacle to the box does not give secure grounding. Notice the space between the receptacle ears and the box ears (about ⅛ of an inch). Because the screw is a loose fit in the receptacle mounting strap, there is no good ground. This is why the grounding wire goes to the receptacle grounding screw.

Figure A-4 shows the receptacle mounted in the box. Even though the mounting strap does not touch the box itself, the receptacle is effectively

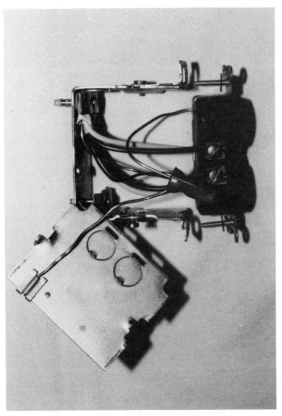

Fig. A-1. Wiring a receptacle in a gangable box.

Fig. A-3. Showing why grounding wire is needed when box is not flush with wall. Notice the wires have a modified S curve in the box.

Fig. A-2. Receptacle ready to be pushed into box.

Fig. A-4. Receptacle mounted in box.

Fig. A-5. Auxiliary fuse panel. Requires 230-V feeders including neutral. Fuses are time delay.

grounded. If the box was surface mounted as a "handy box" is, then the receptacle mounting strap would *contact* the box itself and would not need a grounding wire to result in a ground.

EXPLANATION OF VARIOUS DEVICES

At the top in Fig. A-5 are type S fuses, the center is the fuse adapter to adapt these fuses to the regular fuse panel. The two arrows at the left point to the two main terminals that feed the panel (230 V). The feeder neutral goes all the way around to the right and under one of these screws on the neutral bar. These are all time delay fuses.

At the top of Fig. A-6 is a service-entrance cable box connector. The second row shows Romex connector, BX connector, Thinwall connector, Thinwall connector, compression type. The third row shows BX or Greenfield connector, knockout plug, lock washer, and setscrew thinwall connector. The fourth row shows Thinwall "one-hole" mounting clip, setscrew thinwall connector, and thinwall mounting clip. At the bottom is a piece of Romex

Fig. A-6. Assortment of devices.

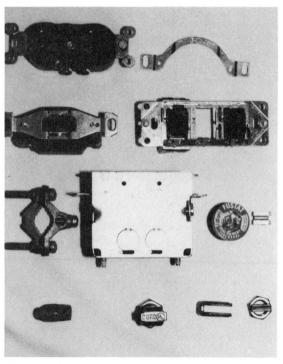

Fig. A-7. Assortment of devices.

with ground and a piece of Romex *without* ground. Do *not* use Romex without a ground.

At the top Fig. A-7 is a duplex receptacle, mounting strap for a plate such as for a phone, "snap" switch, this has a porcelain body (very rare), interchangeable devices (switch and receptacle), ground clamp for water pipe, box that is gangable, Fustat, pound on clamp for box, wirenut, split clamp for heavy wires (notice the UL marking), clamp taken apart.

FOREWORD

All Wiremold products are designed for interior use in dry locations only, as defined in Article 100 of the National Electrical Code.

WIREMOLD® SURFACE METAL RACEWAY SYSTEMS

Eleven raceway systems for complete interior wiring installations, mounted on walls, ceilings, floors, and above ceilings.

Three smaller raceways are primarily for extending conductors from point to point.

Six larger raceways offer a wider choice of wire capacities. All have removable covers, expediting original wiring and possible changes.

Two Pancake® raceways for overfloor installations to bring power and lighting, or telephone and signal wiring to away-from-wall locations without channeling into floor surface.

PLUGMOLD® MULTIOUTLET SYSTEMS

Six Wiremold surface metal raceways are designed to hold receptacles and other devices within the raceway. When used this way they become Plugmold multioutlet systems. They may be field-wired (2100, G-3000, G-4000, G-6000) or prewired at the factory—2000 Wired Sections; 2000 or 2200 with Snapicoil® receptacle harnesses.

TELE-POWER® POLES AND QUICK-E-POLES®

Standard Tele-Power Poles carry electrical and communications circuits in separate compartments from overhead wiring systems to away-from-wall locations. Variety of models meet architectural and aesthetic requirements; choice of finishes and colors, and variations in cross-section, electrical and communications cable carrying capacity. All Tele-Power Poles are available without power wiring, allowing the poles to be used for all communications or electronics wiring.

WIREMOLD ODS® OVERHEAD DISTRIBUTION SYSTEMS

Surface metal raceway systems installed overhead, above or below a dropped ceiling, distribute electrical power to ceiling lighting fixtures, and power and communications wiring to points of use via Tele-Power Poles and Quick-E-Poles. ODS systems provide a quick connect/disconnect capability for poles and lighting fixtures, and switches.

GLASS PLUG FUSES

- Escape vent for hot gases caused by short-circuit; prevents dangerous arcing often caused if gases could not escape.
- Amp rating is visible through window on color-coded insert.
- Meets Fed Specs: W-F831, Type 1; W-F7918, Type 11, Style A, Class 1; MIL-F-15160, Style F14, Characteristic A.

No.6700-15

No.6700-20

GLASS PLUG FUSES

125V AC ONLY			
CAT. NO.	AMPS	INSERT COLOR	WINDOW SHAPE
6700-10	10	Yellow	Hex
6700-15	15	Blue	Hex
6700-20	20	Orange	Round
6700-25	25	Red	Round
6700-30	30	Green	Round

TAMP-PRUF™ TIME-DELAY TYPE "S" FUSES

No.6710-15

- Special thermal cut-out provides time-delay, permitting normal current surges (like motor and appliance start-ups) without needless blowing—in accordance with limits set by UL Standards.
- TAMP-PRUF™ Type "S" design prevents by-pass tampering, as by insertion of coin shaped slugs.
- Improperly-rated fuses cannot be substituted, as each fuse will fit only its proper fuseholder or adapter.
- Adapter screws into standard Edison-base fuseholder or socket; locks in place so it can't be removed, so only the proper Type "S" fuse will fit.
- Cap is color-coded for amp rating, which is printed next to window.

No.6710-20

TYPE "S" FUSES

125V AC ONLY			
CAT. NO.	AMPS	CAP COLOR	WINDOW SHAPE
6710-10	10	Brown	Hex
6710-15	15	Blue	Hex
6710-20	20	Orange	Round
6710-25	25	Green	Round
6710-30	30	Green	Round

No.58015-SA

TYPE "S" ADAPTERS

CAT. NO.	FOR FUSE SIZE
58015-SA	10A, 15A
58020-SA	20A
58030-SA	25A, 30A

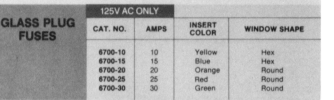

Illustrations on Pages 240 through 263 are courtesy of Leviton, C.

FUSES, FUSEHOLDERS AND KNIFE SWITCHES

NON-RENEWABLE CARTRIDGE FUSES

- Zinc fuse link melts faster than any other good conductor.
- One-piece link soldered directly to ferrule or blade for best conductivity.
- Link visibly soldered to ferrule (60A or less) for quick continuity check.
- Link and knife blade flow soldered into one rigid element (70A & higher).
- Ferrules and caps are crimped around entire edge of tube to assure cylindrical shape for best contact with fuseholder.
- Inert powder in tube surrounds link to dissipate heat safely upon operation of fuse.

No.58100-NON

No.58060-NON

No.58015-NON

250V OR LESS, AC ONLY					
CAT. NO.	AMPS	CAT. NO.	AMPS	CAT. NO.	AMPS
58010-NON	10	58035-NON	35	58070-NON	70
58015-NON	15	58040-NON	40	58080-NON	80
58020-NON	20	58045-NON	45	58090-NON	90
58025-NON	25	58050-NON	50	58100-NON	100
58030-NON	30	58060-NON	60		

PORCELAIN FUSEHOLDERS ("CUTOUTS") FOR CARTRIDGE FUSES

- Two-piece bronze fuse clips.
- Brass terminal and terminal screws.
- Fuseholders rated over 30A have clamp terminals.
- Meet Federal Specification W-P-870c.

No.8900

No.8906

No.8913

250V			DIMENSIONS (INCHES)† ★		MOUNTING HOLES
CAT. NO.	TRADE NO.	AMPS	LENGTH x WIDTH	SCREW SPACING	
SINGLE POLE, MAIN LINE					
8900	256930	30	3-3/4 x 1-3/8	3/8 x 3/4	2
8901	256960	60	5 x 1-1/2	31/32 x 7/8	2
8902	2569100	100	8-5/8 x 2-3/16	1-7/8 x 3/8	2
DOUBLE POLE, MAIN LINE					
8903	296530	30	3-3/4 x 2-3/4	1-1/4 (W)	2
8904	296560	60	5 x 3-5/16	1-1/2 (W)	2
8905	2965100	100	8-5/8 x 4	2-3/8 x 1-13/16	4
TRIPLE POLE, MAIN LINE					
8906	216530	30	3-3/4 x 4	2-1/2 (W)	2
8907	216560	60	5 x 4-7/8	3 (W)	2
8908	2165100	100	8-5/8 x 6	2-3/8 x 3-3/4	4
DOUBLE POLE, SINGLE BRANCH					
8913	193530	30	4-7/8 x 2-3/4	2-3/32 x 1-1/4	3
8914	193560	60	6-3/4 x 3-5/16	2-3/4 x 1-1/2	3

†Length and Width are Overall. Screw spacings are along center lines. L x W. to place oblique arrangement: single axis indicated by (L) or (W).

★ Consult factory for availability.

COMBINATION AND INTERCHANGEABLE DEVICES**

INTERCHANGEABLE DEVICES

- Heavy duty phenolic or urea housings; switches have protection against dust.
- Completely interchangeable with other lines of similar devices conforming to NEMA specifications.
- Devices lock into steel mounting straps without requiring screws.
- Terminal screws and Quickwire™ Push-in Terminals accept up to No. 12 copper or copper clad wire.
- Metal wallplates meet Federal Specification W-P-455a.
- Switches and mounting straps meet Federal Specification W-S-893c.

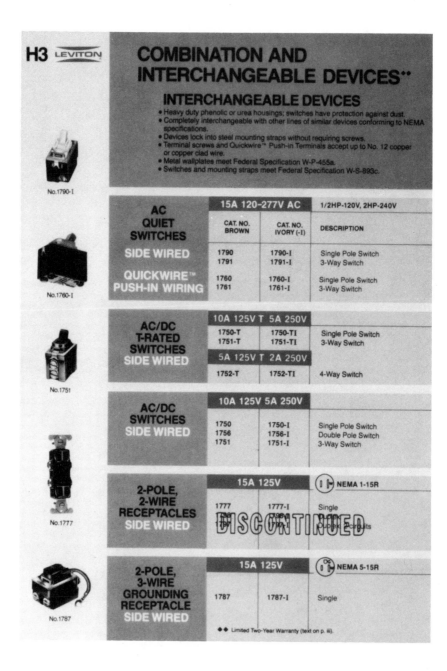

No.1790-I

No.1760-I

No.1751

No.1777

No.1787

AC QUIET SWITCHES	15A 120–277V AC		1/2HP-120V, 2HP-240V
	CAT. NO. BROWN	CAT. NO. IVORY (-I)	DESCRIPTION
SIDE WIRED	1790	1790-I	Single Pole Switch
	1791	1791-I	3-Way Switch
QUICKWIRE™ PUSH-IN WIRING	1760	1760-I	Single Pole Switch
	1761	1761-I	3-Way Switch

AC/DC T-RATED SWITCHES SIDE WIRED	10A 125V T 5A 250V		
	1750-T	1750-TI	Single Pole Switch
	1751-T	1751-TI	3-Way Switch
	5A 125V T 2A 250V		
	1752-T	1752-TI	4-Way Switch

AC/DC SWITCHES SIDE WIRED	10A 125V 5A 250V		
	1750	1750-I	Single Pole Switch
	1756	1756-I	Double Pole Switch
	1751	1751-I	3-Way Switch

2-POLE, 2-WIRE RECEPTACLES SIDE WIRED	15A 125V		NEMA 1-15R
	1777	1777-I	Single
			Duplex Circuits

DISCONTINUED

2-POLE, 3-WIRE GROUNDING RECEPTACLE SIDE WIRED	15A 125V		NEMA 5-15R
	1787	1787-I	Single

** Limited Two-Year Warranty (text on p. iii).

COMBINATION DEVICES** LEVITON H2

SPECIFICATION GRADE

No. 5211-I

No. 5218-I

No. 5214-I

No. 5227-I

No. 5213-LBI

SWITCH 10A 125V T, 5A 250V, RECEPTACLE 15A 125V — NEMA 1-15R

AC/DC T-RATED COMBINATION DEVICES	CAT. NO. BROWN	CAT. NO. IVORY	DESCRIPTION	FEED
	5211†	5211-I	Single Pole Switch & Receptacle	Common
	5211-SP	5211-ISP	As above, SEE PACK	
	5221	5221-I	Single Pole Switch & Receptacle	Separate

SWITCH 10A 125V T, 5A 250V, RECEPTACLE 15A 125V — NEMA 5-15R

	CAT. NO. BROWN	CAT. NO. IVORY	DESCRIPTION	FEED
	5219	5219-I†	Single Pole Switch & Grounding Receptacle	Common
	5220	5220-I	Single Pole Switch & Grounding Receptacle	Separate

SWITCHES 10A 125V T, 5A 250V

	CAT. NO. BROWN	CAT. NO. IVORY	DESCRIPTION	FEED
	5212	5212-I	2 Single Pole Switches	Common
	5212-SP	5212-ISP	As above, SEE PACK	
	5212-2	5212-2I	2 Single Pole Switches, Grounding	Common
	5214	5214-I	2 Single Pole Switches	Separate
	5215	5215-I	Single Pole & 3-Way Switches	Common
	5216	5216-I	Single Pole & 3-Way Switches	Separate
	5217	5217-I	2 3-Way Switches	Common
	5218	5218-I	2 3-Way Switches	Separate

SWITCH 10A 125V T, NEON PILOT 1/25W 125V

	CAT. NO. BROWN	CAT. NO. IVORY	DESCRIPTION	FEED
	5227	5227-I	Single Pole Switch & Neon Pilot Light	Common

SWITCH 10A 125V T, INCANDESCENT PILOT 75W 125V

	CAT. NO. BROWN	CAT. NO. IVORY	DESCRIPTION	FEED
	5213-LB	5213-LBI	Single Pole Switch & Incandescent Pilot Light, less Bulb	Common

†250 V Switch rating not applicable.
◆◆ Limited Two-Year Warranty (text on p. iii).

FUSES, FUSEHOLDERS AND KNIFE SWITCHES

UNFUSED NEUTRAL

30A 125V

CAT. NO.	TRADE NO.	DIMENSIONS (INCHES)†		MOUNTING HOLES
		LENGTH x WIDTH	SCREW SPACING	
SINGLE POLE, MAIN LINE				
8401	2965-0	2-7/16 x 2-9/16	1-25/32 (L)	2
DOUBLE POLE, SINGLE BRANCH				
8400	1935-0	3-5/8 x 2-1/2	2-9/32 (L)	2
DOUBLE POLE, DOUBLE BRANCH				
8404	3115	3-1/16 x 3-1/16	1-1/2 (L)	2
8402	2587-0	6-5/16 x 2-1/2	4-1/2 (L)	2
TRIPLE TO DOUBLE POLE, DOUBLE BRANCH				
8403	2199-0	6-5/16 x 2-1/2	5-15/32 (L)	2
TRIPLE POLE, DOUBLE BRANCH — FOUR CIRCUIT				
8740	3415	6-3/16 x 3-7/16	3-7/16 (L)	2

KNIFE SWITCHES

- Two-piece copper clips and blade assembly.
- Brass terminal and terminal screws.
- Fused (entrance) switches have brass screw shells.

FUSED (ENTRANCE) SWITCHES

30A 125V

CAT. NO.	TRADE NO.	DIMENSIONS		MOUNTING HOLES
		LENGTH x WIDTH	SCREW SPACING	
DOUBLE POLE, FUSES AT HANDLE END				
8712	205	4-5/8 x 3	3-1/4 (L)	2
DOUBLE POLE, FUSES AT HINGE END				
9161	206	4-5/8 x 3	3-1/4 (L)	2
TRIPLE POLE, FUSES AT HANDLE END				
9148	3205	4-1/2 x 4-1/2	3-11/16 x 1-1/2	4

†Length and Width are Overall. Screw spacings are along center lines, L x W, to place oblique arrangement; single axis indicated by (L) or (W).

★ Consult factory for availability.

No. 8400

No. 8404

No. 8403

No. 8740

No. 8712

No. 9148

PORCELAIN FUSEHOLDERS ("CUTOUTS") FOR CARTRIDGE FUSES (Cont.)

No.8911

No.8909

250V					
CAT. NO.	TRADE NO.	AMPS	DIMENSIONS (INCHES)†		MOUNTING HOLES
			LENGTH x WIDTH	SCREW SPACING	
TRIPLE POLE, SINGLE BRANCH					
8911	804230	30	5-7/8 x 4	3-3/32 x 1-1/4	2
8912	804260	60	8 x 4-3/4	3-15/16 x 1-1/2 x 3	2
DOUBLE POLE, DOUBLE BRANCH					
8915	258730	30	7-3/4 x 2-3/4	4-3/16 x 1-1/4	4
8916	258760	60	10-5/8 x 3-5/16	5-9/16 x 1-1/2	2
TRIPLE POLE, DOUBLE BRANCH					
8909	213530	30	8-7/8 x 4	5-3/16 x 2-1/2	4
8910	213560	60	11-3/4 x 4-7/8	6-3/4 x 2-29/32	4

No.9574

PORCELAIN FUSEHOLDERS ("CUTOUTS") FOR PLUG FUSES

- Brass screw shell, terminal and terminal screws.
- Meet Federal Specification W-F-870c.

No.8721

FUSED NEUTRAL

No.8720

No.8717

30A 125V					
SINGLE POLE, MAIN LINE					
9574	2569		2-5/8 x 2-1/4	1-23/32 x 1-1/2	2
DOUBLE POLE, MAIN LINE					
8719	2965		3 x 2-5/8	1-3/4 (L)	2
DOUBLE POLE, SINGLE BRANCH					
8721*	1935		3-1/2 x 3	2-9/32 (L)	2
DOUBLE POLE, DOUBLE BRANCH					
8716	2587		5-1/8 x 3	4-1/2 (L)	2
TRIPLE POLE, MAIN LINE					
8720	2165		4-1/2 x 2-5/8	1-1/2 x 1-19/32	2
TRIPLE POLE, DOUBLE BRANCH					
8718	2135		6-3/8 x 4-1/2	5-9/16 x 1-1/2	4
TRIPLE TO DOUBLE POLE, DOUBLE BRANCH					
8717	2199		6-3/16 x 3	5-1/2 (L)	2

†Length and Width are Overall. Screw spacings are along center lines, L x W. to place oblique arrangement: single axis indicated by (L) or (W).
*Not UL Listed. ✱ Consult factory for availability.

OUTLET BOX LAMPHOLDERS **

- Medium base.
- Pull chain or keyless.
- Shadeholder groove.
- 4-Terminal models facilitate continuous wiring.
- Pull chain models have bell at end of chain or cord.
- Most models in white porcelain; others available in phenolic or urea plastic.

No. 9875-2

PORCELAIN ONE-PIECE KEYLESS
TOP WIRED

660W 250V			
CAT. NO.	TERMINALS	O.D.	FITS BOX SIZE
† 9874	2 screws	3¾"	3¼"
† 9875	2 screws	4½"	3¼", 4"
9975	2 screws	5¼"	3¼", 4"
† 9875-2	2 6" Leads	4½"	3¼", 4"
49875	4 screws	4½"	3¼", 4"
9883	4 Quickwire push-in	4½"	3¼", 4"

No. 9883

BROWN PHENOLIC OR WHITE UREA KEYLESS

660W 600V				
CAT. NO. BROWN	CAT. NO. WHITE	TERMINALS	O.D.	FITS BOX SIZE
8828	†8828-W	2 screws	4½"	3¼", 4"
8829	8829-W	4 screws	4½"	3¼", 4"

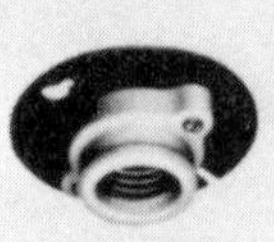

No. 9870

PORCELAIN COVER MOUNTED KEYLESS

660W 600V			
9870 †	2 screws	3½"	3¼"
9931 †	2 screws	4⅛"	4"
9871 †	2 6" Leads	3½"	3¼"

660W 250V			
9873 †	2 6" Leads	4⅛"	4"

Captive Mounting Screws

No. 29816-C

PORCELAIN TWO-PIECE (BODY AND RING) PULL CHAIN REMOVABLE INTERIOR MECHANISM CAPTIVE MOUNTING SCREWS
TOP WIRED

250W 250V			
CAT. NO.*	TERMINALS	O.D.	FITS BOX SIZE
29816-C ▲	2 screws	4½"	3¼", 4"
29816-CM	Interior Mechanism for 29816, 29916 and 49816		
29916-C	2 screws	5¼"	3¼", 4"
49816-C	4 screws	4½"	3¼", 4"

SIDE WIRED

9816-C	2 screws	4½"	3¼", 4"
9816-C2	2 6" Leads	4½"	3¼", 4"

†Meets Fed. Spec. W-L-142a.   *See SUFFIX LETTER descriptions, p. 12.
▲ 2 Captive Mounting Screws
◆◆ Limited Two-Year Warranty (text on p. iii).

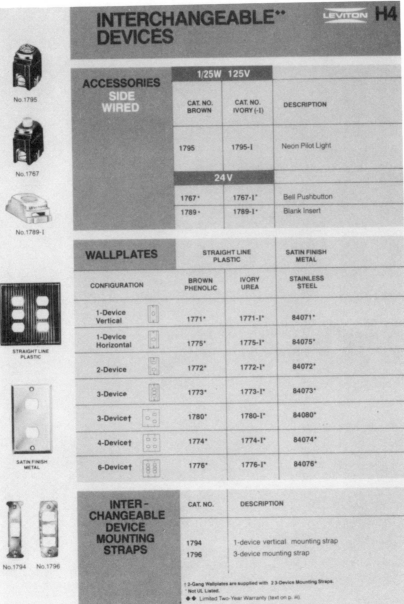

INTERCHANGEABLE** DEVICES

LEVITON H4

No.1795

No.1767

No.1789-I

STRAIGHT LINE PLASTIC

SATIN FINISH METAL

No.1794 No.1796

ACCESSORIES SIDE WIRED

	1/25W 125V		
	CAT. NO. BROWN	CAT. NO. IVORY (-I)	DESCRIPTION
	1795	1795-I	Neon Pilot Light
	24 V		
	1767*	1767-I*	Bell Pushbutton
	1789*	1789-I*	Blank Insert

WALLPLATES

CONFIGURATION		STRAIGHT LINE PLASTIC		SATIN FINISH METAL
		BROWN PHENOLIC	IVORY UREA	STAINLESS STEEL
1-Device Vertical		1771*	1771-I*	84071*
1-Device Horizontal		1775*	1775-I*	84075*
2-Device		1772*	1772-I*	84072*
3-Device		1773*	1773-I*	84073*
3-Device†		1780*	1780-I*	84080*
4-Device†		1774*	1774-I*	84074*
6-Device†		1776*	1776-I*	84076*

INTER-CHANGEABLE DEVICE MOUNTING STRAPS

CAT. NO.	DESCRIPTION
1794	1-device vertical mounting strap
1796	3-device mounting strap

† 2-Gang Wallplates are supplied with 2 3-Device Mounting Straps.
* Not UL Listed.
◆◆ Limited Two-Year Warranty (text on p. iii).

G2 LEVITON STRAIGHT BLADE PLUGS, CONNECTORS AND INLETS

No. 638

No. 649

No. 48646

No. 1511

No. 48642

No. 612

No. 48648

No. 617

No. 113

No. 5385

No. 5442

No. 5006

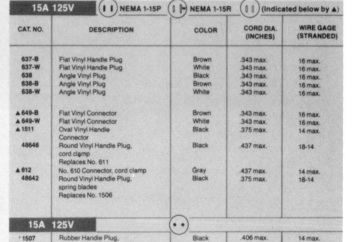

15A 125V NEMA 1-15P NEMA 1-15R (Indicated below by ▲)

CAT. NO.	DESCRIPTION	COLOR	CORD DIA. (INCHES)	WIRE GAGE (STRANDED)
637-B	Flat Vinyl Handle Plug	Brown	.343 max.	16 max.
637-W	Flat Vinyl Handle Plug	White	.343 max.	16 max.
638	Angle Vinyl Plug	Black	.343 max.	16 max.
638-B	Angle Vinyl Plug	Brown	.343 max.	16 max.
638-W	Angle Vinyl Plug	White	.343 max.	16 max.
▲ 649-B	Flat Vinyl Connector	Brown	.343 max.	16 max.
▲ 649-W	Flat Vinyl Connector	White	.343 max.	16 max.
▲ 1511	Oval Vinyl Handle Connector	Black	.375 max.	14 max.
48646	Round Vinyl Handle Plug, cord clamp Replaces No. 611	Black	.437 max.	18-14
▲ 612	No. 610 Connector, cord clamp	Gray	.437 max.	14 max.
48642	Round Vinyl Handle Plug, spring blades Replaces No. 1506	Black	.375 max.	18-14

15A 125V

CAT. NO.	DESCRIPTION	COLOR	CORD DIA. (INCHES)	WIRE GAGE (STRANDED)
* 1507	Rubber Handle Plug, Continental pin blades	Black	.406 max.	14 max.

2-POLE,3-WIRE GROUNDING

15A 125V NEMA 5-15P NEMA 5-15R

CAT. NO.	DESCRIPTION	COLOR	CORD DIA. (INCHES)	WIRE GAGE (STRANDED)
5442	Armored Vinyl Plug	Yellow	.312-.625	18-12
5006	†Armored Plastic Connector		.260-.625	14 max.
48648	Vinyl Handle Plug, cord clamp Replaces No. 615	Black	.437 max.	18-14
617	†Vinyl Connector, cord clamp	Gray	.437 max.	16 max.
113	Rubber Plug, vinyl blade/terminal/ cord clamp inner assembly Replaces No. 5384	Black	.396-.562	18-14
5385	†Rubber Connector, cord clamp	Black	.312-.625	14 max.
5239	Motor Base Inlet			
4937	No. 5239 on weatherproof wallplate	No. 10 max. solid copper or copper clad		

†With double-wipe brass contacts for maximum conductivity and plug blade retention.
*Not UL Listed; for replacement use only.

No. 123-I

No. 111

No. 5087

No. 48643

STRAIGHT BLADE PLUGS, CONNECTORS AND INLETS

 G1

"DEAD-FRONT" REQUIREMENTS BY UL

The ANSI/NFPA 1978 National Electrical Code, adopted by Underwriters' Laboratories, Inc., states the following, in Article 410-56 (d):

"All 15- and 20-ampere attachment plugs and connectors shall be so constructed that there are no exposed current-carrying parts except the prongs, blades, or pins. The cover for wire terminations shall be a part, which is essential for the operation of an attachment plug or connector (dead-front construction)."

Accordingly, NEW DEAD-FRONT PLUGS replace those no longer listed by UL.

ALL DEVICES ON THESE PAGES (SECTION G) ARE DEAD-FRONT.

- Plugs have brass blades, connectors have brass contacts, for maximum electrical conductivity.
- Armored devices have heavily plated steel shields and cord clamps.
- Plastic devices are molded of phenolic or urea to resist grease, oils and acids.
- Vinyl devices have high impact resistance; resist chipping, breaking, cracking, grease, oils and acids.
- Rubber devices resist cold, abrasion, grease, oils, acids and impact.
- Motor base inlets have heavy-gauge brass blades and phenolic bases on rust-resistant nickel plated steel casings and flanges; complete with mounting screws.

2-POLE, 2-WIRE

10A 125V on No. 18-2 SPT-1 3A 125V on No. 20-2 XT	PARALLEL CORDS ONLY	NEMA 1-15P Non-Polarized	NEMA 1-15P Polarized		
CAT. NO.	**DESCRIPTION**		**COLOR**	**CORD DIA. (INCHES)**	**WIRE GAGE (STRANDED)**
123	Flat Plastic Easy-to-Wire Plug (no need to strip wire) Carded — 2 per card		Brown	No. 18-2 SPT-1 or No. 20-2 XT only	
123-I	Same as No. 123		Ivory		
*123-P	Same as No. 123, POLARIZED		Brown		
*123-PI	Same as No. 123-P *Packed 500 Bulk		Ivory		

15A 125V	NEMA 1-15P	NEMA 1-15R	(Indicated below by ▲)		
111	Rubber Plug, vinyl blade/ terminal/cord clamp inner assembly Replaces No. 5084		Black	.296-.562	18-14
▲5087	Rubber Connector, cord clamp		Black	.296-.562	14 max. ▲
48643	Short Flat Vinyl Plug Replaces Nos. 763, 763-A, 749, 1400, 184		Brown	.375 max.	18-14
48643-W	Same as No. 48643 Replaces Nos. 763-I, 763-AI, 749-I, 1401-I, 184-I		White	.375 max.	18-14
48643-E	Same as No. 48643 Replaces No. 1508		Black	.375 max.	18-14

GFCI DEVICES**

SURE-GARD III, THE MOST ADVANCED GFCI RECEPTACLE BUILT TODAY!

- Compact 1⅜" body design; nylon high-abuse face.
- Complete with matching-color wallplate.†
- Exclusive LED Indicator Light on certain models.
- All models are designed for feed-through application.
- Every GFCI receptacle is subjected to special torture-test-chamber cycles of eight hours of cold and heat extremes from −31°F to +158°F.
- Available with UL Listed Hospital Grade, High Abuse Receptacle; certified Corrosion Resistant, with Cupro Nickel exposed metal parts.
- Pre-stripped wire leads for easy installation.

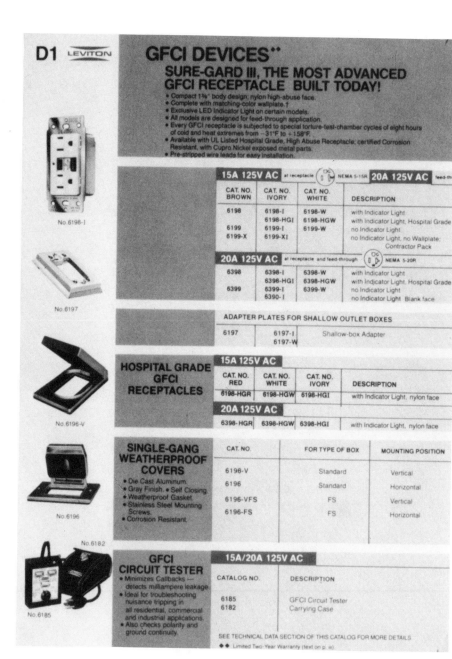

No. 6198-I

No. 6197

No. 6196-V

No. 6196

No. 6182

No. 6185

15A 125V AC at receptacle NEMA 5-15R **20A 125V AC** feed-thru

CAT. NO. BROWN	CAT. NO. IVORY	CAT. NO. WHITE	DESCRIPTION
6198	6198-I	6198-W	with Indicator Light
	6198-HGI	6198-HGW	with Indicator Light, Hospital Grade
6199	6199-I	6199-W	no Indicator Light
6199-X	6199-XI		no Indicator Light, no Wallplate; Contractor Pack

20A 125V AC at receptacle and feed-through NEMA 5-20R

6398	6398-I	6398-W	with Indicator Light
	6398-HGI	6398-HGW	with Indicator Light, Hospital Grade
6399	6399-I	6399-W	no Indicator Light
	6390-I		no Indicator Light Blank face

ADAPTER PLATES FOR SHALLOW OUTLET BOXES

6197	6197-I 6197-W	Shallow-box Adapter

HOSPITAL GRADE GFCI RECEPTACLES

15A 125V AC

CAT. NO. RED	CAT. NO. WHITE	CAT. NO. IVORY	DESCRIPTION
6198-HGR	6198-HGW	6198-HGI	with Indicator Light, nylon face

20A 125V AC

6398-HGR	6398-HGW	6398-HGI	with Indicator Light, nylon face

SINGLE-GANG WEATHERPROOF COVERS

- Die Cast Aluminum.
- Gray Finish. • Self Closing.
- Weatherproof Gasket.
- Stainless Steel Mounting Screws.
- Corrosion Resistant.

CAT. NO.	FOR TYPE OF BOX	MOUNTING POSITION
6196-V	Standard	Vertical
6196	Standard	Horizontal
6196-VFS	FS	Vertical
6196-FS	FS	Horizontal

GFCI CIRCUIT TESTER

- Minimizes Callbacks — detects milliampere leakage.
- Ideal for troubleshooting nuisance tripping in all residential, commercial and industrial applications.
- Also checks polarity and ground continuity.

15A/20A 125V AC

CATALOG NO.	DESCRIPTION
6185	GFCI Circuit Tester
6182	Carrying Case

SEE TECHNICAL DATA SECTION OF THIS CATALOG FOR MORE DETAILS.

** Limited Two-Year Warranty (text on p. x).

No.285

No.5206

No.5051

No. 5054-2

No.55054

No.275

3-POLE, 3-WIRE

30A 125/250V	NEMA 10-30R	NEMA 10-30P	• FOR DRYERS		
CAT. NO. BLACK	CAT. NO. GRAY (-GY) OR WHITE (-W)	DESCRIPTION		TERMINAL TYPE	WIRE GAGE (AWG)
5207	5207-GY	Flush Mount Receptacle		Pressure	4 max.
5055		Flush Mount Receptacle for 4" square outlet box		Lay-In	4 max.
5054-2	5054-2W	Surface Mount Receptacle		Lay-In	4 max.
5054		Surface Mount Receptacle		Screw	4 max.
	285-3†	Gray Power Supply Cord			10/3 SRDT
287		Right Angle Phenolic Plug		Screw	

50A 125/250V	NEMA 10-50R	NEMA 10-50P	FOR RANGES		
5206	5206-GY	Flush Mount Receptacle		Pressure	4 max.
5051		Flush Mount Receptacle for 4" square outlet box		Lay-In	4 max.
5050	5050-W	Surface Mount Receptacle		Lay-In	4 max.
	284-3†	Gray Power Supply Cord			6/2, 8/1 SRDT
287		Right Angle Phenolic Plug		Screw	

3-POLE, 4-WIRE GROUNDING

30A 125/250V	NEMA 14-30R	NEMA 14-30P		
278	278-GY	Flush Mount Receptacle	Pressure	4 max.
55054	55054-W	Surface Mount Receptacle	Lay-In	4 max.
276		Panel Mount Receptacle	Pressure	4 max.
5434-3†		Power Supply Cord		10/4 ST
275		Right Angle Phenolic Plug		

50A 125/250V	NEMA 14-50R	NEMA 14-50P		
279	279-GY	Flush Mount Receptacle	Pressure	4 max.
55050	55050-W	Surface Mount Receptacle	Lay-In	4 max.
277		Panel Mount Receptacle, wired ground side	Pressure	4 max.
277-7		Panel Mount Receptacle, wired neutral side	Pressure	4 max.
5436-3†		Power Supply Cord		6/2, 8/2 SRDT
275		Right Angle Phenolic Plug		

†Dash number indicates length of cord in feet (3′ lengths are used in this listing). Other available lengths are 4′, 5′, and 6′, indicated by changing dash number to -4, -5, or -6, respectively. Example: 284-5 is a 5-foot cord. Consult factory for special-order lengths.

SEE TECHNICAL DATA SECTION OF THIS CATALOG FOR MORE DETAILS.

INCANDESCENT LAMPHOLDERS

The lampholders in this section are designed to meet a wide variety of applications. Leviton's extensive engineering and manufacturing facilities can provide custom designed devices for special applications. For complete information consult your local Leviton Sales Representative.

ALL DIMENSIONS IN THIS SECTION ARE IN INCHES.

METAL SHELL LAMPHOLDERS

See Technical Section for typical dimensions of Electrolier, Short Electrolier and Standard metal shell lampholders.

No.8002
No.19980
No.10083-16
No.9842
No.9346
No.6098
No.8004
No.9843
No.7090
No.19980-M
No.501

MEDIUM BASE FINISHES

A SUFFIX MUST BE ADDED TO EACH BASIC CATALOG NUMBER TO INDICATE THE FINISH DESIRED.

Finishes on Aluminum:

FINISH/COLOR	SUFFIX
Bright gilt/Brass	-BG
Polished gilt/Brass	-PG
Unfinished/Aluminum	-AL
Polished/Aluminum	-NI

Finish on Brass:

Bright dip/Brass	-BR

Example: 8002-PG is a Pull Chain Lampholder with an Aluminum metal shell and cap, with a polished gilt (brass color) finish.

CONSULT PRICE LIST FOR AVAILABILITY OF FINISHES.

CAT. NO. RATINGS	DESCRIPTION
8002 250W 250V	Pull Chain — Standard. Single Circuit. 1/8 IPS tapped bushing w/set screw.
19980 660W 250V	Pull Chain — Electrolier. Single Circuit. 1/8 IPS tapped bushing w/set screw.
10083-16 250W 250V	Removable Turn Knob—Electrolier Single Circuit. 1/8 IPS tapped bushing w/set screw.
7070 250W 250V	Removable Turn Knob — Electrolier 2-circuit, 3 terminal. 1/8 IPS tapped bushing less set screw.
7090 250W 250V	Removable Turn Knob — Electrolier. Two-circuit. 1/8 IPS tapped bushing w/set screw.
9842 250W 250V	Key-Standard. Single Circuit. 1/8 IPS tapped bushing w/set screw.
9346 250W 250V	Key-Electrolier. Single Circuit. 1/8 IPS tapped bushing w/set screw.
6098 660W 250V	Push Thru — Electrolier. Single Circuits. 1/8 IPS tapped bushing w/set screw.
8004 660W 250V	Keyless — Electrolier. Single Circuit. 1/8 IPS tapped bushing w/set screw.
9347 660W 250V	Keyless—Short Electrolier. Single Circuits. 1/8 IPS tapped bushing w/set screw.
9843 660W 250V	Keyless — Standard. Single Circuit. 1/8 IPS tapped bushing. Less set screw.

INTERMEDIATE BASE
(Same finishes as above.)

CAT. NO. RATINGS	DESCRIPTION
512-3 75W 125V	Non-Removable Turn Knob. Single Circuit. 1/8 IPS tapped bushing, w/set screw.
501 75W 250V	Keyless. Single Circuit. 1/8 IPS tapped bushing, w/set screw.

METAL SHELL LAMPHOLDERS - INTERIORS

MEDIUM BASE

- Phenolic body.
- Aluminum screw-shell.

LAMPHOLDER	CAT. NO. INTERIOR	LAMPHOLDER	CAT. NO. INTERIOR
8002	8002-M	9842	9842-M
19980	19980-M	9346	9346-M
10083-16	10083-M	6098	7080-M
7070	7070-M	8004	8004-M
7090	7090-M	9843	9843-M

No.8827-C

No.9716-C

No.9726-C

No.9816-C

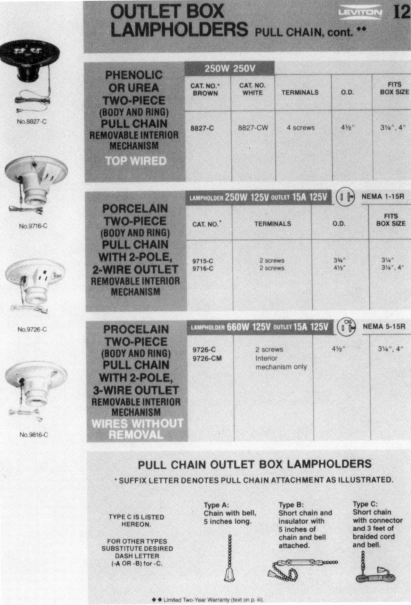

PHENOLIC OR UREA TWO-PIECE (BODY AND RING) PULL CHAIN REMOVABLE INTERIOR MECHANISM TOP WIRED

250W 250V				
CAT. NO.* BROWN	CAT. NO. WHITE	TERMINALS	O.D.	FITS BOX SIZE
8827-C	8827-CW	4 screws	4½"	3¼", 4"

PORCELAIN TWO-PIECE (BODY AND RING) PULL CHAIN WITH 2-POLE, 2-WIRE OUTLET REMOVABLE INTERIOR MECHANISM

LAMPHOLDER 250W 125V OUTLET 15A 125V			NEMA 1-15R
CAT. NO.*	TERMINALS	O.D.	FITS BOX SIZE
9715-C	2 screws	3¾"	3¼"
9716-C	2 screws	4½"	3¼", 4"

PROCELAIN TWO-PIECE (BODY AND RING) PULL CHAIN WITH 2-POLE, 3-WIRE OUTLET REMOVABLE INTERIOR MECHANISM WIRES WITHOUT REMOVAL

LAMPHOLDER 660W 125V OUTLET 15A 125V			NEMA 5-15R
9726-C 9726-CM	2 screws Interior mechanism only	4½"	3¼", 4"

PULL CHAIN OUTLET BOX LAMPHOLDERS

* SUFFIX LETTER DENOTES PULL CHAIN ATTACHMENT AS ILLUSTRATED.

TYPE C IS LISTED HEREON.

FOR OTHER TYPES SUBSTITUTE DESIRED DASH LETTER (-A OR -B) for -C.

Type A: Chain with bell, 5 inches long.

Type B: Short chain and insulator with 5 inches of chain and bell attached.

Type C: Short chain with connector and 3 feet of braided cord and bell.

◆◆ Limited Two-Year Warranty (text on p. iii).

RECEPTACLES

POWER RECEPTACLES

LIMITED TEN-YEAR WARRANTY
PREMIUM SPECIFICATION GRADE

- UL Listed to accept aluminum or copper conductors; clearly marked "AL/CU."
- Heavy gage double-wipe bronze contacts for maximum conductivity.
- Terminals color coded for easy identification, faster wiring.
- Complete with mounting screws.
- Flush mount devices fit single or 2-gang outlet boxes, except Cat. Nos. 5055, 5051, 278, 279
- Surface devices have concentric knockouts for 3/4" and 1" conduit, and cord clamp adjustable for cable size and back or bottom entrance positions.

No.5371

POWER SUPPLY CORDS

- Rugged vinyl cable with break-resistant molded-on right angle plug.

No.5375

DUAL POWER ATTACHMENT PLUGS

SPECIFICATION GRADE

- Each plug supplied with L-shaped 30 amp blade and flat 50 amp blade; interchangeable blades eliminate need for stocking separate 30- and 50-amp devices, simplify and reduce inventory.
- DEAD FRONT right angle construction.

No.932

2-POLE, 3-WIRE GROUNDING

30A 125V		NEMA 5-30R	NEMA 5-30P			
CAT. NO. BLACK	CAT. NO. GRAY (-GY)	DESCRIPTION	TERMINAL TYPE	WIRE GAGE (AWG)	CORD DIA. (INCHES)	
5371	5371-GY	Flush Mount Receptacle	Pressure	4 max.		
5375	5375-GY	Surface Mount Receptacle	Lay-In	4 max.		
	932-3	Power Supply Cord , 3 ft.		10/3 ST		
930		Right Angle Vinyl Plug	Screw	6 max.	.687-1.000	
30A 125V		ANSI C73.13	FOR RECREATIONAL VEHICLES			
7313		Flush Mount Receptacle	Pressure	4 max.		
50A 125V		NEMA 5-50R	NEMA 5-50P			
5373	5373-GY	Flush Mount Receptacle	Pressure	4 max.		
5377	5377-GY	Surface Mount Receptacle	Lay-In	4 max.		
	934-3	Power Supply Cord , 3 ft.		6/2, 8/1 ST		
930		Right Angle Vinyl Plug	Screw	6 max.	.687-1.000	
30A 250V		NEMA 6-30R	NEMA 6-30P			
5372	5372-GY	Flush Mount Receptacle	Pressure	4 max.		
5376	5376-GY	Surface Mount Receptacle	Lay-In	4 max.		
	933-3	Power Supply Cord , 3 ft.		10/3 ST		
931		Right Angle Vinyl Plug	Screw	6 max.	.687-1.000	
50A 250V		NEMA 6-50R	NEMA 6-50P			
5374	5374-GY	Flush Mount Receptacle	Pressure	4 max.		
5378	5378-GY	Surface Mount Receptacle	Lay-In	4 max.		
	935-3	Power Supply Cord , 3 ft.		6/2, 8/1 ST		
931		Right Angle Vinyl Plug	Screw	6 max.	.687-1.000	

No.273-25

No.930

No.5378

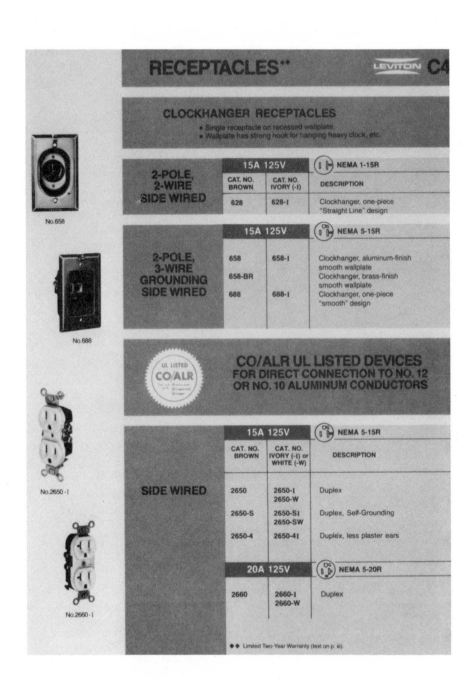

CLOCKHANGER RECEPTACLES

- Single receptacle on recessed wallplate.
- Wallplate has strong hook for hanging heavy clock, etc.

No. 658

2-POLE, 2-WIRE SIDE WIRED	15A 125V		NEMA 1-15R	
	CAT. NO. BROWN	CAT. NO. IVORY (-I)	DESCRIPTION	
	628	628-I	Clockhanger, one-piece "Straight Line" design	

No. 688

2-POLE, 3-WIRE GROUNDING SIDE WIRED	15A 125V		NEMA 5-15R	
	658	658-I	Clockhanger, aluminum-finish smooth wallplate	
	658-BR		Clockhanger, brass-finish smooth wallplate	
	688	688-I	Clockhanger, one-piece "smooth" design	

UL LISTED CO/ALR

CO/ALR UL LISTED DEVICES
FOR DIRECT CONNECTION TO NO. 12 OR NO. 10 ALUMINUM CONDUCTORS

No. 2650-I

SIDE WIRED	15A 125V		NEMA 5-15R	
	CAT. NO. BROWN	CAT. NO. IVORY (-I) or WHITE (-W)	DESCRIPTION	
	2650	2650-I 2650-W	Duplex	
	2650-S	2650-SI 2650-SW	Duplex, Self-Grounding	
	2650-4	2650-4I	Duplex, less plaster ears	

No. 2660-I

	20A 125V		NEMA 5-20R	
	2660	2660-I 2660-W	Duplex	

◆◆ Limited Two-Year Warranty (text on p. iii).

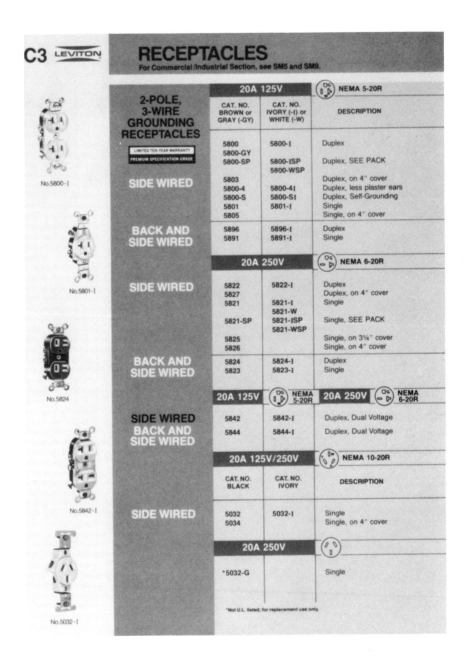

C3 LEVITON

RECEPTACLES
For Commercial/Industrial Section, see SM5 and SM9.

No.5800-I

No.5801-I

No.5824

No.5842-I

No.5032-I

2-POLE, 3-WIRE GROUNDING RECEPTACLES

LIMITED TEN-YEAR WARRANTY
PREMIUM SPECIFICATION GRADE

	20A 125V — NEMA 5-20R		
	CAT. NO. BROWN or GRAY (-GY)	CAT. NO. IVORY (-I) or WHITE (-W)	DESCRIPTION
SIDE WIRED	5800 5800-GY 5800-SP	5800-I 5800-ISP 5800-WSP	Duplex Duplex, SEE PACK
	5803 5800-4 5800-S 5801 5805	5800-4I 5800-SI 5801-I	Duplex, on 4" cover Duplex, less plaster ears Duplex, Self-Grounding Single Single, on 4" cover
BACK AND SIDE WIRED	5896 5891	5896-I 5891-I	Duplex Single

	20A 250V — NEMA 6-20R		
SIDE WIRED	5822 5827 5821	5822-I 5821-I 5821-W	Duplex Duplex, on 4" cover Single
	5821-SP	5821-ISP 5821-WSP	Single, SEE PACK
	5825 5826		Single, on 3¼" cover Single, on 4" cover
BACK AND SIDE WIRED	5824 5823	5824-I 5823-I	Duplex Single

	20A 125V NEMA 5-20R	20A 250V NEMA 6-20R	
SIDE WIRED	5842	5842-I	Duplex, Dual Voltage
BACK AND SIDE WIRED	5844	5844-I	Duplex, Dual Voltage

	20A 125V/250V — NEMA 10-20R		
	CAT. NO. BLACK	CAT. NO. IVORY	DESCRIPTION
SIDE WIRED	5032 5034	5032-I	Single Single, on 4" cover

	20A 250V		
	*5032-G		Single

*Not U.L. listed; for replacement use only.

256

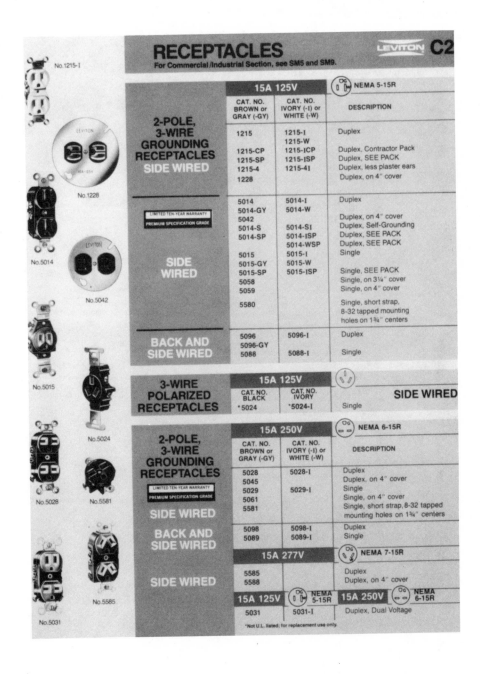

RECEPTACLES
For Commercial/Industrial Section, see SM5 and SM9.

LEVITON C2

2-POLE, 3-WIRE GROUNDING RECEPTACLES SIDE WIRED	15A 125V		NEMA 5-15R
	CAT. NO. BROWN or GRAY (-GY)	CAT. NO. IVORY (-I) or WHITE (-W)	DESCRIPTION
	1215	1215-I	Duplex
		1215-W	
	1215-CP	1215-ICP	Duplex, Contractor Pack
	1215-SP	1215-ISP	Duplex, SEE PACK
	1215-4	1215-4I	Duplex, less plaster ears
	1228		Duplex, on 4" cover
SIDE WIRED	5014	5014-I	Duplex
	5014-GY	5014-W	
	5042		Duplex, on 4" cover
	5014-S	5014-SI	Duplex, Self-Grounding
	5014-SP	5014-ISP	Duplex, SEE PACK
		5014-WSP	Duplex, SEE PACK
	5015	5015-I	Single
	5015-GY	5015-W	
	5015-SP	5015-ISP	Single, SEE PACK
	5058		Single, on 3¼" cover
	5059		Single, on 4" cover
	5580		Single, short strap, 8-32 tapped mounting holes on 1¾" centers
BACK AND SIDE WIRED	5096	5096-I	Duplex
	5096-GY		
	5088	5088-I	Single

LIMITED TEN-YEAR WARRANTY
PREMIUM SPECIFICATION GRADE

3-WIRE POLARIZED RECEPTACLES	15A 125V		SIDE WIRED
	CAT. NO. BLACK	CAT. NO. IVORY	
	*5024	*5024-I	Single

2-POLE, 2-WIRE GROUNDING RECEPTACLES	15A 250V		NEMA 6-15R
	CAT. NO. BROWN or GRAY (-GY)	CAT. NO. IVORY (-I) or WHITE (-W)	DESCRIPTION
SIDE WIRED	5028	5028-I	Duplex
	5045		Duplex, on 4" cover
	5029	5029-I	Single
	5061		Single, on 4" cover
	5581		Single, short strap, 8-32 tapped mounting holes on 1¾" centers
BACK AND SIDE WIRED	5098	5098-I	Duplex
	5089	5089-I	Single

LIMITED TEN-YEAR WARRANTY
PREMIUM SPECIFICATION GRADE

	15A 277V		NEMA 7-15R
SIDE WIRED	5585		Duplex
	5588		Duplex, on 4" cover

15A 125V NEMA 5-15R	15A 250V NEMA 6-15R		
5031	5031-I		Duplex, Dual Voltage

*Not U.L. listed; for replacement use only.

Left margin captions:
No.1215-I
No.1228
No.5014
No.5042
No.5015
No.5024
No.5028
No.5581
No.5585
No.5031

COMBINATION AND INTERCHANGEABLE DEVICES

COMBINATION DEVICES

- Available with AC Quiet Switches or AC/DC Switches.
- Devices with AC Quiet Switches have break-off fins for conversion to separate feeds (except switch/pilot light combinations).
- AC Quiet Switches have silver-cadmium oxide contacts, receptacles have double-wipe contacts, for maximum conductivity.
- All devices side-wired; terminal screws accept up to No. 10 copper or copper-clad wire.
- All devices accept standard duplex receptacle wallplates.
- All switches have framed toggles to inhibit dust collection.

LIMITED TEN-YEAR WARRANTY
PREMIUM SPECIFICATION GRADE

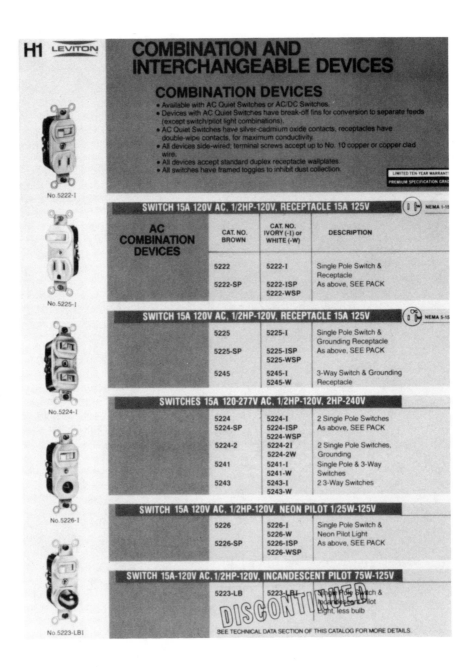

No. 5222-I

No. 5225-I

No. 5224-I

No. 5226-I

No. 5223-LBI

SWITCH 15A 120V AC, 1/2HP-120V, RECEPTACLE 15A 125V				NEMA 1-15
AC COMBINATION DEVICES	**CAT. NO. BROWN**	**CAT. NO. IVORY (-I) or WHITE (-W)**	**DESCRIPTION**	
	5222	5222-I	Single Pole Switch & Receptacle	
	5222-SP	5222-ISP 5222-WSP	As above, SEE PACK	

SWITCH 15A 120V AC, 1/2HP-120V, RECEPTACLE 15A 125V				NEMA 5-15
	5225	5225-I	Single Pole Switch & Grounding Receptacle	
	5225-SP	5225-ISP 5225-WSP	As above, SEE PACK	
	5245	5245-I 5245-W	3-Way Switch & Grounding Receptacle	

SWITCHES 15A 120-277V AC, 1/2HP-120V, 2HP-240V			
	5224 5224-SP	5224-I 5224-ISP 5224-WSP	2 Single Pole Switches As above, SEE PACK
	5224-2	5224-2I 5224-2W	2 Single Pole Switches, Grounding
	5241	5241-I 5241-W	Single Pole & 3-Way Switches
	5243	5243-I 5243-W	2 3-Way Switches

SWITCH 15A 120V AC, 1/2HP-120V, NEON PILOT 1/25W-125V			
	5226	5226-I 5226-W	Single Pole Switch & Neon Pilot Light
	5226-SP	5226-ISP 5226-WSP	As above, SEE PACK

SWITCH 15A-120V AC, 1/2HP-120V, INCANDESCENT PILOT 75W-125V			
	5223-LB	5223-LBI	Single Pole Switch & Incandescent Pilot Light, less bulb

DISCONTINUED

SEE TECHNICAL DATA SECTION OF THIS CATALOG FOR MORE DETAILS.

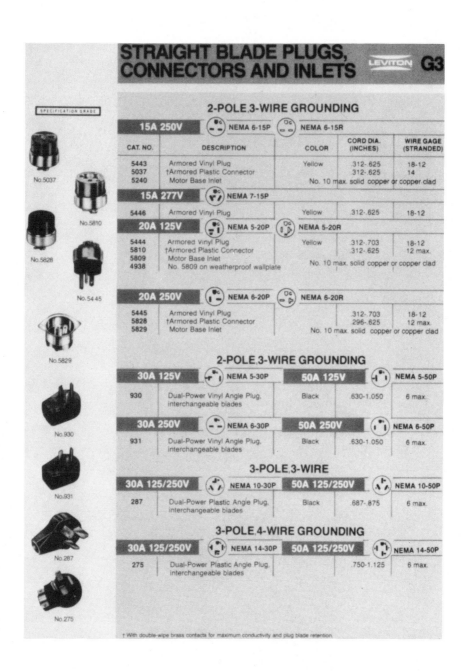

2-POLE,3-WIRE GROUNDING

15A 250V — NEMA 6-15P — NEMA 6-15R

CAT. NO.	DESCRIPTION	COLOR	CORD DIA. (INCHES)	WIRE GAGE (STRANDED)
5443	Armored Vinyl Plug	Yellow	.312-.625	18-12
5037	†Armored Plastic Connector		.312-.625	14
5240	Motor Base Inlet	No. 10 max. solid copper or copper clad		

15A 277V — NEMA 7-15P

5446	Armored Vinyl Plug	Yellow	.312-.625	18-12

20A 125V — NEMA 5-20P — NEMA 5-20R

5444	Armored Vinyl Plug	Yellow	.312-.703	18-12
5810	†Armored Plastic Connector		.312-.625	12 max.
5809	Motor Base Inlet			
4938	No. 5809 on weatherproof wallplate	No. 10 max. solid copper or copper clad		

20A 250V — NEMA 6-20P — NEMA 6-20R

5445	Armored Vinyl Plug		.312-.703	18-12
5828	†Armored Plastic Connector		.296-.625	12 max.
5829	Motor Base Inlet	No. 10 max. solid copper or copper clad		

2-POLE,3-WIRE GROUNDING

30A 125V — NEMA 5-30P   50A 125V — NEMA 5-50P

930	Dual-Power Vinyl Angle Plug, interchangeable blades	Black	.630-1.050	6 max.

30A 250V — NEMA 6-30P   50A 250V — NEMA 6-50P

931	Dual-Power Vinyl Angle Plug, interchangeable blades	Black	.630-1.050	6 max.

3-POLE,3-WIRE

30A 125/250V — NEMA 10-30P   50A 125/250V — NEMA 10-50P

287	Dual-Power Plastic Angle Plug, interchangeable blades	Black	.687-.875	6 max.

3-POLE,4-WIRE GROUNDING

30A 125/250V — NEMA 14-30P   50A 125/250V — NEMA 14-50P

275	Dual-Power Plastic Angle Plug, interchangeable blades		.750-1.125	6 max.

† With double-wipe brass contacts for maximum conductivity and plug blade retention.

SPECIFICATION GRADE

No.5037
No.5810
No.5828
No.5445
No.5829
No.930
No.931
No.287
No.275

53501-I

5501-I

5501-8I

5501-2I

AC QUIET SWITCHES

- Quiet, safe mechanical action in any position.
- Large-head terminal screws backed out and staked for fast wiring; accept up to No. 10 copper or copper clad wire.
- Back-wiring clamps accept up to No. 10 copper or copper clad wire.
- Quickwire™ push-in terminals on certain models provide quickest wiring; accept up to No. 12 solid copper or copper clad wire.
- Large silver-cadmium oxide contacts for maximum conductivity.
- Heavy gauge rust resistant steel mounting strap.
- Shallow design for maximum wiring room.
- Convenient washer type break-off plaster ears for best flush alignment.
- Captive mounting screws for fast installation.

For Commercial/Industrial Section, see SM3.

STANDARD TOGGLE BACK & SIDE WIRED	15A 120-277V AC		1/2HP-120V, 2HP-240V
	CAT. NO. BROWN or GRAY (-GY)	CAT. NO. IVORY (-I)	DESCRIPTION
LIMITED TEN-YEAR WARRANTY PREMIUM SPECIFICATION GRADE	53501	53501-I	Single Pole
	53502	53502-I	Double Pole
	53503	53503-I	3-Way
	53504	53504-I	4-Way
	20A 120-277V AC		**1HP-120V, 2HP-240V – RED COVER**
	53521	53521-I	Single Pole
	53522	53522-I	Double Pole
	53523	53523-I	3-Way
	53524	53524-I	4-Way

STANDARD TOGGLE SIDE WIRED	15A 120-277V AC		1/2HP-120V, 2HP-240V
LIMITED TEN-YEAR WARRANTY PREMIUM SPECIFICATION GRADE	5501 5501-GY	5501-I	Single Pole
	5501-8	5501-8I	Single Pole Hospital Call
• Hospital Call Switches turn on when toggle is pulled down, have 3-foot braided nylon cord.	5502 5502-GY	5502-I	Double Pole
	5502-8	5502-8I	Double Pole Hospital Call
	5503 5503-GY	5503-I	3-Way
	5504 5504-GY	5504-I	4-Way
	20A 120-277V AC		**1HP-120V, 2HP-240V – RED COVER**
	5521 5521-GY	5521-I	Single Pole
	5522 5522-GY	5522-I	Double Pole
	5523 5523-GY	5523-I	3-Way
	5524 5524-GY	5524-I	4-Way

GROUNDING STANDARD TOGGLE SIDE WIRED	15A 120-277V AC		1/2HP-120V, 2HP-240V
LIMITED TEN-YEAR WARRANTY PREMIUM SPECIFICATION GRADE	5501-2 5501-2GY	5501-2I	Single Pole
	5502-2 5502-2GY	5502-2I	Double Pole
	5503-2 5503-2GY	5503-2I	3-Way
	5504-2 5504-2GY	5504-2I	4-Way

SWITCHES ♦♦

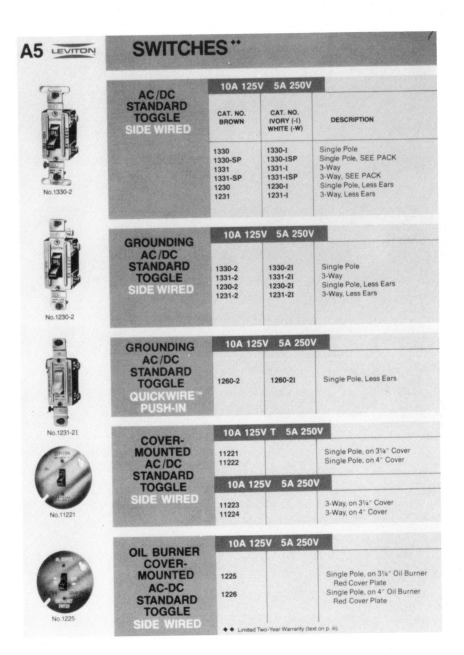

AC/DC STANDARD TOGGLE
SIDE WIRED

10A 125V 5A 250V		
CAT. NO. BROWN	CAT. NO. IVORY (-I) WHITE (-W)	DESCRIPTION
1330	1330-I	Single Pole
1330-SP	1330-ISP	Single Pole, SEE PACK
1331	1331-I	3-Way
1331-SP	1331-ISP	3-Way, SEE PACK
1230	1230-I	Single Pole, Less Ears
1231	1231-I	3-Way, Less Ears

No.1330-2

GROUNDING AC/DC STANDARD TOGGLE
SIDE WIRED

10A 125V 5A 250V		
1330-2	1330-2I	Single Pole
1331-2	1331-2I	3-Way
1230-2	1230-2I	Single Pole, Less Ears
1231-2	1231-2I	3-Way, Less Ears

No.1230-2

GROUNDING AC/DC STANDARD TOGGLE
QUICKWIRE™ PUSH-IN

10A 125V 5A 250V		
1260-2	1260-2I	Single Pole, Less Ears

No.1231-2I

COVER-MOUNTED AC/DC STANDARD TOGGLE
SIDE WIRED

10A 125V T 5A 250V		
11221		Single Pole, on 3¼" Cover
11222		Single Pole, on 4" Cover

10A 125V 5A 250V		
11223		3-Way, on 3¼" Cover
11224		3-Way, on 4" Cover

No.11221

OIL BURNER COVER-MOUNTED AC-DC STANDARD TOGGLE
SIDE WIRED

10A 125V 5A 250V		
1225		Single Pole, on 3¼" Oil Burner Red Cover Plate
1226		Single Pole, on 4" Oil Burner Red Cover Plate

No.1225

♦ ♦ Limited Two-Year Warranty (text on p. iii).

No.1210

SURFACE MOUNTING AC/DC FRAMED TOGGLE
BOTTOM WIRED

- Slotted Phenolic or Urea Cover snaps in place.
- Wood screws furnished for mounting.

10A 125V 5A 250V		
CAT. NO. BROWN	CAT. NO. IVORY (-I)	DESCRIPTION
1210	1210-I	Single Pole

CO/ALR UL LISTED AC QUIET SWITCHES
FOR DIRECT CONNECTION TO NO. 12 OR NO. 10 ALUMINUM CONDUCTORS

UL LISTED CO/ALR
For use with ☐ Aluminum ☐ Copperclad ☐ Copper

No.2651

FRAMED TOGGLE
SIDE WIRED

15A 120V AC		1/2HP-120V
CAT. NO. BROWN	CAT. NO. IVORY (-I) WHITE (-W)	DESCRIPTION
2651	2651-I 2651-W	Single Pole
2653	2653-I 2653-W	3-Way

15A 120-277V AC		1/2HP-120V, 2HP-240V
2654	2654-I	4-Way

No.2651-2

GROUNDING FRAMED TOGGLE
SIDE WIRED

15A 120V AC		1/2HP-120V
2651-2	2651-2I 2651-2W	Single Pole
2651-4	2651-4I	Single Pole, Less Ears
2653-2	2653-2I 2653-2W	3-Way
2653-4	2653-4I	3-Way, Less Ears

** Limited Two-Year Warranty (text on p. iii).

GENERAL FEATURES OF LEVITON WALLPLATES

- Meet Federal Specification W-P-455a, except plastic plates for Interchangeable Devices (1771 Series).
- Conform to NEMA and ANSI Standards.
- Non-combustible.

- Easily cleaned
- Individually wrapped together with matching-color metal mounting screws that are enclosed in extra internal envelope to prevent plate from being scratched.

STANDARD SIZE

| Toggle Switch | Duplex Receptacle | Single Receptacle | Power Receptacle |

- Available in a large variety of NEMA cutouts, in Smooth Plastic, Straight-Line Plastic and Satin Finish Metal.

LARGER SIZE

Standard   Extra Deep

Mid-Way®   **Oversized**   **Extra Deep**

- MID/WAY® Wallplates are used where the devices are to be mounted in the new, larger-size outlet boxes with greater cubic volume. Mid-Way Wallplates serve as economical "Goof Plates," covering wall damage.

- OVERSIZED Wallplates are ¼" higher and ¼" wider than standard wallplates. They are used to conceal more serious wall damage than could be hidden by the extra ¾" coverage of the Mid-Way Wallplates.

- EXTRA DEEP Wallplates are standard height and width. They offer a full ¼" depth, as do the Mid-Way and Oversized, and are used to assure a flush-to-wall fit despite the protrusions of particular devices in certain installations, where extra height and width are not needed.

- Aid compliance with new 1978 NEC requirement that switch wallplates cover wall openings completely and seat against wall (Article 380-9).
- All Leviton Larger Size wallplates listed are a full ¼" deep, to insure a clean fit flush with wall, despite protruding devices.

PLASTIC

Smooth   Straight Line

- Molded of urea or phenolic; match colors of Leviton wiring devices exactly.
- Full .100" thick, with reinforcing ribs for added mechanical strength at points of greatest stress.

METAL

- Easily removed transparent plastic film protects surface of plate during installation and/or painting of wall.
- See Technical Data Section for descriptions of metal alloys used.

** Limited Two-Year Warranty (text on p. iii).

RACO

No. 7601

No. 7602

No. 7604
Brkt. setback ¼"

No. 7603
Brkt. setback ½"

No. 7605

3⅛" DEEP

Raco No.	ACCESSORIES		Cubic Inch Cap.	No. of Cable Pri-Outs	Std. Pkg.	Wt. Per C
	Brackets	Other				
7601	—	nails, Rammit clip	18.0	4	100	31.1
7602	—	nails	18.0	4	100	30.9
7605	FP		17.8	4	50	39.4
7604	BP — ¼" setback		17.8	4	50	49.8
7603	BP — ½" setback		17.8	4	50	48.7

MULTI-GANG SWITCH BOXES

On multi-gang switch boxes, clamps cover all pri-outs.

No. 7490

No. 7491

2-GANG SWITCH BOXES, 2⅝" DEEP
22.5 cubic-inch capacity

Raco No.	ACCESSORIES			No. of Pri-Outs	Std. Pkg.	Wt. Per C
	Brackets	Clamps	Other			
7490	NP	Yes	Nails	8	25	43.6
7491	FP	Yes	—	8	25	42.9

Illustrations on Pages 264 through 287 are courtesy of Raco, Inc.

RACO

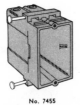

No. 7455   No. 7487

2⁹⁄₁₆" DEEP — 13.5 cubic-inch capacity

Raco No.	ACCESSORIES		No. of Cable Pri-Outs	Std. Pkg.	Wt. Per C
	Brackets	Other			
7455		Nails	4	100	28.3
7487		Saddle, ears, clamps	4	50	34.4

No. 7554   No. 7555   No. 7541   No. 7540 Brkt. setback ¼"   No. 7529 Brkt. setback ½"

2⁷⁄₈" DEEP — 16.0 cubic-inch capacity

Raco No.	ACCESSORIES		No. of Cable Pri-Outs	Std. Pkg.	Wt. Per C
	Brackets	Other			
7554	—	nails, Rammit clip	4	100	29.9
7555	—	nails	4	100	29.7
7541	FP		4	50	37.3
7540	BP — ¼" setback		4	50	47.8
7529	BP — ½" setback		4	50	46.9

THERMOPLASTIC "SOFT" BOXES

No. 7354, 7301   No. 7355, 7302

2⁹⁄₁₆" DEEP — 16.0 cubic-inch capacity

Raco No.	ACCESSORIES		No. of Cable Pri-Outs	Std. Pkg.	Wt. Per C
7354	—	nails, Rammit™ clips	4	100	19.2
7355	—	nails	4	100	19.2
7301	—	nails, Rammit™ clips	4	100	21.5
7302	—	nails	4	100	21.5

RACO

3½″ DIA., 2⅛″ DEEP

No. 7118

No. 7918

CEILING BOXES

14.0 cubic-inch capacity

No. 7123

No. 7923

No. 7121

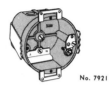

No. 7921

Raco No.	ACCESSORIES			No. of Cable Pri-Outs	Std. Pkg.	Wt. Per C
	Brackets	Clamps	Other			
7118	NP	Yes	nails	4	50	42.1
7918	NP	Yes	nails, grd. plate	4	50	44.6
7123	JP	Yes	—	4	50	46.2
7923	JP	Yes	grd. plate	4	50	48.8
7121	Saddle, ears, clamps			4	50	39.0
7921	Saddle, ears, clamps, grd. plate			4	50	41.3

3½″ DIA., 2⅛″ DEEP

SET-UP BOXES WITH ADJUSTABLE BAR HANGERS

14.0 cubic-inch capacity

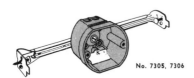

No. 7305, 7306

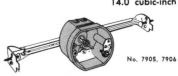

No. 7905, 7906

Raco No.	ACCESSORIES		Bar Adjustment Range	No. of Cable Pri-Outs	Std. Pkg.	Wt. Per C
	Clamps	Other				
7305	Yes	—	11½″-18½″	4	25	64.8
7905	Yes	grd. plate	11½″-18½″	4	25	66.3
7306	Yes	—	19½″-26½″	4	25	75.3
7906	Yes	grd. plate	19½″-26½″	4	25	77.8

STEEL COMPRESSION

rain and concrete tight

CONNECTORS

Patent No. 3,616,522

COUPLINGS

INSULATED THROAT CONNECTORS

Patent No. 3,616,522

STEEL SET SCREW

concrete tight

CONNECTORS

No. 2002-04   No. 2005-08   No. 2140-46

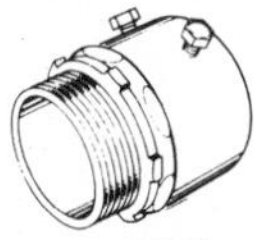

COUPLINGS

No. 2022-24   No. 2025-28   No. 2150-56

INSULATED THROAT CONNECTORS

No. 2122-24   No. 2125-28   No. 2160-66

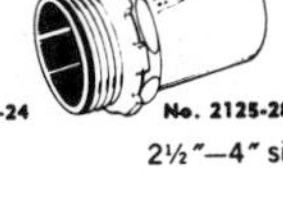

E.M.T. (Thinwall) FITTINGS

Cat. No.	Size	Quantity Unit Ctn.	Quantity Ship. Ctn.	Wt. per 100
2902*	½"	50	500	9.1
2903*	¾"	25	250	14.9
2904*	1"	25	100	22.8
2905	1¼"	5	25	47.0
2906	1½"	—	20	52.0
2908	2"	—	20	71.3
2940	2½"	—	10	163.0
2942	3"	—	5	250.0
2944	3½"	—	5	300.0
2946	4"	—	5	350.0
2922	½"	50	500	10.8
2923	¾"	25	250	18.4
2924	1"	25	100	27.2
2925	1¼"	5	25	37.3
2926	1½"	—	20	45.0
2928	2"	—	20	104.0
2950	2½"	—	10	238.0
2952	3"	—	5	334.0
2954	3½"	—	5	405.0
2956	4"	—	5	475.0
2912*	½"	50	500	9.2
2913*	¾"	25	250	16.3
2914*	1"	25	100	24.0
2915	1¼"	5	25	48.3
2916	1½"	—	20	58.0
2918	2"	—	20	82.5
2960	2½"	—	10	163.0
2962	3"	—	5	250.0
2964	3½"	—	5	300.0
2966	4"	—	5	350.0
2002*	½"	50	500	9.1
2003*	¾"	25	250	14.0
2004*	1"	25	100	20.7
2005	1¼"	5	25	37.8
2006	1½"	—	20	45.2
2008	2"	—	20	63.4
2140	2½"	—	10	117.5
2142	3"	—	5	166.9
2144	3½"	—	5	225.0
2146	4"	—	2	249.4
2022	½"	50	500	9.5
2023	¾"	25	250	15.5
2024	1"	25	100	16.3
2025	1¼"	5	25	41.0
2026	1½"	—	20	45.5
2028	2"	—	20	71.1
2150	2½"	—	10	144.0
2152	3"	—	5	196.9
2154	3½"	—	5	264.0
2156	4"	—	2	306.3
2122*	½"	50	500	9.2
2123*	¾"	25	250	14.3
2124*	1"	25	100	19.1
2125	1¼"	5	25	39.0
2126	1½"	—	20	50.0
2128	2"	—	20	67.0
2160	2½"	—	10	129.8
2162	3"	—	5	179.0
2164	3½"	—	5	210.0
2166	4"	—	2	252.0

*Hardened steel, extruded locknut.

2½"–4" sizes of steel set screw connectors & couplings also UL listed for IMC.

PRESSURE CAST COMPRESSION

rain and concrete tight

CONNECTORS

COUPLINGS

INSULATED THROAT CONNECTORS

PRESSURE CAST SET SCREW
concrete tight

CONNECTORS

No. 2602-04   No. 2605-

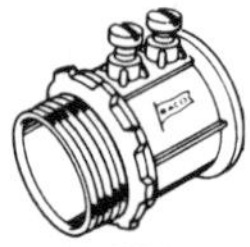

COUPLINGS

No. 2622-24   No. 2625-

INSULATED THROAT CONNECTORS

No. 2612-14   No. 2615-

2½"–4" sizes of die cast set screw connectors & couplings also UL listed for IMC & rigid conduit.

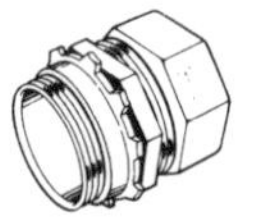

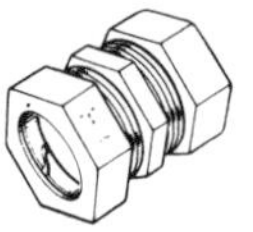

Cat. No.	Size	Quantity Unit Ctn.	Quantity Ship. Ctn.	Wt. per 100
2802**	½"	50	500	8.3
2803**	¾"	25	250	13.1
2804**	1"	50	200	21.8
2805	1¼"	25	100	36.0
2806	1½"	10	40	53.0
2808	2"	5	20	80.0
2822	½"	50	500	11.3
2823	¾"	25	250	16.8
2824	1"	50	200	27.8
2825	1¼"	25	100	43.6
2826	1½"	10	40	67.3
2828	2"	5	20	90.5
2812**	½"	50	500	9.3
2813**	¾"	50	200	21.0
2814**	1"	25	100	37.0
2815	1¼"	25	250	13.2
2816	1½"	10	40	53.0
2818	2"	5	20	81.0
2602**	½"	50	500	5.9
2603**	¾"	25	250	9.2
2604**	1"	50	200	14.4
2605	1¼"	25	100	28.0
2606	1½"	10	40	39.0
2608	2"	5	20	54.7
2640	2½"	—	12	92.0
2642	3"	—	12	125.0
2644	3½"	—	6	163.0
2646	4"	—	6	200.0
2622	½"	50	500	6.5
2623	¾"	25	250	10.4
2624	1"	50	200	14.0
2625	1¼"	25	100	28.9
2626	1½"	10	40	38.0
2628	2"	5	20	54.1
2670	2½"	—	12	108.0
2672	3"	—	12	125.0
2674	3½"	—	6	165.0
2676	4"	—	6	200.0
2612**	½"	50	500	6.0
2613**	¾"	25	250	10.0
2614**	1"	50	200	15.0
2615	1¼"	25	100	28.0
2616	1½"	10	40	39.0
2618	2"	5	20	55.0
2680	2½"	—	12	92.0
2682	3"	—	12	125.0
2684	3½"	—	6	163.0
2686	4"	—	6	200.0

**Extruded locknut.

TWO-PIECE CONNECTORS

die cast zinc

Cat. No.	Size	Quantity Unit Ctn.	Ship. Ctn.	Wt. per 100
2702	½"	100	400	5.8
2703	¾"	50	500	8.8

OFFSET CONNECTORS

die cast zinc

COMPRESSION

1952	½"		50	13.0
1953	¾"		25	22.5
1954	1"		25	32.0

SET SCREW

1762	½"		50	11.0
1763	¾"		25	17.0
1764	1"		25	24.0

INDENTER

1752	½"		50	9.9
1753	¾"		25	16.4
1754	1"		25	21.3

90° SHORT ANGLE CONNECTORS

malleable iron

Cat. No.	Size	Quantity Unit Ctn.	Ship. Ctn.	Wt. per 100
2072	½"	25	100	17.0
2073	¾"	25	100	27.5
2074	1"	5	25	44.0

malleable iron
INSULATED THROAT

3072	½"	25	100	19.5
3073	¾"	25	100	27.4
3074	1"	5	25	44.5

Precisely locates box on ceiling joist or stud

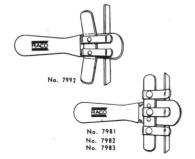

No. 7992

No. 7981
No. 7982
No. 7983

FOR 4" DIA., 1⅝" CEILING BOXES

Raco No.	Description	Unit Ctn.	Ship Ctn.	Wt. Per C
7992	½" setback	2	10	51.0

FOR 4" SQUARE AND SWITCH BOXES

7981	¼" setback	2	10	53.0
7982	½" setback	2	10	53.0
7983	⅝" setback	2	10	53.0

BRACKETS, CLAMPS AND GROUND PLATE

RAMMIT™ CLIPS

Spring-steel clip allows device screw to be pushed in box and tightened with a few turns.

BP BRACKET

Mounts on front of stud. Spurs hold box for easy nailing. ¼" or ½" setback.

FP BRACKET

Mounts on side of stud. Spurs hold box for easy nailing.

NP BRACKET

Mounts on side of stud. Includes staked, serrated nails canted for easy nailing.

JP BRACKET

Bracket with spurs for ceiling mounting. Elongated holes for toe-nailing.

#7 CLAMP

For non-metallic sheathed cable.

GROUND PLATE

Metal plate offords grounding safety. Plate fastened to box with center screw. Ground wire of cable attaches to green hex head screw.

On multi-gang switch boxes, clamps cover all pri-outs.

No. 7546

No. 7545

No. 7552
Brkt. setback ¼"

2-GANG SWITCH BOXES, 2¹⁵/₁₆" DEEP — 27.5 cubic-inch capacity

7546	NP	Yes	Nails	8	25	51.8
7545	FP	Yes	—	8	25	51.3
7552	BP	Yes	¼" Setback	8	25	62.3

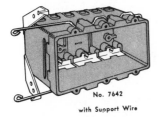

No. 7642

with Support Wire

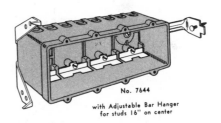

No. 7644

with Adjustable Bar Hanger
for studs 16" on center

3-GANG SWITCH BOXES, 2½" DEEP — 34.0 cubic-inch capacity — 33⅜" x 5²⁷/₃₂" x 2½"

Raco No.	Brackets	Clamps	Other	No. of Pri-Outs	Std. Pkg.	Wt. Per C
7642	FP	Yes	—	12	10	61.5

4-GANG SWITCH BOXES, 2⅝" DEEP — 48.0 cubic-inch capacity — 3⅝" x 7²¹/₃₂" x 2⅝"

7644	FP	Yes	—	16	4	111.0

FLEXIBLE METAL CONDUIT ARMORED BUSHED CABLE

90° CONNECTORS
malleable iron

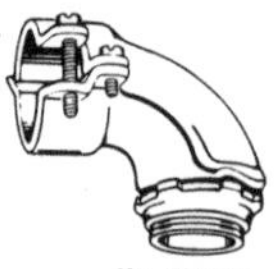

No. 2204-05

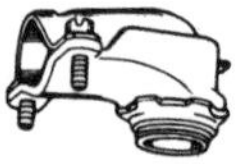

No. 2201-03

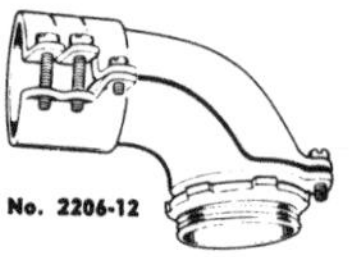

No. 2206-12

Cat. No.	KO Size	Flex. Met. Size	Quantity Unit Ctn.	Quantity Ship. Ctn.	Wt. per 100
2201*	½"	⅜"	50	100	16.1
2202*	½"	½"	25	100	22.7
2203*	¾"	¾"	25	50	26.6
2204*	1"	1"	—	25	45.8
2205	1¼"	1¼"	—	10	70.6
2206	1½"	1½"	—	5	125.0
2208	2"	2"	—	5	199.6
2210	2½"	2½"	—	1	516.7
2212	3"	3"	—	1	809.4

INSULATED THROAT
malleable iron

No. 3204-05

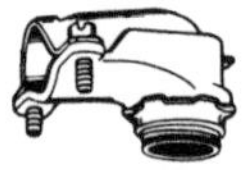

No. 3201-03

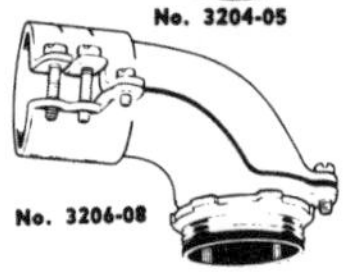

No. 3206-08

Cat. No.	KO Size	Flex. Met. Size	Unit Ctn.	Ship. Ctn.	Wt. per 100
3201*	½"	⅜"	50	100	13.5
3202*	½"	½"	25	100	21.9
3203*	¾"	¾"	25	50	27.5
3204*	1"	1"	—	25	46.0
3205	1¼"	1¼"	—	10	78.0
3206	1½"	1½"	—	5	122.5
3208	2"	2"	—	5	204.0

die cast zinc

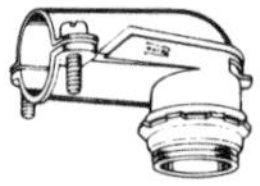

2701	½"	⅜"	50	500	9.5
2692	½"	½"	25	100	13.5
2693	¾"	¾"	25	100	19.0

*Hardened steel, extruded locknut

45° CONNECTORS
malleable iron

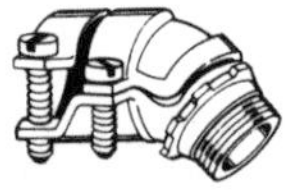

2221	½"	⅜"	25	100	14.5
2222	½"	½"	25	100	20.0
2223	¾"	¾"	25	50	27.0

TWO SCREW CLAMP
malleable iron

Cat. No.	KO Size	Flex. Size	Quantity Unit Ctn.	Quantity Ship. Ctn.	Wt. per 100
2173	¾"	½"	25	100	21.4
2183	¾"	¾"	25	100	21.0

die cast zinc

2632	½"	½"	25	250	9.4

Physical dimensions of armored bushed cable vary between manufacturers. Select connectors by physical dimensions of the cable.

ARMORED BUSHED CABLE

Physical dimensions of armored bushed cable vary between manufacturers. Select connectors by physical dimensions of the cable.

malleable iron

Cat. No.	Size	Quantity Unit Ctn.	Ship. Ctn.	Wt. per 100
2181	½"	50	500	7.5

die cast zinc

| 2511 | ½" | 100 | 1000 | 4.3 |

DUPLEX
malleable iron

| 2111 | ½" | 25 | 100 | 17.0 |

NAIL-UP
stamped steel

| 2252 | ⅜" | 100 | 1000 | 1.7 |
| 2253 | ½" | 100 | 1000 | 2.2 |

NONMETALLIC SHEATHED CABLE

die cast zinc

Cat. No.	KO Size	Cable Size	Quantity Unit Ctn.	Ship. Ctn.	Wt. per 100
2711	½"	2#14, 2#12, 3#14 or 3#12 with or w/o ground	100	1000	5.5

plastic

U. S. Patent 3788582
Canadian Patent 984476

| 4711 | ½" | 2#14, 2#12 or 2#10 with or without ground. | 100 | 500 | 1.3 |

with reversible clamp
die cast zinc

| 2863 | ¾" | 3#12, 3#10 & 2#8 | 50 | 500 | 12.0 |
| 2864 | 1" | 4#12, 3#12, 4#10, 3#10, 3#8, 2#8, 2#6 & 2#4 | 25 | 100 | 19.5 |

ALL PURPOSE
die cast zinc

also for 3/8" flexible metal conduit

| 2661 | ½" | 2#14, 2#12 or 2#10 with or without ground. | 100 | 1000 | 5.5 |

NON METALLIC CABLE PROTECTOR

steel

Cat. No.	Quantity Ship. Ctn.	Wt. per 100
2710	200	9.0

OVAL CABLE CONNECTORS

die cast zinc

Cat. No.	KO Size	Cable Sizes	Quantity Unit Ctn.	Ship. Ctn.	Wt. per 100
2853	¾"	3 # 8, 3 # 6	25	100	10.0
2854	1"	3 # 6, 3 # 4	25	100	16.9
2855	1¼"	3 # 2, 3 # 3	25	100	23.5
2856	1½"	3 # 1/0, 3 # 2/0, 3 # 1	—	25	35.0
2858	2"	3 # 3/0, 3 # 4/0	—	25	48.0

OVAL OR ROUND CABLE
die cast zinc
with reversible clamp

Cat. No.	KO Size	Cable Size	Quantity Unit Ctn.	Ship. Ctn.	Wt. per 100
2863	¾"	3 # 10, 3 # 6, 2 # 6, 2 # 4 & 2 # 2	50	500	11.6
2864	1"	3 # 6, 3 # 4, 2 # 4 & 2 # 2	25	100	19.5

UNDER GROUND FEEDER CABLE CONNECTOR
steel

Cat. No.	Hub or Trade Size	Nominal Cable Size	Grommet Opening	Quantity Unit Ctn.	Ship. Ctn.	Wt. per 100
2462	½"	2 # 14, # 12	.225 x .425	25	100	16.0

WATERTIGHT CONNECTORS

die cast zinc

Cat. No.	Hub or Trade Size	Nominal Cable Size	Grommet Opening	Quantity Unit Ctn.	Ship. Ctn.	Wt. per 100
2464	1"	3 # 8	.410 x .690	10	100	32.0
2474	1"	3 # 6	.500 x .780	10	100	32.0
2484	1"	3 # 4	.530 x .840	10	100	32.0
2485	1¼"	3 # 3	.560 x .930	10	50	48.0
2475	1¼"	3 # 2	.600 x 1.000	10	50	48.0
2465	1¼"	3 # 1/0	.650 x 1.100	10	50	48.0
2486	1½"	3 # 2/0	.720 x 1.250	—	25	80.0
2476	1½"	3 # 2/0	.760 x 1.330	—	25	80.0
2466	1½"	3 # 3/0	.870 x 1.480	—	25	80.0
2488	2"	3 # 2/0	.850 x 1.350	—	10	80.0
2498	2"	3 # 3/0	.865 x 1.375	—	10	80.0
2468	2"	3 # 4/0	.960 x 1.550	—	10	80.0
2478	2"	3 # 4/0*	1.130 x 1.780	—	10	80.0

Physical dimensions of service entrance cable vary between manufacturers and with type of jacket. Select connectors by physical dimensions of the cable.

CONDUIT ENTRANCE ELLS

pressure cast
aluminum

Cat. No.	Size	Quantity Unit Ctn.	Quantity Ship. Ctn.	Wt. per 100
2332	1/2"	10	50	20.1
2333	3/4"	10	50	25.6
2334	1"	5	25	52.3
2335	1 1/4"	2	10	102.7
2336	1 1/2"	1	5	129.8
2338	2"	1	5	160.0

OVAL CABLE ENTRANCE CAPS

cast aluminum

Cat. No.	Cable Size	Quantity Unit Ctn.	Quantity Ship. Ctn.	Wt. per 100
2430	3 #8, 3 #6, 3 #4, 2 #4 & 1 #6, 3 #3, 2 #3 & 1 #5, 3 #2, 2 #2 & 1 #4, 3 #1, 2 #1 & 1 #3	5	25	37.9
2420	3 #1/0, 2 #1/0 & 1 #2, 3 #2/0, 2 #2/0 & 1 #1	—	10	73.3
2440	3 #3/0, 2 #3/0 & 1 #1/0, 3 #4/0, 2 #4/0 & 1 #2/0	—	10	95.2

OVAL CABLE SILL PLATES

cast aluminum

Cat. No.	Cable Size	Quantity Unit Ctn.	Quantity Ship. Ctn.	Wt. per 100
2470	3 #3/0, 2 #3/0 & 1 #1/0, 3 #4/0, 2 #4/0 & 1 #2/0	—	10	82.3

With sealing compound and 2 screws.

OVAL CABLE STRAPS

steel

Cat. No.	Max. Cable Size	Cable Size PVC Jacket	Cable Size Neoprene or Braided Jacket	Quantity Unit Ctn.	Quantity Ship. Ctn.	Wt. per 100
2441	.453 x .812	3 #6, 3 #4, 2 #4 & 1 #6	3 #8, 3 #6, 2 #6 & 1 #8	100	1000	2.2
2442	.625 x 1.047	3 #2, 3 #1, 2 #2 & 1 #4, 2 #1 & 1 #3	3 #4, 3 #3, 3 #2, 2 #4 & 1 #6, 2 #3 & 1 #5, 2 #2 & 1 #4	100	1000	2.6
2443	.828 x 1.438	3 #2/0, 3 #3/0, 3 #4/0, 2 #2/0 & 1 #1, 2 #3/0 & 1 #1/0, 2 #4/0 & 1 #2/0	3 #1, 3 #1/0, 3 #2/0, 2 #1 & 1 #3, 2 #1/0 & 1 #2, 2 #2/0 & 1 #1	50	250	10.8
2444	.984 x 1.703	—	3 #3/0, 3 #4/0, 2 #3/0 & 1 #4/0, 2 #4/0 & 1 #2/0	50	250	12.3

1½" DEEP WITH ARMORED CABLE CLAMPS

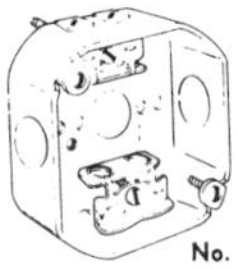

No. 153

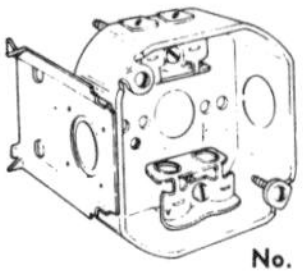

No. 157

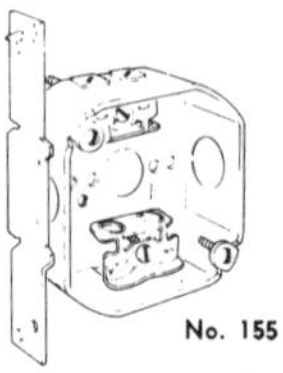

No. 155   15.5 cubic-inch capacity

Raco No.	Universal No.	ACCESSORIES			KNOCKOUTS				Std. Pkg.	Wt. Per C
					SIDES		BOTTOM			
		Clamps	Brkt.	Ears	Conduit	Cable	Conduit			
153	54151-X	2-X	—	—	2—½"	4	1—½"		50	57.3
155	54151-FAX	2-X	FA		1—½"	4	1—½"		50	71.0
157	54151-JX	2-X	J	—	2—½"	4	1—½"		50	73.0

2⅛" DEEP WITH NON-METALLIC CABLE CLAMPS

No. 165

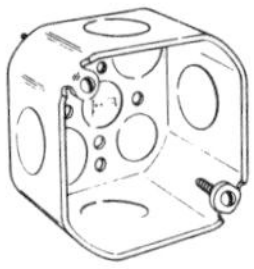

No. 166

No. 167

21.5 cubic-inch capacity

Raco No.	Universal No.	ACCESSORIES		KNOCKOUTS				Std. Pkg.	Wt. Per C
				SIDES		BOTTOM			
		Clamps	Brkt.	Conduit	Cable	Conduit			
165	54171-½	—	—	4—½"		5—½"		50	66.9
166	54171-¾	—	—	4—¾"		3—½" 2—¾"		50	66.9
167	54171-SP	—	—	2—½" 2—¾"	—	3—½" 2—¾"		50	66.9

2⅛" DEEP WITH CONDUIT KO's

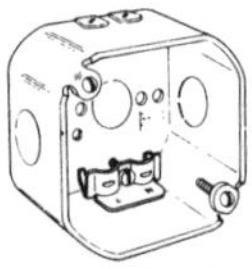

No. 175

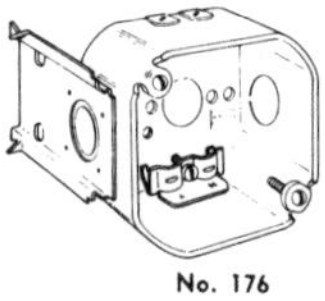

No. 176

No. 177
Bracket
Setback ⅝"

21.5 cubic-inch capacity

Raco No.	Universal No.								Std. Pkg.	Wt. Per C
175	54171-N	2-L	—	2—½"	4	1—½"			50	71.1
176	54171-JN	2-L	J	2—½"	4	1—½"			25	82.7
177	54171-FAN	2-L	FA	1—½"	4	1—½"			25	81.8

RACO

11½″ TO 18½″

Rigid M
Patent No. 2,809,002

No. 920-921   No. 924-925   No. 922-923   No. 926-927

Raco No.		Stud	Clip	Std. Pkg.	Wt. Per C
920	(With staked nails)	Yes	—	50	37.3
924	(No nails)	Yes	—	50	36.3
922	(With staked nails)	—	Yes	50	33.4
926	(No nails)	—	Yes	50	31.9

19½″ TO 26½″

921	(With staked nails)	Yes	—	50	47.4
925	(No nails)	Yes	—	50	45.4
923	(With staked nails)	—	Yes	50	43.4
927	(No nails)	—	Yes	50	41.8

4″ OCTAGON SET-UP BOXES   ADJUSTABLE BAR HANGERS

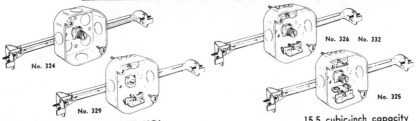

No. 324

No. 329

No. 326   No. 332

No. 325

15.5 cubic-inch capacity

1½″ DEEP WITH CONDUIT KO's

Raco No.	Universal No.	Box No.	Bar Hanger No.	Clamps	Stud	Std. Pkg.	Wt. Per C
324	54151-HU	125	920	—	Yes	25	88.6

1½″ DEEP WITH NON-METALLIC CABLE CLAMPS

326	54151-L-HU	146	920	2-L	Yes	25	91.7
329	54151-L-HUC	146	922	2-L	—	25	89.8
332		146	921	2-L	Yes	25	101.0

1½″ DEEP WITH ARMORED CABLE CLAMPS

325	54151-X-HU	153	920	2-X	Yes	25	93.5

2⅛″ DEEP WITH NON-METALLIC CABLE CLAMPS

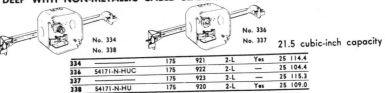

No. 334
No. 338

No. 336
No. 337

21.5 cubic-inch capacity

334		175	921	2-L	Yes	25	114.4
336	54171-N-HUC	175	922	2-L	—	25	104.4
337		175	923	2-L	—	25	115.3
338	54171-N-HU	175	920	2-L	Yes	25	109.0

LIQUID-TIGHT FITTINGS

90° CONNECTORS

malleable iron

INSULATED THROAT

malleable iron

Cat. No.	Size	Quantity Unit Ctn.	Quantity Ship. Ctn.	Wt. per 100
3421	⅜"	25	50	20.0
3422	½"	25	50	21.6
3423	¾"	10	50	32.1
3424	1"	5	25	61.2
3425	1¼"	5	25	103.9
3426	1½"	2	10	144.6
3428	2"	1	5	206.0
3430*	2½"	—	1	500.0
3432*	3"	—	1	625.0
3436*	4"	—	1	950.0
3541	⅜"	25	50	21.0
3542	½"	25	50	31.0
3543	¾"	10	50	39.0
3544	1"	5	25	59.1
3545	1¼"	5	25	101.1
3546	1½"	2	10	141.0
3548	2"	1	5	207.0
3550†*	2½"	—	1	500.0
3552†*	3"	—	1	625.0
3556†*	4"	—	1	950.0

*Captive, steel grounding ferrule; other sizes have removable ferrule.

† Connector with insulating bushing

Liquid-tight connectors available with external ground lug; consult factory for price and delivery.

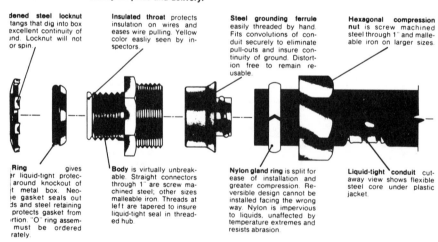

dened steel locknut tangs that dig into box excellent continuity of ind. Locknut will not or spin.

Insulated throat protects insulation on wires and eases wire pulling. Yellow color easliy seen by inspectors.

Steel grounding ferrule easily threaded by hand. Fits convolutions of conduit securely to eliminate pull-outs and insure continuity of ground. Distortion free to remain reusable.

Hexagonal compression nut is screw machined steel through 1" and malleable iron on larger sizes.

Ring gives er liquid-tight protec- around knockout of t metal box. Neo- ie gasket seals out ds and steel retaining protects gasket from irtion. "O" ring assem- must be ordered rately.

Body is virtually unbreakable. Straight connectors through 1" are screw machined steel; other sizes malleable iron. Threads at left are tapered to insure liquid-tight seal in threaded hub.

Nylon gland ring is split for ease of installation and greater compression. Reversible design cannot be installed facing the wrong way. Nylon is impervious to liquids, unaffected by temperature extremes and resists abrasion.

Liquid-tight conduit cutaway view shows flexible steel core under plastic jacket.

CONDUIT ENTRANCE CAPS

sand cast aluminum

THREADED

for rigid or IMC

Cat. No.	Size	Quantity Unit Ctn.	Quantity Ship. Ctn.	Wt. per 100
2302	1/2"	10	50	26.7
2303	3/4"	10	50	37.3
2304	1"	5	25	53.2
2305	1 1/4"	—	10	61.6
2306	1 1/2"	—	5	103.8
2308	2"	—	5	135.8
2310	2 1/2"	—	1	475.0
2312	3"	—	1	475.0
2314	3 1/2"	—	1	787.5
2316	4"	—	1	1000.0
2320	5"	—	1	6225.0
2324	6"	—	1	5962.5

CLAMP TYPE

for rigid, IMC or EMT

Cat. No.	Size	Quantity Unit Ctn.	Quantity Ship. Ctn.	Wt. per 100
2402	1/2"	10	50	31.9
2403	3/4"	10	50	40.0
2404	1"	5	25	66.2
2405	1 1/4"	—	10	65.4
2406	1 1/2"	—	5	110.0
2408	2"	—	5	207.5
2410	2 1/2"	—	1	487.5
2412	3"	—	1	472.9
2414	3 1/2"	—	1	643.8
2416	4"	—	1	720.8

SLIPFITTER

for rigid or IMC

Cat. No.	Size	Quantity Unit Ctn.	Quantity Ship. Ctn.	Wt. per 100
2372	1/2"	10	50	28.3
2373	3/4"	5	50	35.4
2374	1"	4	20	67.0
2375	1 1/4"	—	10	58.8
2376	1 1/2"	—	5	101.7
2378	2"	—	5	190.6
2380	2 1/2"	—	1	450.0
2382	3"	—	1	458.3
2384	3 1/2"	—	1	812.5
2386	4"	—	1	804.2

No. 2372-74   No. 2375-86

COMBINATION

set screw

for rigid or IMC

Cat. No.	Size	Quantity Ship. Ctn.	Wt. per 100
2358	2" pipe, 1 1/4" head	5	88.8
2359	2" pipe, 1 1/2" head	5	108.8
2362	2 1/2" pipe, 2" head	5	205.0

OPENING INFORMATION for all insulators used on conduit entrance caps shown on this page.

Size	No. and Dia. of Openings	Size	No. and Dia. of Openings
1/2"	4-19/64"	2 1/2"	3-7/8", 1-1", 3-1 9/16"
3/4"	2-3/8", 3-13/32"	3"	4-1 1/8", 3-1 3/4"
1"	2-7/16", 3-1/2"	3 1/2"	4-1 1/8", 3-1 3/4"
1 1/4"	2-7/16", 3-1/2"	4"	4-1 1/8", 3-1 3/4"
1 1/2"	2-19/32" 1-7/16", 3-3/4"	5"	Solid transite plate
2"	2-3/4", 3-1", 1-17/32"	6"	Solid transite plate

A thin flash covers all insulator openings.

1½" DEEP WITH CONDUIT KO's

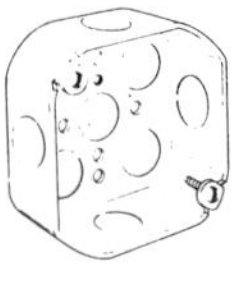

No. 125 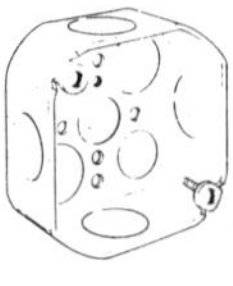   No. 126    No. 127 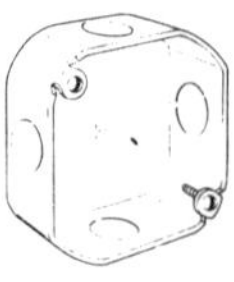   No. 135 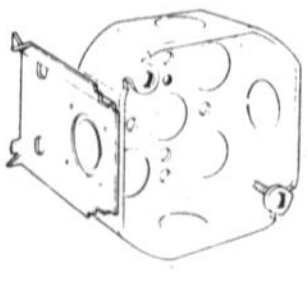   No. 158 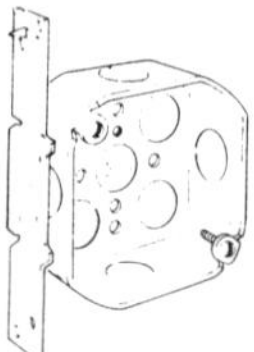   No. 161

15.5 cubic-inch capacity

Raco No.	Universal No.	ACCESSORIES Brkt.	KNOCKOUTS SIDES Conduit	KNOCKOUTS BOTTOM Conduit	Std. Pkg.	Wt. Per C
125	54151-½	—	4—½"	5—½"	50	52.0
126	54151-¾	—	4—¾"	3—½", 2—¾"	50	52.0
127	54151-SP	—	2—½", 2—¾"	3—½", 2—¾"	50	52.0
135		—	4—½"	—	50	53.6
158	54151-J½	J	4—½"	5—½"	50	63.9
161	54151-FA	FA	3—½"	5—½"	50	63.0

1½" DEEP WITH NON-METALLIC CABLE CLAMPS

15.5 cubic-inch capacity

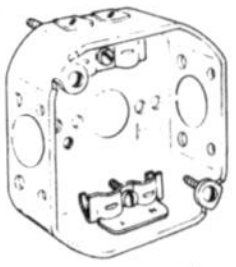

No. 145 with nail holes 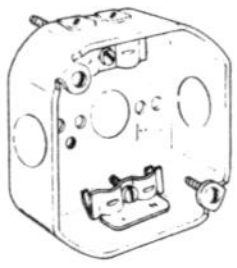   No. 146 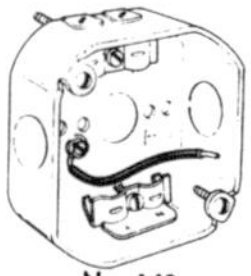   No. 148 insulated #12 grounding pigtail

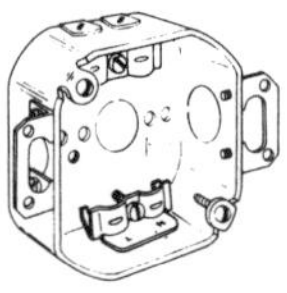

No. 150 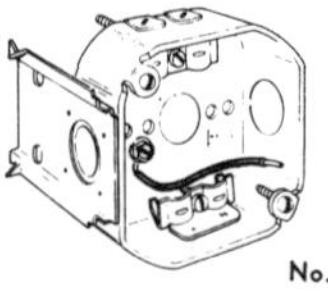   No. 154 insulated #12 grounding pigtail 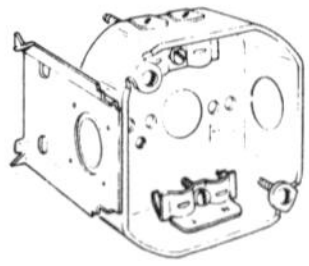   No. 160   No. 164

Raco No.	Universal No.	ACCESSORIES Clamps	Brkt.	Ears	KNOCKOUTS SIDES Conduit	Cable	KNOCKOUTS BOTTOM Conduit	Std. Pkg.	Wt. Per C
145		2-L	—	—	2—½"	4	1—½"	50	54.7
146	54151-L	2-L	—	—	2—½"	4	1—½"	50	55.8
148		2-L	—	—	2—½"	4	1—½"	50	61.0
150	54151-NE	2-L	—	Yes	2—½"	4	1—½"	50	58.7
154		2-L	J	—	2—½"	4	1—½"	50	71.8
160	54151-JL	2-L	J	—	2—½"	4	1—½"	50	66.8
164	54151-FAL	2-L	FA	—	1—½"	4	1—½"	50	66.4

![RACO]

No. 292.   No. 286   No. 287   No. 290   No. 291   No. 293

3.9 cubic-inch capacity

½" DEEP WITH NON-METALLIC CABLE CLAMPS

Raco No.	Universal No.	ACCESSORIES			KNOCKOUTS		Std. Pkg.	Wt. Per C
		Clamps	Ears	Stud	Conduit	Loom or Cable		
292	36115-9	2—#9	Yes	—	3—½"	4	50	28.2

¾" DEEP WITH NON-METALLIC CABLE CLAMPS

286	36125-10-S	2—#10	Yes	Yes	—	4	50	37.2
287	36125-10	2—#10	Yes	—	1—½"	4	50	33.4

¾" DEEP WITH ARMORED CABLE CLAMPS

5.0 cubic-inch capacity

290	36125-12-S	2—#12	Yes	Yes	—	4	50	39.4
291	36125-12	2—#12	Yes	—	1—½"	4	50	35.9

6.0 cubic-inch capacity

½" DEEP WITH CONDUIT KO's

293	56111	—	Yes	—	5—½"	—	50	35.2

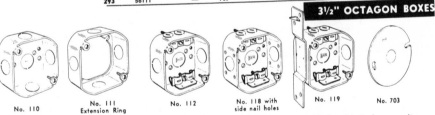

No. 110   No. 111 Extension Ring   No. 112   No. 118 with side nail holes   No. 119   No. 703

11.8 cubic-inch capacity

1½" DEEP WITH CONDUIT KO's

Raco No.	Universal No.	ACCESSORIES		KNOCKOUTS			Std. Pkg.	Wt. Per C
		Clamps	Brkt.	SIDES		BOTTOM		
				Conduit	Cable	Conduit		
110	24151-½	—	—	4—½"	—	1—½"	50	43.4
111	25151-½	—	—	4—½"	—	1—½"	25	37.2

1½" DEEP WITH NON-METALLIC CABLE CLAMPS

112	24151-L	2L	—	2—½"	4	1—½"	50	46.8
118	—	2L	—	2—½"	4	1—½"	50	46.8
119	24151-FAL	2L	F	1—½"	4	1—½"	25	56.8

Fits 3¼" or 3½" Box

703	24C6	Flat, ½" KO		100	17.7

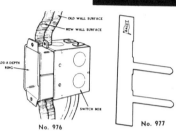

No. 970

No. 976

No. 977

Raco No.	DESCRIPTION	Std. Pkg.	Wt. Per C
970	Switch Box Support	50	14.0
976	Add-A-Depth Ring with 2-1⅛" long screws included	25	11.8
977	Grip-Lok	200 Pcs.	2.9

3¾" x 2" SWITCH BOXES

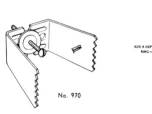

No. 403   No. 404   No. 405   No. 415   No. 417   No. 418   No. 419

6.5 cubic-inch capacity

4" x 4" x 1"
14.8 cu. in. Cap.

1" DEEP — NON-GANGABLE

Raco No.	ACCESSORIES		KNOCKOUTS		Std. Pkg.	Wt. Per C
			ENDS			
	Clamps	Brkt.	Conduit	Cable		
403	—	D	1—½"	2	25	38.2
404	1-Q	D	1—½"	2	25	40.0
405	1-Q	D	—	4	25	41.9
415	2-Q	D	—	4	25	64.6
417	—	D	2—½"	4	25	66.2
418	2-Q	D	2—½"	4	25	64.6
419	Adapter plate for Nos. 415, 417, 418.				100	5.7

4" x 2" SWITCH BOX

No. 622
Nail Holes

1½" DEEP — GANGABLE WITH CONDUIT KO's

10.0 cubic-inch capacity

Raco No.	KNOCKOUTS		Std. Pkg.	Wt. Per C
	EACH END	BOTTOM		
	Conduit	Conduit		
622	1—½"	1—½"	50	46.6

No. 860

No. 861

No. 863
No. 867
No. 868

No. 864

No. 865

No. 866

Raco No.	Universal No.	DESCRIPTION	Std. Pkg.	Unit Pkg.	Wt. Per C
860	58C1	Blank	100	25	10.3
861	58C6	½" KO	100	25	9.9
863	58C5	Single Receptacle 1-13/32" D.	100	25	8.8
864	58C7	Duplex Receptacle	100	25	7.5
865	58C30	Toggle Switch	100	25	10.1
866	58C40	Despard, 3 Device	50	10	15.8
867	58C4	For 20 Amp. Receptacle 1-19/32" D.	100	25	8.3
868	———	30 Amp. Twist-Lock Single Receptacle 1-23/32"	100	25	8.4

1½" DEEP

No. 880

No. 640

7.3 cubic-inch capacity

Raco No.	Universal No.	KNOCKOUTS			Std. Pkg.	Wt. Per C
		EACH END	EACH SIDE	BOTTOM		
640	4800	1—½"	3—½"	3—½"	50	36.3
880	48-C-1	Blank, For 640 Box			50	12.3

1⁵⁄₁₆" x 1⅝" DEEP

No. 426

No. 427

Raco No.	No. of Gangs	Length	Cubic Inch Capacity	CONDUIT KNOCKOUTS			Std. Pkg.	Wt. Per C
				Each End	Each Side	Bottom		
426	1	3¾"	6.5	1—½"	2—½"	2—½"	2	40.8
427	2	5¾"	10.0	1—½"	2—½"	2—½"	1	60.7

FOR BARE GROUND WIRE

malleable iron

Cat. No.	Water Pipe Size	Tap Wire Size Minimum	Tap Wire Size Maximum	Quantity Unit Ctn.	Quantity Ship. Ctn.	Wt. per 100
2520	½"- ¾"-1"	No. 8 Solid	No. 4 Stranded	25	50	17.0

bronze alloy

Cat. No.	Water Pipe Size	Tap Wire Size Minimum	Tap Wire Size Maximum	Quantity Unit Ctn.	Quantity Ship. Ctn.	Wt. per 100
2504	½"- ¾"-1"	No. 10 Solid	No. 2 Stranded	25	50	20.8
2505	1¼"-1½"-2"	No. 10 Solid	No. 2 Stranded	—	25	45.3

FOR BARE ARMORED GROUND WIRE

malleable iron

Cat. No.	Water Pipe Size	Tap Wire Size Minimum	Tap Wire Size Maximum	Quantity Unit Ctn.	Quantity Ship. Ctn.	Wt. per 100
2530	½"- ¾"-1"	No. 8 Solid	No. 4 Stranded	25	50	20.5

bronze alloy

Cat. No.	Water Pipe Size	Tap Wire Size Minimum	Tap Wire Size Maximum	Quantity Ship. Ctn.	Wt. per 100
2507	½"- ¾"-1"	No. 10 Solid	No. 6 Stranded	25	35.5
2508	1¼"-1½"-2"	No. 10 Solid	No. 6 Stranded	25	71.5

FOR RIGID CONDUIT OR E.M.T.

bronze alloy

Cat. No.	Water Pipe Size	Conduit Hub Size	Quantity Ship. Ctn.	Wt. per 100
2531	½"- ¾"-1"	½" or ¾" E.M.T. & ½" Rigid	25	46.0
2532	1¼"-1½"-2"	½" or ¾" E.M.T. & ½" Rigid	25	69.8

FOR RIGID CONDUIT

bronze alloy

Cat. No.	Water Pipe Size	Conduit Hub Size	Tap Wire Size Minimum	Tap Wire Size Maximum	Quantity Ship. Ctn.	Wt. per 100
2512	½"- ¾"-1"	½"	No. 10 Sol.	No. 6 Stranded	25	39.9
2513	½"- ¾"-1"	¾"	No. 10 Sol.	No. 2/0 Stranded	25	49.0
2522	1¼"-1½"-2"	½"	No. 10 Sol.	No. 6 Stranded	25	64.4
2523	1¼"-1½"-2"	¾"	No. 10 Sol.	No. 2/0 Stranded	25	48.3

Clamps reversible for ground rods

COMBINATION COUPLINGS

RIGID TO E.M.T. SET SCREW steel

Cat. No.	Size	Quantity Unit Ctn.	Quantity Ship. Ctn.	Wt. per 100
1432	1/2"- 1/2"	25	100	14.6
1433	3/4"- 3/4"	25	100	27.0
1434	1" -1"	—	25	37.7

RIGID TO E.M.T. THREADED/COMPRESSION malleable iron

Cat. No.	Size	Unit Ctn.	Ship. Ctn.	Wt. per 100
1352	1/2"- 1/2"	25	100	11.2
1353	3/4"- 3/4"	25	100	16.3
1354	1" -1"	25	100	23.5

FLEXIBLE TO E.M.T. malleable iron

Cat. No.	Size	Unit Ctn.	Ship. Ctn.	Wt. per 100
1941	1/2" to 3/8"	25	100	13.0
1942	1/2" to 1/2"	25	100	16.0
1943	3/4" to 3/4"	25	100	26.0

RIGID TO FLEXIBLE malleable iron

Cat. No.	Size	Unit Ctn.	Ship. Ctn.	Wt. per 100
1552	1/2"- 1/2"	25	100	18.5
1553	3/4"- 3/4"	25	100	25.0
1554	1" -1"	—	25	34.0

REDUCING WASHERS

stamped steel
size stamped
on each piece.

Cat. No.	Size	Quantity Unit Ctn.	Quantity Ship. Ctn.	Wt. per 100
1365	3/4"- 1/2"	200	1000	0.9
1366	1" - 1/2"	100	1000	1.7
1367	1" - 3/4"	100	1000	1.4
1368	1 1/4"- 1/2"	100	500	2.7
1369	1 1/4"- 3/4"	100	500	2.3
1370	1 1/4"-1"	100	500	1.9
1371	1 1/2"- 1/2"	50	250	3.5
1372	1 1/2"- 3/4"	50	250	3.3
1373	1 1/2"-1"	50	250	2.8
1374	1 1/2"-1 1/4"	50	250	6.0
1375	2" - 1/2"	50	250	5.2
1376	2" - 3/4"	50	250	4.9
1377	2" -1"	50	250	4.5
1378	2" -1 1/4"	50	250	4.0
1379	2" -1 1/2"	50	250	3.1
1380	2 1/2"-1"	—	50	11.7
1381	2 1/2"-1 1/4"	—	50	10.5
1382	2 1/2"-1 1/2"	—	50	9.7
1383	2 1/2"-2"	—	50	7.5
1384	3" -1 1/4"	—	25	13.8
1385	3" -1 1/2"	—	25	15.5
1386	3" -2"	—	25	15.5
1387	3" -2 1/2"	—	25	10.4
1389	3 1/2"-2"	—	10	25.0
1390	3 1/2"-2 1/2"	—	10	21.9
1391	3 1/2"-3"	—	10	16.3
1392	4" -2"	—	10	32.1
1393	4" -2 1/2"	—	10	27.9
1394	4" -3"	—	10	23.1

BEAM CLAMPS

No. 2500
stamped steel

No. 2510-2538
malleable iron

Cat. No.	Size	Max. Load Lbs.	Quantity Ship. Ctn.	Wt. per 100
2500	1"	125	100	12.4
2524	1"	335	100	22.1
2534	1"	335	100	22.0
2536	1 1/2"	525	50	49.5
2538	2"	750	25	90.4
2510	2 1/2"	900	25	127.4

	A	B	C	D	E	F
			Dimensions			
2500	1 13/16"	1/4-20	5/8"	21/32"	1 1/2"	1/4—20 x 1"
2524	1 3/16"	1/4-20	21/32"	13/32"	1 13/32"	5/16—18 x 1 1/4"
2534	1 3/16"	10-24	21/32"	13/32"	1 13/32"	5/16—18 x 1 1/4"
2536	1 3/4"	5/16-18	11/16"	1 1/2"	1 3/8"	3/8—16 x 1 1/4"
2538	1 7/8"	3/8-16	15/16"	2"	1 7/8"	1/2—13 x 1 1/4"
2510	2 11/32"	1/2-13	31/32"	2 3/8"	2 3/32"	5/8—11 x 1 1/2"

CONDUIT CLAMPS

size stamped on each piece

stamped steel

Cat. No.	Rigid Size	EMT Size	Trade Size	Quantity Ship. Ctn.	Wt. per 100
2042	3/8"- 1/2"	1/2"	0	100	5.0
2043	3/4"	3/4"	1	100	7.0
2044	1"	1"	2	100	8.6
2040	—	1 1/4"	2 1/2"	100	10.0
2045	1 1/4"	1 1/2"	3	100	11.0
2046	1 1/2"	—	4	100	14.2
2048	2"	2"	5	50	21.0
2047	2 1/2"	2 1/2"	6	25	22.7
2049	3"	3"	7	25	26.3
2050	3 1/2"	—	8	10	32.1
2051	4"	4"	9	10	53.8

WITH BOLTS stamped steel

Cat. No.	Rigid Size	EMT Size	Trade Size	Ship. Ctn.	Wt. per 100
2052	3/8"- 1/2"	1/2"	0	100	7.3
2053	3/4"	3/4"	1	100	9.4
2054	1"	1"	2	100	10.9
2041	—	1 1/4"	2 1/2"	100	12.8
2055	1 1/4"	1 1/2"	3	100	13.2
2056	1 1/2"	—	4	100	16.3
2058	2"	2"	5	50	23.3
2057	2 1/2"	2 1/2"	6	25	27.8
2059	3"	3"	7	25	33.8
2060	3 1/2"	—	8	10	38.8
2061	4"	4"	9	10	70.0

KNOCKOUT SEALS

NOTE: Each set includes two seal discs, one bolt and one nut, in a plastic bag.

steel

Cat. No.	Size	Quantity Unit Ctn.	Quantity Ship. Ctn.	Wt. per 100
1042	1/2"	100	1000	1.6
1043	3/4"	100	1000	1.9
1044	1"	50	500	2.5
1045	1 1/4"	50	250	3.2
1046	1 1/2"	50	100	4.8
1048	2"	25	100	6.3
1037	2 1/2"	1 set	10 sets	28.7
1039	3"	1 set	10 sets	62.5
1040	3 1/2"	1 set	10 sets	65.6
1041	4"	1 set	10 sets	78.6
2570	1 3/8"x 3/8"	100	500	5.1

FIXTURE EXTENSION

steel

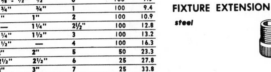

BRACKETS

Note: Setbacks given below are the general rule. Exceptions are indicated by the catalog number.

"A" BRACKET — Positions against side and face of stud. Bracket set back ⅝" on Handy Boxes.

"B" BRACKET — Mounts on face of stud. Bracket set flush on 4" Square and set back ⅝" on Handy and Switch Boxes.

"D" BRACKET — Flat, bracket side on Non-gangable Switch boxes. Very rigid. Gauging notches at ⅜", ½" and ⅝".

"FA" BRACKET — Side mount bracket with spur and back up flange for extra rigidity. Bracket set back ½" on octagon and ⅝" on handy and switch boxes.

 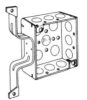

"FH" BRACKET — Side mount bracket with barbed hooks that drive in face of stud. Exceptionally rigid bracket. Bracket flush on 4" square boxes and set back ½" on switch boxes.

"J" BRACKET — For any area where box need not be centered between studs. 2 spurs, slotted holes for toe-nailing. Bracket set flush with gauging notches at ⅜" and ½".

"W" BRACKET — Mounts on side and face of stud.

"S" BRACKET — Non-gangable switch box with flat sides extended to double as bracket. Pair of holes for nailing straight or on angle. Option of staked, angled 16d nails. Gauging notches at ⅜", ½" and ⅝".

CLAMPS

L CLAMP—
For non-metallic cable.

#10 CLAMP
(Ceiling Pan)
For non-metallic cable.

#9 CLAMP
(Ceiling Pan)
For non-metallic cable and non-metallic conduit (loom).

X CLAMP—
For armored cable

#12 CLAMP
(Ceiling Pan)
For armored cable

BN CLAMP—
For non-metallic cable

"Q"®
QUICK CLAMPS
Pat. Nos. (U. S.) 2,458,409-2,556,977-2,564,341-2,706,647-RE 23,720 (Canadian) 472,982-472,983-486,331-492,565

For non-metallic cable.

No screws needed.

286

1½" DEEP WITH CONDUIT KO's

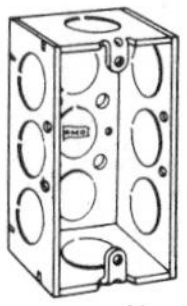

11.5 cubic-inch capacity

No. 650

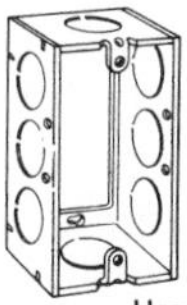

No. 653
Handy Box Extension

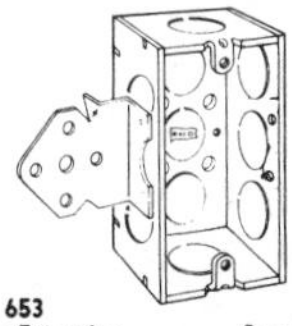

No. 654
Bracket welded ¾"
from face of box.

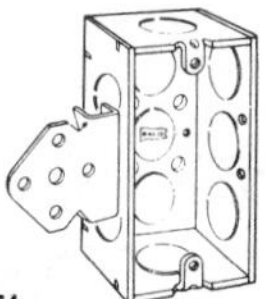

No. 655
Bracket welded ¼"
from face of box.

Raco No.	Universal No.	Brkt.	KNOCKOUTS			Std. Pkg.	Wt. Per C
			EACH END	EACH SIDE	BOTTOM		
650	58351-½	—	1—1½"	3—½"	3—½"	50	49.3
653	59351	—	1—1½"	3—½"	—	50	39.9
654	58351-B-½	B	1—1½"	3—½" One Side	3—½"	50	57.3
655	58351-B-¼	B	1—1½"	3—½" One Side	3—½"	50	59.3

1⅞" DEEP WITH CONDUIT KO's

13.0 cubic-inch capacity

   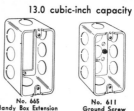

No. 660

No. 661

No. 662

No. 663

No. 665
Handy Box Extension

No. 611
Ground Screw

Raco No.	Universal No.	Brkt.	KNOCKOUTS			Std. Pkg.	Wt. Per C
			EACH END	EACH SIDE	BOTTOM		
660	58361-½	—	1—1½"	3—½"	3—½"	50	48.8
661	58361-A-½	A	1—1½"	3—½" One Side	3—½"	50	65.1
662	58361-FA-½	FA	1—1½"	3—½" One Side	3—½"	50	60.6
663	58361-¾	—	1—¾"	2—¾"	2—¾"	50	49.8
665	59361-½	—	1—1½"	3—½"	—	50	40.8
611	—		1—½"	3—½"	3—½"	50	49.4

2⅛" DEEP WITH CONDUIT KO's

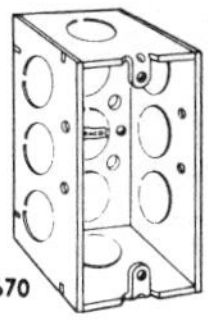

No. 670

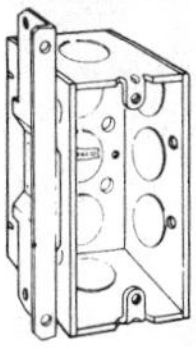

No. 671

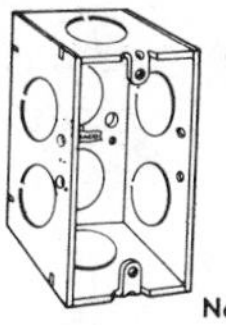

No. 674

No. 678

16.5 cubic-inch capacity

Raco No.	Universal No.	Brkt.	KNOCKOUTS			Std. Pkg.	Wt. Per C
			EACH END	EACH SIDE	BOTTOM		
670	58371-½	—	1—1½"	3—½"	3—½"	50	62.7
671	58371-A-½	A	1—1½"	3—½" One Side	3—½"	50	79.5
674	58371-¾	—	1—¾"	2—¾"	2—¾"	50	64.8
678	58371-FA-½	FA	1—1½"	3—½" One Side	3—½"	50	73.5

Glossary

accessible—Capable of being removed or exposed without damage to walls or to the building structure.

ampacity—Current-carrying capacity if electric conductors are expressed in amperes.

attachment plug (plug cap)—Device to be plugged into a receptacle to connect a portable appliance to electricity.

bonding—Joining two parts made of metal to form a solid connection.

bonding jumper—A connection of two metal parts that are possibly separated from each other by a distance, but must be connected at all times. Example: jumper around a water meter to provide continuity if and when the meter is removed.

bonding jumper, main—Jumper from neutral bar in service-entrance panel to the panel itself to effectively ground the metal of the panel itself.

branch circuit—The circuit conductors from the fuse or circuit breaker to the current usage point (receptacle).

branch circuit, individual—A circuit having only one piece of utilization equipment (electric range, etc.).

building—A separate structure standing alone or cut off from adjacent structures by solid walls or fire doors.

cabinet—An enclosure containing wires, devices (breakers or fuses). May be surface mounted or flush with the wall surface.

circuit breaker—A device to open a circuit automatically or manually when needed to protect wiring leaving such a device

concealed—Not accessible without damaging the building structure. This includes wires in conduit or tubing.

conductor—Any wire or bus bar capable of carrying electricity. May be bare, covered (but not insulated), or insulated.

connector, pressure (solderless)—A terminal end to be attached under a screw or pushed onto or into a mating terminal end. The wire is inserted in the hollow end and this end is crimped.

This makes a secure electrical connection by pressure only.

continuous load—A load which continues for more than three hours.

dead front—Having no live parts exposed. The cover on a breaker panel, for example.

device—Any unit carrying current but not using that current. Examples: switch, receptacle, thermostat.

disconnect—Main switch for service equipment, large motors, air conditioning equipment, etc.

enclosed—So designed that persons cannot contact live parts. A metal box or a fence around outside high voltage parts.

equipment—Any part of an electrical installation: fittings, devices, switches, appliances, etc.

exposed—So situated that persons might accidentally touch live parts.

fitting—Any part of an electrical installation that has a mechanical rather than electrical function.

ground—A connection to the earth, either accidental or intentional.

grounded conductor—A conductor intentionally grounded.

grounding conductor—The wire from the equipment to the established ground. Also called *grounding electrode conductor*.

ground fault circuit interrupter—A device for the protection of persons to detect and interrupt very small current leakages.

lighting outlet—A connection to an outlet for holding a bulb or installation of a fixture.

location, damp—A location partially protected by overhanging awnings, roofs, and locations such as barns and some basements.

location, dry—A location not subject to dampness.

location, wet—Underground or in contact with the earth or saturated with water.

neutral conductor—A conductor that carries *only* the current that is unbalanced as the neutral conductor in a service-entrance cable serving a dwelling.

outlet—A point where current may be taken such as a lighting outlet or a receptacle outlet.

overcurrent—An excess of current over the full load capacity of a wire or motor.

overload—Equipment using more amperes than its rating or a wire carrying more amperes than its ampacity, such as a short circuit or ground fault.

raceway—Any channel to carry wires or bus bars. Includes large square surface raceways, conduit and thinwall.

receptacle—A contact device for accepting attachment plugs.

service—Conductors and equipment to supply power to a wiring system such as a house from the utility or other source of power.

service drop—Overhead wires from the utility to the premises.

service equipment—Disconnect, main breaker or fuses, the distribution panel also containing breakers or fuses.

service lateral—Underground wires from the utility to the premises.

switch—A device for connecting or disconnecting current using equipment.

thermal protector—A protective device, usually automatic to protect a motor or motor/compressor from burnout.

TERMS NOT DEFINED IN THE CODE

AWG—American Wire Gauge such as No. 14 wire, No. 6 wire, etc.

bushing, conduit—Metal or plastic screwed-on end of conduit or other fitting to protect insulation on wires from abrasion.

bushing, other—1) For reducing the size of a pipe thread to accept a smaller fitting. 2) A fiber bushing such as that supplied with BX to protect insulation on the wires from abrasion.

BX—Armored bushed cable having two or three insulated wires plus a bonding wire. It is flexible and is used in house wiring.

carbide drill bit—A drill for concrete to make holes for anchors and access through walls for conduit, wires, or cable.

code—The National Electrical Code.

configuration—Arrangement of slots in a receptacle or blades on an attachment plug as being different from others.

continuity—A complete path for current as through a fuse or wire.

dead—Having no electric current in a wire or device. Not attached to a source or power or being disconnected.

die—A tool to cut threads on a piece of round stock as a bolt.

drywall—Plasterboard consisting of two cardboard outside layers having a plaster core, ⅜-inch, ½-inch, and ⅝-inch thick.

Edison base thread—The standard thread found on light bulbs and plug fuses.

elevation—Height above a reference point such as a floor. Example: Toggle switches are installed at a 48-inch elevation.

enclosure—Enclosed cabinet or box to hold live electrical parts.

feedback—A source of current other than the obvious or usual route. In control circuits there are sometimes more than one source of current. Turning one switch off may not "kill" all wires in the equipment.

ferrule—A sleeve, usually of brass, used in various types of waterproof, flexible conduit fittings.

fill—Amount of space in an electrical box that wires may occupy without crowding.

fish—To push or pull cable inside hollow walls or through attics while attempting to snag the end and retrieve it and through an opening in the wall.

fuseblock, pullout—Type used in 60-A fused service-entrance panels. Has plastic front with fuse clips on the back. When this block is removed from its recess, the fuses are absolutely dead and can be changed with complete safety.

fused disconnect—A device having fuses in a cabinet. Also an externally operated switch to disconnect the power from the equipment served by the disconnect. Note: If the switch is correctly wired the fuses will be dead.

fuse—A link in the circuit which is purposely weak to protect wiring and motors from pulling too high amperage and burning out. Fuses are accurately calibrated to "blow" at their specified rating.

hickey—Rigid conduit bending tool. This looks like a pipe tee with one side cut away. A section of pipe is the handle and the hickey is hooked over conduit. By prying down on the handle the conduit can be bent.

hot—Energized wire, motor or other piece of equipment. Another word used is "live."

I.D.—Inside diameter, such as of a pipe or conduit.

knifeblade—Referring to a type of fuse having the contacting ends flat and wide as a knife is. These fit in between two like surfaces held together tightly to give good contact. Also refers to a style of switch having similar but longer "knifelike" blades fitting between similar surfaces at one end and hinged at the other, operated externally.

knockout—Round, partially punched out openings in junction boxes and cabinets. Any one of these can be "knocked out" to provide a hole for a fitting.

locknut—A threaded flat piece of metal similar to a thin nut which screws on a box fitting which was inserted through a knockout opening. This locknut secures the fitting in the opening.

meter socket (base)—A casting having electrical connections designed to accept a utility meter by plugging it into four knifeblade acceptors inside the base, much like plugging in an attachment plug into a receptacle.

mouse—A tool handmade by coiling up wire solder to form a small heavy weight having a loop to tie on a line.

name plate rating—A metal plate on equipment such as an air conditioner or motor which gives current draw in amps, the voltage required, name of manufacturer and sometimes but not always, the horsepower.

new work—Electrical wiring installed in buildings not yet finished, but having partition framing and enough other work finished for the electrician to complete rough-in work.

normal—A condition of a switch or other piece of equipment when it has neither pressure, vacuum, electricity or any other motive force acting upon it.

nut driver—A hand tool that looks like a screwdriver, but having a socket in place of a tip. This socket fits nuts on electrical parts and is turned like a screwdriver to loosen or tighten nuts. Many ¼-inch socket sets have such a handle, but they have various sockets to fit different size nuts. The nutdriver has only one size.

O.D.—Outside diameter as on conduit or tubing and pipe and copper tubing. Sizes listed for these tubing and pipe type items are called nominal because they are not the actual measured size. Example: Rigid conduit is called half inch and has an internal diameter of 0.622 of an inch and the outside diameter of nearly ⅞ of an inch.

old work—Installation of electrical wiring in a finished building that makes it necessary to fish wire and cable inside finished walls by cutting flooring, removing baseboards, and doing other cutting and patching.

open—A break in the continuity of a circuit or certain wire that makes it impossible for current to flow. A broken wire. To turn a switch so that it breaks the circuit.

overload—Excess current greater than the device or equipment is designed for.

panel—A cabinet with its component parts such as a breaker, fuse panel or service-entrance equipment.

parallel—Having two or more separate paths for electricity to travel. Lights in a house are wired in parallel (any light is able to be turned off or on without affecting any others).

photocell—A device that senses light and darkness and closes contacts when its "eye" senses darkness.

pry-out knockout—A knockout in a metal box that does not have to be *knocked out*, but is pried out by inserting a small screwdriver in a slot provided and prying or twisting to remove.

Romex—Brand name of nonmetallic sheathed cable made by Rome Cable Co., Rome, New York. Used extensively in house wiring.

sash chain—Used by some electricians and others as a mouse.

series—Having only one path for electricity to travel. The current has to go through each device in turn to get back to its source. The type Christmas lights where one bulb removed shuts off all the others.

series-parallel—A combination of both wiring arrangements together.

service head—Special fitting at the top of the service mast or top of entrance cable to keep out rain.

short—A condition where both wires of a cord become bare and touch each other, causing an arc, or a motor wire becomes bare and touches the case, causing an arc. Both conditions will blow a fuse (or should) if you did a good wiring job. The act of causing a short.

switched—Having a switch (manual) to control the light or receptacle or other device or appliance.

tap—A tool having threads on it like a bolt, but having slots lengthwise so the threads have cutting edges that will cut a thread in a drilled hole to accept a bolt or screw.

tester—A tool for testing for electricity (voltage

tester) or a tool for testing for defective circuits that are incomplete or wired improperly (continuity tester, this tester uses batteries and must *not* be used on live wires).

thinwall—Correct name is electrical metallic tubing (EMT). This is thinner than rigid conduit and is very popular to use.

time lag—Applied to special fuses that hold on the current in rush when motors start, but will blow when needed.

timer—An electrically controlled device that turns equipment or lights on and off at timed intervals.

type S—Fuses that have this designation applied have the time-lag feature built into them.

upstream/downstream—Upstream means the location of a device or other item closer to the power supply than another device or item. Downstream means a device or item farther away from the power supply than a second device or item.

Underwriters Laboratories, Inc.—A national testing lab that test, among other things, electrical equipment, cords, devices and any other items that carry electricity.

vise grips—A type of pliers that will grip and lock onto any item and hold it for you. It can be released at will.

voltage to ground—Voltage registered when prods are touched to the hot wire and a grounded wire or the earth directly.

volts—Electrical "pressure" such as 12 V, 24 V, 115 V, 230 V.

Index